A Note on the Author

Duncan Fallowell was born in Middlesex in 1948. He travels a good deal, contributes to many journals, and is the author of two novels, *Satyrday* and *The Underbelly*. He has a flat in the Notting Hill district of London.

TO NOTO

TO NOTO

OR LONDON TO SICILY IN A FORD

DUNCAN FALLOWELL

BLOOMSBURY

First published in Great Britain 1989
Copyright © Duncan Fallowell 1989
This paperback edition published 1991
The moral right of the author has been asserted

Bloomsbury Publishing Ltd, 2 Soho Square, London W1V 5DE

A CIP catalogue record for this book
is available from the British Library

ISBN 0 7475 0769 4

10 9 8 7 6 5 4 3 2 1

Typeset by Hewer Text Composition Services, Edinburgh
Printed and bound in Great Britain by
Cox and Wyman Ltd, Reading, Berkshire

To Natale

Festina Lente

CONTENTS

PREFATORY NOTE

I'd like to thank warmly all those mentioned in the text for their help. Special thanks are due to the Rt. Rev. John Satterthwaite the Bishop of Gibraltar, the Hon. Julia Stonor, Bunny Dexter, Sarah Gilbert-Rolfe, Sir Harold Acton, the Rev. Peter Blackburn, Franco Amoroso, my mother and father Mr and Mrs T. E. Fallowell, Christopher Walker, Joanna Gill, Von Whiteman, Prof. Rosario Tinè, Salvatore Corleone, Count Tasca; to the late Helmi Whipp Pfeiffer for her unique brand of support; to the late Sir Sacheverell Sitwell at whose home the idea first took seed; to Kris Mancuso, the Principessa Costanza Camporeale, the Baronessa Renata Pucci Zanca, Natale Maganuco, Toby Moore, all of whose sweetness and generosity opened many doors; and to Justin Wintle, Polly Halliday, Glyn Alban Roberts, and Nicholas Jones-Evans in whose Welsh houses most of the manuscript was written.

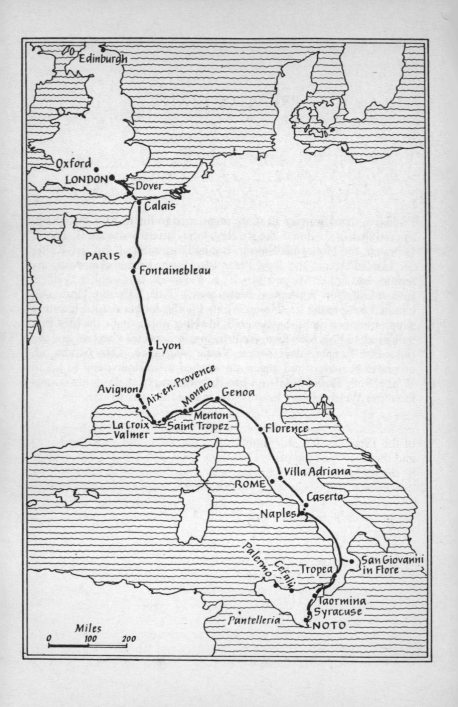

Edinburgh

Oxford
LONDON   Dover
                Calais

PARIS
        Fontainebleau

Lyon

Avignon   Aix-en-Provence
                Monaco   Genoa
          Menton
La Croix Saint Tropez
Valmer   Florence

                          Villa Adriana
            ROME
                          Caserta
        Naples

              Palermo   San Giovanni
                Cefalù Tropea   in Flore

                          Taormina
                          Syracuse
      Pantelleria   NOTO

Miles
0   100   200

1

Slow Start
(a visit to Sir Sacheverell Sitwell)

Midwinter. About noon on an icy day in the heart of England. The sky is blue and sunshine glitters across frosty fields as we approach Weston, a small village deep in tractor mud, lost in the uneventful county of Northamptonshire. The through-road is dominated by a long high wall which is the colour of bruises near the pavement, rising by degrees to a greyish, greenish gold. If followed, this wall leaves the main road, curves round to the left under bare trees, and we arrive at a pair of wrought-iron gates and a Victorian lodge. The gates are jewelled with frosted spiders' webs – among them is repeated the Greek motif of the palmette. From here a short drive travels over a humpback bridge, carrying you forward at an oblique angle, between lawns and milky pools of snowdrops, into a large square of gravel in front of Weston Hall.

It is not a large house and it is in good working order, 17th century in origin, 18th century in atmosphere, gently gothickised at the beginning of the 19th; considerable outbuildings gather mysteriously behind it; and there is about the place something tongue-in-cheek, as if it might be the set for an Agatha Christie melodrama. Since 1930 this has been the home of Sir Sacheverell Sitwell, poet, traveller, writer of curious prose rhapsodies on artistic subjects, younger brother of Edith and Osbert and the only one of them still alive.

The door is opened by the housekeeper, Gertrude Stevenson. She is petite with curly grey hair and a soft voice, and wears a brooch at her neck, but her sweetness of manner conceals a sturdy character. Behind her in the hall, despite his years, bobs Sir Sacheverell, wearing what Wyndham Lewis once described as Sachie's 'look of sedate alarm'. He is surprisingly tall and thin; his frame winds about like a convolvulus en route to the ceiling. And when he doesn't look alarmed, he looks amused. He twinkles – a man different from the rather tight-lipped portrait by Graham Sutherland which hangs in the hall. He is genially ill-at-ease and in the drawing-room says 'Would you like a sherry or

somefing? Those are jolly nice shoes. Aren't shoes a dreadful price
now? Were those expensive?'

'Mmm.'

'It's worth it in the end, isn't it, paying more. What am I looking
for? A cigarette. Oh, here we are. Do you want a cigarette?'

'No thank you. What's that incredible smell?'

'Is there a lovely smell of some kind? I wouldn't know. Smoking
destroys one's sense of smell. Perhaps it's that plant over there which
I'm told smells very nice.'

I approach a bush in a pot and have a good sniff. 'Yes, it reminds
me of being very young. It's the sort of smell you bump into when
you're crawling about in the garden.'

'It's supposed to be a first cousin of the orange blossom,' he
explains.

The drawing-room is dull gold, dull pink, creamy and white, well
lit, comfortable, with portraits, books, plants and a carved fireplace
in which logs flame and glow. There are photographs of 2 beautiful
women on a table against the wall. A copy of the *Almanach de Gotha*
lies carelessly on a causeuse.

'I love the snowdrops in your garden.'

'They really are the last word in elegance, aren't they?' he says,
subsiding into a dull gold, winged chair beside the fireplace. 'Luckily
I haven't had to buy any new shoes lately. I used to go to the last
great shoe-maker. He's dead now. But my younger son realised what
a wonderful shoemaker he was and had a whole fleet of shoes built
and it's like having antiques by Chippendale. He could sell them for
quite a large sum of money.'

'I brought you some more of those chocolates by the way.'

'My goodness, thank you. They really are the best chocolates I've
ever tasted, especially the white ones.'

Gertrude comes in to say that lunch is ready when we want it. She
takes charge of the chocolates and adds in an aside 'I'm so grateful
to you for introducing Mr Sachie to those chocolates. Sometimes he
won't eat – but he'll eat those. I tell everybody to bring them now.'

'What's Gertrude saying? I rather missed it,' he says. Actually he
says 'raver missed it', having the peculiarity of pronouncing 'th' as 'v'
or 'f' (which I'll occasionally indicate). And his voice is produced not
in the throat or nose but at the front of the mouth. Yet its tone is rich,
without any twittering preciousness, and the intonation is Edwardian,
even though he uses many of the throwaway idioms of the 1920s.
Occasionally a smoker's rasp cuts across it and quite often short
coughs. The speed of his talk is uneven with rapid spurts.

'You pronounce "th" as "v" or "f". Is that a Sitwell thing?'

'You noticed that, did you? I just don't hear it. My bruvver and sister never had it. And there wasn't a Sitwell way of speaking, not like there was a Bloomsbury one – they used to moon away on sofas in the most appalling manner.'

'I wonder why Virginia Woolf went mad.'

'I dunno. Er, it's always a mistake to mention it, because of relations, but I think it must've been in the family, don't you?'

'I think she was worshipped too much as well.'

'And a lot of tiresome lesbian women were fond of her.'

'Were they?'

'Well, I think so, yes. Got her worked up.' His face creases with mirth and a chuckle turns into a cough. 'Did I tell you that story about Diaghilev? My bruvver and I used often to have supper with Diaghilev at the Savoy. This was during the war – the First War – and I was always having to catch the late-night train saying "I must go, I've got to get back to Aldershot". And Diaghilev said "Alors, qu'est ce que c'est, cette Aldershot? Votre maîtresse?" . . . He could hardly speak English and my French is simply appalling. The only English words he was ever heard to speak were "More chocolate pudding". But I can read French very well. That's one thing I can do.'

'I can't read it very well. I can speak it very badly.'

'I can read it because foreign writers interested me mainly, when I was young. Balzac I used to like reading terrifically. And Flaubert's *Salammbô* is a wonderful masterpiece – like a film. It's about Ancient Carfage. I found a translation of it – this is one of the sort of keystones of my childhood – in the Post Office at Eckington in Derbyshire where my family lived. It was an extraordinary find in a way. It had an enormous influence on me. The language was so magnificent and strange.'

'Do you know, I've never read Proust. It's one of the things I've not done.'

'I haven't read it since I was about 29.'

'And I've never read *1984*.'

'No, I've never read that,' he says.

'You haven't? I thought I was the only person who hadn't. I haven't read *Brave New World* either.'

'No, neither've I.'

'And I haven't read *Lord of the Flies*.'

'Who wrote that?

'William Golding. He won the Nobel Prize.'

'Did he really? I don't know him. Now listen, there's luncheon . . .'

The dining-room looks out to lawn, hedges, trees. We sit at one end of the table which is fairly long but not one of those very long ones. Gertrude has laid the starter in a dish, a salad of salmon, eggs, and tomatoes, and we help ourselves.

'Have you been very busy writing lately?' he asks.

'I have.'

'And the cash is flowing in, is it, sort of fing?'

'I don't know that the cash is flowing in.'

'I've rather stopped at the moment myself. You see, the ghastly thing is I've written over 80 books, which is really too appalling, isn't it?'

'How did you manage it?'

'Well, I always come down at ½ past 8 for breakfast. I usually wake up about 7 actually. Sometimes ½ past 6. Then I would sit upstairs in my bedroom, which is the only room in which I used to write, and write every morning until about ½ past 12. Then I have a siesta after luncheon. Then I would generally try in the evenings after tea to write until about 7.'

'Aren't you still writing poems?'

'Yes. I was writing one this morning. But poetry is much less trouble than writing prose. You can write poems beside the fire for example. You can sit very comfortably in a chair and meditate.'

'And poetry is economical these days – shorter poems.'

'It isn't economical as far as proceeds go. I've never heard of anybody making a living out of writing poems. In fact it's a dead loss where that's concerned. Which is really the point of it, I suppose. But the marvellous thing about *manuscripts* . . . is that they count as chattels and therefore, if you sell them, you don't have to pay tax. My wife sold her letters from my sister for £6000 to the Texas Library at Austin who buy up manuscripts like lunatics and pay enormous amounts. So seriously, don't forget that.'

'What do you think of your first book?'

'I can't for the life of me remember what it was.'

'*The People's* something. I looked it up.'

'Oh, yes, *The People's Palace*. I was fearfully young and it shows my strong socialist principles at the time. When I was at Balliol my great hero was Trotsky. I was in a very rebellious mood and I'd just come out of the army and I honestly don't think I was studying anything at all and the authority was tiresome, so I sent myself down after 2 terms. Will you have some wine? I think it's Italian. Verdicchio . . . Is it all right to drink?'

'Very good.'

'There's a wonderful drink called the Singapore Sling – have you ever had one?'

'Yes, I had one in the Strand Hotel in Rangoon.'

'Those are very acceptable, aren't they? I've not been to Burma.

People who've had to do with Burma tell me the females are very pretty there.'

'They smoke cigars . . . I've not been to Venice.'

'Haven't you really? Venice really is the greatest experience in the world. When I was about 12, I was in Venice and had terrible bronchial trouble. And Dr van Someren used to attend to me. I remember being fascinated by his red chalk pencils which is the sort of fing that interests you when you are 10 or 12. Meanwhile he was having the most fearful time with Baron Corvo who was staying wiv 'im. I've really travelled almost everywhere I've wanted to go. I was very lucky there. But I now feel as if I've hardly been even in London. Can you understand that? I used to love the Café Royal. I remember so well the lavatory attendant. He met absolutely everybody – in their off moments. He was called Sigismondo Pandolfo Malatesta and he really was descended apparently from the Malatesta family and very very proud of that. They were the tyrants of Rimini. Next time you're passing through Rimini, you ought to stop and have a look at the wonderful Malatesta tombs.'

Gertrude comes in to take the first course plates and says to him 'Now you're to eat plenty.'

He twitches and replies 'For some extraordinary reason I can't get *The Lambeth Walk* out of my head.' He hums a snatch.

'That's because we were singing those old songs last weekend,' she says.

'You must remember *The Lambeth Walk*, do you?' he asks, humming a further snatch for my benefit. 'It was the last good Cockney song.'

'I drove along it once. It's all demolished.'

'Is it really?' he remarks in an upcurve. 'Gertrude is highly musical. She can sing practically all the popular tunes from the last ¼ of a century – as well as the previous quarter.'

'I need Henrietta to teach me,' she says self-deprecatingly. 'That's Mr Sachie's grand-daughter. Well, you are not going to believe this but I'm going to tell you. You know who Mick Jagger is, don't you?'

'Oh yes.'

'Well, his granny was my mother's bridesmaid. I tell everybody. His mother came from Derbyshire where Mr Sachie comes from and where I come from.'

'Eckington,' says Sachie with a nod.

Mrs Stevenson puts a steak & kidney pie in the centre of the table and dishes of potatoes, carrots, peas, and I say to her 'I interviewed him once. It was tea-time and he'd just got out of bed.'

'What a life,' she says, throwing up her eyes.

Sachie motions me to take food and says 'Max Beerbohm had a

sister who was a nun and who made a great career for herself by writing a music-hall song which had a terrific success. She went on being a nun but lived off the proceeds for the rest of her life. I remember having lunch with him at Rapallo. There was a procession outside. It was Mussolini going past. And Beerbohm said "There goes the Black Bottom".'

'I suspect you're musical too.'

'I'm not a musician. I've certainly written a lot about music. At the moment I'm stuck on Domenico Scarlatti. I think he was the great master of music for the harpsichord like Chopin was for the piano. He has such an extraordinary variety for one fing. And some of it is deeply, almost upsettingly passionate. He has the most extraordinary changes of mood which are very fascinating.'

'Wasn't he Sicilian?'

'His father was. Alessandro. But where music's concerned, and I know it's fearfully impertinent to say so but, um, I'm not really awfully fond, well, of Beethoven, you know . . .' He seems truly contrite at this, looking uneasily at his plate. Then he continues 'But I really like music more than anyfing else, so I like almost any form of it. I've got some wonderful songs of Gershwin over there, sung by Ella Fitzgerald. And I used to like going to nightclubs. You go to nightclubs, do you?'

'I do.'

'Very wise . . . If you give me your glass I'll give you some more wine. How long is it since we last met? About a year?'

'18 months?'

'You see, my memory is getting bad, isn't it?'

'Did you go to that nightclub in Paris, Le Boeuf sur le Toit?'

'Yes, I went with Cocteau. He more or less ran it. And he taught me to say when one's in a restaurant, and the dish is shown to you before being served "Merci, c'est bien resemblant." Meaning "Thank you, yes, it really quite looks like whatever it's supposed to be." I went to Paris to see poor Modigliani. You know his pictures, do you? And the poor fing was in the most terrible state.'

'What was the matter?'

'Well, he was dying. From tuberculosis and malnutrition and everyfing else. And his wife – well, she wasn't his wife, she was his mistress – he died – and she was going to have his baby and she threw herself out of the window and so that was the end of that. And I bought 2 pictures from him for £4 each which is really shaming and I'd almost sooner it wasn't mentioned. But I think he died about a fortnight later. One of these pictures went for £160,000 not long ago. Which is appalling, isn't it, and shaming and dreadful, don't you think it is?'

WALK Calgary's world of
international, national and local DESIGN

DESIGN DISTRICT

Phone 780.993.2273~www.zotmedia.com~E-mail:postcards@zotmedia.com~Edmonton AB~ ◆ ©2004~NOT FOR RESALE

DESiGN DISTRICT

1 Brew Brothers Brewery, Restaurant & Taproom
Rebuilt Beers Brewed on Premise, Live Music, Secluded Deck, Free Internet (WiFi), Private Parties, Games Room.
607 11th Ave N.W. • www.brewbrothers.com

2 Contempa Carpet Company
Carpet – hardwood – ceramic – Vinyl.
Tailor your lifestyle with Contempa Carpet Company.
1315 11th Avenue S.W. 403-245-4353

3 Chintz & Company
Sumptuous sofas, interior textiles & home couture, eloquent crockery and candle light, fountains ponds and interior décor.
1238 11th Avenue S.W. 403-245-3449

4 Kai Mortensens's
Your custom upholstery, drapery, designers and more
- Come see what makes us Calgary's unusual furniture.
1235 11th Avenue S.W. 403-245-5751

5 The French Connection
Offering beautiful French & Swedish antiques, giftware and sumptuous Ives Delorme linens. Experience the ultimate.
1222 11th Avenue S.W. 403-263-4344

6 City Tile Design Studio
We showcase a collection of stone, ceramic, porcelain, glass, metal & artisan tile that is guaranteed to fit your style.
1220 11th Avenue S.W. 403-244-7171

7 Designers Choice Kitchen & Bathrooms Ltd.
20 year exquisite kitchens & bathrooms from custom design to installation featuring Miele, Sub Zero, Wolf.
1218 11th Avenue S.W. 403-229-1900

8 Robert Pashuk Architecture
Robert Pashuk has recently opened this storefront location specializing in contemporary commercial and residential design.
1217 11th Avenue S.W. 403-270-9376

9 Maria Tomás
Calgary's retail design source center. Textiles, upholstery, window treatments, custom design, Farrow & Ball Paint & Paper.
1015 11th Street S.W. 403-233-9055

10 Prints Charming
Your wall decor store featuring fantastic custom framing and thousands of fine art posters.
1409 11th Street S.W. 403-229-0220

11 Century Floor Covering (Carpet one)
When it comes to flooring, nobody does it better. The largest showroom, best installations, expert management service.
1115 11th Avenue S.W. 403-245-1115

12 the art of hardware
Your wall decor... unique kitchen and bath faucets, hand crafted knobs to any décor.
1001 10th Avenue S.W. 403-244-0960

13 B.A. Robinson Lighting & Bath Center
Calgary's premier lighting and bath showroom serving...
940A 9th Street S.W. 403-245-9637

14 Webster Galleries Inc
Since 1979, eclectic range of Canadian artists work, superior framing facilities contained in 10,000 square feet.
812 11th Avenue S.W. 403-263-6500

15 18 Panache for Living
A blend of unique and exceptional furnishings, custom framing, artwork, jewelry and personal accessories.
1210 11th Ave. S.W. 403-263-1543

16 Domicile
Contemporary furniture for your active lifestyle. Join us in creating a functional and enjoyable design.
715 11th Avenue S.W. 403-262-9780

17 Harrison Galleries
Representing the art of local, regional and internationally renowned artists, the gallery carries an extensive collection of traditional and contemporary artwork.
709a 11th Avenue S.W. T2R 0E3 229-0088

18 20 Harringer Kiss Gallery
Specializing in provocative contemporary artwork be emerging and mid-career artists. Custom framing available using the latest designs in frames and mirrors.
101, 1111-11th Ave. S.W. 403-228-4889

'Yes, but it happens all the time. The picture would go for much more now.'

'One of the most beautiful paintings in the world is in the Louvre. *Gilles* by Watteau. It really is the masterpiece of the 18th century. And if you look at Gilles carefully, Watteau has painted red in the corners of his eyes – as if he's been weeping. Chagall said that the *pants* of Gilles always made him want to cry. And somehow they do have that effect on one. The pants are – '

'Poignant pants.'

'Yes. There is something terribly moving about Gilles's pants . . . When were you born?'

'1948. September 26th.'

'That means you are 51 years younger than me. I was born in 1897. I read a long article *Had Queen Victoria A Sense Of Humour?* the other day. There was a grand diplomatic reception and one of the foreign diplomats was so overcome that on departure he kissed his own hand instead of hers. And that made her quite hysterical with laughter apparently.'

The sun has melted the frost on the lawn in several large circular patches. These patches glow a rich green under the blue sky and everywhere outside is touched with gold sunlight which pours diagonally into the dining-room.

'What is your earliest memory?'

'Oh my goodness. Honestly I can't remember. It was so long ago. I remember the Russo-Japanese War very well. That was 1905. The Russians lost. We were all dreadfully surprised. But my chief childhood memory is how much I hated going back to school.'

'Prince Charles is a great advocate of Queen Victoria's sense of humour.'

He coughs and says 'My encounters with members of the Royal Family have been few and far between. But I did drive once down a crowded street with Queen Mary and she did lower the window and say "Why don't you cheer, you little idiots!" Which is really quite funny, isn't it? Almost my only other encounter was when I went to a wedding when I was about 7 and Queen Alexandra was there looking very beautiful but very enamelled. Do you know, I upset my lemonade into her black silk ear-trumpet. And she was delighted. She laughed and laughed and laughed. I felt I should've adored her if I'd known her better.'

'I like the story of the Queen Mother saying at lunch to the Queen "Don't have a second glass of wine, dear. You've got to rule this afternoon."'

He chuckles. He chuckles frequently in an infectious staccato which creases up his whole face. He doesn't usually laugh outright but will take the chuckle to its absolute limit, at which point it judders and sometimes turns into a cough.

'What about when you did the Companion of Honour?'

'That was almost embarrassingly easy. I found myself seated chatting with the Queen and eventually I thought it's not possible, it can't be her – but it was. I was told I must bow twice on admission to the presence and twice on the way out and I absolutely forgot on leaving but I don't think it mattered very much. I do remember when I was in the Grenadiers, we had to go on guard at Buckingham Palace and the band was playing and we saw an absolutely furious face at the window. It was King George V. The band had got it into their heads to play the March from *Prince Igor* and he was onto it like that!' (snapping his fingers). 'He sent down a message, saying Stop it now and never again! So the poor fings had to stop it in the middle and they were rather offended by that too.'

'What didn't he like about it? That it was Russian?'

'That it was Russian. And he wanted the Maidens' Chorus from *The Maid of the Mountains* or somefing . . . Do have some more pie.'

'Have you got lots of things like the Companion of Honour?'

'I've got about . . . 2 honorifics.'

'What's the other one?'

'The Freedom of the City of Lima. The grand object of all travel is to get to Angkor. Did you manage to get there?'

'No.'

'Poor old Angkor, it's out of bounds now. I've been there twice. It's absolutely enormous. You can walk for miles. Heaven knows what it was really all about but it was always uninhabited and built apparently to placate their gods and therefore nobody ever slept there. They slept in reed huts some distance away. That makes it very haunted in a way.'

Gertrude enters unobtrusively with a steamed chocolate pudding. 'I'll bring some more sauce,' she says, putting the pudding on the table, 'in case you . . . want more sauce.' Then she says to me sotto voce 'He doesn't eat enough. But he loves this. There's always method in my madness.'

'What's Gertrude saying? I missed that,' he says, flickering in consternation as if a plot might be afoot.

'I was saying how much you like this. And I make a special chocolate cake too,' she continues to me. 'Osbert's recipe.'

'What's special about it?' I ask.

'Nothing. Mrs Gubbay guarded the recipe and only cooked it for Queen Mary but since Queen Mary was a great friend of Osbert's,

Mrs Gubbay condescended to give it to him. And he condescended to give it to me. But the silly thing is – *exactly* the same recipe is in Lady Maclean's Cookbook!' And with a soft cackle, Mrs Stevenson withdraws.

There is silence as each communes with his plate of chocolate pudding. Spoons clattering against china and quietly champing jaws emphasise the hush on the brows of ruminant beings. Eventually Sachie looks up and, with his green eyes in their expression of surprised enquiry, asks 'Is there anywhere you particularly want to go at the moment?'

'Russia. Sicily. Brazil. Lisbon. Sulawesi. Costa Rica. Malacca.'

'I haven't been to Russia. There's a marvellous Russian who lives near here called Igor Winogradoff who married the daughter of the famous Lady Ottoline Morrell. Well, his mother's Norwegian. I asked him if he remembered Moscow before the war – the First War – and he said he remembered how wonderful the chocolate shops were. He was about 8 or 9 at the time.'

Gertrude rematerialises with the extra chocolate sauce.

'Who's that out there, Gertrude, strolling along the garden path?' he asks.

'It's somebody Bernard's just gone out to. He's in charge of putting in the trees. Will you have a little more?'

'Thank you, dear . . . Fine, that's enough . . . There's a very charming young man let loose in London drawing-rooms now called Azimat Guirey. Have you met him? He's a direct descendant of Genghis Khan. Strange to think of him being in London drawing-rooms. He's a Moslem. He's done the pilgrimage to Mecca. And apparently he lives near Dublin which is awfully curious.'

'How can he be a direct descendant of Genghis Khan?'

'I dunno. Have a tiny drop more wine.'

'No, I'm fine, thanks, Sachie.'

'Oh, have a tiny drop more.'

'Just a dash. I tell you what I wanted to ask you. Did you ever happen to meet Swinburne? He died in 1909.'

'No, I never met him.'

'You were too young.'

'Yes. But Sir Edmund Gosse we knew, who was a kind of doyen of English letters. And he was a great friend of Swinburne's, which was Gosse's attraction from our point of view.' He pronounces *doyen* (as he pronounced *Prince Igor*) in the French manner. 'I must tell you a funny story about Evelyn Waugh and his first interview. Evelyn was a little boy in knickerbockers, I suppose about 10 years old, and Gosse said to him "Where are those little knees going to carry you?", looking at the knickerbockers, you see. And Evelyn said "Wherever I damn well want to go." And then Gosse said "Ah, the confidence of youth to be able to envisage a prearranged destination." It's a wonderful Victorian sentence, isn't it?'

We leave the dining-room and return to the fireside. The sky has clouded a little and the daylight begun to fade. Sachie bends his limbs in various places and puts himself back in the winged armchair with piles of books round its legs. I wonder if the house is haunted.

'No, not haunted at all. But since my wife died, I do get very nervous sometimes. That's a photograph of her over there.' He indicates with a long thin finger a pretty, rather saucy-looking woman. 'I absolutely refuse to spend a night in this house by myself. Gertrude and her husband live in the village and so her husband comes to sleep here at night . . . I was thinking in the middle of the night last night about all the people I've been in love with in my life. There were 5 of them. And I'm not going to give any names.'

'Your sister didn't marry. And your brother was homosexual and didn't marry. You were the only one to be conventional in that sense, to marry and have children.'

'That's true,' he says, adding with alarmed eyebrows 'but extreme normality can be very unpleasant. Dean Cunningham, an ancestor of mine, had, I discovered recently, 20 sons. And they were all by the same wretched woman too. Can you imagine anyfing more hideous?'

'There don't seem to have been many aunts, uncles, cousins in your childhood.'

'No, well, my father couldn't stand the sight of my mother's relations. I inherited this house from an aunt. All the characters in here' – he extends an arm like a piece of driftwood – 'all these boring portraits, are relations.'

Gertrude appears with coffee and says 'Am I interrupting?' She hands Sachie the chocolates and he makes an enormous noise unwrapping the golden box from its paper coverings.

'Have one, Gertrude. You know you adore the white ones,' he says.

'No, I won't have one now.'

'Are you feeling all right? You don't look awfully well.'

'Of course I'm feeling all right,' she declares, then goes out.

I say 'If you have blood pressure or heart problems, you're not supposed to eat chocolate. It speeds you up. Have you ever had heart problems?'

'Yes.'

'You have? And did they tell you not to eat chocolate and salt?'

'I can't remember. I went into the army when I was 18 but never

went to war because I had a bad heart. I've always had a bad heart.'
He adds lugubriously 'I know someone who's going to Japan. I wish
I was going to Japan.'

'I looked you up in *Who's Who*. It said you were Lord Lieutenant
of Northamptonshire.'

'Now wait a moment – I was Sheriff, wasn't I?'

'Oh, is that what it was? Probably I've got it wrong.'

'Was I a lord lieutenant as well? We must ask Gertrude. She's been
with me for well over 50 years – and she and her husband together for
well over 100. I was certainly a sheriff.' (It turns out I was in error – he
was Sheriff, not the Lord Lieutenant.) 'Which involves sitting in court
and listening to cases and walking in fearfully boring processions and
it's also very expensive because you have to entertain the judges and
all that sort of fing.'

'So why did you agree to do it?'

'I can't imagine. It must've gone to my head or somefing.'

'Is this a particularly social county?'

'In the north of Northamptonshire more. They go in for hunting
up there. Which I've never gone in for. And I do suffer a great deal
from loneliness because my poor darling wife is no longer here. I
was so marvellously happily married for 56 years which is quite a
time. During the night she made this rather curious noise and her
eyes opened and rolled back. They said she'd had a massive cerebral
haemorrhage which was a very good thing because if it hadn't been
massive Georgia might've been reduced to a vegetable. Being old is
awfully tiresome, you know. And if you've had a very happy life, it's
so awful it only happens once.' The clock strikes the half hour with
a high pure ping. 'But my eyes have got very much better now that
I'm older. I saw a famous eye-specialist called Dr Ida Mann and she
said – your eyes will improve enormously as you get older. And that
has happened . . . I've never had any religious feeling of any sort,
have you?'

'Not through the usual channels.'

'I can't believe in the Virgin Birth or anyfing of that sort, can
you?'

'Good Lord, no – and if it did happen it was surely a misfortune,
not something to celebrate.'

'The local vicar came to see me and I had to explain that I thought
Our Lord was an ordinary human being but a very wonderful one and
leave it at that.'

'Do you think you've changed as you've grown older?'

'I think I've become stupider. I think it's inevitable as you get older.'
He has another chuckle here.

'But does contemplating the modern world depress you? Old people often say it does.'

'Well, in some ways it's encouraging, isn't it? There's a young man near here, about 10 miles away, called Hawkins and he became completely paralysed and deaf and dumb. Then about a month ago they opened his head and took out the biggest cerebral tumour there's ever been and he's perfectly all right now. Got his speech back and everyfing. It's almost unbelievable. And it's wonderful to be alive, you see, apart from anyfing else.'

'Would you say you've learned anything particularly?'

'I've certainly learned a lot, yes. Having travelled so much, I have a most marvellous knowledge of works of art, really more I think than almost anybody else I know, without wishing to throw my weight about. And I have a most extraordinary accumulation of knowledge on rather unusual subjects like . . . snuffboxes.'

'I really meant more in the personal sense.'

'Well, one realises as one grows older that one's been dead wrong about people. Often mistaken them entirely. Would you like to wash your hands or anyfing? No, well, I'm going to retire for a second and be back in 2 minutes. I've got to go and wee as they say.'

Edith, Osbert and Sacheverell were the offspring of an odd couple from Derbyshire. Sir George Sitwell presided over the family's shrinking iron and coal money and also wrote, among other things, a history of the 2-prong fork. His wife, Lady Ida, overfond of gambling, became entangled with money lenders. When Sir George refused to pay her debts, she went to prison; upon her release 10 weeks later, he announced that he would forgive her.

When Sir George died, his elder son Osbert inherited the baronetcy, the estate at Renishaw, the castle of Montegufoni in Tuscany, and everything else. And when Sir Osbert died, Sacheverell became the baronet but Osbert divided the property between Sachie, Sachie's eldest son and Osbert's Maltese companion in such a way as to prevent any one of them being able to live in the grand style Osbert himself had enjoyed. Sacheverell had been much looking forward to spending his last years with his wife at Montegufoni. So when Osbert, by-passing his brother, left Renishaw and Montegufoni to Sachie's elder son but with no money to maintain the latter, this can be seen as a gesture of spite. Perhaps this is why Weston Hall has about it an air of Arcadian exile.

When Sachie returns I say 'Your father is usually presented as an ogre – but he seems to have had charm too.'

'I'm so glad you think so. Because it's time Papa stopped being maligned. I think really in some ways he was a much nicer character than Osbert. My father had this wonderful manservant called Henry Moat who used to say "To-night, Sir George, you are dining alone. And you couldn't want for better company." '

'Why do you think your brother broke up the inheritance?'

'Osbert probably rather resented my getting married because he and I had been living very happily together in Chelsea. But Montegufoni was originally a mad idea of my father's and it has always had this megalomaniac effect on people. It is now a loony bin. No, perhaps we shouldn't say that. It is now a rest home. And when he bought it, over 100 people were living there, sort of camping in it. It was a complete village really. Perfectly ridiculous. We used to go there every Easter. There's a room in it painted by Severini which is raver nice.' Sachie waves his long hands about near his ankles and eventually finds what he is looking for, his packet of cigarettes. 'Having been brought up a good deal in Italy, I very much prefer Spain.'

'Why's that?'

'I dunno. The Italians are too agreeable in a way.'

'And what are the Spanish? Disagreeable?'

'They're more difficult until you get to know them. You won't have a cigarette? The Sicilians are quite like the Spaniards in this respect. Have you been to Noto?'

'No. Where's that? Japan?'

'Sicily.'

'Is it really? It sounds so strange.'

'Well, it is strange in a way, a wonderful, forgotten baroque town.'

'I very much want to go to Sicily.'

'You do, do you?'

'Yes. I want to find the Lago dei Palici,' I say.

'What's that?' he asks.

'It's a lost mythological lake of black water somewhere in Sicily.'

'Sounds fascinating.'

'*Doesn't* it sound fascinating. I read about it somewhere. There are strange phenomena – birds die if they fly over it for example. It is supposedly the birthplace of Castor and Pollux.'

'Well, you must certainly find it. And you must go to Noto which is all gold. And very sleepy, remote and wonderful with old palaces and baroque churches and terraces. And surrounded by lemon groves and almond groves in the sun . . .'

For a few moments neither of us is in icy midwinter Northamptonshire. We are staring into a fireplace of glowing logs, in a daydream that is half memories, half fantasies. The Golden City. And the Black Lake . . . Then he says 'I was a great admirer of D'Annunzio. And I still can't help being one either.'

'A very unfashionable figure.'

'*Very* unfashionable, yes. All the more reason for liking him. I thought he was such a wonderful writer. We are now talking about when I was 20. I went to see him at Fiume. He had seized the city – and held it. I went with my bruvver and we had dinner several times wiv D'Annunzio. Then we had dinner another night wiv 2 Garibaldi veterans in red shirts . . . It's getting quite dark now . . . I must close the shutters in a little while.'

The frost has stayed on the trees all day.

'I'm now hibernating and I go to bed fearfully early. I mean, about a ¼ to 9. But then I read an enormous time in bed, you see. I never put my light out until ½ past 10 or 11. But in this awful climate one really is more comfortable in bed, in the country. I've formed an enormous personal attachment to my electric blanket. Have you got one? No, well, you'll find as you get older that you really do have to keep warm.'

'Do you have any vices?'

'Well, obviously selfishness. Jealousy is a big one . . . jealousy of people who've had an undue amount of success.'

'You've not had success?'

'Not nearly the success I've deserved.'

'What is the success you deserve?'

'. . . Well, I think I ought to be known as a really first-rate poet, which I am, although I say it myself . . . And I'm certainly fearfully greedy. Think how much I like those chocolates. I'm very partial to foie gras, are you? And caviar. But many's the long day since – have you had caviar lately? If one's being taken out, it's fearfully bad manners to ask for caviar now, isn't it. And champagne I'm very fond of, are you? It's one of the great inventions of human beings. I think I better close the shutters. Then Gertrude will come and pull the curtains in a minute.'

He rises like a crane from a lawn, and with surprising vigour and an almighty din, slams and bars the shutters against the gathering night. Gertrude comes in, piles more logs on to the fire, and says to me 'Lady Egremont was here last week,' as if I know the woman in question.

'She's still going strong,' says Sachie. 'But one's friends are all dropping off very fast now. Not that I insist women be my age. In fact I quite like them to be 35. Now will you have a whisky & soda?'

'Why don't you introduce Mr Fallowell to Buster?'

'What, dear?'

'To Buster . . . Buster's Mr Sachie's oldest friend.'

'He sent me a wonderful magnum of champagne. He owns the Harrods of Cincinnati. Now have we got his address? He's been a friend of mine since – well, we met at the Villa Trollope in Florence in 1907 when we were both 10. It was a sort of hotel and both our families were staying there. Or was it at the Royal Hotel in San Remo? He's American. We played with lead soldiers.'

Gertrude is going through an address book with great concentration, unable to find the address, and says curtly 'I did ask you to write it down to save me the trouble.' He becomes flustered, picks up a book at random, dives into it, pretending to be fully absorbed by what it contains until the moment of her irritation has past.

'You've got down here a recipe for lumbago,' she says. 'On a lump of sugar put 1 drop of oil of cloves, 1 drop of juniper, 1 drop . . .' Her voice trails away but the address hunt continues. Notebooks and address books in other parts of the house are drawn into the search and meanwhile I finish my drink and prepare to leave.

'Will you sign this book for me?'

'I certainly will,' he says. 'Is it a book of mine incidentally?'

'Yes. *All Summer In A Day*.'

He signs it in a loopy hand. Gertrude sees me across the hall to the front door. Suddenly there is cold on my face and stars in a jet sky and silence in every direction. The car door makes a loud clunk in the clean cold air. I say goodnight to her and while the car crunches on gravel and pulls away into the black night, the last golden squares of illumination are disappearing from the house as Gertrude completes the closing of the shutters.

2

Decision

A number of years passed. Life was awful, wonderful. But the thought of Noto remained in my mind. A secret unpolluted world in benign sunshine, grand but small, a place of escape, glamour, of porticoes and gardens and fountains, of personal adventure, all integrated and waiting for me, magical, tantalising. The Golden City. And its macabre opposite, the Black Lake – no less tantalising.

Noto was mentioned, albeit briefly, in several guidebooks. But the Lago dei Palici, so ancient and sinister, wasn't in any of them. I was beginning to think I'd imagined it entirely when one rainy afternoon, in a secondhand bookshop in Hay-on-Wye, I came across *Sicily: the New Winter Resort: an Encyclopaedia of Sicily* by Douglas Sladen (London, Revised Edition, 1908). First I looked up Noto.

. . . Noto Antica . . . is called 'the mediaeval Pompeii' having been deserted since its destruction by the great earthquake of 1693 . . . Modern Noto is one of the handsomest cities in Sicily. Its buildings, including the cathedral, all built since the earthquake, are very fine.

That was all. Whereas to my great surprise, on the Lago dei Palici there was considerably more.

The Dei Palici were a pair of indigenous Sicilian deities whom some have attempted to identify with Castor and Pollux. They could give an asylum to fugitive slaves, and important oaths were taken beside their bituminous springs to be made especially binding. Doubtless it was for this reason that Ducetius, who tried to form an anti-Greek Sikel league, established his capital first at Menae, the modern Mineo, and second at Palica, both overlooking the lake. Freeman (History of Sicily, vol. 1) *discusses the Palici at great length. There was a superb temple here dedicated to the Dei Palici, who were declared to be the sons of Zeus and Aetna (or Thalia). Virgil speaks of the 'pinguis et placabilis ara Palici'. The Greeks said that Zeus, having made the nymph with child, made the earth open up to conceal her from the wrath of Hera, and when the time came for her to be delivered, the children came up through the earth. The natural phenomena here are very remarkable. A little lake 500 yards round contains the spring from which a rich and nauseous black oil comes up, which Fazello says is very deadly to animals. These exhalations in the neighbouring territory of Favorotto produce a mirage called the Fata Morgana. The evil atmosphere of the lake must be exaggerated, for the Sicilian railways have lately established a ferryboat over the lake so that the phenomena may be observed.*

This entry was accompanied by a very poor faded photograph which carried the subtitle *The Lake of the Palici, the oldest sanctuary in Europe.* This surely must be an exaggeration. The oldest sanctuary in Europe, I always thought, was the site of Stonehenge, with the 'invisible' Woodhenge nearby even older (older than the Pyramids in fact). Doesn't this make Woodhenge the oldest architectural religious site in the world? And indeed – no, let's keep to the matter in hand. Clearly the Lake of the Palici is a very fascinating place which has somehow disappeared from the traveller's map. According to Sladen it is near the small town of Palagonia which *is* marked and is not terribly far from Noto, so . . .

A couple more years passed. Life was dull, brilliant. Then I decided to go, and one morning in London, I jumped into my midnight-blue Ford Capri and set out for Noto.

3

London to Fontainebleau

It is spring, the opening of the year, the perfect time to drive south. What I like about this journey – down through France, along the Riviera, down through Italy, across to Sicily and to God knows what – is that it's adventurous but not outlandish, not *Through The Hindu Kush On Stilts* or *Hulloalloalloa: The People Of The Atoll*. One will not have to have a dozen injections and on arrival wave good-bye to all considerations of personal hygiene. Mind you, I've been outlandish. I've done a fair bit of shitting my heart out in No Man's Land. But not this time. Not this morning. This one's going to be civilised. With bidets. Ever so slightly . . . familiar. This one you can do. I can do. And yet, it is far from being a banal surrender to what is ordinary – for we shall be taking a route through the most remarkable region of the planet: Europe.

Things which conspire to prevent us getting away:

(1) Inertia. Personally, however, I find it takes more will-power to stay put than it does to move around. Man is designed for movement.

(2) Money. Managed to grab some at the 11th hour but nearly had to call the whole thing off.

(3) A cold. The sting at the back of the nose and the sharp dribble down the back of the throat began just 24 hours ago and now, on the morning of departure, it's in full flood.

(4) Wheel-clamping. Park outside the front door in Lennox Gardens while loading up and swallowing a last cup of tea proffered by Bunny, my American landlady. The clampers arrive and have to be persuaded off my wheels. Try to blind them with science: 'I'm leaving for Noto, you know, this very second.' 'Where's that, mate? Japan?' 'No, it's not Japan. I keep telling people it's not Japan.' The clampers say they've heard it's a rough Channel crossing to-day. Thanks a million but I'm not afraid of a few waves. 'Are you *sure* you don't want me to come?'

asks Bunny. 'Positive, darling. And don't forget to give the cat *meat*.'
'Bon voyage!' Her smiling figure recedes into the distance behind the
car, then we (you and I, that is) turn a corner.

(5) Death. As I tootle along to the petrol station, a woman in a red
BMW almost kills me by shooting across the junction of Whitehead's
Grove with Sloane Avenue. She doesn't even give me a glance, the
cow. Quite apart from death or coma, there would be something truly
soul-destroying in having a car crash, however minor, within the first
5 minutes of this great enterprise.

In addition to luggage and presents (books, jam, marmalade, Christmas
puddings – yes, I know it's spring but they always go down well on the
Continent – Christmas puddings is something they don't have, like
crumpets, parsnips, watercress, custard, mint sauce, Marmite and
horseradish), I'm carrying large phials of J. Collis Browne's Mixture
(because it contains liquid extract of opium, excellent for a long drive
with cold) and car spares. My father suggested fanbelt and lightbulbs,
and Stavros, who serviced the car a couple of days ago, suggested in
addition (since the Capri is no longer young) spare clutch cable and
throttle cable (also useful against bandits in a crisis). What about a
spare diaphragm? Too late, we're full of petrol, it's time to roll, 11
a.m., much later than I'd intended, so into first gear and off we go
. . . Sneeze! Schlurrup, sniff . . .

Yes, it's a fine spring morning in London, sunny, with big fluffy white
Constable clouds and several blotches of doomier grey/purple John
Martin clouds in a soft blue sky. Careening round Hyde Park Corner,
we are brought to a halt by the compacted presence of other cars. This
gives us time to ogle the hideous, gauche bulk of the Intercontinental
Hotel, for which they not long ago demolished a group of grand belle
époque houses. Will they never stop making these terrible errors of
judgement? The managing class which makes these decisions has no
understanding of aesthetics. Another recent horror story is British
Telecom's ripping out and selling off of the traditional red British
phone boxes, an act of breathtaking coarseness of mind. Who *are*
these cretins in charge of our world? Come smoothly out of the
junction and flow down towards Victoria and Vauxhall Bridge Road.

Things which conspire to prevent us getting away:

(6) Traffic jams.

(7) Not knowing where you want to go.

(8) Wanting too much, i.e. wanting to go in 2 directions at once

(this is called conflict), e.g. wanting to go abroad – and wanting to stay at home and kick in the faces of British Telecom's Board of Directors.

Traffic is appalling – detour through Belgravia and Pimlico – past the neo-stucco of Bessborough Gardens, an interesting corner of London with many fine new buildings of various sorts, including a new tempietto. Over the Thames and curve round the Oval.

Things which conspire to prevent us getting away:

(9) London's suburbs. Because London has been bigger longer than any other city, its suburbs are old and endless with narrow roads. Camberwell Green, Peckham High Street – these are still recognisably 17th-century village centres with many of the original country buildings much overlaid. Very charming but very dense and one can lose one's way . . . Switch on radio. *This is Radio 1 News* (to a background of funky pop music). *A huge radioactive cloud is hovering over vast areas of Scandinavia. An alert sounded this afternoon at a nuclear plant near Stockholm. It was first thought to be an escape of gas from the plant at Forsmark 100 miles north of Stockholm, but that's now been discounted. Denmark, Norway and Finland have also reported increased levels of radioactivity* (pop music fades out). *Roger Milne, the nuclear energy correspondent of* New Scientist *magazine, says the Swedes have pinpointed the source as a reactor in the Soviet Union: 'The Swedish ambassador in Moscow has pointed the finger very firmly at a station called Ignalina which is a very large nuclear power station northwest of Moscow in the old Baltic republic of Lithuania. It's the Russians' largest graphite-moderated nuclear plant. This particular reactor design is peculiar to the Russians and it's regarded generally in the West as being inherently less safe than a lot of Western nuclear technology.'*

. . . Oh God. What's going on now? . . . I tell you, this planet is in the hands of maniacs. None of us is safe. Now a radioactive cloud is beginning to drift across Europe! Keep calm, Duncan, keep cool. The BBC has promised updates . . . Fuck, I'm lost. Must've taken a wrong turn . . . Where the hell am I? Turn off radio. No more horrors please. Not until I've found myself. . . . Yes, here we go, right I think I'm OK . . . . . Yes . . . . . but ooooooooo – urgh – a nasty accident, a *nasty* one at Queen's Road by the railway bridge. A red car and a grey car, head-on collision, mangled across the road, and red double-decker buses clamber up on to the pavement to get by. Blood and petrol dribble across the tarmac in morning sunshine. This journey can only get better . . .

Deptford Town Hall is a superb baroque building with soldiers on the front of it – they presumably have plans to pull it down.

Things which conspire to prevent us getting away:

(10) Shocking news.

I steel myself and tune in Radio 4. Mary Goldring is reporting on an artificial agricultural oasis which the Saudis are developing. *There are cows wherever you look*, she says, a note of consternation in her voice, *17,000 of them in the middle of the desert!* Up Blackheath Hill, it starts to get posh. Traffic jam. *The greening of the desert also includes growing wheat which costs 12 times what it would on the open market!* But Prince Abdullah says that, despite the fall in oil prices, Saudi Arabian reserves held in the United Kingdom and the USA are still rising . . . Unaccountably the traffic jam dissolves away and we are in the spacious realm of Blackheath. Green, sun, mist – but no trees on the heath itself. This is because the dead were buried in lime here during the Black Death. But on the rim of it are many fine houses with mature gardens overflowing with daffodils. 2 hitch-hikers. Not stopping. Hitch-hikers can be fun if they are solo. But never pick up a double act – unless you are a triple act – which would mean 5 in the car which is too many anyway. And if you stop for a solo and another pops out from behind a tree, *do* have the gumption to drive away and leave the deceitful buggers standing there.

The Black Prince Interchange. I look at the sky and see not celestial infinity but a radioactive realm buzzing with invisible death. Passing under the strutted flyovers of the M25, the world's longest urban orbital, we see on the left what looks like a 19th century prison. It resembles a string of abandoned French châteaux, boarded up, ready for demolition, but very beautifully grouped in the landscape. So many modern architects seem to design a building indoors then go out and slap it down without reference to anything else around it – unlike the earliest builders who orientated their buildings not only to the landscape but to the stars. A merely self-referential structure is alienated; were it a human being it would be classified as insane.

After Snodland and crossing the Medway Valley, one at last begins to leave the megalopolis and have an intimation of countryside. Very uncomfortable ringing noise in ears as we pass under electric cables strung across the M2. There's something to be researched about overhead cables giving out electroweirdness to innocent dwellers-by. And not only do pylon lines screw up the brain – the inner landscape – they screw up the outer landscape too. Bury the blighters. The radio

has offered no more on the Death Cloud – presumably all the top brass
are rushing for their satin-lined nuclear shelters while we poor sods
have to take it full in the face. Now an AIDS counselling programme
comes on – weirder and weirder . . . Will there be anything left for
that Great New Year's Eve Party in 1999? No wild animals that's for
sure. We are driving into the future as we hurtle along the road –
we are the tip of an unleashed arrow –

Things which conspire to prevent us getting away:
    (11) Diseases worse than colds.
    (12) Fear of novelty. Not applicable in my case.
    (13) Fear of going it alone. Ditto. Ra-ra-rah! Big head . . . One
slows to a crawl in a welter of white and luminescent orange cones.
Woman's Hour to-day is spotlighting battered parents, especially women
who've suffered at the hands of their sons. Apparently it's an overlooked
thing, with everyone so obsessed with incest. A faint blue mist hovers in
the green and twiggy spring countryside under a crisp sun. The leaves
aren't out on the trees, but when they are, the English countryside is
characterised by things nestling in it, buildings sunk in gardens and
lush folds, obscured by foliage and verdant banks.

Things which conspire to prevent us getting away:
    (14) Inability to procure what one needs to depart. In this case,
white cotton shorts. You can find shorts in synthetics and mixes but
not all-cotton. Not even in Harrods. Not even in Lillywhite's. Which
is simply outrageous in a so-called civilised capital. Some of us can't
wear synthetics. Because they give us prickly heat – under ordinary
circumstances, let alone in a hot climate. Once in India I developed a
flagrant groin rash through wearing synthetics, which vanished when
I donned cotton. Dover. The boat sails at 3 . . . Up on the poop
here, looking at the white cliffs and thinking of Dame Vera Lynn, I
marvel at the beautiful and surrealistic spectacle of this site. White
Regency terraces low to the left and beyond them a modern white
pyramid. A radar installation, radio masts, and a castle on the clifftop.
The waving slice of the cliffs themselves, blue sky behind. There is
virtually no rubbish in the eye. The diverse elements, from ancient
to futuristic, are arranged in the spacious vista with an exceptional
sense of dramatic fitness, and constitute the most successful example
I know of landscaping complex modern amenities. For Englishman and
foreigner alike, it is a majestic introduction to the United Kingdom.
But we are going the other way thank heavens!
    The ship is of the Townsend-Thoresen Line and called the *Spirit*

of Free Enterprise. I'm not too happy about the name – in my present mood it evokes visions of planetary desolation brought about by uncontrolled short-term exploitation of natural resources. The ship squats motionless in a basin of green water. Disco music crackles over the tannoy. Up here, out on the poop, there's a fresh breeze which blows the faint clouds of music into nothingness.

Things which conspire to prevent us getting away:

(15) Drowning. A sub-division of (5), but it always passes through one's mind on boats.

(16) Insularity. It's terrible leaving the island by boat. There is always a tearing sensation. You don't get it with aeroplanes – with aeroplanes you have only the death fear. But as the boat stirs and froths in its basin and begins to edge backwards towards the bar and open water, one is slowly torn from the matrix of home. And yet, falling too easily into routines, one is always arranging departures, to prevent the skin growing over eyes and ears and nostrils and heart, to prevent the staying becoming suffocation – because enwrapment is the opposite of enrapture. This of course is pre-Chunnel consciousness. Will one be more blasé after the Channel tunnel has opened?

Away . . . . trail of foam on a lightly choppy sea . . . . Parties of French school children are returning home from the Land of Pop Music. They are dressed alike, not in uniform but in the same casual costume: baggy trousers rolled an inch above the ankle to expose coloured socks, and baggy jackets with sleeves reaching down to the second knuckle of the fingers. Lots of pronounced French noses. The French girls – the boys to a lesser extent – behave like high-spirited adults. They give a very passable impersonation of their sophisticated elders. The boys shuffle more than the girls – except one who appears to be a young and intelligent homosexual and who has advanced as far as the girls in knowingness and expertise of demeanour and so prefers to be with them. Already it is a different world one is in.

I saunter off to buy a couple of bottles of Laphroaig whisky and have a final cup of British tea – the tea turns out to be a cultural humiliation, dead brown water which dribbles out of a nozzle into a cup when you press a button. The milk is sealed in a miniature plastic tub – at least this prepares one for the maltreated milk one has to cope with virtually everywhere on the Continent. Once off the island, it's difficult to find real milk with which to make real tea. In Germany and Italy the milk has a brown tinge and the texture of motor oil. Change money. Foreign money seems so flimsy after British money, especially the coins . . . . .

The ship is sliding through haze . . . . . The island tension relaxes . . .
One can do anything. One can be anybody . . . A kid I saw eating a giant
Toblerone bar from the Duty Free Shop is now vomiting it up over the
rail. But the wheel clamper was wrong. It is not a rough crossing.

The line of France emerges from the haze. The prospect of Calais
is ugly compared to that of Dover, a light industrial mess along a
low sandy shore with towerblocks on the pleasure beach. Down in
the belly the drivers start up their cars, buses and lorries, blowing
poisonous exhaust into each other's radiators. Then slowly the hatch
winches down, a spear of light (the sky of France) expands into an exit
and one by one we roll off the ship, over a ramp and on to foreign
soil. Freedom.

Passport and customs hardly exist and I'm bowling along on the right
hand side of a French road almost before I realise it. Compared to
England, the sign-posting here is brilliant – in fact French roads are
crowded with things to read. The French hate to be lost. Everything
must be identified, signified. For a Frenchman, hell is a place where
one is lost; whereas for an Englishman, to be able to get lost every
so often is crucial to his peace of mind.
    Just outside Calais a hitch-hiker in a black sombrero is holding up
a board which says 'Italy'. No thanks. Far too ugly. He wears a Zapata
moustache and faded jeans, a hippy of uncertain age, the kind of figure
who hardly exists any longer in Britain but who is much to be met with
in Europe – there's loads of them in Germany.
    It's kilometres now instead of miles – this makes distances seem
shorter . . . God, the north French countryside is a bore. And God, the
French are hysterical drivers. Twice as many French die on the road as
British. Once behind the wheel their customary desperation fulminates
into rampant rabies of the road. Here's one now, look, swooping up
behind, *right on to my bumper*, for fuck's sake, get back, get *back*! I can
see in the mirror that the silly arse is frantic beyond belief, especially
because he's divined I'm British, throwing his hands in the air, flashing
his headlights – there he goes now, overtaking me on a bend, the prat –
oh, it's a woman with a child loose in the back, s-t-u-p-i-d bitch . . .
Dismal drizzle on a soul-less landscape of prairie farming . . . . .

Péage (the toll on French motorways). After the beastly drivers, the
second shock is having to pay to use the motorway. This means that

if driving alone, as we are, with a right-hand drive, we must stop the car, undo the safety belt, get out, walk round the bonnet, press the button for the ticket (the French for some reason use the words 'ticket' and 'stop' and 'parking' on roads), get back into the car, do up the belt, the barrier lifts, and off we go down the slip road on to the motorway. Since toll gates interrupt the autoroute every so often, on a long drive this necessity refreshes the head and stretches the legs. As for travelling alone in general, things happen when you travel alone. The couple – unless it has children – creates its own prophylactic, sealing it off from outside influences and approaches. The rest of the world assumes that personal search ends with the couple. Whereas the traveller alone will have much offered him. Or her.

The toll barrier lifts. I drive through the turnpike and we're off! No, we're not . . . A squat gendarme in a navy blue mac has waved me over to the side. He asks questions, gets me to open up the car, and starts going through my bags with languid thoroughness, smiling sweetly to himself. They often stop travellers a little way into French territory, just as you think you've got away with it and begin to relax. With an exaggerated expression of astonishment, he indicates 2 large plastic people lying on their sides across my rear seat. They smell frightful. I explain that these models belong to Ms Anna Moody, a friend of mine who has a boutique in Saint Tropez (my French is feeble but a crisis always tunes it up; and another thing I've noticed – the more fluently one speaks a foreign language the worse one's accent becomes, because if you are absorbed by what you are communicating, you don't have time to think about pulling the mouth around in the correct manner). He seems inclined to saw the bodies open. He touches them (they are newly made from some resinous plasma, and sticky) and lifts his fingertips to his nostrils where they remain while cogitation takes place. But he veers off towards a brown leather grip which contains shoes and jars of marmalade. Do my 2 bottles of whisky exceed the allowance? I wonder, guilt exuding from my temples in droplets. Eventually his reconnaissance draws to an end. He says I can close up, and with true courtesy apologises for deranging me.

'Vous cherchez quoi, monsieur?' asks the innocent abroad.

'Stupéfiants, monsieur,' he replies with a sardonic curve of the mouth.

'Ah, vous êtes trop tard, monsieur. Je suis trop grand maintenant.'

I used to take all the drugs. Heroin I took for 3 weeks in Penang to find out. I didn't like heroin. I much preferred opium. Heroin was like living under water. Warm water. But when I floated off across the Bay of Bengal to Madras, leaving the drug behind, I don't recall

any withdrawal symptoms, perhaps because I was so full of alcohol
and blues (early designer pills by Smith, Kline & French). We were
wild. It was fun. Usually. But now most drugs get in the way rather
than help. These days I get stupefied by reality.

Drizzle clears. Late afternoon sun comes through the cloud in peachy
patches. Put the car clock forward an hour (I don't wear a wristwatch)
and suddenly it's later. There is a great deal of information along the
banks of French motorways, including illustrations, to explain what
you're shooting through. In fact the French motorway system is a
whole world in itself with shops (overpriced souvenirs and examples
of local produce), many petrol stations, and picnic lay-bys.

    Switch on the radio for Death Cloud update – Radio 4 still loud
and clear. A panel of pundits are discussing the Futurist exhibition
in Venice – Marinetti and his night drive through Paris – while I
eat sandwiches and flapjacks from Justin de Blank, Walton Street
(superb) . . . Vast incandescent cherry of sun descends on the right
into mist, wide open fields, abandoned slagheaps like black pyramids,
an occasional clump of trees and rooftops clustered round a church
steeple, an occasional slowly rolling tractor, lines of pylons . . . French
pylons are more like people than are English ones – they have little
Thalidomide arms, large heads, erect terrier ears . . . . . War graves.
Les champs de la Bataille de Somme. My mother's father fought there
and in Flanders. My father's parents were Methodists and pacifists
. . . . . The BBC News says that all evidence points to a disaster in
Russia but that the Russians are silent. Another item announces the
discovery of a huge but invisible object midway between the Earth and
the edge of the observable universe. Could be a black hole; could be an
enormous concentration of galaxies, they say; could be cosmic string.
It has been detected because 2 images of the same quasar have been
observed in the sky, which means that light from a single source has
been bent by the gravity of some object: we are seeing round both
corners. Given the degree of separation of the images, astronomers
deduce that the thing bending this light must be absolutely colossal
. . . More war graves. Deep slug of Collis Browne's Mixture . . . Then
a pale full moon shows up on the left like a macaroon in a sky of misty
lavendery grey . . . Slot in a tape and flow creamily towards Paris at
90 m.p.h. as Jacki Wilson gives full throat to *Here Comes the Night*.

But we are not going to Paris. Not even to see Gilles's pants. We are
going to give those pants a wide berth because the Périphérique will

be jammed and it's our intention to fall further south before bedtime.
I've only been to Paris once. To interview Mick Jagger. Flew in at
lunchtime, met him at teatime, flew out at dinnertime. It was a sunny
afternoon, I remember, but the light didn't penetrate very far into the
modern bowels of the Hotel Warwick off the Champs Elysées. The
press agent, a young Cockney with very long eyelashes, had spent much
of his day in the lift because Mick Jagger was occupying a large suite
at the top, while people who wanted to see him accumulated at the
bottom, waiting in the bar with increasingly round shoulders, eating
endless bowls of garlic biscuits and black olives and gherkins, drinking
endless beers or whisky & sodas as the clock slid slowly round and the
barmen replaced each other.

2 p.m. 2.30 p.m. 'Yeah, don't worry. Mick knows you're here.' 3 p.m.
'Mick's just getting up. Shouldn't be too long now.' 3.30. 4. 'Yeah,
Mick's got up now – just let him get some coffee down, some breakfast.'
4.30. 4.45. 'You can go up now.'

'Who, me?'

'Yeah. What's your name again?'

As the lift moved silently and greasily skyward, Jaggerward, the
question which formed itself was 'Why am I so nervous?' because
the style around there was *looseness*. Mick Jagger's face, it turned out,
was exceedingly loose. The lips really were all they've been cartooned
as, and hung in mid-air like disembodied giblets some way off the
rest of him going 'Yeah, Alan . . . yeah . . . yeah . . .' as the press
agent flitted about trying to be loose *and* specific. The star's hair
was long which did nothing to lift a visage upon which gravity had
such a tremendous grip. That he was prepared to meet a stranger in
this crumpled 'first-thing-in-the-morning' condition says much for his
self-possession.

In my embarrassment my first words were 'You've got something
on your front tooth.'

He gave me a fatigued, sideways look and said 'That's me diamond.'

The diamond in his tooth was the only jewellery he wore. He
didn't need it. It was entirely overshadowed – wrong word – by his
white-tiled smile (when he remembered to switch it on) which blotted
out everything else in a spasm of good humour.

'I have to keep remembering which country I'm talking to,' he said,
'because you know you go from Japan, Spain, England, America and
they're very different in what they want to know. The Germans like
to talk politics. The Spanish just want to talk about football and I told
the Spanish bloke I wasn't interested in football, which is a lie, and
that really fucked his whole interview, poor guy. But I didn't want to

talk football for half an hour, fucking hell. The Americans obviously want to know about the music. And the English, they go round and round and round and then it comes to sex which is really all they want to talk about.'

'All right. I've got a sex question. How did you discover the facts of life?'

'God! That's a sudden question. Let me think – yeah, I was told by the kids at school. Then I started masturbating. Then I started fucking. Then I . . .!'

'And here's an American question. In what way were the Rolling Stones important?'

'I'm probably the last person to go on about it. They must've done something, coz first of all . . . in America and here in Europe there is a tremendous sense of . . . I don't know what it is, but there's a sense of something out there. And perhaps like . . . there's a closing of the generation gap. People bring their children to see the Stones and . . . that's what they do. Not everybody, but I mean they do it. I think the Stones were part . . . I mean, they weren't the most important part even, but they were a part of . . . that period.'

Could one get looser than this? But you should remember that in the Stones' heyday to be articulate was not à la mode because it implied you hadn't been taking enough drugs to totally flab out your mind.

'Do you take drugs still?'

'That's faded.'

'Health food then?'

'No! I hate health food. I eat like crazy but I don't eat junk food either. I don't like junk food. If I did, I'd eat it probably. I'm 9 stone 8 and I really eat. If you're doing a lot of physical stuff, like 3 hours before you go on, I eat a huge plate of pasta and that's completely burnt off. Protein, steak, is like not apparently the thing any more. It's carbohydrates now – it burns quicker – anyway that's what all the footballers and athletes do, so that's what I do.'

He was wearing sporty clothes, a red V-necked football jersey trimmed in white, green cotton trousers with box pockets up the legs, purple socks, black and grey running shoes. The harsh colour-scheme drained vitality from his complexion.

'You're very sporty at the moment.'

'That's the thing this year. This top is Aberdeen Football Club. They gave it to me. And these trousers are what the young gay boys are wearing in London. I dyed them green myself.'

'Have you got any phobias?'

'Not that I can think of. Have you?'

'I don't like bats in an enclosed space.'

'I don't, er, I mean, I've never been with bats in an enclosed space but I'm sure I wouldn't like it if I had.'

'What's your greatest failure?' (*Think: God, I sound so rude and abrupt. Loosen up, Duncan.*)

'Um . . . . Riding roughshod over people without thinking. While I'm riding roughshod I should be thinking "Hey, I'm riding roughshod" but I forget because there's so much to do – that's my excuse.'

A waiter came onto the balcony where we sat and put glasses of beer and fizzy water on small paper mats on the table.

'Did you fight with your father when you were an adolescent?'

'Yeah. Well, he was bloody awful. So disciplinarian. He was a school teacher. I have a very good relationship with my parents now.'

'When did your father calm down?'

'When I started making a lot of money, dear.'

'Are you careful with money?'

'Not at all.'

But he is. According to the barman downstairs, Jagger paid his personal bar bill daily in order to keep tabs on it.

Mick added 'Paul McCartney's been very businesslike. And so has George Harrison – funnily enough.'

'And what about the future?'

'Yeah, oh yeah. I was always a science fiction freak. And I like the idea of satellite communication. I look forward to being able to tune in to sort of 180 TV stations in the middle of the Caribbean Sea – for a very modest cost.'

'I meant – your future.'

'I'd love to do some acting but I don't get offered very good parts because there are a lot better actors around than me . . . I'd probably be involved in politics if I were an American citizen which I'm not and am very unlikely to be because I don't have to be. In America there's dialogue. There is a dialogue between . . . I mean I have a dialogue with the Kennedys, right? A dialogue with them. Of course they want things from me and I want things from them. But there's dialogue, which you wouldn't get in England.'

While trying to work out if there were any Kennedys left, I asked 'You mean you meet the Kennedys at parties?'

'We meet and talk about politics. I mean I talk to Jerry Brown who's a bright guy. I mean he's bright. He may be a bit stupid in some ways – but you know what I'm saying? He asks what do you think, Mick, and I'll say what the fuck is this, Jerry? I mean coz he's got information that I don't have and there's, you know . . .'

Dialogue?

'. . . dialogue. If I was an American I'd probably be getting in there.'

'Do you ever use your songs to get in there?'

'No, my songs are all about girls and food and . . . sex and drugs . . . and touring and . . .'

'Do you find yourself moving in a huge aquarium of celebrities?'

'No, not really. I mean, I have some friends who are just . . . unemployed.'

'I read somewhere that you spent a lot of money on beauty treatments and things for your complexion.'

With a disparaging roll of his eyes, he turned his head like a sleepy old iguana and said 'Does it look like it?'

And that has been my only experience of Paris.

But I'd like to take the opportunity to salute it, a great city which I have yet to experience and where many of the greatest works of 20th century English Literature had first to be published because of the puerility of Great Britain and America. To the glorious sanity of the French in art and sex we shall in due course come. But my God, they couldn't produce a band like the Stones in a million years. Good on you, Mick!

Leave the motorway at Senlis, pay the toll, take the Meaux-Melun route to Fontainebleau. It is now dark and on these long straight roads of rural northern France I am repeatedly flashed by oncoming motorists. Ah, I've forgotten to paint my headlamps yellow in accordance with French custom and they, quite rightly, will give me no peace until I've done so. Pull over and rummage in boot for the small bottle of translucent yellow paint which is always kept there. I apply it by torchlight on bended knee – yellow drips down the glass like liquid jaundice.

Roll into Fontainebleau (a town of dreamy, faded elegance) feeling tired and wuzzy from the rhume but wide awake (Americans call this 'being strung out') and make for the Hôtel de Londres in the Place Charles de Gaulle opposite the palace. Also in this square is the Club of Physical Harmony and a beautiful gateway in rusticated stone, blocked up alas with concrete.

The Hôtel de Londres is a charming neo-classical building in grey and white, with shutters, and a Greek key pattern on its iron balconies. Most important of all, it has parking within the gates. This is crucial when you have a car full of luggage, carrier bags, plastic people. After a long drive the last thing you want to do is haul that lot upstairs just for a night. In Europe, if parking in the street, you must leave *nothing* on show in the car. The attitude is – if you do, you deserve to lose it.

A Frenchman at the desk, his heavy-lidded eyes full of world-weariness and a melancholy detachment born of seeing so many tired and excited travellers come and go, and knowing that he must remain fixed in this place, with this wallpaper, for ever – he gives me a slip of paper to fill in and the key to Room 3. The room faces the palace which is floodlit gold against a black sky. There is a double bed painted green and blue, pretty fake furniture and wallpaper covered with birds the colour of dried blood. A washbasin and bidet in a large plasterboard box with folding plastic door occupy the middle of the left wall and knock out a large chunk of what would otherwise be a delightful room. In this box there is a white striplight which howls with displeasure when turned on. I know people like that.

Ablute as best I can, for there is no soap, and walk into the town on unsteady legs past small restaurants full of yacking, noshing French. It's a balmy evening and suddenly we are in that café world with its casual fluctuations between indoors and outdoors. There is always activity, because the French are vivacious, experts at busy-doing-nothing. And the eye-contact. A profound relief expresses itself in my stomach and ribcage at being in the world of permissible eye-contact (i.e. a world of human adventure) and away from that mustn't-look-mustn't-touch British code. Permissible eye-contact detenses the street.

Dislike eating alone in restaurants, so my first meal in France is a takeaway hamburger. The boy handing out the food has bitten his nails down to the quick. His finger-ends are puffs into which are pressed narrow slivers of fingernail. But the taste of the hamburger, judging from what the rhume allows to come through, is delicious. On the opposite pavement, strutting waiters are stacking café chairs at the end of another day. In the Boulevard de Magenta is a second stone gateway, free-standing, with pediment and wrought-iron gates closing a secret domain. I put my nose through the bars but can make out little in the leafy scented darkness beyond the streetlamps . . .

Remove the bolster from the bed and take the square pillows out of the wardrobe and plump them up against the headboard of flowered brocade. Slide into the fresh white cotton sheets and, despite having only moments ago brushed my teeth, have several slugs from the flask of whisky/brandy mix brought up from the car (kept somewhat in check by the day's pace, the rhume is now streaming out of me – but I don't want to take any more Collis Browne's Mixture because in excess it constipates). Open the Gideon Bible at random for some synchronicity (it's a 3-in-1 text, English/French/German, and the English fortunately is the Authorised King James Version). Luke 12, Verses 54/56. *And he*

said also to the people, When ye see a cloud rise out of the west, straightway
ye say, There cometh a shower; and so it is. And when ye see the south wind
blow, ye say, There will be heat; and it cometh to pass. Ye hypocrites, ye
can discern the face of the sky and of the earth; but how is it that ye do
not discern this time?

Reflections. When first I started coming south I stayed at the Hôtel de Londres. Then I discovered cheaper accommodation, also with off-street parking, in the rue Île de France, in the Hôtel Île de France, an exotic establishment run by Africans and Vietnamese in an old merchant's house. They had a lush garden, overgrown, mossy, with broken statues. They also had a fierce Alsatian dog which would be let off its chain at night, so that if you took it into your head to retrieve something from the car in the early hours . . . Small French hotels often have dogs. This can be off-putting. But the worst example I ever came across was in a small hotel in Edinburgh – they had 2 Doberman Pinschers, said 'They can't get out', but you'd see through the glass of the dining-room door these 2 killers snarling at you with dripping fangs . . . Anyway, the Hôtel Île de France cleaned up the garden, cleaned up the house, put up their prices, and so I transferred to another hotel in the same street run by Chinese from Hong Kong. Who soon began to hoist their prices too. And before long these amusing honky-tonk hotels in the rue Île de France were no cheaper than the cosy Hôtel de Londres with its perfect façade and position opposite the palace and rum London iconography in the dining-room. So now I come here again. Its particular drawback is that there are no curtains at the windows, only nets. I'm therefore obliged to hang up the counterpane on the net hooks in order to cut out the streetlamps and prevent dawn waking me (stupidly I have forgotten that there are shutters!).

More slugs of whisky/brandy and swab my nose with a mouchoir. There is always something secret and snug about the night stop at Fontainebleau. It is a caesura in one's life, a night that is carefree. Why is it so good to get away? Simply to escape the constraints of personality? Of what everyone, including oneself, has decided one is? England, having an ancient, populous and highly-evolved society, is psychically very dense. But here – now – one is naked – elemental – breathing more freely. Being elemental is a weight off one's mind. Islands . . . We are off the island. For an islander abroad is absolute; for a mainlander, merely relative. Islanders combine intense symbiosis with reserve. A mainlander can walk to Peking or Machu Picchu, but an islander is always subconsciously aware of being physically circumscribed in his home place. Lack of physical space increases psychological

space between people. English (individualist) and Japanese (collec-
tivist) have in common: gardens, monarchy, inventiveness, hypocrisy,
phlegm, ancient culture and advanced culture simultaneously, tattoos,
a predisposition to stomach upsets when abroad, an avoidance of
eye-contact. And what about the Sicilians? But rolling sumptuously in
my dark fresh cotton world, I realise that clouds are not respecters of
frontiers, watery or otherwise, and as the Death Cloud comes our way,
I wonder if there will be anything left of Europe by the morning.

4

Fontainebleau to La Croix Valmer

The palace floats in bluish morning mist with pale gold sun above. Clouds arrive after breakfast and my cold is in the way, but who cares? I am always in the highest glee setting off south in the morning from Fontainebleau. Dead squirrel . . . dead cat . . . dead rabbit smeared on the road through the forest which has begun to leaf, creating another mist, a green one.

On to the motorway, the A6, the Autoroute du Soleil. Cédez le passage. An overcast but animated sky – and it's dry. Lyon 381 kms. Why do the English add an 's' to Lyon and to Marseille when the French do not? Slot in the Screaming Blue Messiahs, hard driving music at this delicate hour, too hard, eject it, and continue in a fresh alive silence. The European motorway system is a joy – you can zip along runways of Zen detachment to fabulous places almost without realising it. Travelling in hyperspace must resemble this, moving into a smiling nothingness and allowing the destination to suck you to itself.

Speeding south, little rents of blue appear in the overlapping eiderdowns of cloud, and as we come singing over a hill near Joigny, the motorway curves far far far ahead in Hogarth's serpentine line of beauty through an immense landscape under an immense sky, le paysage de l'Auxerrois with few hedgerows, occasional clumps of trees in an undulating ocean of green, brown and yellow stripes. It has the bleak, sullen look of mechanised farming.

Start chatting to myself in French – the nasal and guttural timbres of French are not found in Italian which is accordingly much easier for the English to pronounce. Car going well, 80 m.p.h. slipping up to 90, smooth, with a discernible ear-pricked cockiness though it's only a 1.6 engine. The road is quiet, it's a Friday, but having only 2 lanes in each direction one is kept alert by the need to overtake lorries.

Slot in *Cléopâtre* by Berlioz, sung by Janet Baker. What a voice. Is it good or bad? The reedy high notes come through loud and clear –

but such panache (+Colin Davis, London Symphony Orchestra)! The dying sequence, with curious Philip Glass perpetuum mobile on strings, keeps its tautness until the final expiration deep in the orchestra, after which I realise I have been driving on automatic pilot, unaware of the road, my upper attention absorbed by the exit of Berlioz's romantic heroine.

The open road, where one is anonymous, unreachable, cleansed . . . . .

Cloud gathers into pregnant puffs of purplish grey. A few large raindrops fleck the windscreen with almond-shaped dashes of water, oil and dirt. Pull off motorway into the Aire de Montmorency to go to the loo. I see a man come out of the Ladies', which startles me, until I realise it is a woman. Mannish lesbians, like effeminate homosexuals, are very visible in France. This one, with short steel-grey hair and grey anorak, smokes a cigarette and studies intently a roadmap opened out upon the bonnet. Her girlfriend, who is pretty and blonde, tosses her long hair about, laughing delightfully.

The glory of this day's drive is to pass through the landscape, Arcadian and harmonious, of north Burgundy. This landscape also has mystery, i.e. it is vast and intimate at the same time. Huge forests and wooded hills, low odd-shaped escarpments brindled with spinneys and gorse, field stripes receding to a blue-haze horizon. Trees accumulate in the recesses of the landscape like body hair in groins. Cowslips and dandelions grow along the verge of the motorway and birds of prey fly across it. The grass is very green in meadows supporting cream cattle and trees in blossom. Here and there red roofs, steeply pitched, sometimes pierced by dormer windows, gather about church spire or venerable château. The windows of the houses have shutters of weathered white, eau-de-nil or washed-out lavender paint. But the settlements are not numerous. A million shades of green are pregnant with the lushness which will break forth in a few weeks' time. Northern Europe has an air of profound moisture and its inhabitants either have the rosy-cheeked dairy-farm look or the hardy, sinewy, buttoned-up, windswept look. An absence of pylons allows the beauty, the benevolent drama, the rare sense of nature in cultivated but uncontaminated exercise, to prevail. The soul does not soar up. It soars out, across sylvan distances. Ugliness is beauty flawed, beauty attacked. First there is beauty. Then afterwards ugliness. Ugliness, unlike beauty, does not exist in its own right. Anything all-of-a-piece is beautiful. A thing-in-itself cannot be ugly.

I sing aloud and talk to myself of sexual matters. Eat the final cereal flapjack. There is a lack of cereals in the French diet. They never have cereals for breakfast. Muesli does not exist here. Only recently have French bakers introduced brown bread – but it's lead-weight brown as if to say 'If you want your bread brown, you get it *totally* brown and it's kept over there in a special basket in the weirdo corner.' It looks so unattractive that I've never seen anyone buy it including me – the patter of the boulangerie (deux ficelles, trois baguettes, un restaurant) continues as normal. I'm not one of those who consider the French kitchen the *ne plus ultra* of food. It's deficient not only in cereals but also in fresh vegetables and fruit. They eat much 'salad' by which they mean a rag of lettuce drenched in a lip-smacking dressing. Far far too much cheese (it's delicious), egg and meat. Everything is accompanied by sticks of bad white bread which looks as though it's spun from cellulose. All of which compounds to a heavy claylike stodge in the bowels.

Wash flapjack down with slug of Perrier. It's wise to keep a bottle of water in the car. When driving alone you have to unscrew the top by jamming the bottle in your crotch, opening it with one hand while continuing to steer with the other. Many of the bottles are plastic but the Perrier is glass and I often think – oh God, if I were to have a car crash now, my genitalia would be sliced to ribbons.

Over 3 hours on the road. The spirits slump and I realise I need lunch. Pull over and fill up with petrol. The attendant, who is Oxfam thin with lank greasy black ringlets about his ears, tries the usual trick of declaring I need a complete change of oil. I look him in the eye and suck in one cheek – this makes him twitch. Buy cheese, a box of Minizza (baby imitation-pizza biscuits which sound unpleasant and are addictive), a bag of madeleines aux fruits (small butter sponges with raisins), Hollywood chewing-gum. Only buy essentials on the motorway – prices in these knick-knackeries are often double what they should be. Coffee from a dispenser is excellent. The cakes leave behind a curious sensation, registered by the tongue, as if the teeth have been coated with an abrasive chemical.

. . . Passing under lots of electric cables . . . Partage des Eaux: the water now runs south to the Mediterranean whereas a moment ago it ran north to the Channel. As if to demonstrate this, the road tilts down towards Beaune and another immense vista opens up, this time across a tattier, drier, more industrialised region. The motorway is joined by another, the number of lorries markedly increases, and Burgundy flies into the past.

..... Hum of contented car. The partage des eaux is fine for water but for us humans the real division is Lyon. When Lyon is behind you, you've cracked the journey, but the last 100 kms to that town is a real effort. I've been listening to *Elektra* by Richard Strauss whose music is extremism within convention, emotional but safe. *Wer glücklich ist wie wir, dem ziemt nur eins: schweigen und tanzen!* sings Birgit Nilsson, then she dies. Gap in text as author goes mentally dead – which is his way of dealing with the last 100 kms before Lyon.

Lyon, the Birmingham of France. Can anyone amazing have ever been born in Lyon? A Mozart or a Shakespeare? Or a Jackie Wilson? Come to that, was anyone amazing ever born in Birmingham? This isn't cultural snobbery but a serious question about the effect of environment on the soul. Lyon is built upon hills, giving it an advantage over Birmingham, and the Lyonnais have opted for full-blown modernism so it's quite dramatic in a way, an urban landscape full of liveliness but hateful to live in. The motorway runs along the river through the centre of town and is always jammed at holiday time (which is not to-day. One holiday I was caught in a 60-km jam centred on Lyon. You don't make that mistake twice). The city stinks. You might think it's your engine fouling up but it's Lyon fouling up. The French, being so olfactory, seem not to mind. And the best is saved for last – the ELF Oil Refinery on the right as you leave the conurbation. It's a killer, massive drums alongside the road, with plenty of pong. It's a tarry pong, not actually disagreeable. Appearing on the right now is the Rhône, in full flood from snow melts.

Nous entrons sur les autoroutes du Sud de la France. Bonne Route ... I'm very happy to be on no other road than this. The Mediterranean, like a great bowl of warm saliva, is within spitting distance. This is now the A7, second limb of the Autoroute du Soleil. Pull into lay-by for pee and catch the sweet perfume of newly mown grass, surely the last time I shall smell it for many months. A high is establishing itself across Europe. Sky is opal blue and 2 aeroplane vapour trails intersect making an X almost as wide as the firmament itself.

As one drives south very nearly a whole season concentrates itself into a day. Everything is noticeably more out down here (but then, it always is: a warm climate exteriorises). Overtaken by a white

Rolls-Royce from Switzerland, a Corniche with a soft top. White cars
are said to have the fewest accidents, red cars the most. Contemplative
lorry drivers flick balls of snot out of their windows as they bowl along.
At 4 p.m. we are warm and breezy, window down, music up, but the
wind blows most of the music away and it doesn't matter . . . Les
châteaux de la Drôme . . . Montélimar (reminds me of *Apple Duffs*
by George Harrison) . . . The landscape has developed the rocky,
untidy Mediterranean look, the houses have taken on the orange-tiled
Roman farm villa look, and the first Provence cypresses appear, the
most beautiful and characteristic tree of the south, dark green fingers
pointing to the sky (they're called Tuscan cypresses in Italy).

Driving on motorways is far less wearing on the shoes than driving
on other roads because the feet don't move much. It's one of the
reasons the feet can start dying on you. Numb from the ankles down.
Or waist down. Or neck down. Or neck up. Or buttock ache. Or all
of it. These long drives take people different ways. I have numb feet
and buttock ache. Put on Chuck Berry and jiggle bum around, then
stop off for coffee where I'm approached by 2 German hitch-hikers
with yellow hair, red faces, heavy backpacks, filthy clothes. They are
exceedingly smelly and happy and untouchable and I tell them that
regretfully I am unable to do what they so keenly suggest . . . Mistral
begins to blow violently down the Rhône corridor . . . Here's a very
new post-modern turnpike, a mighty flattened arch with 2 concrete
pylons in the centre. It is a folly, an example of the French trying very
hard to be up-to-date. But follies are appealing.

What is this business of going south? Returning to the warm belly
of the mother? But the south can be wild, anarchic, inhospitable too.
Maybe it is an atavism from the ice-age when south was where one
went to escape the advancing ice. Certainly my cold feels much
easier. But:

> O tell her, Swallow, thou that knowest each,
> That bright and fierce and fickle is the South,
> And dark and true and tender is the North.
>   (Tennyson)

Orange is the first town of the south. No town has a more beautiful
name. The Prince of Nassau was so charmed that he named his royal
house after it, whence the name found its way to the Protestant
group of Northern Ireland. Louis XIV said that Orange contained
the noblest wall in his kingdom and it does, the great wall of the
Roman theatre . . . Scriabin's 3rd Symphony takes one into a cloud
of sound that includes the car but is not limited to the car. Effort

is over for to-day. One is simply floating south in a warm cloud of sound . . . . .

Barcelona 438 kms. But we're not doing the Iberian route. We're doing the main route, the central route, the spine of Europe.

(1) Purpose of journey: to drive to Noto.

(2) Purpose of driving to Noto: to travel down the spine of Europe.

(3) Purpose of travelling down the spine of Europe: to see it now, as it is, non-magically. To clear away the deceitful magic of travel brochures and nostalgia. To stay fluid. Travel is a way of preventing the formation of deadening crusts about one's soul. Though it can be a trap. Some people travel to escape – to maintain a deadening crust of superficial impressions, to live only on the surface because to live deeper is painful for them.

(4) Purpose of all that stuff in (3): the pursuit of magic. All travel is the pursuit of magic.

(5) Purpose of the pursuit of magic: to get one's rocks off.

The spine of Europe, which begins in London and ends in Noto (actually it begins in Edinburgh and passes through York and Oxford but we're not going that way), runs down through Paris, south through Avignon, along the coast and down through Italy to Sicily. Either side of the spine are the rest. Thus:

The spine has been formed over a long period. Britain has the most highly evolved prehistoric culture in Europe and Europe's only truly intercontinental city. Italy is Rome and its empire. Sicily is Ancient Greece. France made itself the continental crossroads with cafés, boulevards and the arts of pleasure.

Ella Fitzgerald sings Cole Porter's *Ridin' High* VERY LOUDLY. Is it possible to make love to someone – to really make love to them – and not want to possess them completely, body and soul? Physical love, this dynamic of giving and using, generosity and greed, high/low, exhaustion/dissatisfaction . . . Love is fullness – and emptiness. Avignon, cité des papes, and the worst crime rate in France (Paris 2nd, Marseille 3rd). And here we are at our first turn-off, Cavaillon, because we're going to stay with some old friends, the Schmidts of Roussillon.

Irmin Schmidt is a post-modern composer, born in Berlin. All music is his resource. And he's read everything. Just as I am a voracious consumer of music but read always with an ulterior motive, so he is free voraciously to consume the word, but can only listen to music analytically. He is one of my connections with the mentality of the European avant-garde which, assuming thorough technical grounding, says that the artist can have that complete identification with his art which brings freedom, that in-the-bone seriousness which brings detachment, that the artist must not be afraid to let his inner voice be his outer voice, that the artist *dares* . . . Such a mentality is hardly to be found in Britain, as far as music or writing are concerned, though it does arise in the military field (the motto of the SAS being 'Who dares wins'). All 20th century British writers and composers have lagged behind, have had what Cyril Connolly called 'the gentleman complex' which kept them in a state of infantilism on the great questions, the great emotions, the great audacities. Who are the important figures in modern English literature? Conrad – Polish. Joyce – Irish. T. S. Eliot – American. Whom have the British produced? Evelyn Waugh: the meanness of his sympathies is, with the passage of time, eating into his books like dry rot into an apparently sturdy structure. Graham Greene: he might have been a great novelist but for his Catholicism. A writer cannot afford to be cranky about religion or politics if he hopes to be taken seriously. After all, a writer aspires to sanity. W. H. Auden – lovely stuff, but too cosy? Too cuddly? Or is Auden the one English genius of 20th century literature? The teddy bear finally makes it as high art? Oh, but I'm forgetting the Glorious Daemon, the Great David – Mr Lawrence. He was most definitely the real thing. So my theory should be revised, perhaps.

Irmin has for years been building a house, Les Rossignols, in a sloping field near Roussillon, the red ochre hill village (not to be confused with the département), because he can't bear living in Cologne any more or indeed anywhere in Germany. His father was a Nazi and all that Hitler stuff churns Irmin up inside – he's not very good at doing the amnesia trick. This is not only a humanitarian response but also a cultural one since the Nazi experience cut Germany off from the richness of its own culture. The new German model has more in common with America or Japan and he finds this equally distasteful.

Their house has a fine view of hills with Gordes and its château up on the left horizon. When a big cheque arrives Irmin and his builders start another room. The house is far from finished, and perhaps will always remain so because Irmin has grandiose plans – new ideas parturiate from completed ones. But the roof's on, the walls are plastered, the plumbing and heating and electric wiring are in. At one time you'd eat your lapin au vin surrounded by breeze blocks and electric cables strung through the place like a gigantic fishing net. The electrical system was especially awe-inspiring and every day revealed within itself new circuits trembling on the lip of disaster. Yet there were no electrocutions because Irmin's wife Hildegard – blonde, beautiful, efficient *and* warm – had not only the esoteric knowledge but also the absolute confidence which, by refusing to treat with the negative quantities in this world, allowed the positive energy to flow. Both Gibbon and Smollett refer to 'the adage that the German genius lies more in the back than in the brain' but Hildegard has plenty of both. She not only runs the family and household but also all Irmin's professional affairs (while he meditates in bed on the great questions, the great audacities, or unblocks a drain) as well as managing the group of musicians called Can in which Irmin figures on keyboards. A remarkable performance from her.

Irmin likes to go to bed late and sleep late. He and I talk long into the night over red wine in front of the great log fire. 'It's traditional to have a pile of juniper logs,' he says, 'to throw one on occasionally because juniper wood makes an especially beautiful perfume.' He knows how to eat, has developed a large belly (emphasised by his shortness) since moving to the country, and is the only man I know who can smile convincingly through gold-rimmed spectacles. We've had many magnificent conversations – one of the best was while walking round Oxford at sunrise under the influence of opium – but I can't recall a blind thing either of us ever said on these occasions. We talk in English because my German is non-existent. Their daughter – modern multilingual Sandra – giggles helplessly at my appalling French which is off-putting. Every time I launch into a French sentence, this fresh young girlish laughter castrates me and I swing defiantly, pathetically back into English.

To-night however I do remember what we talked of – the nuclear disaster in Russia – not at Ignalina, it transpires, but at another reactor further south – an explosion releasing a huge amount of radioactivity into the atmosphere of eastern Europe, now drifting west. The inhabitants of Russian cities near the disaster have red eyes, irritated skin, cracked lips, and their ears are ringing. The Russians have asked for extra food supplies from the Common Market which of course always has mountains of stuff left over, rotting in sheds, turning to dust in freezers. The whole situation – especially the lunacy of politicians – gives me insomnia.

While we are sitting outside the Bar Tabac this morning in sunshine on plastic chairs (the latest virus to hit Europe is plastic tables and chairs outside cafés) a group of chi-chi bohemian Germans arrive and are very at home at the next table, talking jovially with the owners of the café and with the most tramplike of the locals (you prove how 'in' you are by your ability to exchange banter with this ragged creature who hangs around the little square being pretentiously penniless). Suddenly I feel uncomfortable, an outsider among these brilliantly relaxed Europeans. They seem to know all about life and how to live it – and I don't. A pang of loneliness hits me, and a shiver of insecurity. Also la bourgeoisie artistique – both French and German – who live in the Luberon rather kill the authenticity of the place with easy fashionable clothes and open-plan cottages and cars and trendy children and super-knowing rural *good taste* and dishwashers, trying to be *real* around a Provençal hill village with which they otherwise have absolutely no connection. Hildegard and Irmin are saved from this by: (a) Lack of money (b) Their slight dottiness a l'Anglais.

. . . Madame Seydelmann was very sweet, an old lady with a brooch worn over the neck button of her blouse. She used to run the Galerie Le Castrum in the vieux village on the path up to the neglected church. When I first visited her she was reading a German translation of *Orlando* by Virginia Woolf. She told me that Samuel Beckett wrote *Waiting For Godot* in Roussillon while waiting for the Second World War to end.

'He worked for a farmer *there*,' she said pointing from her high window to a spot on the warm wide hummocky plain below, 'and Beckett says he'll never return because it was the worst time of his life. After the success of *Waiting For Godot*, journalists came down here to ask about Mr Beckett's past and the farmer said he didn't know a Mr Beckett but there was a very strange and he thought *English* man who had worked for him but who never spoke to anyone and there was no making him speak either.'

I bought from her a tiny dark picture on a large white ground: *Moon, Mandolin, Mask* by Iwaya, a Japanese painter of L'Ecole Noire, the school of Black Painting in Paris.

This was during one previous springtime when I rented a peculiar house in the vieux village from a rich German sculptor called Christian Weiser who doesn't sculpt any more because he makes so much money out of property. This house was a sinister Alice-in-Wonderland creation built into the ramparts on an ascending twist, with a salon d'été and a salon d'hiver. I wrote in the salon d'été with my travelling sheet of green baize flung across the centre of a refectory table 14 feet long. It's the only house I've ever felt persecuted by. It knocked my head, elbows, stubbed my toes, tripped me up. Suddenly I would find myself disorientated because of the mazelike layout – mazelike in 3 dimensions – or would unaccountably lose things. One night – I'd been tense, in the middle of writing a novel, out of sight of the beginning, not in sight of the end, and what's more smoking cigarettes with Nils Letallec though I'd given up 3 years before, and it was an extremely unusual novel anyway – but this night I woke in terror some time after 2 a.m. Slight noises became emphatic, laden with malign import. I turned on the light – but the terror increased. I was trembling, my musculature tightening up like a cloth being twisted, tighter and tighter, and sweat was forced out of my body in a slow but inexorable acceleration of panic. The tension emanated from a point at the top of the belly where the ribs begin. Often I have tension at this point but never before had it spread so aggressively through the whole system. It was as if I'd been seized by something outside myself. And then – oh horror – my twisted heart started to miss beats. And the missed beat would be followed, after an interval when all the stars stood breathlessly in their tracks waiting to see whether I'd survive into the next moment, by a beat so strong that my torso would be jolted upwards, as if a frantic animal were in there trying to kick out through the ribcage. Thus . . . Boom-boom boom-boom boom-boom then nothing (I shall die!) . . . . . BOOM! My heart no longer had anything to do with me. In a fever of cold sweats, almost delirious with fear, I clambered out of bed and drank heavily from a bottle of whisky, forced myself to pace up and down, tried to think of nothing as the irregular pattern swung me over queasy voids and terrorised me with the prospect of imminent death. Eventually the alcohol won and I fell asleep from exhaustion. The prospect of imminent death is very exhausting. I shall never stay in that house again.

And couldn't stay another night. The next morning, drained and depressed, I packed my bags, to the mistral's bastinado outside, went down the hill, out of the village, and through fields to Hildegard and Irmin's familiar portal. They'd shot off along the motorway to Zurich or somewhere but Sandra and Sieglinde, Irmin's sister, were there and the mistral blew and blew and blew. Tight gusts of neurotic noise beat ceaselessly about Les Rossignols and buffeted the hillsides, a wetless wind blowing the landscape into abstraction under a hard blue sky. The outdoor scene was cruel, needle-sharp, composed of clean shapes, dry dustfree volumes, flat colours. It is an odd characteristic of the mistral that it doesn't arouse dust but removes it from the world. And as it continued to blow, a Chekhovian atmosphere built inside the house – bored, restless, waiting. There was something intensely silly about that wind! At night there was a chill and the log fire was piled high. The mistral had blown down a power line and there was no power in the house. The deep freeze dripped in the cellar, leaking its gory contents like a white upright coffin. I lay on my bed reading Byron's Letters by candlelight but the flame wavered maddeningly which was the mistral forcing itself in through fissures.

The French courage proceeds from vanity, wrote the larky lord, *the German from phlegm, the Turkish from fanaticism and opium, the Spanish from pride, the English from coolness, the Dutch from obstinacy, the Russian from insensibility, but the* Italian *from* anger . . .

Unexpectedly the mistral stopped. That is to say, one was not aware of its dying, only that it had died. There was an eerie silence in the small hours, a sense of the world being returned to humans, no longer an abstraction, but organic now, of varying connections, distinctions and pulsations. I blew out the candle to sleep but was uneasy, nerve-endings prickly – then the damn nightingales started up. Twitter twitter tweet tweet, an insufferable din outside the window, in my very ear. One was obliged to go out there and lob stones. One after another stones crashed into the bushes. I paused, listened. At long bloody last there was peace and quiet.

Go visiting:

(1) Hiram Winterbotham. I met him through his partner Daniel whom I bumped into, drinking on the terrace of the Café Grégoire in Apt (the local town, nothing extraordinary but, like all French towns round here, very charming with a vivid life of its own; Apt's speciality is sugared fruit; and it is the birthplace of photographer Bernard Faucon). Daniel asked me where I was staying and I said with friends but also renting a house in Roussillon belonging to a German sculptor.

'Oh, *that* house,' he said. 'Did you notice anything weird about it?'

I feigned ignorance.

'Well, nobody stands it for long. A racing driver and his girlfriend used to stay there and I'd go up for, you know – ' A leer came over his rubbery, boozy, amiable features and a glint into his eye. 'None of us *ever* had a decent night's *sleep* in that house. So we decided to investigate and discovered that, in the Middle Ages, whenever the village was invaded, the defences were always breached at that point, that's where they'd come in, and naturally there'd be lots of slaughter. The house is built over a pile of death.'

Now I telephone and Daniel says come round for a swim. Hiram, inheriting money from a Gloucestershire textile company, moved to France with Daniel, built a house at Rustrel in the modern style, big glass windows, flat roof, sharp corners, white cement walls since become dull and rain-stained, and established a tree and shrub garden of many species. He is the world expert on black bamboo.

As I arrive 2 people are leaving. They introduce themselves as 'Sally Westminster' and 'Jeremy Fry' and drive away. Wearing a tracksuit which has seen better days, Hiram sculpts the air with his hand and says 'Come in, come in! Do you know why the brothel has disappeared from everywhere in France except Lyon? . . . Then I'll tell you. Basically because people get it for nothing nowadays. However the only people who need to get it quickly and will pay for it are commercial travellers away from home – and Lyon is the main intersecting point in the whole of France for commercial travellers.'

We wander into the garden which is wooded, with pools of sunlight, full of unexpected thorns and prickles. 'This monkey-puzzle tree is the Australian variety from Norfolk Island – it was given to me by a man who later went up a mountain and disappeared – just like that. Do you know why turtles have all but vanished from the Mediterranean? Then I'll tell you. They eat jellyfish. And they've been eating plastic bags by mistake. Do swim in the pool.'

I take off my clothes and slip naked into the icy, green, slimy water. When I get out – which is soon – Daniel says 'Did you know that the ex-headmaster of Rugby lives over that way? Apparently he stood up at one of those prize-giving days with all the parents there and announced to the assembly that he was chucking it all in to go and live in France with a young man. His wife was stunned.'

(2) Sir Angus Wilson. Saint Rémy de Provence is another ordinary French town full of charm, ½ an hour south of Avignon, but it has pretensions to style and is less intimate and conspiratorial than Apt. Nostradamus was born there, Gounod composed there for a while, Van Gogh painted there – for a while. Angus Wilson and Tony Garrett, after 30 years in Suffolk, came to live on the top floor of a modern block of flats off the main square. The flat has windows and sliding glass doors on 3 sides, a wide, railed balcony running round it, grand views of craggy limestone upland and the roofs of the town spread out below.

Sir Angus, gripped by a comfy sofa, looks as though he's on the point of pushing his tubby form out of it – but never does.

'I came here because I write out of doors and I *loathe* bad weather and I love the sun and I like to get sunburnt.'

'But why move to a penthouse when you suffer from vertigo?'

'. . . Um, that's a very good question,' says Sir Angus, drawing his brow into a frown.

'We're still working on it,' says Tony, looking raffish in a chocolate pinstripe suit.

'You could sit with your back to the railings,' I suggest.

'No, I couldn't. I'd think all the time that a mountain was going to come and strangle me.'

He looks rather sunburnt already. In fact his head is a splendidly coloured object: white hair, red face, yellow teeth, blue eyes. Tony brings in the tea and goes off to burrow in some cardboard boxes.

'Perhaps I could sit on the balcony with something over my head,' wonders the knight, 'because I'm not frightened of falling down. I'm frightened of falling up. That's why I find New York difficult because I think I'm going to be sucked upwards. Do help yourself to one of these.'

With a gourmet bishop air, Sir Angus proffers a box of small meringues glued together with jam. The flat is full of half-emptied cartons and packing cases. Pictures and mirrors lean against walls. Books are piled in corners. They are still moving in.

'I will miss the rose garden and the English countryside enormously but I do find all that hypocrisy about homosexuality and so on very hard to swallow. They were quite awful in Suffolk when Tony was forced out of his job as a very good probation officer, saying how much everyone liked him but really he couldn't be allowed to continue in the circumstances – just because he didn't hide our relationship.'

Sir Angus removes a meringue from his mouth by swallowing it and continues 'My only surviving brother lives in Cannes – his wife's French. He's well over 90. I had 5 brothers and I was the youngest and I had 2 gay brothers who were entirely 20s people and one of them took cocaine for pleasure.'

'Cocaine used to be called whacky dust in those days.'

'Did it? I never had anything to do with drug-taking.'

'I did, but I was never sufficiently organised to get addicted to anything.'

'I must say that the advent of drugs in America in the 60s seems to me a wholly healthy thing. That brittle macho American spirit was rather intolerable at one time but with drugs a softness came into American life which was thoroughly good. Oh, I love America!'

'What about the macho spirit down here in the Mediterranean?'

'I find one can usually get round that with some culture talk. By the way,' and he raises his eyebrows in emphasis, 'I've come to France not to retire but to write. All the English writers worth thinking about have done that at some point.'

'I believe Lawrence Durrell lives over there beyond Nîmes.'

'I believe he does,' says Sir Angus, starting on another meringue. 'I've never known Lawrence Durrell and I've never tried to get to know him because . . . it's just so *sad* when one remembers how good he *used* to be and I made the mistake of saying so in a review. Mind you, people do say – and they've a perfect right to say – that I haven't quite fulfilled all that might have been hoped for.' But as the knight scans the cake-box it appears not to worry him. 'I love France. It was the first country I went abroad to by myself which was after my mother died when I was 15. But what you do get here a bit and very much in Italy is almost a pidgin language when they speak of cultural things and it's usually er – '

'A load of waffle?'

'Precisely. And that you don't get very much in England. But what I'm glad to leave behind is all that . . . anti-culture which is the fashion now, this great revival of Benthamism and sensible economic values.'

'There's one thing worse than a government that's not interested in culture – a government that's *terribly* interested in culture.'

'Yes, that's awful. But we don't often get that in England, do we!'

'Don't think we've ever had it. You get it with ideology. What we get are the puritans wanting to make everything illegal.'

Is he going to get up from the sofa? Yes . . . . . No.

'The backlash,' he sighs. 'All my brothers were totally without any business sense. And I certainly have none. The whole of it is total boredom to me. Partly because I've never had much money – and resent it.'

'You can sell your manuscripts.'

'I've already done that. They're in Iowa City.'

'It's tax-free because they're classified as chattels.'

'That's right. That I do know. Come on, you should've had 10 cakes by now,' fuffles Sir Angus. Sugar falls down his jersey.

An electric storm rolls along the top of the distant hills seen from Irmin's studio at 5.30 p.m. Lightning throws gold daggers into the horizon. The thunder and lightning are far off and give a sense of peace. I have stayed at Les Rossignols in winter. One night, returning along the motorway from a Marseille discothèque, I was caught in the only electric snowstorm I've ever heard of. The snow was sudden and very heavy, rushing into the car headlights and making me dizzy. One could see only a few feet ahead on the deep white track, except when flashes of lightning floodlit a fiendish purple the whole of the Rhône valley and Luberon mountains. The car pirouetted several times, simply revolved on the road surface despite my crawling pace and being the flash silver low-slung Datsun Z (a hand-me-down from my sister). I only made it back by entering a patch of rainfall – which must have been the explanation of the lightning. A snowstorm and a rainstorm had been travelling side by side.

The next day, Sunday, a house was burning fiery orange on the snowy horizon. I watched a robin dancing on a pile of logs near the front door. And on Monday a thick plume of sperm-white smoke rose into the cold blue sky above the burnt house, flattening out at a certain height into a T shape, and from the centre of the crossbar another plume began to rise, so that the configuration of smoke became in due course a gigantic crucifix in the sky above the smouldering ruins of the house. To ventilate the smoke from our fire, I opened the front door and the robin flew in from the logs. Immediately the large grey cat had him. Then the small black & white cat picked up the corpse and retreated with it into the ground-floor bathroom and under the bath for a chew, making an unpleasant little mess of blood and feathers. Robins sometimes murder each other.

The Bonfils family have the small farm next door. Once while walking I made the mistake of putting a foot over the invisible line which divides Bonfils land from Schmidt land. The dogs, my God, hell let loose on paws! The south of France like Italy is a land of small holdings, and walking in the countryside is made tiresome by these groups of hysterical dogs which rush at you every ¼ mile. The French love their dogs as weapons – which makes walking on the beach a trial too.

Monsieur Bonfils and his son Serge speak with fruity, singing Provençal accents (vang et pang for vin et pain) but she, Jeanne, is from Paris and in consequence can sometimes be seen out for the day in a little hat, or on the crest of a hill in huge sunglasses and a turquoise kaftan while her husband is indoors eating in his vest.

Serge calls the British 'les gibines' after the GB sticker on cars. He is getting married to Anne. A few days before the wedding the bride had an accident in the kitchen which blew off her eyebrows, but art has triumphed over disaster. There are to be 2 ceremonies, the important one at the Mairie, then another at the church. Both bride and groom leave from the same place, the Bonfils farmhouse. This amazes me but Irmin says 'They would leave from the same house in Germany too. We don't have that very formal thing any more.'

'It's not formality. It's natural for them to come from separate places.'

At least the bride and groom leave for the Mairie in separate cars. Anne is bountifully fluffed in white – with veil. Serge is in a tight bum-freezer cream silk jacket with cream silk bow-tie. I am given the honour of driving him and his mother to the Mairie. They pull my windscreen wipers away from the screen and fix pink bows to them, then both sit in the back chatting to each other while I play chauffeur. When the wipers are switched on, the pink bows describe 2 arcs in the air which is very eye-catching and ingenious-French. The cars drive off in procession, honking repeatedly as we go and on entering the narrow streets of the village the sound is amplified to terrific volume.

The ceremony at the Mairie, with sombre reference to La République under an immobile tricolour, is very moving. You're not allowed to use cameras here. Then it's up to the church for a more off-the-cuff happening. The church is pretty but very plain (the Church is poor in France, though not far from here a charismatic priest, Dom Gérard Calvet, brother of the Bordeaux wine merchant, has collected enough support to build a new monastery of strict Benedictine observance in solid gothic. To see this 'new gothic' structure rising stone by stone on the mountainside at Le Barroux is a rare post-modernist sight).

You're permitted to take photographs in the church and lots do as the curé delivers his sermon on the metaphor of building a marriage the way you would a house. He thinks Serge is a builder. When someone tells him the groom's a farmer, the curé says 'Oh. But the sermon is still true.' The service is simple – vestigial in fact. Afterwards we file up the aisle to kiss the bride and groom 3 times each. Then you kiss them 3 times each as you arrive at the reception – which is back at the farm on grass among trees. All this kissing makes for an excellent atmosphere. The wedding cake arrives from L'Isle-sur-la-Sorgue in the back of a van and is a model of the church tower made out of what looks like sponge fingers. Everyone says bravo and claps. Food is often applauded in France – it's their way of saying grace. Snacks start to circulate. Then you must kiss the bride and groom 3 times each before leaving. I have to leave early because I don't want to be too late at La Croix Valmer on the coast. To-morrow I must open up the house and go shopping – this is my parents' house near Saint Tropez where we are spending Easter. I do my kissing, say goodbye to the Bonfils family, to the Schmidt family (Hildegard says 'Be careful of Sicilians, they all carry knives!'), and arrange to meet Irmin some weeks later, with Micky and Tschöntsch, on the terrace of the Carlton Hotel in Cannes during the Film Festival. Jeanne presents me with a wedding decoration, a flower made from wire and lace and pink & white sugared almonds, saying 'Pour la route!' She is wearing a deep smile and a cheeky little hat. As I honk, wave, and slowly snake the car between cherry trees, the disco in the open-sided barn pounds out *I'm Your Venus* by Bananarama.

It's a fine afternoon and the overland route to Aix-en-Provence seems the best idea, picking up the motorway there. Feeling marvellous – the world is vivid and full and easy. The first landmark is the semi-abandoned hill village of Lacoste which climaxes in a wilderness of trees and jagged battlements, the ruins of the Marquis de Sade's château. Chancing to be up there alone on the day a book I wrote, *April Ashley's Odyssey*, was published in London, and lacking a convenience, I celebrated by having a crap in the open air hidden among bushes (up at the ruin past the village, the terrain is wild and overgrown, with a monumental quarry behind, which looks as though Abu Simbel had been let down into the ground rather than raised up). This act, in an aerial wilderness which had been part of de Sade's domain, led to sexual excitement and I went in search of someone, anyone (there are such moments), with whom to share it, but the site was deserted. Then I threw back my head and laughed like a hyaena. I shall mention defecation from time to time. Nature it was who committed us to this daily event, an event which becomes even more significant when travelling in foreign parts, so that any obsessiveness resides in the *avoidance* of mentioning it. Besides, in busy lives, it is often a moment for significant reflection. If the English and Americans were more relaxed, less squeamish about the body, they would have bidets – as any civilised society should. But for them the bidet is a confession of uncleanness – they would rather have the reality of uncleanness. More will have to be said on British horror of the body when we visit the beach.

The landscape, looking towards Bonnieux from Lacoste, with Bonnieux rising like an ancient noble city up the side of its mountain, is perfect. The scoop of the plain between is one of cultivated variety, with trees, vineyards, crops and stone houses naturally disposed, and nowhere has crude modern development been allowed to interfere. This is the landscape which the crusaders must have seen. It is a marvel of romantic conservation, hushed in the mellow afternoon heat. On the other side of Bonnieux the car trampolines out of a pothole and there's a sick crack as the head of one of Anna's plastic models snaps off.

We join the motorway at Aix, the A8, La Provençale (which branches from the Autoroute du Soleil above Marseille). Soon after, looms the elephantine white bulk of Mont Sainte Victoire in les paysages de

Cézanne. Mount Victoria, as I call it, is the sentinel of the Côte d'Azur. Once past it you can feel the sea. Pop into a motorway shop for a carton of milk for tea on arrival.

Leave the motorway at Le Muy where, at the tollgate a few years ago, a gust of mistral blew off my car door when I opened it to get out. It is a treacherous wind, starts and stops abruptly, can blow continuously for days or in short uneven spurts.

40 kms to Saint Tropez. Still quiet here at this end of the Côte. Even during Easter it's not unbearably packed and quietens down again immediately afterwards. Only July and August are jammed. Whereas from Cannes to Monaco it's a fight for the greater part of the year.

The non-evergreens are out. Approach coast via a dangerous road through steep forested hills which at one point offers a brief magical glimpse of sea and Saint Tropez, a natural teaser, as if even the landscape round here had been designed by a clever queen in Paris. Beware oncoming overtakers – 'Saint Tropez' in the air makes French drivers even more violently exhibitionistic than usual. The only things on the road which they respect are bicycles (bicycling being the national sport!) (The reason why the centre parting has survived in France is because of bicycling – when you bicycle headfirst into a wind of your own creation the result is a centre parting.)

Sainte Maxime is heralded by the Parc de Sport et Loisirs, built in the countryside for maximum desecration. The Mediterranean tradition does not value countryside. Its terrain is often threatening and infertile. Any opportunity to subdue and 'civilise' it they take. Sainte Maxime is exploding with holiday flats and studios, is covered with placards and cranes, and has become a typical modern Côte d'Azur resort of old buildings all but overwhelmed by stacks of modern flats – a pattern which culminates at Monte Carlo. The Saint Tropez district is the only exception to this, although Menton has survived pretty well too.

Pop the last sugared almond into mouth and turn right along seaboard. Saint Tropez with its citadel above shows unmistakably on the left across the gulf, glowing curded yellow, gold, hot rose in the face of the setting sun. It disappears as the road runs back from the sea and we speed past Port Grimaud (an extravagant fake built in the style of a Provençal harbour town where TV star Joan Collins lived) to the large roundabout with the Géant Casino supermarket in the centre. Gassin surrounded by ilex woods looks magisterial and aloof on its hill. On to La Croix Valmer, currently undergoing expansion with a new shopping centre slap in the middle. Take the small road up behind the Post Office – up – up – with crepuscular sea views on right and left – still on – still up – to Super Valmer, a small development of houses where our place is, Les Sauges, built into the bosom of a forested hill.

There is development below but none above and it is peaceful. As far as one can make out, the other houses at the site are empty – quite often the case. Steps down to front door, unlock shutters and fold back, unlock security gates in metal lattice, unlock front door itself, and go in – sniff that peculiar, appealing smell of warm closed-up house waiting – and walk across the pale blue and pink carpet to the French windows, open them, unlock another pair of security gates, more shutters, out onto the top terrace and whoosh – there you are – the view. The view.

Given depth and substance by a cypress on either side, and seen across a small garden which each time I come looks more prolific than I remember it, the view this evening is filled with a ghostly, pensive light, last light of day, first light of stars. A line of forested hills descends from right to left in 7 undulations to the sea which is lake-smooth and the colour of lavender, with slashes of cherry red, reflecting the final sunset flare behind the hills. The small port of Cavalaire animates the distance, a gay miniature with swags of harbour lights glimmering in the still water. A few lights in the hills betray grander villas among trees and wisps of firesmoke drift slowly from their gables. Beyond, almost on the horizon, the Îles d'Hyères show above the waterline like the dark humps of a sea monster, and on the left of the Île du Levant, the white beam of the Phare du Titan shoots its regular, reassuring pulse. Astonished that this view should always be here, waiting with serene patience for one's return, I turn back in with a moist eye to make a cup of tea and already it's as if I've never been away. But views are inimical to writing. For that, I like to get a table against a plain wall with door to left or right of me – you can't write with your back to the door. And out of direct sunlight. Direct sunlight's no good.

In absentia the house is looked after by Roy, Brenda and Nick Ainsworth who live down in the village with monster dogs. Roy has been up to turn the place on a bit and put new ice in the fridge. I must switch on the heating to chase out any damp, and start the business of unpacking, traipsing up and down stairs while working through a pot of tea and box of Beurré Nantais biscuits.

Turn on the TV – it's the Benny Hill Show dubbed into French. Oo la la, panties and naughtiness, very popular here. I stand the 2 plastic models, one without a head, in front of it and take a chair onto the terrace where after the thigh-gripping sunset there's now to be had a fresh spring night with moon above like a ball of burning magnesium. A fine mist has arisen and it catches and diffuses the moonlight which glows in the scene with a brilliant yet peaceful luminosity. To-morrow I'll say Happy Easter and the holiday begins. In the meantime . . . sleep well.

5

Super Valmer/Saint Tropez

La Croix Valmer, which is considerably further south than Florence, is where the Emperor Constantine saw a cross in the sky AD 312 and as a result converted the Roman Empire to Christianity. In 1852 Charles Tousennel explained that what had really been seen was not a cross but the flight of a phoenicopter, i.e. a flamingo. La Croix Valmer faces southwest on the Presqu'île de Saint Tropez and so gets a better deal on the sun than Saint Tropez itself. Until recently it was a very quiet commune with a few dozen old villas in sumptuous gardens and several religious communities.

Our house, one of a group of 16 collectively known as Super Valmer and built above a swimming-pool, is constructed in 'the traditional style': pink cement walls, orange rooftiles on a pitched roof, wooden shutters, tiled floors, solid wood window frames with small panes of glass. It is a modern cottage, with inside a beautiful wooden staircase whose balusters wave, suggesting the sea, and to my mind look Minoan. There are 4 bedrooms, 2 bathrooms, a simple kitchen with good heavy wood furniture in it, and a 'séjour' done in pale blue and pink by my mother. This is not a practical colour scheme but it echoes the evening colours outside, producing an ethereal effect at sunset seen through the French windows at the southern end of the room.

Super Valmer is the last site on the climbing road which turns to rubble track hereafter and continues joltingly along the crest of the Massif des Maures all the way to Bormes-les-Mimosas. The massif wraps around us here an uninterrupted cloak of ilex (the short cork oak – Mediterranean trees, like Mediterranean people, are low on the ground). There are wild boar in these hills and hunters sometimes shoot humans by mistake. It is a Wagnerian backdrop against which the houses appear to float. Most of the lower coastal lands are in a flood of development but it stops here, as if the waters of exploitation can rise no higher.

The hills also provide shelter for wild cats and cover for burglars.

The house was burgled once – hence the security gates. Also I've been car burgled so many times I've learned my lesson. This is what you do. Never carry a GB sticker – or whatever your nation is. Do not clean the car inside or out – spruceness invites crime. Don't leave anything on show or covered up – make sure you have a removable stereo. Empty the glove compartment and leave it open. Also beware of groups of people flagging you down – some Arabs tried to do this to me by standing in the road. I accelerated.

Next day I open all the windows to air the house. Then I put away the vases of artificial flowers which my mother dots everywhere. While doing this I hear a harsh sawing noise without. Leaping on to the terrace, I see Vincent the gardener sawing down a tree in one of the neighbouring gardens to the left. My body experiences an unpleasant physical sensation as if one of its own ribs is being taken out. Vincent throws up his arms helplessly. There's nothing we can do. The owners of the house want to maximise their view. But a view is not indecent exposure. The owners of the older properties understood this and sunk their villas in trees. But the new people – if the slightest frond intrudes upon their view, they want it removed.

Retreating within, I turn on Radio Côte d'Azur – *loud* – look around the kitchen to see what needs buying and calm myself with a shopping list. Food of course. More powder for the dishwasher. Otherwise the place is pretty well stocked. Plenty of bug sprays in tall canisters and insect powders in puff drums. Ants, mosquitoes, wasps are the main problem. You'd be eaten alive if you were Franciscan about it. A bongo player I knew, Rebop, a friend of Irmin's, he slammed his hand on an insect the moment he saw it. He came from Africa where you can't afford to be sentimental about such things.

The wildlife isn't terrifically hostile here. Geckoes, praying mantises, small scorpions, the occasional snake, bumble bees. What you must watch out for is the inch-long hornet. There are various mutants too, creepy things which aren't quite grasshoppers or cicadas or cockroaches or locusts. One of these mutants is especially loathsome. It begins to crawl up the hillside in June, a large green flightless mini-robot on stick legs searching out juicier leaves on higher ground – it finds our jasmin leaves particularly toothsome. One is compelled by an atavistic fear of mutants to spray these horrors, and observe their death spasms. The spray has a curious smell like old tea.

I want to stay here until my parents arrive after Easter – so how to occupy myself? Régine, dragon empress of the night who has lent her name to nightclubs in many of the world's upmarket cruisy spots, is opening one in Saint Tropez – and a second in London (where her first London venture flopped). So I phone *Woman's Journal* to see if they're interested and they are and then London phones Paris and the people in Paris say great, because Régine is in Saint Trope *right now*, probably choosing barmen, and Paris will ring me in La Croix Valmer to fix up the time and place. Excellent. Thoroughly satisfied with my morning's work, I cook spaghetti for lunch then go on to the terrace and lie in the sun, waiting for the phone to ring. It is 70°F in the shade, much more in the sun, bliss. Thoughts drift. Not only is La Croix Valmer further south than Florence but if you laid Mexico across Europe it would stretch from London to Istanbul. The world is not the shape we imagine. Reality and documentary reality differ – as do documentary reality and imagined reality. I'll tackle the shopping reality when the shops open at 4.

There's a shuffle among oleanders at the side of the house and a ra-ra voice I recognise. Opening eyes into glare I discern Peter Preissner pierced by flashing sunrays. A Danish girlfriend follows. They are terrace-hopping in the district. I ask if he's hopped onto Helmi's terrace and he says he's not allowed there any more – she has accused him of stealing her paintings. Coming in to mix them drinks, the room is black. In the south there is free movement between indoors and outdoors – except for light which is extremely contrasted between them. In the north this is reversed – there is no free movement between indoors and outdoors, except for light which differs little in intensity between them.

Peter says 'I must go back to Germany soon but I hate to do it because the sight of the German flag at the border makes me feel sick' (his father was in the SS).

The girlfriend says 'The Germans think the Danes are stupid. And the Danes think the Germans are monsters.'

They drive off to another terrace on another hillside and I go down to the shops – halfway down is the other great view hereabouts: east across the Gulf of Saint Tropez with Gassin up on the right in its crinoline of green, and purple hills receding to the very Alps themselves which on a clear day like today stand sharp on the horizon like crunched white paper. This view makes me feel terribly 'abroad'.

In La Croix Valmer there is the old high street and at the top end of it the new shopping centre. Only in France would you find a shop called Chipette et Titi. Here it is, in the new shopping centre, selling lingerie, bonneterie, and bijoux, not my needs right now, maybe later at partytime. Buy fresh flowers for the house – miss the English spring flowers which are not available down here. Instead there are irises, daisies, roses. The mimosa is finished but the judas trees and fruit blossoms are out, and the corporation gardens are bright with primulas and pansies. Muesli – you can't buy. Onions – yes, the white virginal

French onions. Look in at the post office where 6 people are already waiting so I move on because in my experience French post offices are even slower than Indian ones. Buy *Var Matin* at the Maison de la Presse and the superbadtaste magazine *Hara Kiri*. Camembert – when fresh and uncut it smells, as you've probably noticed, like sperm with a dash of hazelnut. Look for 'au lait cru' on the box to ensure it hasn't been made from pasteurised milk. Those camemberts which have are among the world's most disgusting objects – the consistency of jelly, the odour of feet, lumpy in the mouth. Also open the wrapping to see if there is any discoloration round the edge – this has an unpalatable ammoniac taste. If it looks as white as snow, buy it, cut out a small segment and leave the box in the sun for an hour or so. It will be perfect . . . . . Er, I've run out of money. Down here it just goes. The French miracle: turning money into water. There are bargains to be had – bottled beer is astoundingly cheap, so are plain drinking glasses, cotton sheets, underpants and socks. Otherwise the south of France is expensive, with the world's greatest concentration of rich people living here.

The richest I've met so far is Sammy Johananoff, about 60 years old, of distinguished Levantine appearance, short and stout, with sleek grey hair, a brush moustache, and a bad leg. But where does his money come from? No one could say. Michelle Grant was staying there, at Sammy's Villa Neptune, and invited Alexander Weymouth and myself to her birthday dinner. The villa had a beautiful floodlit garden with an atmosphere of bodyguards.

Blonde, blue-eyed Michelle, looking ever-lovely in a diaphanous creation, asked 'Do you like this watch Sammy bought me for my birthday? One of the diamonds fell off in the pool and got lost – but it's still pretty, don't you think?'

A striped face of pink and gold. Cartier of course. Actually there were 2 pools, both at 30°C, and a waterfall you could switch on and off. In the kitchen Sammy had a gaggle of Chinese cooks. Dinner was served in the garden on an oval table made from fossilised shells, laid with modern silver, ugly green bubble glasses, and paper napkins. The food was very good – salmon flown down from Scotland, etc. One of the courses, I forget which, was served with Sammy's Special Sauce 'which I always make myself' (he has not forgotten what it is to labour): coriander, hot red pepper, garlic, olive oil.

Mozart was playing in the trees and halfway through Sammy said 'Be quiet now, everyone. I want to listen to this passage of the Sinfonia Concertante.' It was clearly an order. Everyone shut up, even the voluble Italian music professor in a denim suit. Sammy tilted back his head, let his lids drop, and simulated transport. The professor tried to do the same but was even less convincing. The rest of us were embarrassed and although the word was eventually given and conversation permitted to resume, this assertion of authority meant that the party was never comfortable again.

Later, on the terrace with brandy, he asked 'Do you know my great friend Edward Heath?' I had to deny having that pleasure and we traded pomposities and platitudes on the state of the world and the nature of reality, after which he said 'I enjoyed that. I don't often have good conversation.'

None the less there was something appealing about Sammy, a sense of loneliness. He had around him colleagues, guests, employees, servants, women – maybe even a wife somewhere – but his existence seemed without companionship. On the other hand, he was tough meat.

Tea at Les Sauges. Hearing a woof, I open my eyes. It's the Alsatian of Roger and Nadine a few houses away. So I'm not alone up here any longer. Roger comes across and I tell him I'm making for Sicily. He says 'Vraiment, Monsieur Duncan, vous êtes un globetrotter. Mais gardez les voleurs dans le sud.' He adds that recently he was in Tunis visiting an Arab friend who taught at the university there and was shocked to discover that his friend, previously so open and civilised, could talk about nothing but the glories of Muslim Fundamentalism.

This evening I call on Helmi. She is in her 70s, a painter, and although very dirty, she has such a forceful and attractive character that she's become in quite a short time one of my dearest friends. With her you can be *totally* yourself – she dislikes it if you are not. She rules over the Domaine du Cambon which has grown up around her in an eccentric and picturesque manner. The house is up a long drive full of boulders and ravines. It is buried in woods and plants, cavelike, with a purple sitting-room, a green and gold dining-room, a black and white striped conservatory, and a kitchen of mind-blowing filthiness. In the woodland round about, there are a half dozen or so smaller houses, built in a ramshackle fairytale manner, painted nursery colours, filled with mosaics made from broken plates/tiles/Perrier bottles, jazzy furniture covers, and decorated with Helmi's hessian wall hangings on which she's painted, in a bold yet subtle style, mythological creatures and invented flowers. There is a swimming-pool, cracked and unused, lined with red mosaics, presided over by a troll from whose gigantic erect penis, when switched on, springs a fountain. Huge insects in rusting metal may be encountered in the undergrowth. The Domaine du Cambon is unique, a Hansel & Gretel mescalin fantasy, and it's beginning to disintegrate. The plants which penetrate the dwellings at every point are taking over.

And Helmi's house is cleaned only if a visitor decides to do it. But the peacocks thrive.

Jo Gill first introduced me to Helmi but I came to know her well when I rented one of the strange cottages. The facts about her are few. She was born in Estonia and has that east European mannerism of describing people as 'of good family', 'of quite good family', 'of not very good family'. She studied at the Ecole des Beaux Arts in Paris. When World War II broke out she was stranded in Cairo where she painted pornographic wineglasses for King Farouk. Then one day in a café she met a Frenchman who asked her to return to France with him. She said 'But I'll never get a visa.' And he said 'You will if you marry my son.'

Helmi said to me 'It was a dream. I thought this cannot be true. But it was. Jacques agreed to his father's idea. Jacques' mother was a Plantagenet – but in Jacques the line had degenerated completely. We didn't make love – but I was faithful to him! After I married, I had nothing, nothing at all. We were married in the Lutheran Church in Cairo and while the ceremony was taking place I was thinking "Oh God, I hope they don't recognise me", because you see not long before, in this same church, I'd married a German. But he had fled to Australia.'

Jacques's father took them to his land, a hill between Gassin and La Croix Valmer, and said to her 'Choose where you would like your house.' Incidentally this story only makes sense if you assume that Helmi was Jacques's father's mistress – which she always denies. The father built them a house, ½ architecture, ½ art, overseen by Helmi and decorated in her own peculiar style of botanical Picasso-Byzantine.

She is not a great artist but she is a genuine one. Her painted hessian sheets (there are now several hundred up there), especially the naturalist fantasies, have an exuberant spontaneity and rightness. Then one day, alas, she was regressed by a hypnotist who had a chemist shop in Sainte Maxime and she discovered that in a previous life she'd been a painter at the court of Montezuma in Mexico. What's more, this painter was male and had married Montezuma's daughter. Helmi's hangings went Aztec overnight. The result was remarkable pastiches, lacking the originality of what had gone before. However Prince Montezuma in Madrid got to hear of these developments and gave her a decoration.

Soon after I came to know her, Jacques – tiny, sweet, feathery – died, and Helmi was left with the peacocks, the faithful dog Cocku, and the domaine. She seemed stronger than she was. She is prey to Slav melancholy. And has very little money – the estate was never in her possession. So the winters are hard. But in the summer unconventional people come to stay in the crazy cottages, those who don't mind sharing their bedrooms with mice, lizards, beetles, plants, woodworm. Many of the local notabilities have abandoned her – there is a doctor in Saint Tropez whose first question, if anyone went to him with food poisoning, was 'Have you been dining at Helmi's?' But he never asks this question now. Once she cooked one of the peacocks for Christmas dinner. A guest said 'How could you? It was so tame,' and Helmi replied 'Oh, it was half dead already.' I asked her what peacock meat tasted like and she said 'Very good. Very tough.' And the dinners continue, marvellous dinners, with old faithfuls and new discoveries.

I recall one dinner in late August during a violent thunderstorm, blue and violet lightning, torrential rain. Who was there? Allon Bacon, an Englishman with a flat on the port at Saint Tropez. He has hair of grey waves and often sports bare chest in the season with leather waistcoat and amulet on thong round neck. His catchphrases are 'It's fun, isn't it' and 'When I was in rep . . .' But he isn't an actor. He says he's a writer, a composer, a painter. What he's really hooked into is 'healing'. Some people think he's a terrible fraud because he uses words like 'destiny' a great deal but I find him very amusing company. He is the only man I know, apart from William Burroughs, who carries spray Mace in his bag.

At this torrential dinner he said 'There aren't many writers who heal. I'm one of the few. But these women *keep on* phoning me up – do they think I'm Mr Fix It? Did you hear me on the radio yesterday? The chap was good, he handled it well. With healing, if you're not handled properly, you can come across as a right Charlie . . . By the way, is 8 important to you?'

'No. Why do you ask?' I never know if he's serious.

'Because I just saw a figure 8 standing on your shoulder. It usually means 2 lives interlocked.' He's uneasy, nervous of the storm.

'Ooo, let's hope so.'

'That must be me,' declared Bunny Dexter, my American landlady, who was also at this dinner.

'It's *not* you,' I replied with emphasis. She's always wanting it to be her and sometimes this makes me wild. But she is a dear friend too, full of energy and capable of great kindness. In fact some would say her sympathetic faculty is overdeveloped. She is addicted to what the French call 'la vie snob' in an artless, eager American way which can raise English eyebrows. Her other addiction is food and her mother sends her giant jars of peanut butter from Florida in case she's not getting enough. Bunny is one of those numerous American women who have passionate and trying relationships with hot fudge sauce, ice cream, chocolate cake, brownies and Coca Cola, as a result of a gooey childhood. Her mane of wuzzy yellow hair and plentiful teeth have become distinctly noticeable in the Place de l'Ormeau where for the last few summers she's been renting Lord Bangor's house.

What were we eating? A tasty Estonian stew – avert your eyes from the world's filthiest kitchen, unwashed plates and glasses! I tried to wash the glasses but the stuff wouldn't come off. They need to be soaked in white spirit. Pudding was damson tart, the jam full of stones. The pastry base was so hard that it wasn't susceptible to knives or any other form of division and was abandoned in favour of a German cellophane cake brought along by Katherine, a black girl helping Anna at the shop. Although it was late August, they both had colds.

'I feel I'll never have another man again!' bubbled Anna, then raising her glass she declared 'To absent lovers!'

'To absent lovers!' bellowed the table amid thunderclaps.

'Come for a drink at the Byblos,' suggested Bunny, casting blue omnivorous eyes over the intractable tart.

The Byblos I call the Dead Loss. The most fashionable hotel in the south of France with fur bar, Martian swimming-pool and Middle Eastern antiques, it promises so much and nothing ever happens there.

August is a strange month on the Côte. It goes on for ever, stretching like chewing-gum. And the second half always has a thundery tristesse. But the reason I'm recollecting this particular dinner is not because of the unusual violence of the thunder and lightning, nor because of the dense sheets of rain, but because just before the party broke up there was an almighty explosion, as though a cannon had fired in the next room. The film broke – everything went black and froze for a moment – then Helmi shouted 'A thunderbolt!' Lit up by lightning, Allon Bacon looked as though it were he personally who'd been struck – I remember thinking it odd that a man so au courant with the cosmos should be so ill-at-ease with the elements – but Helmi was outside immediately, wading through the torrents with a torch, punching back the lightning, looking for the damage. This was only slight. The thunderbolt had knocked out the electricity box near the house. But a very characteristic memory of her.

When you call on Helmi you just go – these days she is always there. It's dry and chilly to-night. A small round moon stands directly above her house like a spiteful ping-pong ball. I tap on the glass of the French windows under a leafy porch and Cocku explodes with barks, then becomes gentle. Inside, Helmi is sitting beside the log fire, wearing a woolly hat and grubby knitted housecoat, huddling close to the flames like a troglodyte in its lair. There are no lights

on. The rest of the house is dank and black, filled with the smell of
her hangings. She laughs but does not look surprised to see me. Her
cheek when I kiss it has the softness of chamois leather. I open my
wine and we drink, talking of old friends.

'I saw Peter this afternoon. He sends you his love.'

'He takes my paintings – then gives me his love!'

'Did you have many visitors this winter?'

'It was a bad winter. Do you want something to eat?'

'No, I've eaten.' This is untrue but I don't want to tell her I'm
eating with Jo Gill to-night. 'I'll bring up some pizzas in a day or so.
I'm trying to get hold of Régine.'

'Why?'

'She's opening a nightclub.'

'Oh, that's all nonsense. Give me your hand.' She looks at my
hand. 'Very interesting,' she says. 'Interesting' and 'not interesting'
are Helmi's way of saying 'good' and 'bad'. 'You will have great
success.' I beam with pleasure – I never fail to believe her. Then
she grabs my thumb in her horny hard hand and twists it backwards
and forwards quite aggressively, saying with a chuckle 'But so weak
. . . so weak . . .'

Jo Gill, an Englishwoman who sells property down here, has been
having problems with her boyfriend but her son Simon is staying
which has obviously bucked her. He's very blond and red from
sudden sun and unemployed at present. His last job was selling
advertising space in Ethiopia for a telex directory. 'I only ever made
one deal by wearing my Old Etonian tie,' he says. 'That was in
Karachi. And the deal fell through. God, Eton was a loathsome
experience.'

Jo asks after Helmi and I eat but feel myself slumping. It has been
a full day. Z z z z z z z z z z z . . . . .

Paris was supposed to be ringing me about Régine, yes? But they
haven't, so next morning I phone London again who give me the
Paris number which I phone. Paris takes my number here, saying
London never gave it to them, and promise to ring me back to-day
or to-morrow. I'm ranting at the ceiling about berloody Parisians!
when Chris and Juliet Richardson walk through the door – they're
staying a couple of nights. She's pregnant and glorying in it. 'Want
any weeding done? I love to bend,' she says.

'Yes,' I say, not being one of nature's weeders – although there are
times when it can be curiously satisfying, like squeezing blackheads
from a lover's back. 'But in the south you can't weed until after rain
or watering, because the sun hardens the soil. So unpack first – and
I'll get the sprinkler out.'

Jo joins us for dinner and brings me a tube of Biotherm Dermo-Active Anti-Wrinkle Cream Protection Factor 2. 'You have to pat it over the crows' feet,' she advises. I do and immediately look years younger. 'What's happened to Ivor?' she asks (Ivor Bartels, thaumaturgical masseur).

'He's living in Paris. I told him I'd been in Berlin for Sylvester and he said that the East Germans had turned round the statue on top of the Brandenburg Gate, so that it faces east instead of west. He's full of these bits of information. He said he did a lot of reading during his identity crisis.'

Dinner coincides with the sirocco which rains pink mud from Africa over everything. And Christopher and I talk late into the night, continuing what seems to be the theme of the last couple of days by remembering old names from the dawn of history. Poosie Murdoch, Willy Lewisham, Rupert Keenleyside, Chandos Gore-Langton, Martin Lanigan-O'Keefe. Where are they now? And for that matter, where are *we* now?

Next day Chris and Juliet leave in their pink mud car. And of course Paris hasn't rung back about this interview and I've been in most of the time but don't want to be tied to the house, so ring Paris again and they say yes, Régine definitely is in Saint Tropez and they'll ring her now and ring me back and I say will you really? and they say they really will. Low cloud moves in from the southwest, skimming the roof of the house and obscuring the hills behind. I do some physical jerks on the terrace, then go and sweep the front of the house where I encounter Charlotte Dent. She and Gerard used to have the house next door but have now bought a tumbledown at La Garde Freinet with a shattering view at the end of *miles* of shattering unmade road (Gerard's father incidentally is one of the last Victorians and in the 1920s wrote a newspaper article saying that the tank would never replace the horse until a sporting use could be found for it).

'We've got water now up at the ruin!' declares Charlotte joyously. 'They had to drill down 550 feet for it – that's the height of Big Ben, isn't it? Will you come and see us?' And she's off.

Roger and Nadine leave – they wave good-bye from their car as I take the rubbish up to the collection point at the end of the road. The sun comes out, hot and surprising in the clammy gloom, then goes in again. Wisteria at the front and side of the house has suddenly burst into leaf.

Quite alone up here. An unexpected clarity and tearful composure come over me . . . Alone – the excitement of the journey reasserts itself. I feel myself expanding. Expansion is 360° penetration. Which is why it feels so good. Take from the bookcase Auden's *Collected Shorter Poems* and read it straight through. The 1930s poetry is flashy and trite. The best comes after World War II – the voice is more intimate and true. *Alone.*

> *Each lover has a theory of his own*
> *About the difference between the ache*
> *Of being with his love and being alone*

The phone rings. I fall on it. But it isn't Paris. Sarah Gilbert-Rolfe tells me that I have an invitation to the Naples Music Festival in the second half of May through her husband's friend who knows Claudio Abbado's wife *terribly* well. Inspired, I phone John Satterthwaite, the Bishop of Gibraltar, in London, to find out the name and address of his man down there. The Bishop says 'He's called Peter Blackburn and he's a delightful sun-loving bachelor.' So Naples is suddenly looking rosy.

The weather clears up in time for sunset . . . Bands of shocking pink fluff against a pale blue sky, and flooding upwards from below the papaya-coloured incandescence of the plunging sun. Long weals of violet creep across the sea. Night drifts into the landscape like a darkening vapour. The most wonderful thing about Super Valmer at night used to be its swimming-pool with underwater lights glowing a luminous green-blue and throwing Circean light up into the leaves and branches of the surrounding trees. It was an extraordinary spectacle, like an arrival from outer space which had sunk itself into the woods below the house. But now the committee (composed largely of Britishers, alas) which runs the common parts of Super Valmer has decided that the pool must not be lit after dark – because it encourages swimming at night! Why do the Britishers have to bring their shrivelled-up attitudes down to the Mediterranean? One comes to France to escape that anti-life neurosis. The British are terrified of the Dionysiac, of anything getting out of control. The only Dionysiac event in the British calendar is the Notting Hill Carnival which always puts the authorities into a panic (although New Year's Eve is increasingly wild). As a result of the general repression and attitude of denial fostered by the ruling class in Britain, the Dionysiac (in the absence of wars and empires) emerges in a random way, making the country especially prone to outbursts of irrational or class violence and yobbery . . . I try to have the committee's decision on the pool lights reversed but am told that I'm not allowed to attend the meeting.

Woke up this morning to a loud noise like a xylophone being played – it's rain bubbling on the tiled roof. Throw open bedroom shutters to find the house suspended in cloud and relentless rain. When it rains down here, it *rains*: heavy, fast, vertical. Nice has a higher annual rainfall than London but on fewer days. Once when I was living in the south of France for most of the year, it rained *solidly* from the end of April to halfway through June and from the end of September until Christmas. It was so bad in October that I rented the Bangors' house down in Saint Tropez simply to get out of cloud (where I discovered that Marjorie Bangor has the girlish foible of slipping small pieces of used tissue under the cushions where she's been sitting). Even the French were impressed by the rain that year – and it is a matter of pride with the French never to be impressed by anything, since it implies lack of experience. The French like to be cool. Consequently they probably have a higher percentage of silly little farts in their population than any other nationality, e.g. deliberately walking across the road right in front of your car, seeing you but not looking at you, and walking that bit more slowly on purpose. British rudeness is often a question of forgetting or avoiding the other party, but the French can be actively rude.

French arrogance is a product of French insecurity. They have been conquered so many times, especially by Britain and Germany. They are very self-opinionated too. When this clashes with French cool, it can result in something called the French Fit. Should this happen to one of your Gallic friends, lie him or her on the back, put the feet up, a cold flannel across the brow, and stroke the temples with an unvarying rhythm, saying in a low sweet tone 'It doesn't matter that you're not 100% cool, it doesn't matter that you got it wrong, it doesn't matter that you don't know everything.'

I park at the Citadel and walk down through drizzle to the Maison de la Presse in the rue des Commerçants. Brigitte Bardot right on cue brings her battered white van to a slushy halt, jerking it up onto the pavement, and stalks into the Casino supermarket next door. Saint Tropez is looking like a Dufy. It always does, whatever the weather. A couple of large white plastic motor yachts loom in the mist, floating silently against the quay, while a few folk occupy the cafés along the port which have begun to open under dripping tarpaulins in preparation for Easter. Saint Tropez loves to think that behind the razzamatazz it is still a real fishing village. But it isn't. It is always posing for you. I like it best on a windy, rainy November or February day, almost closed down, half a dozen shops open and 2 cafés, secret yet superbly self-conscious. To-day all the shops are open and in Villebrequin I find what I've been looking for: a pair of shorts in fine cotton, perfectly simple, no designer effects, and not knee-length which so many of them are at present. I choose a royal blue pair.

Giving a lift to the MacKeogh kids, who've just arrived for Easter, I ask them what they do when the weather's bad and one of the girls says 'Mummy's brought this 1200 piece jigsaw.' I ring Paris again and after pressure they agree to give me Régine's private number. This is headway. London rings to say they've got my La Croix Valmer number wrong, so I give it to them again, and after putting down the phone, think: if they've got my number wrong, how can they ring to tell me so? Then I ring Régine directly at her house. She isn't there and they say phone back later.

The other thing you can do when it rains is watch TV. Stylistically French television is amateurish and still in the 1950s – everything looks cardboard, not electronic. But the content can be surprising. I couldn't believe *Sexy Follies* which came on at 10.30 p.m. one night, une émission de girlie titillations such as you'd never find in a British club let alone on television. The British will permit much on the TV screen in the interests of reality, *if the story demands it.* But the idea of showing the naked body for its own sake, for *pleasure*, oh God, that's TOTALLY UNACCEPTABLE. *Sexy Follies* included 5 complete to-the-muff strips – a nurse, Scheherazade, a slave girl, a housewife with repair man, the first I missed. Brilliantly done. Very healthy. Except that the repair man didn't take off a stitch. Come on, boys, your turn.

Another attractive quality in the French is that, although they enjoy their food and drink so much, they are *lean.* Unlike Italians who tend to wallow in their appetites, the French are honed, economical, mean. They turn everything to account – dandelion leaves in the mesclun for example. Their leanness and economy is typified by the face of Voltaire who lived on 3 hours' sleep a night and who, as is well known, died eating his own excrement. These thoughts are provoked by a TV programme I'm watching right now about the next Ice Age. The panel of glaciologists are all in their 50s and 60s and what a fine array of cheekbones, tanned skin, sunken eyes, expressive mouths they present. Yet another attractive French feature – they don't overdo capped teeth. They age well. But the French woman can be too honed. French chic can be too hard, Italian chic is sexier and so, funnily enough, is English chic, although chic of any sort is basically unsexy. Spanish chic is impressive but wooden. The Germans don't have chic – they just throw the skis in the back of the Audi. Like the Americans and the Japanese, the Germans have marketing instead of chic. For chic, you require not any old urban culture but a high urban culture, a rich metropolitan focus which has endured through time.

I'm in the kitchen now, throwing an omelette together, and hear an Italian film on the box. Whisk in hand, I pop my head round the door of the séjour to discover that the film is Russian, *Alexander Nevsky*, mercifully undubbed (unlike the Italians, the French will not dub a masterpiece). For me Russian has the most beautiful *sound* of any language. It sounds like Italian plus backbone. Italian sounds lively but soft, its yolks spilling everywhere. A pasta language. French sounds pretty, especially when spoken by children, sometimes fussy when spoken by adults. Oriental languages, especially Chinese and Japanese, sound ugly and boring. Arabic sounds ugly and interesting. German sounds uncouth. Dutch and the Scandinavian languages sound uncouth and silly. Spanish sounds like German cooked in olive oil.

While forking down the omelette, there's a power cut. Quite common hereabouts. And since the house is powered entirely by electricity, including the central heating (a fireplace was to have been built but never was), the result is semi-disastrous. A damp chill takes about 6 minutes to penetrate the entire building. Candlelight ripples in the dark. Then the phone rings – I fall on it. Michael Miller, an old school chum, calling from London.

ME: I thought you were Régine.
MICHAEL: Ray who?
ME: Doesn't matter. I can hear Gilbert & Sullivan in the background.
MICHAEL: It's *The Mikado* on TV. My father's watching it.
ME: What's the weather like in England?
MICHAEL: You know – those damp dark English spring days.
ME: Same here.
MICHAEL: Really?
ME: Total sog. And now there's been a power cut. I can't even make a cup of tea.
MICHAEL: Perhaps you should come home.
ME: Oh, no, God, it's not that bad. I can always sing to myself.
MICHAEL: Last week I went to the library of London University in Russell Square. They have a list there of collective nouns. A never-thriving of jugglers, an eloquence of lawyers, a disworship of Scots –
ME: Of what?
MICHAEL: People from Scotland. A murder of crows, an incredibility of cuckolds. (*Laughter*) A laughter of ostlers. They're in *The Transactions of the Philological Society* 1909. I came across them when I was doing my research on Rochester. A blush of boys, a desert of lapwings –
ME: Oh, that's entirely mad.
MICHAEL: Yes, they're all fairly mad. That's why I went to look them up. Many of them are from the Middle Ages. A ffyttynge of beggars. Double 'f' of course, like your surname used to have. A dronkship of cobblers.

ME: I thought it was a load of cobblers.

MICHAEL: No, a dronkship. Vicki de Lambrey died last week. Heroin overdose.

ME: Another weirdo from the 60s bites the dust. Soon there won't be enough weirdoes to go round. Poor old Vicki.

MICHAEL: Apparently he phoned the police just before he died, saying it was murder. Talking of weirdoes, I was in a pub and this man handed me a note which said *My name's John. I like to be strangled.* So I asked him if it was true and he said 'Not strangled to death. Just within an inch of my life. It's a real turn-on, not being able to breathe.' A tabernacle of bakers, a rag of maidens, a route of wolves, pronounced rout, an observance of hermits, a blast of hunters, a charm of goldfinches, a temperance of cooks . . . . .

I go out on to the terrace where the rainmist has suddenly lifted and there's a wind up. The beam from the Phare du Titan pulses reassuringly again and overhead clouds lurch across a fierce moon with Frankensteinish effect. The mistral blows me to sleep and next morning when I open the shutters, it's still blowing – blowing the landscape into a diamond-hard clarity of blue, yellow, green. Halfway down the hill, the Alps show up crisp and pert, describing an exact line where their white caps bite into the sky. The mistral whips the waves, but the following day the sea is full of rubbish, brown weed dragged up from below by the turbulence.

London rings to say it's all arranged with Régine! So I ring Régine's villa again and the secretary says she can't come to the phone right now but who am I, what's the subject of my call? I say it's about the interview already *agreed to*, and they say cán I ring to-morrow? Deep sigh of exasperation . . .

Anna rings. She's arrived! I arrange to deliver the plastic people and have dinner with her to-night. This evening the sinking sun covers everything with gold and after it's gone the sky turns cobalt blue like a summer night. The temperature drops. The mistral drops. A young moon is tucked behind a hill and one horn of it rises up hugely, the colour of Ogen melon which is odd because usually on a post-mistral night the sky is very black and the moon and stars very white. A shooting star streaks with long tail – and another! They are messages in bottles from other worlds.

Apologising for the loss of one head, I hand over the 2 models. Anna breaks off the other head and says they both look happier now. She is Hungarian – from Bradford, Yorkshire. Her parents fled the Russian Invasion of 1956.

'Jacques is in London visiting Michel,' she says. Jacques is Jacques

Picard, a fashion expert from Paris and one of the easiest Frenchmen
I know, and Michel is Michel Lupo, an Italian homosexual who's
murdered 4 people and tried to murder 2 more. Jacques is visiting
him in Pentonville Gaol.

'Did Jacques ask him why he did it?'

'Of course. Michel said he'd had everybody in London, New York,
Paris, he'd been everywhere, and not even the prospect of Yves St
Laurent's new collection excited him any more, so he turned to murder.
I tried to have an affair with an Italian once. It was all right at first.
Then it went funny. The Italians are so fucked up with guilt. And
they always come too soon because most of them don't have much
sex, it's all talk.'

Her hair is in corkscrews and she looks 20 – but she's almost
double that. Anna is very pretty when she dresses 20. But when she
dresses 30, 35, she's really beautiful. We walk to Le Gasimple to
eat and she sketches me on the tablecloth (made of brown paper)
with crayons (which are on every table alongside the salt & pepper).

'Are you in love?'

'Yes, I'm in love with lots of people,' she says. 'It's because if I love
someone I always love them.'

'So do I – but I mean an upsetting, passionate love which transforms
you because you aren't thinking of yourself because you're obsessed
with the other.'

'Yes, I'm fed up with one-night stands, one-week stands. My problem
is I like muscle, 17-year-old muscle – when the tummy muscles are like
the little squares of a chocolate bar. See that boy sitting behind me –
I've had him. I like muscle *with* intellect, that's the real problem.
How's Helmi? There are plenty of gorgeous hunks around but I want
a relationship. I was really hurt to-day. Someone said I didn't look a
day over 30.'

She tears off the coloured sketch. It's good. A little wonky but she's
caught something sad, slightly bewildered in my eyes. Then our salads
arrive.

'I've had a lot gigolos,' she continues. 'But not for money. Even
gigolos have to do something in their spare time. I had one – he stole
my wallet. I knew it was him. Then he invited me out for dinner and
paid for it with *my* money. Still, it was only 60 quid, who cares. We
had fun. And when my other money ran out, he ran out. I knew he
would. But every year there's new muscle.'

'Now I know what that glint is in your eye: the quest for perfection.'

'Now, it's the Bandol Rosé. Are you going to the opening of
Régine's?'

'Yes, and I'm supposed to be interviewing her but I'm not having much luck.'

'She's in town.'

'Oh yes, she's always in town. But she's not in touch.'

'Jacques tells me that the *hot news* for men this year is – sideboards are back! I like your black suède shoes – they haven't made it down here yet.'

Good Friday. Ring Régine again and they ask what it's about and I say I'm the man who rang yesterday about the interview which has already been arrangé arrangé arrangé, and they say if I want an interview I should ring Paris and I say I've already done that and they say anyway Régine isn't there, would I ring later? I'm going mad, I'm going mad, why am I bothering with this creep? Need the money of course. The phone rings – I fall on it and it's a girl from a company in Fréjus who gabbles so fast I can't understand.

'Can you speak English?'

'A leetle.'

'What do you want?'

'I want to sell you a kitchen.'

'I've got a kitchen. C'est pas possible avoir deux cuisines dans une maison de cette taille.'

'Ah, monsieur, merci beaucoup et bonne journée.'

I must say, Good Friday doesn't seem very religious so far, and all the shops are open but they're full of brown and white chocolate animals so that's something. Take 2 pizzas from La Bergerie and wine to Helmi. A peacock is displaying its tail at a giant grasshopper in rusted iron by the front steps. Peacocks have been observed to make sexual advances to the most inappropriate things – donkeys, wire fences, trees. We eat at the mosaic table under the porch and after lunch Helmi reads the dregs of my Turkish coffee. 'Ah . . .' she breathes, looking at me with sanpaku eyes, 'I see a woman with an arm upraised. This is victory. And you will have a lot of money. But you are worried about something. How is your work going?'

'OK . . .'

'You have to get cracking. It is important if you are artist to *give* yourself to your work and not worry if it is good or bad but to do it. Do you have any success?'

'Little bit.'

'An artist should have some success – not too much but some. It makes him stronger.'

At the edge of her terrace a rotting plaster statue is gradually revealing the pins and chickenwire over which it was constructed. The sea is visible beyond the woods. The pop of a tennis ball against rackets carries from a villa hidden down there among the trees. When Helmi dies, something profoundly unshitty will have gone from here. Modern Saint Tropez is so slick and calculating. But Helmi is the opposite of that – dirty, careless, straightforward, alive. I come upon 2 dogs stuck together in the drive. They've had their passion and are now stuck. They present a pair of very lugubrious faces to the car and hop awkwardly out of its way.

A glorious sunny morning. It puts me in a ballsy, carefree mood, so, naively optimistic, I again take up the Régine thread, ring the villa and they say what is it about and I say it's about this . . . interview, and they say can I call back later? And I say but *I keep calling back later* and anyway *c'est tout arrangé avec Paris, avec Londres, avec Régine aussi!!!!!* And they say hang on a minute. (I use 'they' in the singular because I have the sense of never having spoken to the same person twice in these calls.) Then a voice returns to the phone and says can I be there at 5.30 to-morrow afternoon?

Christ.

Miraculous.

Penetration at last.

Phone Anna and arrange to meet her at the beach, the free bit next to the Aqua Club on Pampelonne. Take the African road – I call it this because the massed umbrella pines along it make the district how I imagine east Africa to look. Take the left fork at Le Grand Garage de La Croix Valmer and keep on winding, past generous Edwardian villas, past the Parc Hotel, grand and cheap among palms, behind gates, past the abandoned convent and the green-roofed Villa Allelujah in a mass of purple judas trees, past the neo-classical religious house in cream stucco on the right. This delightful sequence of buildings is highly redolent of the 1920s. As the road twists among the woods, sea vistas open and close in every direction. A few clouds form dark mobile patches on the hillsides. But eventually the pink cement of Les Hauts de Gigaro flashes into one's eye like loud farting at an opera. The cancer of development has broken out with a vengeance.

Until now, the Presqu'île de Saint Tropez, the hilly peninsula where the Massif des Maures tumbles into the sea, and which embraces the villages of Ramatuelle, Gigaro, Gassin, La Croix Valmer, as well as Saint Tropez itself, was an exception to the story of Mediterranean despoliation. It was a place of green-topped cliffs, mixed woodland

and flowery glades, where vineyards and country lanes came right
down to the beaches along which bamboo or pine forest grew, and
where, below the woods, small farms and villas left each other room. It
remains a place of great beauty, a remarkable oversight which retains
a rustic character by the skin of its teeth – the hinterland of its great
beach of Pampelonne is still rural Provence. Among all the famous
postwar resort names, only here has the cement death been kept at
bay. But suddenly it's vanishing.

Because it's been hitherto unmolested, people assume that the
Presqu'île is protected. It isn't. There is one small protected headland,
Cap Lardier. All the rest is up for grabs and disappearing fast. From
Sainte Maxime to Cavalaire the builders are ogling the fields and
woods, hungry to develop. Gigaro, so miniature, secluded and perfect
5 years ago, has been ripped apart. La Croix Valmer, the worst offender
on the Presqu'île, is rapidly becoming a pink suburb. France has no
organisation which resembles the National Trust. Given that all building
permits are in the hands of local mayors who, generally speaking, are
closely associated with those interests who are happy to see maximum
development, the only chance for survival appears to be the creation of
a National Park to cover the Massif des Maures. Away from the coast
the Massif is almost untouched, though increasingly threatened.

One final twist in the road and the whole of Pampelonne spreads out
below, ahead, with the Alps glistening in the distance. There is no finer
prospect on earth. Descend between vineyards, with the first vineleaves
sprouting on the ugly fists, to the southern end of Pampelonne, utterly
unspoilt until recently when a foul mass of indigestible pink shit called
the Village Vacance Leo Lagrange was put up here. Thanks, Leo.
Anyone for nitroglycerine?

Park almost on the beach among celandines and the white bells
of wild garlic. The bamboo is just beginning to sprout, showing fine
blades of green among the fawn shafts. Sheep munch the shore scrub,
controlled by a sane black dog and windswept shepherd. Last week
flamingoes landed here.

Anna has bivouacked in the sand with Axel and Philippe and I
join them, carefully beating round my spot to clear any sandflies.
If the sandfly bites you, you can catch Leishmaniasis, a debilitating
AIDS-like disease which is sometimes fatal and which is caused by
the transmission of the parasite *Leishmania donovani* from sandfly to
man. Other names for the disease are Kala-Azar, Dum-Dum Fever
and Black Fever, and it is now endemic along the entire Mediterranean
coast, having arrived from the Third World. Incidence has recently
shot up in Europe but tour operators remain silent on the subject.

Before settling into bronzification, I do a quick recce. Pop across to say hullo to the beautiful Roger on Les Palmiers Plage – he gives me a Pee-Pee (pamplemousse pressé). At Aqua there are 2 raving queens from New York City to whom Bunny introduced me one year. The one in leopardette swimming trunks and red wig which clashes with black hair at the back of his neck talks obsessively about AIDS, jack-off parlours and strawberry-flavoured condoms. Another American, Tom Murphy, who says 'Kahn' instead of 'Cannes', is also here with a party. He's getting on a bit but likes to keep in shape and so is really pissed off about the Russian nuclear disaster. I invite him to my Hot Brown Lunch on Sunday. He can't make it and invites me the following week but I'll have gone by then.

'Where are you going?' he asks.

'Sicily.'

'Good idea. Stay clear of that fucking cloud. Taormina used to be wild when Truman lived there.'

'The President?'

'No, Capote.'

He's drinking a new invention, peach champagne, which sounds vile and tastes delicious, *the* thing this year (it later spreads all over the world). Anna, who's very up-to-the-minute in these matters, is wearing a strand of coloured wool round her wrist which is apparently also *the* thing this year. Last year *the* thing was a cigarette case holding 6 cigs for the beach. 3 red white and blue Martini aeroplanes give a cracking display over the sea. The waves are light and lazy. The aroma of suntan oil drifts along the sand. A couple of Italian transsexuals trundle up to Anna and start rapping in semi-lunatic fashion. 'Tutto dentro, tutto dentro!' one of them repeats obsessively.

And then of course there are the mums and dads with kiddies. This is the most free and easy beach anywhere. All ages, all sexual tastes, all colours, all statuses freely mingle in all states of undress. No surprise that 'France' and 'frankness' come from the same root. A nudist family with small children disport themselves happily beside a couple of amorous gays, old men with penises like dried-up orange peel, big-titted mamas lying splat upon the sand (in French a woman with large breasts is 'une laitière') or the granny with nymphette boobs (she's had a breast job and proudly displays her pert rubberoid hooters to the plage, though they don't at all go with the rest of her). A group of blond German teenagers play beachball and tits and cocks are flying all over the place – then they tire and lie lithe upon towels, sunkissed buttocks uppermost. What saves the Mediterranean morally – despite its heritage of machismo, guilt, matriarchism – is its pagan simplicity, the physical ease which underlies everything. Which underlies even the fantasies of the Church. In every case where a Christian rite is moving, it is because one discerns behind it a deeper, older, more intelligent impulse which Christianity has merely upholstered. Christianity died out in its country of origin but prospered in the west. The coming of Christianity brought the Dark Ages. Therefore Christianity grew up in an *uncivilised* environment. This explains much of the abominable brutality of the Church. But what can explain the absurdity of its propositions?

We could do with some of this unworried pagan elegance in Britain. The British, as a society, really are pathetic when it comes to sexuality and the human body. In France and Italy, specific sexual behaviour is not considered appropriate for law-making and the basic law of assault is sufficient for most purposes. But Britain has the most complex set of anti-sex laws in the world. The British can't even get past their ruling class a decent programme of sex-education in schools. In Britain 45 per 1000 teenage girls become unwantedly pregnant compared to 14 per 1000 in the Netherlands where sex education is compulsory from an early age. According to one survey, ¾ of Swedish 9-year-olds understand how a baby is born whereas the majority of British children of the same age think it comes out of the anus, navel or mouth. In Britain everything about the subject has to be private, furtive. No wonder bondage is so big in Britain. Definition of bondage: can't take yes for an answer.

The British associate sex with violence. Whenever an MP calls for control on representations of violence in the public domain (television or videos for example), sex is always attached to it. Whence comes this painful pairing? Violence is often the result of sexual blockage – so why block it further? The British as a society are terribly worried by sex and their political system permits into positions of authority only those who view sex negatively.

One good thing about the arrival of AIDS is that it has forced everyone to be more honest about sex. The British ruling class loves AIDS for a different reason. It has enabled them to launch a general programme of propaganda against all sexual behaviour outside the private marriage bed. Laws against male homosexuality have been further tightened. Homosexuality has always figured prominently in British law. The age of consent for homosexuals is, barbarously, 21 years old, leading to cruel and pointless prosecutions. French and Italians ask 'Why do the British feel that the heterosexual impulse in their males is so fragile that it must be protected in this way?' In an imploding world, everyone is a member of a minority. Tolerance of differences becomes crucial to survival.

The Nanny Complex is to love what the Gentleman Complex is to the arts in Britain: SMOTHERING. The French are imaginative and open in love – eye-contact reveals a world teeming with intimate possibilities. Everyone in London tries to avoid everyone else's eyes – this is symptomatic of general avoidance and physical shame. Irrational fear of the body produces sexual shame. Whence comes this British fear of the body? From fear of emotion? The British disguise it with irony, phlegm, jokiness. Phlegm, which is fear of emotion, becomes fear of the body which may arouse it. Bashfulness is sexy but paralysis is tragic.

Why do the British have all these anti-sex laws? It can only be the result of a deep sex anxiety. But they should learn to ease up a little because sex rejection is far more damaging psychologically than seduction. Thank God Britain is a member of the EEC – healthy, mature, relaxed influences will flow to it from Europe. Think what a nasty fetid vicious puritanical and prurient little backwater Britain would otherwise become. I expect I shall have to return to this subject during the Italian phase of the journey.

Anna and I arrange to go to the parturition party for Régine's club tonight, especially since I'm doing the interview to-morrow. Back at the house I turn on the box – *Apostrophes*, a literary programme with peak viewing figures. They're discussing sodomy in 17th century China. Bunny Dexter phones.

'Guess what?' she begins, 'Grace Lau took some S&M photos of Michel Lupo – she could've been killed! The police interviewed her. Why aren't you in Sicily yet?'

'I'm having a moochabout here. It's a sort of staging post.'

'Can I come to Sicily with you?'

'Désolé but no. To night Anna and I are going to the opening of Régine's.'

'I'm jealous, I'm jealous!'

Bath. Change. Brush teeth with Ultrabrite Fluor (au goût sauvage). Eat. Brush teeth again. Driving into the world's smartest fishing village at night is always special – except at holiday times when traffic jams can prevent you doing so until the early hours of the morning. It's now about 11.30 p.m. but the traffic is not heavy. 3 yachts, too big to come into port, are lit up with strings of lights in the Gulf on the left, just past the torpedo factory. Ahead the Citadel is floodlit, and throbs a warm coppery gold above the town, and overhead a huge tilting semi-circle of moon glows dull red, the colour of plum jam, all in a black velvet night. Simply out of this world.

The port is ⅔ filled with boats but there are no orange people yet (these are the *orange*-tanned international high-lifers with bleach-*blond* hair, plenty of *gold* ornaments, and *white* clothes – they begin to congregate here in June. Another local speciality is women with posteriors hanging

out of their shorts – there are a few round since it's unusually balmy
for an Easter night).

The town is exquisitely pretty with the artificial atmosphere of a
mockup in a film studio – at night even the stars have a painted-on
look. The film is always running, whatever the weather or season.
Everyone knows they're on camera, even the garage mechanic and
bank cashier. Everyone looks marvellous even when they look ugly.
Everyone is searching for the marvellous. In summer Saint Tropez
has the greatest concentration of deliberately beautiful people in the
world. It always extends sexual promise, a chance encounter leading
to fulfilment. It is the perfect size for sexual intrigue and social
reverberation. More diverse and less constricting than a village, it
has none of the anonymity of the town. It is possible to be secret
but not possible to pass unnoticed – unless you choose not to pass
at all. Rows of tourists at the cafés sit facing outwards, all hoping to
catch a glimpse of myth made flesh. Will someone spot them? Will
they spot someone? Will someone whisk them away to a place where
they no longer have to be responsible for themselves?

The problem is – only the ruthlessly carnivorous can win here. This
is because a town in which everyone is simultaneously on stage and
in the audience tends to be self-cancelling. Saint Tropez has been
numbed by its own legend. That wishful-thinking girl over there –
amazing-looking, with the flop-forward throw-back hair – if her
future walked by, she'd not recognise it. She's too involved in flopping
forward and throwing back, the come-on followed immediately by
the withdrawal into aloofness. So many beauties trapped in this
predicament make Saint Tropez the ultimate resort: pure form, no
content. Like many other places of legendary gratification, Saint
Tropez finds it difficult to give. Life is replaced by image, and image
freezes. Narcissism, cock-teasing, a too knowing vanity, prophylactic
conceit, these factors eventually make beauty ugly. It's one of the
hardest towns to pick people up in – unless you're Cecil B. de Mille or
just want a safe-sex quickie in the bushes or hotel room. So somehow
nothing ever *really* happens in Saint Tropez – you come here with
people who've happened elsewhere. I love it – but could never stay
here in the season. I have to be along the coast a bit, up in the hills
a bit, because when you are not in the mood for Saint Tropez you
are absolutely *not* in the mood.

The nightclubs here, even the zany and opulent Caves du Roy at
the Byblos, are small. We hope Régine's, which is opening under
the name New Jimmy'z, will be bigger. The French idea of a good
party is mass asphyxiation. They call it ambience. Régine's crush is
frightful. Lots of people with flop-forward throw-back hair in smoky

red and purple light. Jazzy clothes, giraffe-print upholstery. Throats, lips, cigarettes. And of course drinks of mind-boggling expensiveness after to-night. Can't see any famous. Everybody keeps looking round for famous. Discover that there are *children* of the famous here – which is my recipe for a *truly terrible* happening. What you don't want in your club, magazine, restaurant, or whatever, is the *children* of the famous. Believe me, it's the kiss of death.

Crushed against the wall by a gang of raucous obnoxious nonentities, I say 'This isn't worth it. They're not even pretty. Although the upholstery sort of matches your zebra skin evening bag.'

'It's not zebra skin. It's printed cow. Yes, let's go to Le Bal,' says Anna.

Régine lives at the Villa Byzance on the chemin de Sainte Anne, just before the Chapelle Sainte Anne where Mick and Bianca Jagger were married in the far-off balmy palmy swami days. You drive up a rough track, press a buzzer, and a pair of white wooden gates opens into a short drive of pinkish gravel and a large garden of palm trees, cypress, flowers and lawn. Ahead is a pool, with inflatable armchairs in see-through plastic and a man on a lounger dead to the world. The house hides behind ivy and bougainvillaea on the right. Like most villas round here it's in the Provençal farmhouse style with tiled roof and shutters. I'm on time, 5.30 p.m. A man with ragged hair is speaking on an outdoor phone under a loggia. He looks up, asks me what I want, then carries on talking down the phone. Eventually he rings off and says 'That was Régine. She's late, she's out on a boat. Can you come back at 7?'

The temptation to slice him up with 4 letter words and not come back at all is intense. But I've invested too much energy in this crap to withdraw now. The silly frog fart offered no apology of course.

At 7, a woman waves me across to the villa but tells me to wait outside for a moment. She disappears inside, 10 minutes later coming out, and saying would I please wait just 5 minutes, and disappears across the lawn. I sit on a low wall in the dimming light, staring at a young gardener in swimming-trunks tying up palm fronds as protection against the mistral, get thirsty, wait about 15 minutes, then the secretary comes out and says could I wait just 2 *more* minutes, so I wait another 10 minutes, and eventually Régine herself totters out barefoot in a designer rugby top of broad green and white stripes, waving her arms, saying désolée, désolée but there have been so many phone calls.

The first thing I say is 'Are you Régine?' because there are lots of waving women in Saint Tropez who look like this. And she says yes. And I say 'Should I come in now?', not feeling very confident that the moment has arrived. And she says yes, waving me towards a verandah and 2 wicker chairs.

The first thing I notice on sitting down are her eyebrows – fine purple lines drawn on at an angle above her eyes (to say 'above' the eyes may sound obvious but you never know in Saint Tropez; in its frantic search for originality, you may find eyebrows being worn below the eye this season; Régine is in a position to wear her eyebrows any place the pencil will go). But she's not talking to me. She's not even looking at me. She's talking to her secretary (a man with an indoor complexion the colour of uncooked pastry) about getting Cristal – perhaps I'm to be given a glass of champagne as softener. It's been a hot day, a hot evening, and I'm parched. Now she looks at me. Then, as if not liking what she sees, looks immediately down at the floor which, in the sitting position she's adopted, is between her knees. I seize my opportunity and say 'Where do you come from?'

'I am Polish originally. But you know what I can do? I can send you my biography.'

'I'd prefer you to tell me yourself. Now that I'm here.'

'Yes?' She laughs a faint nervous laugh, which one soon realises is characteristic, and pulls a funny face.

'And how many nightclubs do you have?'

'I have 17.'

The secretary appears with a portable telephone saying he's got Cristal. Not champagne but a person. Régine gives the excuse-me-so-sorry-but-what-can-I-do? expression, takes the phone and plunges down the mouthpiece. References to a dinner party. Placido Domingo and *La Traviata* are mentioned. Then some Marrakesh talk which sounds very businessy and important.'

'I haven't got much time, I've got a big night to-night,' says Régine, encouragingly.

'Why nightclubs?' I slam back, clinging to the subject.

'Coz I'm a nightlife person. I was a barmaid in Paris. And in 1953 decided to make a disco dance. Because I like to dance and make people move. It was only 12 years ago that I start to be international.'

She speaks English with that French timbre that sounds like a sinus problem. She lisps slightly. She often produces a thin girlish giggle which doesn't quite reach her eyes. The eyes flit all over the place as if searching for what *else* might be going on right now. Her hands twist nervously over each other or she pulls at her red hair. There are 5 basic complexions: blond (e.g. Scandinavian), brown (e.g. average mouse), dark (e.g. Celtic or Italian), black (e.g. African) and ginger, e.g. Régine. She is one of the ginger people. Her hair is bright bottle

red, she is covered with freckles from head to toe, and her eyes are –
it's difficult to say. I retain no clear impression of their colour. Pale
tea? Speedy, haunted, here but not here, Régine clenches and gives
you *all* of herself for 2, maybe 3 sentences, then she's gone again.
And she's charming, yes, despite everything, and perhaps the charm
comes from this unexpected air of nervousness.

'When did you leave Poland?'

'I never leave Poland. I was born in Belgium.'

'What sort of family?'

'From good family. From good Jewish Polish family. But my father
was a little bit crazy for gambling.'

'Of all the famous people you've met, who was the most charismatic?'

'Purfirio Rubirosa. He was real gentleman. He told me very early you
can become international because every time when I present somebody
to you they ask me about you afterwards, you have something in you
which makes the contact.'

Secretary comes forward with portable telephone. Régine excuses
herself and talks – in fact a woman at the other end does most
of the talking with our hostess slotting in the occasional 'formi-
dable' and 'd'accord'. Inside the house, the secretary is working at
a glass dining-table with tubular metal chairs. Various big gold bits
are dotted about in the main room and big china bits and chunky
glass bits. Sofas in front of the fire. Lived-in but impersonal, a
workaday office atmosphere. Framed pictures of hot air balloons on
the wall.

'Where's home for you?'

'When I feel well in a place, it's 'ome. Can be an hotel, can be an
'ouse. I like 'ouses.'

'Is this your house or do you rent it?'

'It's my 'ouse. I don't rent. I buy 'ouses. I have an 'ouse in London
now for my new nightclub which is opening there and it will be a great
success.'

'Why did your first London club fail?'

'We got the membership wrong. Now we got it right.'

'Do you sleep easily?'

'No, I don't like to sleep. 3 hours a day is enough.'

'Do you drink coffee to stay awake?'

'No, I don't drink coffee. I drink a little bit tea. I don't drink alcohol.
I don't smoke. I'm a chocolate maniac.' She's drinking from a tray of
tea now and the thing which astonishes me is why am I not being
offered a cup?

The Riviera has a wonderful polarity. Its 2 smartest resorts are

Monte Carlo at the east end and Saint Tropez at the west end. And
they have 2 contrasting styles: black tie in grand urban Monte Carlo,
no tie at all in rustic sexy Saint Tropez.

Régine has a few tugs at her hair and says in her husky lisp 'I like to
put on the wonderful clothes and make the big appearance in Monte
Carlo. I have my club Jimmy'z there and for 15 years I was working
there every night in the summer, living in the Old Beach Hotel, it
was like my 'ouse. But you know, Saint Tropez is more relaxed, more
décontracté, and coming here was a need for me. Have you been to
my New Jimmy'z?'

'Yes. I went to the opening night. It was a bit crowded.'

'Yes. We have decided for next year we are going to have an
enormous glass roof open to the stars.'

'Mmm, fabulous. Have you known loneliness?'

She is sitting forward again with her knees apart, playing with
her fingers, looking at the floor, looking at me. 'Let me tell you,
I am a lonely person – by character. Because I'm a Capricorn.
So I'm working very much all the time to be with people. People
think everybody call me – but no, I have to do the calling. At
the same time I'm very shy also. People don't believe that. I'm
very very shy. Therefore I am forced to make this strong communication. But people don't call me. Always I have to do the
first step.'

So her drive comes from a fear created by shyness but greater
than the shyness, the fear of being marooned within oneself. Here
is a clue to Régine's success: she is tough but not hard, cruel but
not cold. Even the lack of consideration shown to a meagre writer
waiting on the gravel (and who is about to faint from thirst but who is
determined to out-distance her rudeness) is ill-mannered of course but
not malicious, simply that vulgarity of temperament which successful
French people so often develop. We say good-bye and she rushes off
down to the pool, says something to the man on the lounger who
rises from the dead. She takes off her rugby top to reveal an electric
puce bikini which blazes between the palm trees like a couple of laser
beams. Through silently opening wooden gates, I head off to find a
good long drink of fresh orange juice. Incidentally, Régine's second
club in London closed down after a few months. And so did her club
in Saint Tropez.

The Hot Brown Lunch. Lie on terrace in sun waiting for guests. The silence is broken by small sounds amplified in the amphitheatre of hills. Somewhere a little girl says 'Mummy, he stuck his finger in my couscous.' And twiddling the radio tuner I catch the BBC World Service, a station I usually try to avoid. *To-morrow we shall learn what the long-term effect of the nuclear disaster will be on the food chain of Europe.* The announcer says it with a jocular twang as though introducing the next episode of the Archers. We are eating outside.

Radioactivity means no salad of course. Couldn't think of a brown starter, so settled for orange, i.e. Ogen melons from Cavaillon. Be careful about keeping melon in the fridge, especially if sliced. As with strawberries and cucumber, its deceptively quiet perfume will pervade everything. Meat course: a steak and kidney stew with masses of herbs, red wine, vegetables. Jacques Picard congratulates me on the excellence of the Camembert and I say 'Don't you know about leaving it in the sun?' And he says he doesn't. And neither does Lydia Rolland who's just arrived, laden with goodies.

Alexander Weymouth says he's terrified of catching AIDS and I say 'Well, I met your father in the drive at Longleat pruning a tree and *he* said he was terrified of catching AIDS too.'

'That's ridiculous,' says Alexander, 'he's 100 years old. But I had the test and I'm clear and I've got a letter to prove it and I've made all the wifelets have tests and get letters. It's a rule of the club now.'

'Doctors' letters or French letters?' asks Jacques who has a thorough knowledge of English idioms.

What I want to know – can AIDS be passed out through spots? Not that I make a bee-line for spotty individuals, but it's best to be prepared.

For pudding I unveil a new one: Glace McDuncan: vanilla ice-cream with hot chocolate and whisky sauce. Which continues the theme of my previous pudding creation which was a spectacular hit in the Sud: Coupe Fallowell: strawberries piled on vanilla ice-cream and pink champagne poured over. The touch of sweetness in pink champagne makes a perfect connection with the fruit which, as a refinement, may be soaked in a little vodka and sugar the night before.

As for the Glace McDuncan, it's entirely overshadowed by the fruit tart, chocolate tart and cinnamon cake generously brought along by Lydia. I met her through the Bangors when she was about to marry the French novelist Michel Haas – which she did – but he then ran off with the Jesuit priest who married them – and Lydia lost her baby –

but she's now had another baby with someone else and is joyous once more.

Both Lydia and Jacques are unequivocally anglophile which generally the French are not. But the French are helplessly fascinated by a Britain which paradoxically has the most multiracial society in Europe and also the most continuous culture in Europe. According to Anthony Burgess, the French have an inferiority complex about Britain because the English win wars and the French don't, because English is the world language and French isn't. War is irrational, instinctive. The French are discomfited by the irrational in life. Therefore they deal with it irrationally, e.g. their phrase 'vachement chouette' meaning 'absolutely fantastic' but actually meaning nothing. The French believe that to act irrationally is to remove the connectedness between things. But this is not so. In the irrational, the connectedness is poetical, emotional, intuitive. The French distrust intuition – which is why they have no great symphony orchestra.

But one very noble quality in the French is that, unlike my family for example, they do understand what it takes to be a writer, that there are certain difficulties attached to this activity. After the philistinism of the British, this comes as a great support. However there are dangers in a writer being taken too seriously by his country, his friends, his family, the main ones being that it makes him nationalistic and self-important. Also, were one to be held in awe by family and friends because one was a writer, life would be a nightmare. One would be shut out from the world. (Mind you, the French aristocracy can be just as philistine as the British. A relation of Anna de Noailles once said 'She starts quoting Plutarch the moment she comes into the room and I can't have that sort of thing in my house.' Which is a very English remark.)

Allon Bacon says 'I went up to Helmi's to-day. I gave her a bit of a charge-up. I thought she could use a bit.' He walks to the edge of the terrace and looks down. 'Is your pool warm enough for swimming in yet?'

'On hot days. It's too cold to swim in the sea, isn't it?'

'No, it's OK if you don't stay in too long. Swimming in the sea is much better for your aura than swimming in a pool.'

'Bunny went swimming off La Ponche last year and got some used toilet paper in her mouth. It killed her aura for a week.'

There follows a short wine conversation. We're drinking an excellent vin de pays (vin du patron, 14%) from Plan de la Tour. The local wines of Provence have a distinctive herbiness and heat. I'm a great fan of them. La Bernarde and Vignelaure are the smackiest, and Château Minuty can also be fine.

Jacques admires the view, Lydia explains that it's Pardigon Plage, the last natural beach of any size between Marseilles and Genoa and that a golf course and 1500 houses are planned for it. She starts to clear up the plates but I stop her because I like a mess at the end of a party.

The following day my mother and father arrive in the Daimler. They live very well now but 30 years ago it was a story of struggle, crisis, and rebirth. My mother arrives with a huge number of shoes, her main indulgence. My father once counted over 100 pairs. She says she needs them 'because of my feet'. I never suspected they were for her hands. 'No,' she replies with a giggle, 'because my feet are so *terrible*.'

They flob onto the terrace, glazed by the journey, gradually euphoric. We have tea, then unpack the car, then have Buck's Fizz. My father turns on the radio and says 'Hey, listen to this. It's a French version of *The Isle of Capri.*'

After a good night's sleep, the first thing they do is go out to buy flowering plants for the garden. I've done my bit to tidy it up, and cleared the terraces and gravel paths with weed killer (although Vincent later rebukes me for this). William Waterfield, who has a very grand garden at Menton, gave me seedlings and cuttings of judas trees, coronella, acanthus, daisies, etc., but the folks also want geraniums and masses of annuals for immediate colour. This is the third garden – the first 2 were killed off by exceptional winters. We lost a couple of palm trees, 5 mimosa trees, all the bougainvillaea, so now it's conifers and the indestructible, colourful, flowering-all-summer oleander. Jasmin, wisteria and japonica also survived.

When they're down we always eat very well, a different restaurant every night but mostly old favourites like La Bretonnière at Grimaud or La Pergola at Cavalaire – where my mother, after eating a delicious piece of fish, declared 'But I don't like French food.'

SON: Why?

MOTHER: Because I don't like my food always smothered in sauce Everything comes messed-up. You can't taste what you're eating.

SON: But you like here and La Bretonnière.

MOTHER: But La Bretonnière's a superb restaurant. Haute cuisine. They really know how to do it. But most French restaurants don't – but they do it nonetheless. Everything comes so fussed-up and played-about-with.

(Despite continuous propaganda in the British quality press that the food in France is always wonderful, I've come to agree that my mother has a point as far as restaurants go. But where the French win, I think, is in the widespread availability of good quality, freshly prepared food at the cheap bars, inns and caffs.)

SON: Dad, why did you buy a place here?

FATHER: Because I wanted a place in the sun. France is civilised compared to Spain and, contrary to Mummy, I find the French sauces delightful.

SON: Would you ever live down here full-time?

FATHER: Yes, but not –

MOTHER: Not with his wife.

FATHER: Not at Super Valmer.

SON: So having chosen this particular part of France, what do you like about it?

FATHER: It's tout naturel.

MOTHER: It's unsophisticated.

FATHER: Do you mind, dearest? I'm answering the questions.

MOTHER: I answer them faster.

SON: All right. Pass the mike to your wife.

MOTHER: (to husband) I'm better than you. (To son) I'm better than him.

SON: You're supplying the negativity on this one, Mum. Do you like the French?

MOTHER: I like the ones I know.

FATHER: But you don't like many English people either, do you, Celia?

MOTHER: It might be better if I could speak French.

SON: Why don't you learn it?

MOTHER: Because it just doesn't penetrate. I just can't absorb it. It's as simple as that. It's because I've got no brain.

We shoot along the motorway for the tennis final at the Monte Carlo Country Club. At the Beach Hotel we sit opposite a US aircraft carrier for salad. Tennis on clay has a sullen quality, like a tape with drag on it, going a little slower than it should. The socks of the players turn terracotta from the clay dust. Prince Rainier appears in the royal box and my mother says 'Poor man, he's had nothing but problems recently.' They hose the court after 2 sets. Mats Wilander wins.

Then we go to the casino and play roulette. Garnier's building is simply sensational – he built l'Opéra in Paris too – and its leitmotif is the naked woman, painted on ceilings and walls. I've been unable to buy a book here on the architecture of Garnier, just as I was unable in Vienna to buy one on the architecture of Semper. By comparison British 19th century architects are extremely well covered.

Parts of Monaco are still charming but Monte Carlo on the whole is hideous: very undistinguished modern towers. But this central part of Monte Carlo, where the casino is, is being redeveloped in belle époque style. The New Metropole building, replacing the deliciously seedy old Metropole Hotel, is the first block of flats in Monaco to be built with a nuclear shelter. The Café de Paris on the garden square has been demolished and is being rebuilt. All the slot machines from it have been moved for the time being into one of the huge salles of the Casino where they look barbarous and imbecile. Under glittering chandeliers, frescos, pillars, tall gilded torchères, tourists in open-necked shirts, jeans and gym shoes pull warm handles. Even in the salles privées, a tie is no longer necessary, just passport and jacket or jumper. The fruit machines set up a moronic roar that shivers with the sound of falling coins. By accident, by pressing things I don't understand, I win £60 on one of them.

Les Sauges is sublimely peaceful after the clamour and spaghetti tangle of the east Côte d'Azur. My sister rings up to give Dad news of the factory she runs in his absence. And it's time for me to move on. Ring Harold Acton in Florence. Whenever I call him from France he always says 'Oh France! How wonderful! You are so lucky – I wish I were in France – the French – so intelligent!'

Visit Helmi to say good-bye and she asks 'Are you travelling alone?' And I say I'm meeting up with a friend called Von Whiteman at Taormina and she says 'Ah the Germans! If they think something is shit, they say this is shit. But the French and English play games, they have these *manners*. You can have a very good friend with a German. But the French and English are more interesting . . . Do not be too much alone. It's good that you are meeting this German.'

Last night. My parents take me off for a heavenly meal at La Bretonnière, and from the kitchen, between courses, come what the Burmese call 'tongue ticklers'. When we return home I'm impressed by the efficiency of my father's brain. Despite white and red wine and finishing with cognac, he does 2/3 of *The Times* crossword whereas the clues are simply a wuzz to me. It's been a good week with them – no rows – and after I leave, the Straights are coming to stay so they'll have more jolly outings. My mother asks 'This time next week, where will you be?' She is very sensitive to the poignancy of time's passing. My father says he is a survivor, one of the few airmen in World War II who came back. Most of his friends didn't. So he feels lucky to be alive and at night puts his head on the pillow and falls asleep, regardless of what the day did to him – or he to it. Airmen were trained to hypnotise themselves to sleep by concentrating on the image of a red spot. My mother thinks on through the small hours. I like to think that I've inherited my mother's sensitivity and my father's determination and sense of comedy. Only time will tell whether I survive as well as they, with their joie de vivre still brimming.

The moons down here are extraordinary: brown, green, blue, yellow, apricot, and sometimes shining on the still surface of the sea with a luminescence so powerful that it is as if stadium floodlights had been switched on. To-night there is a custard-coloured moon in a navy blue sky. And from this silent perfect picture comes an unearthly whirring sound, a Scops owl, the weirdest sound in the Mediterranean night.

6

The Riviera

A gorgeous lunchtime, blue skies, fresh breeze, a few puffs of white cloud – dark spectacles necessary for driving to avoid itchy eyes. The sea in the Gulf of Saint Tropez is striped and blotched different blues and greens by cloud, weed and wind. Soon after

Sainte Maxime, the coast road becomes tatty with inferior new building and the landscape uninspiring, low, deruralised but not yet suburbanised. Now that Easter is over, most of the villas and flats are locked up. The first stop will be at the Cannes Film Festival to meet Irmin, Micky Karoli (his old colleague from Can) and George Reinhardt, a Swiss entrepreneur. The first stop was to have been at

Saint Aygulf, a district of scrappy pines where lives HRH Don Ferdinando, Duke of Castro, pretender to the throne of the Kingdom of the Two Sicilies, and a businessman. Actually the pretence to this throne is disputed between Don Ferdinando and his young cousin Don Carlos, Duke of Calabria, who lives in Madrid – they both have sons (Don Ferdinando's claims the title Duke of Calabria and Don Carlos's the Duke of Noto) so the dispute will squitter on for many years yet. This sort of thing is a specialised pursuit, like hermetic magic or quantum mechanics, and I don't propose to pursue it further. Besides, I have been unable to contact Don Ferdinando. My letters have gone unanswered (they are Spanish Bourbons, one of the least attractive royal strains). He lives in a house called 'Il Casteluccio'. One always forgives delusions of grandeur in such circumstances.

Fréjus is a little further on, across the Argens river, and on the right are sheep, with tinkling bells, grazing on land marked Terrain Militaire

Accès Interdit. One expects any moment one of the sheep to explode
into the air. Fréjus is an old Roman town with amphitheatre where pop
groups play. But the whole area is a bewildering mess of main roads
best avoided by sticking to the coast where you come directly upon

Saint Raphaël, or what is left of it after the demolition boys and
flat stackers have done their work. No need to linger here, unless
it's a Friday night when they show pornographic films at the local
fleapit. Keep to road marked 'Cannes par le bord de la mer'. The
road becomes increasingly serpentine and the earth grows red. The
Massif de l'Esterel falls into the sea in an uprush of red rocks which
puts one in mind of Mexico or China. As the road swings along the
precipice, the view swings too – don't look at it while driving. This is
where Margot Ingot's parents were killed on their way to the Monte
Carlo Opera House. Halted by traffic lights at

Miramar, the untidy little spot after which so many undistinguished
seaside hotels in Britain name themselves. At these lights stands an
old man eating figs, head sunken into shoulders, long matted grey
hair, leering out of one side of his face as he chews, a Riviera tramp.
You get quite a few down here. Crooks too. Petty crooks, con men, the
dispossessed and the fantasy-struck. The sun attracts shady characters.
Halt for coffee and snack.

La Napoule comes into view. Joggers puff up the hill in baseball caps
and behind them rear modern concrete slabs. And beyond is

Cannes – big flat-stacker territory. That's the first impression of it –
flats – flats – flats like piled-up books and records, white, brown, grey.
From now on all the Riviera towns present this as a first impression –
perhaps all the towns in the world do. The planet is being overrun by
pylons, pipes, roads and flats as governments attempt the doomed task of
keeping abreast of the population explosion. The curious and individual
outline has gone. This is the beginning of the Cannes-Nice-Monaco
stretch of the coast, a long conurbation which is busy all year round.
It has rush hours, for example. Saint Tropez is a green memory.
     At Cannes the Croisette is blocked by the Film Festival whose
chairman this year is Dirk Bogarde. I once read one of his autobiographies. What a phoney. The book hovered fussily at the point where

discretion becomes deceit and reflection becomes self-idealisation. Autobiography should represent a man or woman's attempt to come to grips with the truth of their life but there was no sense of Bogarde daring to do that. Beneath the carefully casual exterior it was all horribly uptight. Bogarde says his great quality is charm. It isn't. It's sadness. An aura of extreme emotional vulnerability gives depth even to his trashiest roles. He is of course the finest British screen actor alive and it's regrettable that he turned his back on his principal gift in order to write demure books. Gérard Départdieu is the *face* of the festival.

Car creeps slowly along the front in evening light. Palm tree trunks are plastered with posters. Everyone's hanging about trying to spot stars, be stars. On the right, smart people in evening dress are climbing an outdoor staircase lined with policemen into the modern festival building (glass and terracotta cement) overlooking the sea. A man runs across the road in front of my car – black bow tie, red shirt, white suit, blaring orange waistcoat – he's late. Flashbulbs pop around the bottom of the staircase, then I'm diverted by police off the Croisette, creep around a bit, until with uncommon luck I chance upon the only parking space left in central Cannes which happens to be at the side of the Carlton behind a chic Mini Minor in metallic prune.

Meet the lads on the Carlton Terrace. It's a madhouse out here.

'We're drinking champagne,' says Tschöntsch which is the name Swiss Georg(e), festively bald with spectacles, usually goes by.

'In that case you can answer a question for my book. What do you think of the Cannes Film Festival? And make it witty. It's got to be witty.'

'Well, I think we're in the wrong place. Everyone's at the Majestic.'

'Have you seen any films?'

Tipped for the Golden Palm is Bertrand Blier's fabulous, irresistible, wildly clever *Tenue de Soirée*.

'*Nobody*'s seen any films,' says Tschöntsch. 'There's no *time* for films. We're doing business. But the Americans aren't here. They're terrified of terrorists.'

'But there's a table of Americans next to us.'

Micky turns and gives them a big smile. The Americans are different colours but speak with the same commercial tone. At least half their conversation is in numbers. It seems that American society is made up of so many cultural groups that the only language they have in common is money. Americans communicate with money not words. Furthermore, although Americans do everything to excess (including good taste), they somehow remain unshaped by what they do. American life lacks the tragic dimension; everything is reduced to flavour-of-the-month. To transform the world according to American ideals would be to remove the historical and mythic underpinning which gives life resonance and meaning. On the other hand European density can become immobilising just as easily as America freedom can become hollowness.

A woman who is the embodiment of animal magnetism joins them. She is enormously fat and pretty with long hair, in a clingy-stretchy dress of horizontal grey and white stripes. Her breasts push out in every direction – under the arms, under the chin – it must be like making love to a waterbed. She's compulsive viewing but what would you cast her as?

The lads agree that she's gross and sexy but Micky says 'I'm not sure that I like Americans.'

'I do. They make things happen,' I say.

'Maybe that's what I don't like about them,' he replies. 'And for sex I think the English girls are best – they know what they want and how to enjoy it when they get it.'

On that uplifting note we go and eat. The woman who runs the back street restaurant chatters about how Serge Gainsbourg always eats there and once got so drunk he peed in his pants and the smell was awful 'but *such* talent, such charisma!' – and there's Dave Brubeck playing in the background. I say *Take 5* is from 1961. Irmin says no, late 50s. Tschöntsch thinks early 60s too. They bet each other a case of champagne – 59 backwards it's Irmin's, 60 forwards it's Tschöntsch's. Tschöntsch says he bets on everything but he has to write them down in a special 'bets' section in his Filofax otherwise he forgets. At the end of the year, he goes through it and rings everyone up. Then we return to the Carlton Terrace screamerama where the fat American girl continues to cause a sensation every time she lifts her drink.

'What about *Gormenghast*?' I ask. 'Have you got the film rights?'

'We have to deal with the family solicitor,' says Irmin, 'who lives in a place called . . . Lostwithiel.'

(When eventually we meet up with Mervyn Peake's sons, it is in an Italian restaurant in Covent Garden called Orso. Fabian Peake is a painter. Sebastian Peake is a wine merchant 'but I'm going to be a poet now. It took me a long time to realise myself because my father was such an overpowering personality who upset me very much. He was a sadist. He used to fire arrows vertically into the air above us and wait. And if I'd been naughty he'd hold my neck between his knees and hit my head, so that I get attacks of breathlessness and claustrophobia to this day.')

I order 2 glasses of champagne, 2 beers – 160 francs. I give the waiter 200 – he says 'I must get change'. We never see him again.

Tschöntsch says 'Look, we're still at the wrong place. This time of night we should be at the Martinez.'

An American woman at the next table, not the fat one, starts talking to me and says 'I used to live in Rome. I don't like Rome – it's too much of a carnival. Now I live in New York. I don't like New York – it's too cruel.'

'I agree. But I *loved* Los Angeles.'

'I don't like Los Angeles,' she says, 'because I'm a street person, not a car person. I thought of Paris – then I remembered the Parisians – ugh! London's great – but there's nowhere to go out at night unless you're under 25. Do you know what?' she asks. 'I can remember all Marlene Dietrich's lyrics – but none of the tunes.'

She's on the third recitation when Micky says it's time to go. We're all staying at his house 40 minutes north of Nice. I shall be there a few days because (1) I like to stay there and (2) I want to visit James Baldwin.

Antibes is quiet as we drive through. The Musée Picasso in the old town is delightful because it's full of fauns, satyrs, centaurs but many of Picasso's large paintings here are rather feeble daubs (he was working here after World War II). Picasso was proud of his body. I have a photograph of Picasso and Braque in 1952. Picasso has his shirt off, his shoulders squared, his chest puffed out, the pose of a short man, a macho Mediterranean fisherman, while Braque looks decidedly northern, ironical, is bigger, heavier, physically more sluggish, wearing shirt *and* jumper *and* scarf and heavy jacket, hands in pockets. It argues against the observation of Picasso's young girlfriend at that time, Geneviève Laporte, who said Picasso's 'only link with the solid world of mortals took the form of laughter . . . or love.'

Graham Greene has a flat in the new town opposite the marina. I visited him a couple of years ago but we won't bother with that now, except to say that, like Régine, he didn't offer me anything to drink.

Turn left just before Nice, direction Digne, with the Var river on the left. Then at Plan du Var turn right along the Gorge de Vesubie to

Cros d'Utelle where Micky and Shirley inhabit a renovated water mill on the bank of the Vesubie river. Pass a spooky convoy coming in opposite direction, travelling slowly (it's after 3 a.m.) with police escort – small box in the middle of a flat trailer – the whole convoy flashing blue and purple lights – very spacey. Presumably it's something nuclear, wouldn't you agree?

The house is at the bottom of a narrow gorge. In winter there is no sun, it is permanently night-time, and this is what Micky loves, the dark electric womb – but in a natural environment. He's gone off cities. I don't remember going to bed but I recall waking up next day to the sound of rushing water, unhooking the curtain from the bedroom window and seeing 2 canoeists flash past in dayglo orange tops. Ouch. Too much vitality for my rather hung-over state. The large stone room downstairs, with giant water wheels at one end, is silent. I make a cup of tea with a Lipton's teabag and wander into the garden, through wild violets, across the single-arch stone bridge to enjoy the brief passage of the sun. The gorge towers up on either side and deciduous trees clinging to its walls make a pale green mist splashed with blossom above the water foaming over white rocks and smooth pebbles. The path up the forested cliffside opposite is fringed with primroses and celandines. The sun goes, the top of the gorge lost in dank cloud. On returning to the house I encounter Shirley sitting in weak shafts of light, holding a mug of tea and munching something. She says 'You can always tell when it's spring because the ants start attacking the jar of honey.'

It is about midday, time for breakfast. Has Tschöntsch returned to Cannes? Indeed did he ever leave it? One thing is certain – Micky and Irmin are still asleep. 'How's George?' I ask. This is another George. George Douglas-Home.

'He's in Milan now,' she says. 'I wanted to visit him but was turned back at the border.' Shirley, who's from Kenya, has been married to Micky for some time but has only recently applied for a German passport. When she becomes an Eek (EEC) all her visa problems will be over. 'There's some bread over there etcetera. I've been reading about the Ugandans,' she says. 'Do you know why the Ugandans are very stupid? Because they are strapped to their mothers' backs for a year which makes them very dependent. Then they go to live with their grandparents who lock them in a dark room for 5 years because it's more convenient. Then, when they get out, they just want to shoot everybody.'

'I see. Is that tea?'

'Yes. And this jam's delicious.' One of my house gifts was a jar of black cherry jam from Fortnum & Mason. Guitou, their big black dog, comes into the room and cats stir on various horizontal surfaces. 'Everything's been terrible,' she continues, giggling and pulling a flowery wrap tighter round herself. 'First I was turned back at the Italian border. Then someone stole £600 from me. Then I had a row with Micky about the Russian cloud. I'd been hanging up washing in the garden and it was a bit wet out there and I came back in in my shoes and Micky freaked out, saying I was walking radioactivity all *over* the house.'

Micky's hypochondria is proverbial – and he's very intelligent which makes it worse. He even convinced himself he had AIDS, complete with sympathetic swellings, on account of one night in Kinshasa years ago. A full blood screen in Baden Baden pronounced him 100% fit but he's still uneasy.

I go to the loo. There's one étron which won't flush away . . . I wait, flush again. It won't go . . . I return in 10 minutes, there it is, I flush again . . . The bubbling water settles and up bobs the tiny turd, irrepressible, buoyant, eternal . . . . .

Evening. Is it dinnertime? Lunchtime? Tea-time? We talk about medicine – Micky is eloquent on the complexities of an elephant tranquilliser he once encountered. We talked about sex and he says 'For me, women are not people. Men are people. Women are – women.' His attitude is not exceptional. In AD 589, the Council of Mainz granted women a soul – but only by a majority of one vote. 'And what is the purpose of your journey?' he asks.

'Well, one of the purposes is to rediscover the Lago dei Palici. Which appears to have got lost. I can't find it in any modern guidebooks but it's in all the old ones as something very special.' I run up to my room and return. 'This is what *Baedeker* 1908 says. *Lacus Palicorum or Lago de' Palici . . . generally 490 feet in circumference and 13 feet deep in the middle. In dry seasons it sometimes disappears entirely. Two apertures (fratres Palici) in the centre emit carbonic acid gas with such force that the water is forced upwards to a height of 2 feet, and the whole surface is agitated as if boiling. Small birds are suffocated in attempting to fly too near the surface across the lake, and horses and oxen experience difficulty in breathing as soon as they enter the water. The ancients regarded the spot as sacred and the peculiar resort of the gods.'*

Next day I visit James Baldwin. Saint Paul de Vence rises magisterially above its battlements like a great lady in a crinoline of stone, looking scornfully down upon the villa-clogged vistas around it. Saint Paul is very touristy now and the whole area has been suburbanised – this is the fate which awaits the Presqu'île de Saint Tropez. It is a muggy day. A slow turbulence in the air above the town suggests the possibility of thunder but there is only silence and the distant whoosh of a French car accelerating on an ascending curve.

Mr Baldwin in a pair of espadrilles shuffles out of his study into the garden and sits under a huge umbrella. He is sniffing and wraps a shawl round his shoulders, concealing a jolly Hawaiian shirt. 'I think

I've got a cold coming on,' he says, 'and this weather doesn't help. It's so heavy.' The myth of the Riviera weather – the sun doesn't always shine in a royal blue sky. Sometimes it shines so brightly that the sky itself is lost in a whitish glare. Or it doesn't shine at all. Or like to-day, the sun is felt hotly and steamily like an infra-red bulb in a greenhouse, a louring presence in a clammy haze.

How did the boy from Harlem come to live here? 'By accident,' he says in a shruggy laconic way which involves raising both eyebrows and staring at something off at the left, as if to say 'Well, don't ask me, how should I know?' He continues 'I'd been very ill in Paris. When I came out of the hospital I was shipped down here by some friends. When I got well, I decided to stay.'

This is followed by a deep coughing fit which rolls in his lungs and violently shakes his body. Physically Baldwin is small. He steps lightly on the ground when he walks and paddles the air with his hands, as if hoping a clump of reeds will show up soon to steady him. Tobacco and watered whisky see him through the day and night. Both products have done something to enrich a voice as full and deep as a beef casserole. The voice and the head from which it issues are at odds with the unassertive body, as if all the certainty in him had swept upwards and concentrated itself above the neck.

'But I first came to France in 1948. To Paris. To live. In fact I didn't decide to go to Paris. I decided to leave New York. It was time for me to leave. I arrived in Paris in November with a one-way ticket and 40 dollars. I don't know how I got through it – I met some people I suppose, got some jobs.'

The despised social group in France is Arabs from North Africa. There is a certain smartness here attaching to a black man. 'That's because there aren't many of us. I wasn't treated badly when I arrived. I simply wasn't noticed. Which was exactly what I wanted.'

But he still lives part of the year in New York. 'I am not an expatriate. My life is dictated by the necessities of working. You have to find a way of making it possible to work – that isn't easy, especially as time goes on. For a writer it's easier to see your society if you remove yourself from it from time to time.'

'As you take the plane from Nice to New York, what goes through your mind?'

'I'm always a little apprehensive because it's going back to territory where your blood is in the soil.'

He has 3 brothers and 5 sisters. Has success drawn him away from them at all?

'Oh no. I know it can happen. It depends very much on what you want. I never wanted to grow away. That boy running around the garden at the moment is my nephew.'

He gets up about noon and works mostly at night. Despite his work obsessions, he is the easiest person to see. The big iron front gate is unlocked. Friends and family, students and strangers pass through. And the French are very French and leave him alone?

'Ya . . .'

'Do you find it easy to make friends with the French?'

His eyes flicker all over the place. His complexion is so black that the whites of his eyes are yellow. He is blinking and not quite comfortable in the beams of interrogatory light.

'Not easy, no. It takes time. But when you have a French friend, you do have one.'

'What do you think of the French on the whole?'

'I'm very fond of them – otherwise one couldn't live here. There's a surface hardness, a certain style, but a real passion beneath it.'

It is peaceful here under the big umbrella in a garden which has been well-planted then allowed to burgeon with unclipped liberty. There are climbing roses everywhere and vines, a vegetable patch, secret corners where bamboo sprouts or a well lies overgrown. Geraniums and bougainvillaea add blotches of brilliant red and purple. Baldwin's property here amounts to a miniature estate, including a lodge by the big gate where his secretary Bernard Hassell lives. Bernard is also black and bounds around stripped to the waist with a gleaming smile, but has for the moment gone to ground. A Doobie Brothers album floats out of his window.

Baldwin's house, like the garden, is in contrast to the highly tailored villas which surround it. The house rambles and crumbles. It has odd rooms and is mildly disorientating inside. It is composed of a thousand decayed shades of brown and fawn and dark red. It feels very natural, though no doubt artifice is required to keep it that way without it altogether falling down.

'Oh, it's just an old stone house,' he says in a manner which combines both modesty and pleasure.

'But you have that talent for knowing when to leave well alone. I met a man from Palm Beach last week who said "You must come to Palm Beach – it's the most manicured place on earth."'

'I can't stand that.'

'Also he has 2 cats and he's had all their claws removed so they won't mark the furniture.'

Mr Baldwin's eyes bulge enormously as if someone has pressed 2 vicious thumbs into the back of his neck. 'But that's *horrible*,' he says.

'He said everyone in Palm Beach takes the claws out of their cats.

Your life here is very much not that. At the same time this is very
fancy territory – do you ever feel guilty about living here?'

'Coming from Harlem, you mean? No, it would be foolish to have
a sense of guilt about that.'

'When did it dawn on you that you were black?'

A look, to which incredulity, fatigue, exasperation and the desire to
instruct all make contribution, passes over his face. 'It happens when
you're very young. It's an accumulation of small moments. You're too
young to put it together. But by the time you're 6 or 7 you know you're
in terrible danger. This frightens you at first. Then it makes you very
bitter and you begin to evolve weapons.'

'When you listen to Mozart do you hear white music?'

'Oh, no, no, no, no, no, no, no!' followed by a terrible cough that
rakes his insides.

'What's the best thing about being black?'

'Well, you are subject to fewer delusions than if you're white. You
have fewer expectations of what the world can do for you and this gives
you a sounder grasp of reality. You have to take people as they are.'

'When did it dawn on you that you were homosexual?'

'When did it dawn on me? I don't know. Everybody's adolescence
is a kind of opaque storm.'

'And why do you think you are?'

'That's a good question too. And I don't know. I knew I was very
strange. A strange black boy. But I was strange on many levels.
Certainly being black and being homosexual adds a handicap to a
handicap – which is why one was so reluctant to realise it. But what
can you do? You can't change your colour. You can't change what
you really are, what you really want. You have to use it – unless you
are prepared not to live.'

'What is the most painful thing about being homosexual?'

'I don't think it differs in that sense from any other kind of
sexuality. Love, pain, sex, involvement – they're all together for
everybody. In my own life it wasn't the detail of sex that threw me –
it was the question of loneliness.'

'You have a awful obligation, especially in your context, to think
in terms of black justice rather than the necessity of the art.'

'That's not entirely true. A bad book doesn't help anybody.'

'So what's the difference between preaching and writing?'

'A very great difference. When you are preaching you have to assume
provisionally that you know what you're talking about. You have to
assume that authority for the moment. But when you're writing, you
don't know anything. You discover things.'

A black man. A homosexual. A writer. An 'ugly' man. There's a quadruple alienation here. His face which appears to have been made from leather and ivory tells the tale of one who has come through. But the anxiety remains. He coughs, throwing back his head, levelling nostrils like a pair of railway tunnels, then says 'Well, one of the difficulties for me has been – you see, I never wanted to allow myself to become bitter. I've had to work very hard sometimes not to, which can lead to an almost willed overestimation of others. But I can't go through life assuming everyone's a cop who's going to beat me up – and that's dangerous too, but there's no life without danger.'

'Do you think of yourself as a simple or a complex person?'

First the frown – then the glorious gap-toothed smile bursts like a firework across his face. 'Well, either way, I'd be making a terrible mistake, wouldn't I?'

Mr Baldwin lights another cigarette.

Back at Micky and Shirley's it is dinnertime? daytime? night-time? Anyway they are drinking and eating at the long table. Irmin is below in the kitchen, doing something creamy in a pan.

'What was he like?' asks Shirley.

I tell her.

Micky beseeches Shirley not to lean her face on the palm of her hand. 'You'll get spots,' he says. 'I do. One touch and I get spots.'

'Chocolate gives me spots,' I say. 'When I left Vienna, my face was scrofulous.'

'Switzerland is the best place for chocolates,' says Micky.

'I prefer Belgian.'

'No,' he replies with determination. 'When you're in Zurich go to Sprüngli. They're much better than Belgian, less sweet, less greasy, smoother. Try and you'll see what I mean.'

(A year later, at Orso, I say to Tschöntsch 'I hear Sprüngli chocolates are the best in Switzerland' and he replies 'No. Teuscher are the best. Their champagne truffles, my God!')

Micky and Shirley's house is one of the dreamiest, most soothing I know. If I stay another day I'll never leave, so Good-bye! Thank you! It's the middle of the day suddenly, after endless dusk-night-dawn – and hot. One needs cool shoes for long drives. I'm wearing lightweight white buckskin lace-ups which seem to do the trick. You don't want running shoes or boots or anything heavy or rubbery unless you want your feet to become puffballs of smelly hotness. At the outskirts of

Nice Arab workers lounge on walls outside factory gates, smoking through their lunchtime, staring at the road.

Edward Lear wrote to Holman Hunt in 1864 . . . *if you want to be quiet anywhere for miles round Nice, and sit down to draw – lo! presently 30 parties of smart young ladies on donkeys immediately surround you – and in a twinkling the ground is white with tableclothes, and liveried servants are opening champagne bottles . . .*

Swoop left onto the Promenade des Anglais, an 8 lane highway with 3 rows of palm trees which curves right round the Baie des Anges. Nice is a great town, its centre in very good condition, although the local mafia are always trying to demolish the important buildings in it and sometimes succeed. They succeeded with the old casino. They are currently trying to demolish the Palais du Mediterranée on the front, a superb 1920s pleasure dome. None the less the 19th century town, the old town and the port all preserve their characters and are full of delight – but we're not stopping because to-day's objective is Menton to find Aubrey Beardsley's tomb. From here on, the coast road splits into the 3 corniches and many fantasy villas survive from an earlier age. Rolls-Royces and Bentleys move serenely round the sharp bends in the sun like glossy misrouted boats. Turn into the Bay of

Villefranche where the Hôtel Welcome is. Tom Driberg used to come here and said that the manager would supply him with 3 or 4 boys a *day*. When it was suggested that this might be physically exhausting he replied 'I only want to *drink* them.' Quite apart from the pleasure this gave him, he believed that sperm had rejuvenating properties. Immediately beyond is

Cap Ferrat where Jean Cocteau lived at the Villa Santo Sospir in the 50s. In soiled bathrobe and yellow scarf he would mix cocktails using recipes he discovered in detective novels. The coast is very rocky here where the Alps drop into the sea and recent building reduces what vegetation there was, so it has a dry look even in spring. More divine villas at

Beaulieu where David Niven used to live – but does one want a rock face shooting straight up the back of the house? Here the road has warning signs – chute de pierres – and the rocks wear snoods. A butterfly, camouflaging itself as a green leaf, is trapped in my windscreen wiper.

Monaco again, looking like a mirage of São Paulo. Rainier receives an enormous slice of everything that's built, so it's not surprising that the place has been handed over to developers.

Tea at the vicarage beside the Anglican church of St Paul's, avenue Grande Bretagne. Such a shame that the British choose to commemorate Saint Paul, the man who took Christianity away from Christ and made it sin-laden. The vicar says 'Johnny Satterthwaite has a marvellous sense of humour – which is fortunate because he has an impossible diocese. The Bishopric of Gibraltar stretches from Finland to Turkey, across to Portugal, and into the Iron Curtain at Budapest. Mind, a lot has gone. No longer churches at Dieppe and Saint Malo, can't afford it. Many consulates have gone. Nice for example. Do you know, there's not one British consul for the *whole* of Sicily? And the British communities abroad have changed. They're not so much retired folk, colonials, invalids, as business people, representatives of toothpaste companies for example. They're mostly pretty ancient down here. But they live for ever in this marvellous climate. We have to shoot them in the end.'

'Is it a grand life for you in Monaco?'

'Somebody said I was sitting next to a prince at dinner the other night – but I didn't notice anything special. There's an old governess left behind I have to visit – down a basement flight of steps, down the hall, a bed in a room $12' \times 6'$ with a cooking-ring in the corner, that's all she has.'

(On a previous visit several years earlier the vicar said 'I tell you who lives along here on the avenue Grande Bretagne, Somerset Maugham's er . . . friend, Alan Searle, who has a young man to look after him, but he is very sorry for himself, always ill, no friends, it's very sad. Perhaps you'd like to visit him?' I phoned Alan Searle – in a frail wavering voice he said he was unwell and about to go into hospital but possibly I could visit him when he came out? I never did and he died in 1985 at the age of 80.) The castle of

Roquebrune flashes up briefly on the left. It is the oldest castle in France and was presented to the municipality by Sir William Ingram. Aromas of jasmin and pine waft through the open car window. On the right is

Cap Martin where Yeats died in 1939 and Le Corbusier was drowned in 1965. And opening ahead, a fine prospect of

Menton where Aubrey Beardsley died in 1898, the most charming resort of the belle époque Riviera. You'd never think 'menton' were French for 'chin' but it is. Its charm lies in the fact that though hemmed in, it is not at all claustrophobic, and that visually it's enchanting and coherent. This is because to a considerable extent its pre-1914 buildings have not been replaced by modern ones. The modern buildings which do exist do not overwhelm. The whole has terrific bravura and restfulness, a rare combination. The old town is Italianate with a staggering complex of churches and staircases piled up at its centre. The 19th century town is dominated by the magnificent meringue of the Winter Palace but is full of further flourishes. And on the far side towards the Italian border is the new marina. The whole works terribly well.

Tarte Tropezienne is excellent – a light sponge generously filled with custard cream. So, thinking it might be equally good, I buy a large piece of fougasse Mentone – and throw it away, a horrible fabrication of aniseed sponge with coloured speckles on the top. Make my way on foot up to the town cemetery, romantically sited high on a rocky platform thick with trees. In my *World Cemetery Guide*, which one day I must get round to compiling, it would have a distinguished place for it's possibly my favourite cemetery of all (although also dear to the memory are Cairo's City of the Dead, Park Street Calcutta, Byton Herefordshire and the two cemeteries by the waves at Saint Tropez and Aberdaron, Wales). None has a more enchanting location, draped in leafy tiers between the mountains and the sea, nor a more touching atmosphere. Several generations of well-to-do Russian and English tubercular victims have here turned to dust. The tomb of William Webb Ellis, who invented rugby at Rugby, is a mass of colour, strung with scarves and rosettes by French rugby fans. But no sign of poor Aubrey Beardsley's resting place. I search and search, round and round, up and down staircases clutching a small cactus in a pot, my votive offering. I don't think he would be found at the very top where several 'streets' of mausolea in classical, gothic or moorish modes form a picturesque citadel.

Eventually, after brushing dead leaves off perhaps a hundred graves, I give up, leave the cactus in the care of Miss Florence Jones (born Stafford 1843, died Menton 1889), and descend from the necropolis to William Waterfield at the Clos du Peyronnet, a plush semi-tropical paradise with Edwardian villa now divided into flats. He gives me a mug of tea and Jaffa cakes. The garden, which I believe was planted by his grandparents and which he tends entirely by himself, is now truly sumptuous and appears to have everything. I ask about snowdrops and he says no, but he does have the Nice snowflake, a leaner species with a bright yellow pin in the centre, growing only between Nice and Menton. He shows me an example. It cannot match the snowdrop for lustre. The snowdrop – so beautiful, so tough.

Then I make my way to a property considerably more dilapidated, the Villa les Colombières, and a great deal larger, with an extensive, disintegrating garden suspended high above the sea, which incorporates a variety of evergreens, terracotta fixtures and dizzy views framed by gazebos, pillars, trees. A terracotta belvedere has plants growing out of the roof; a dried-up cascade terminates in a weed-clogged pool with broken balustrade; yew trees, yew hedges and cypresses perfume the spiralling paths.

The place is owned by an old German widow who gives me more tea, in porcelain cups decorated with myrtle leaves, accompanied by madeira cake. The gardener (there's only 1) comes in to pour it out – he's about 40 with a loose face and affable, nonchalant French manner – while she explains 'I let rooms . . . but it still feels like home . . .' in slow, excellent English.

The Côte d'Azur was at one time a variegated wonderland of 19th and early 20th century domestic architecture, mostly executed with imagination and finesse, often with extravagance. It has largely been swept away, to be replaced by humbler accommodation in more uniform design. But the Villa les Colombières carries on – just. Inside is even more fanciful than out, a Sarah Bernhardt set with turn-of-the-century mosaics and furnishings, trompe l'oeil stonework, and a pillared blue saloon with murals of sea vistas (which continue the exact sealine observed through the windows) and painted art nouveau maidens bending their heads toward the ground. At a long dark table on one side of this evanescent room the German widow stirs the pale lilac-coloured air with her hand and urges me to take another slice of madeira, smiling sweetly saying 'No one else is staying here at the moment . . . Menton is somewhat triste now . . . compared to the old days . . . . .'

7

Menton to Caserta

It is a sunny lunchtime in May and we are driving into Italy, our provisional objective being the most monumental palace in Europe, that of the Neapolitan kings at Caserta, north of Naples. We begin modestly, by taking the coast road out of Menton, forking left past the Paris Rome Café, over the railway track between high old houses and up to the border point. First the French border point, with its smart tricolour, where nothing happens. Then the Italian border point, where the Italian flag is badly frayed down one side. Again nothing happens. A man simply waves me through in a lazy, pre-war Riviera way and that particular ambience is indeed very strong hereabouts. It is the early 1930s and I pull over to the Mussolini building on the right to change money and buy petrol coupons. You can *only* buy them at the border and it is a very good idea to do so because:

(1) Garages in Italy do not accept credit cards, so petrol can be a drain on ready cash.

(2) Coupons give you petrol at a reduced rate.

(3) You also receive a 10,000 lire voucher towards the motorway tolls.

(4) But most of all, you receive a free breakdown service throughout Italy – as many as you need. The Capri has one of the best engines Ford ever made but mine is far from young and this breakdown bonus gives me a great sense of security – no one is more cheatable than a foreign motorist who hardly speaks the language and who doesn't understand cars.

The border post has severe concrete facings but mellow woodwork inside. It's quiet in the lunchtime warmth. There is only one traveller, me. Only one guard – he lethargically turns the pages of an Italian newspaper and every so often sighs disconsolately upon meeting another gloomy headline. And one bright young woman behind a wooden counter. She requires my green insurance card for these coupons – major derangement of luggage trying to locate the bugger –

and after much form-filling she hands me a dossier of coupons, maps and brochures with a smile and tilt of her head. I go for a pee. One of the world's most unpleasant lavatories is at this border – on the French side, a squatter. Swarm of flies in there and shit spread up the tiles where frantic travellers have splatted their desperate diarrhoea.

Crossing into Italy always brings a sense of adventure, of abandon, as of moving into a wilder, more romantic realm. The landscape is relatively unkempt and less built-up on the Italian side and the road is inferior. But soon terraces of glass greenhouses appear, covering the hillsides. They owe their existence to the garden estate at La Mortola nearby, established by the Hanbury family who first persuaded the locals that horticulture could become a way of life.

Hug the coast and you won't go wrong. Which takes one through the centre of Ventimiglia – yes! – mouldering old houses piled up in a mound with washing hanging all over it and nondescript modern building round the base – this warm and savage sight is not at all France. Attempts to build flashy blocks of flats along the shore have not been a success. Where are we going now? Diverted into a back street with little church, char*ming*, look for signs, switch off radio, attention, look for signs. The Italians are far less efficient at signposting than the French – and in France the motorway signs are blue and the main road signs are green, whereas in Italy it's the other way round.

Trams, my dear, good Lord, haven't seen *trams* for years. Where are we exactly? Can anyone help? Slither along the coast, past a shop selling classical statues cast in cement for gardens, past the Residence Bristol, Hotel Britannique, Hotel Florida. Hotels the world over give themselves names deriving from places other than those in which they are, one more aspect of the relentless phoneyism of the tourist industry. The holiday building has continued uninterruptedly from Ventimiglia, but without that gloss of richesse which still survives along the French Riviera. We're staying on the coast road until San Remo where we'll pick up the motorway and whizz past Genoa into Florence. Bordighera . . . is not quite what one expected. The first palm trees in Europe were at Bordighera, planted by the corsairs from Africa in the early Middle Ages. I've never been here before but I always confuse the name of it with Bagheria where I've also never been. Other confusions are:

Cement – Concrete
Petrarch – Plutarch
Menander – Meleander – Meleager
Nostradamus – Paracelsus – Agrippa
Wheat – Corn
West Drayton – West Hartlepool

Walter Savage Landor – Wilfrid Scawen Blunt – Edward Bulwer
 Lytton
(Sarah Gilbert-Rolfe wants me to add to this list 'good' and 'bad')

Also I've noticed Italians cause confusion between the following
English words by pronouncing them identically:

> Peas – Piss
> Shit – Sheet
> Beach – Bitch
> Hungry – Angry

The sea is cerulean blue . . . Coming into San Remo, lovely old
wedding-cake hotels – Hotel Astoria West End, Grand Hotel Londra
. . . 'If you're going through San Remo, stay at the Royal,' said my
father blithely (my parents had a phase of driving all round Europe,
doing the grand hotels and casinos). San Remo is lusher, less garish,
sexier than Cannes, but I'm not staying here to-night so . . . . . we
climb the hill to pick up the Autostrada 10, winding up and up
and jammed behind a town bus which slows right down, farts and
honks loudly at every bend . . . Interval for car exercises – tense
your buttocks, relax, tense your buttocks, relax (bum ache on a long
drive is something to deal with – of course stopping and getting out
is the answer but one can find oneself sucked on by the road, mile
after mile after mile, hypnotised, hour after hour, unable to stop, like
a bloody fool) – stretch the spine upwards, stretch the spine upwards –
you are dangling on a string – sense the bones in your bum – turn
head to left and right, raise shoulders and drop. Repeat. The heat is
beginning to absorb me. Am surrendering to the incandescence. Feel
my soul sinking into it. At the feed road to the autostrada, a municipal
noticeboard says *Goodbye, Arrivederci, Au Revoir, Auf Wiedersehen, until
the next time*.

Now we begin the Great Drive along the coast of Liguria (la regione
dei poeti). Good swig from flask. A road which links the Riviera to
the city of Florence should not be mediocre – this one is a major
engineering feat, many were killed in its construction, no I can't
remember exactly how many, I lost the bit of paper, but drive it and
you'll understand why, a string of tunnels and viaducts through vistas
which burst upon the driver like green and blue explosions. Italian
tunnels are noticeably less well lit than French ones and Italian drivers
noticeably less neurotic. Snack thoughts – dying for a cup of that

delicious Italian coffee and suppose I'll have to buy a couple of those
gruesome dry powdery Italian white rolls with a slice of greasy salami
introduced at one side or the ubiquitous prosciutto/formaggio.

   . . . the Viadotto Taggia swings to the right over a precipitous
landscape, a cream curve on massive concrete brackets and posts. What
is the difference between concrete and cement? Another noticeable
change is that Italian motorways do not carry the cultural information
which French motorways do and although they have quite as many
garages, they do not have those leafy stopping places which are so
useful in France. Feel your seatbones, stretch up, stretch up! But
bum ache no go 'way . . .

   Here's a garage and bar. Pull in, get out, make sure the headlights
are off (all that in & out of tunnels, one can forget). Get talking to an
English Eurohaul lorry driver over coffee – he says you can't drive
the lorry on Sundays or bank holidays in Italy and sometimes not
the day before bank holidays too and he got stuck at Caserta with a
couple of banned days so went down to Sorrento where he met an
English girl who said she was walking along the street in Naples and
someone came up and ripped her little gold chain off her, just like
that, so watch out, mate.

   You can't listen to the radio on this drive because of the tunnels so
I play my home-made tapes of very mixed music. Hills spattered with
hilltop villages pass by, signalling to each other across chasms. Before
the car, to visit a neighbouring village would be a major enterprise.
It is astonishing what people throw from the inside to the outside of
their cars as they drive along. Applecores – OK, biodegradable. But
empty tins too. And *tissues* are always flying out, used tissues. One
has caught on my right wiper blade and I flick it off with disgust.

   Past the uscita for Turin and stupendous Stupinigi . . . past uscita
for Milan, the world's most polluted city (according to a recent survey).
Then the pink towerblocks of Voltri. When are we going to stop *breeding*
so that we don't have to stack people up in this way? Rising up the
hillside, these blocks have been designed with crude geometric shapes
on their façades in an attempt to make them 'interesting'. I once met
Heiner Müller in Berlin. He's an East German by nationality but lives
in both east and west Berlin. In some respects he is very modern, in
others very old-fashioned, and said that the declining population in
West Germany is evidence of its 'death wish'. I violently disagreed.
In an advanced technological society, a declining population is a sign
of health. Curiously, Italy's birthrate is at present the lowest in the
industrialised world.

   Here we are, hanging over Genoa, city of Dickens and Nietzsche
and Sergio Soldano. 'Who?' you ask. Sergio Soldano. He makes the

finest toiletries for men in either France or Italy. 'Why?' you ask. Because of the *smell*. The perfume of the 'black' range manages to be both opulent and fresh, with terrific *lift* in it. Soldano's men's products smell so good that even the Italians haven't heard of him. And the reason we are *hanging* is that the most extraordinary viaduct of all has been built over Genoa, carrying the road hundreds of feet above the city on towering spider's legs. Normally it bounces as one drives across but to-day there is a traffic jam here, producing the occasional ripple and the ineradicable hum of the thought that at any moment it might crack and collapse onto the sharp skyscrapertops far below. We are jammed in the air – then creep forward to a spiral which takes us even higher and, delicate filament that it is, trembles in the wind. Don't look down. Let's concentrate in here. It's all a dream out there beyond the carapace of the car. Swig from flask. Slug of water from bottle. Couple of biscuits. Inch forward round the curve of the spiral and forget that one is supported above the abyss merely by a set of computer calculations. What if they got the sums wrong? Eventually the spiral drives its arm into the rock face and at this point a group of policemen gesticulate to us and to themselves, wearing blue jackets, white leather cross-straps, grey jodhpurs with magenta stripes down the side, pistols, jackboots, caps, motorbikes – Ruritania meets Marlon Brando. But if there's been an accident, there's no evidence of it. And miraculously the traffic clears, the motorway divides and we take the route marked Livorno.

The landscape east of Genoa is more beautiful than that west. Dickens thought it the most beautiful landscape in Italy. Past the uscita for Rapallo and Max Beerbohm; also for Portofino which was the inspiration for Portmeirion in Wales (but Portofino has become banal while Portmeirion remains strange because it occurs exactly on the hinge between fantasy and reality) . . . Carrodano – the Ligurian landscape, which here is free from insensitive building or coarse industrialisation, is the second great unspoilt landscape on this journey (the first being North Burgundy; Provence is often glorious but very interrupted), a region remote but dreamily civilised with villages perched in a dramatic green lushness, each with its exotic church tower. The hills and low mountains, covered by steeply falling verdure, make fascinating folds, as if hands were pushing up beneath heavy bedclothes.

The landscape degenerates after La Spezia, although the mountains above Carrara look very fine, shark grey against a pale blue sky in the late afternoon sun. Italiana Coke factory on left – fuel for burning – very smelly downwind. Motorway divides again. Take arm to Florence, missing Viareggio where Rilke wrote *The Book of Poverty and Death*, and missing Pisa (but mention may be made of the remarkable urine-coloured light in Pisa's cathedral + the phallic graffiti atop the Leaning Tower, its base famous as a place to pick up young soldiers). The road is dry as a bone and the air very clear. Spectacular double viadotto (Viadotto Bolzano 1 and 2) affords splendid views of flooding on the coastal plain. Landscape again takes on a sumptuous aspect and begins to smell of white blossom.

I know Florence reasonably well – it's a great shopping town for the better things, not too overwhelming – and when there I always visit Harold Acton who's the last bastion of etc etc (I don't enter virgin territory until after Rome). On my previous visit to La Pietra, Acton's house, he spoke of the Prince and Princess of Wales's stay. 'They are so charming. They always travel with their own servants. And their butler would bring in all the magazines and newspapers in which they featured and these, hundreds of them, they would spread over the carpet and *pore* over them, especially her. And they wanted *everything* translated. But after a hectic day, he liked to go up onto the roof and paint . . .'

There are 2 kinds of people. Those who go down for breakfast in hotels and large houses and those who have breakfast in their room. Charles would go down for breakfast. Diana preferred to have it in her room. This is a fundamental incompatibility. Incompatibilities spice a relationship.

Pull over at a garage about 35 kilometres from Florence to fill up and the garage man notices some Scotch shortbread open in the car and goes Mm, mm, I'd like one of those. So I offer him one and he takes 2 and I follow him in to pay and he gives me a swig from a bottle of brandy and then starts to pull out pornographic magazines from his desk drawer, saying 'We have little party', laughing, showing white teeth and purple gums, and I think my God, this would never happen in France or England and I can hardly believe it's happening here but we sort of have a little party there and then, and afterwards I return to the car, tired but happy, slot in Toots and the Maytals, and fly into Florence.

In winter I'd stay at the Hotel Porta Rossa, one of the great hang-out hotels, but at this time of year one can use the Pensione Bandini (too cold in winter) in the Piazza San Spirito because the aura of the Oltrano is less touristic. Luckily there's a parking place outside the palazzo at the top of which is the pensione, cheap and grandiose with a high pillared loggia looking west above the city. The old stone heart of Florence was so well built that it remains more or less intact. There have been few incursions – the Palazzo Strozzi had a beautiful 15th century courtyard which was demolished in 1920 to make way for the Odeon Cinema. I leave my bags in Room 6 and with sore eyes walk on to the loggia, rest my arms on the parapet and look outwards above the rooftops, feeling good, thinking of nothing.

Over breakfast I decide to buy a leather bag from a shop I know off the Piazza della Signoria but, on descending to the street, discover that a busy market has sprouted all round my car. This is a problem, not least because I have parked on the pitch of a fruit seller who is now standing in front of me loudly informing me of this fact. He's about 40, hair cut medium short all over in the way Italian men do if they don't want a hairstyle. I can't understand a word he's saying but am more concerned about a king-size bunch of bananas he's shaking in my face. I don't know about you but first thing in the morning is not my brilliant time – in fact I'm often not really rolling mentally until way after lunch – so that this situation is more than I can grasp. One thing is certain. If I become involved with moving the car now I'll never have time to buy my bag – and besides, my luggage is still up in the pensione – so I say 'Impossibile, impossibile!' to whatever he's demanding and walk off. A big mistake. He comes running after me – the market folk stop what they're doing and look to see what will happen. I keep walking, trembling, trying to shake him off, trying to rise above it/him/them/Florence/the World. He is now in a terrible rage, pursuing me with roars, shaking his bananas, spittle at the corners of his mouth. We are this morning's spectacle, me walking white and silent, him following red and noisy. Clearly he'll follow me all the way to the bag shop and may even strike me down beforehand. My nerve breaks first. I turn about, look him in his bulging eyes and say 'OK!' I walk back to the car, agree to move it, although the compress of marketeers seems to make this absurd. And at this point Bananas suddenly changes. Changes completely. He says that I don't have to move the car *at all*. I'm bewildered. No, no, it's fine, he says. How long do I need to go shopping, 1 hour, 2 hours? That's fine . . . Very weird. But I'm not going to argue with him again. Perhaps he simply wanted me to acknowledge my turpitude. B-i-z-a-r-r-e . . .

I set out bagwards, distinctly paranoid, convinced that I've become the victim of a Florentine ruse, that the car will be stolen in my absence or tyres slashed at the very least. Bananas is bound to have dark friends. Walking along the Arno I become mesmerised by the bases of the lamps which line it: shaggy squatting 3-legged crotches. The central lamp-support pierces the crotch and embeds itself in the top of the riverside wall, so as one passes one is repeatedly presented with this representation of something hanging down between squatting shaggy thighs. As usual there is dog shit everywhere and scooters.

Norman Douglas had a theory that the English walk along staring downwards in order to avoid dog shit on the pavement – this is true of me here. Pass a shop displaying antique sepia photographs. One particularly catches my eye – the Palazzo Bonagia in Palermo – a baroque staircase in a courtyard, several figures standing mutely on it in period dress. When I reach Palermo I shall find this intriguing place, so redolent of the south, and find out what goes on there – the photograph suggests many stories. Into the messy Piazza della Signoria crammed with naked statues. Very healthy for Florentine children to grow up surrounded by these cyclopean pricks and bums and tits and balls (though Florence is not a very sexy town).

In the leather shop, while the girl manipulates my credit card, I fondle the bag's wondrously soft and supple flanks. Oh gorgeous thing, you were worth it. But carrying the booty back across the river, I grow uneasy at the car problem ahead and decide to compose myself in the Boboli Gardens, a most enchanting resort behind the Pitti Palace. Decrepitude adds to the romance of its endlessly adventurous pathways. To clip the very tall hedges round the isolotto to-day, the gardeners are using outsize step-ladders painted bright green. This enormous exaggeration in the size of a conventional item makes them appear to be the gardeners from *Alice in Wonderland.*

Struggling back through the crowded market, I discover the car where I left it, oppressed by shoppers on every side but unburgled, unslashed. Bananas comes across, almost joyous – he's kept an eye on it for me. But will it explode when I open the door? No. Is he after money? It seems not. It's all hugs and cheery slaps and, once I've rammed the luggage in the back, he assists me with waving arms to make the only possible manoeuvre which is to *back* out of this turmoil between piles of gaudy goods, past mamas with pushchairs – please God, let me not kill a baby, that really would be the end – shaving the obtrusive corners of stalls and those Latin bottoms and bellies. There is no more than 2 or 3 inches on either side of the car. While handling the wheel with the delicacy of one applying a scalpel to a brain, there breaks upon my concentration a broad Yorkshire accent. 'Eee, you've got a job on your hands there, lad!' and he's gone. I'm sweating all over, tingling at the temples, wet in the small of my back.

But eventually the extraction is accomplished and the car rolls into a proper road with space in it. It's a narrow Florentine side street but it seems like Salisbury Plain to me. The relief . . . Ha, and now I feel *high*, feel that no matter what the Italian traffic flings at me, I shall survive. And I feel a deeper liberation too. Baptism by marketplace. I've interacted, broken through an inner resistance, a holding back from the life around me which always has to be overcome in a new place. Italy is beginning to exert its catalytic influence and from now on I'll know less and less. By the time Rome is behind us, I'll know nothing at all. One more thing. Bananas taught me a lesson in good manners. I was guilty of a coarse territorial infringement. There are few more offensive acts than depriving a man of his workplace. And he wanted me to recognise that. Once I had admitted I was wrong, he was happy. So feeling much less complacent and thoroughly improved, I set off across town for lunch at the Villa La Pietra.

A retainer opens mighty gates to the cypress avenue and the car cruises up patrician gravel to a villa of the Renaissance in gold stone. The house was bought and filled by Acton's father, helped by money from Acton's mother who was the daughter of a Chicago banker. The white-haired butler in white jacket admits me to the salone where on the piano one notices signed photographs from Princess Margaret and the Prince and Princess of Wales. The room is large, high, filled with old gilded pieces, and overlooks the garden. It is also deeply quiet and I listen to the bubbles in my gin & tonic until eventually Harold comes trundling round the door in 3-piece suit and carpet slippers, a slightly insolent smile on his face. I say he looks very well and he says 'That's because I've just come back from Switzerland where I had a prostate operation. That's the only place I travel to nowadays, to Switzerland, for operations.'

'I nearly didn't make it. I was assaulted by a fruit seller.'

'Beautiful, I hope.'

'No.'

'So few of them are.'

'Entirely my fault, I parked on his pitch. Would it be possible to see the garden before lunch? I've never seen it.' Normally this is the first thing one is shown but in half a dozen visits I've not been asked out there, so he puts on a coat and we step through the windows.

'The house was occupied by the Germans during the war, then by the Allied troops, and they knocked most of the cocks off the statues and took them away as souvenirs. It's a terrible shame . . . Here's an enormous statue of Bacchus. His cup fell down the other day. It had been held in place since the 16th century by an oxbone but the bone was eaten away by ants. So now we've put in a steel pin . . . In this open space here the Russian Ballet danced during the First World War.'

'What's that smell?'

'Pig shit. The farmer next door has pigs and they come right up to this fence. Where are you going exactly?'

'Missing Rome. I've been invited to a music festival in Naples – to see a forgotten Liszt opera at the San Carlino.'

'O-o-oh!' There's a warble of relish in his voice. 'It's a wonderful theatre! As the lights go down, everything turns rose pink. And while you are there, you must go to the cloister of Santa Chiara.'

'And then down through Calabria to Sicily. To Noto.'

'Yes, Noto! O-o-oh, you are so lucky.'

'I'd also like to find the Abbey of Thelema at Cefalù which Aleister Crowley set up.'

'I believe his wall paintings are still there. Lots of cocks!'

'And the Lago dei Palici.'

'That I've not heard of.'

'No one has. It's a mystery. Is there anyone you can suggest I visit?' There isn't. 'They've booked me into the Majestic Hotel – do you know it?' He doesn't. 'And I have to contact a woman called Ritzy Accardo – do you know her?'

'No, all the people I knew down there have died. I do have a cousin near Naples but she doesn't speak a word of English or French. The Neapolitan Actons are totally Italian. And she drags this son around with her wherever she goes. He's 30 and just not with it. I don't think he's ever going to be with it. Sicily I haven't been to for more than 20 years. The boys of Taormina are so *brazen*, you know . . . The Whitakers of Palermo have all gone – Bill Whitaker lives in London now. And the Duke of Verdura who went to New York and made a fortune designing jewellery, he died in London not long ago – he was much admired by Andy Warhol. Do you know Norman Douglas's book on Calabria? He'd put a lot of boys in a row and have them tossing off, saying "The first one to come gets a prize." This is the sort of thing I couldn't put in my memoirs. He was fond of *young* people. The slightest shadow of pubic hair put him off . . . It was a terrible winter, you know. We lost several trees here. And now a bug has got into the Tuscan cypress, so I don't know *what* will be left of the landscape by the time that's done. Who else do you hope to see on your travels?'

'Perhaps Gore Vidal at Ravello.'

'Ugh! Gore Vidal! Fifth rate, appalling, can't stand him! Save yourself the trouble . . .'

'What's wrong with him?'

'For a start he thinks he's beautiful. He *really does* think that, can you imagine? I first met him just after the war with Tennessee Williams whom I very much did like. But Gore Vidal – no talent whatsoever. And so . . . full of himself. I can't stand that sort of thing.'

'I like Gore Vidal's story of Joan Crawford trying to be posh when picking up the phone and saying "Whom is it?".'

As if the very mention of Gore Vidal is too much, Harold pauses, unbuttons his coat, and sidles up to a bush for a pee. What is so appealing in Acton is that despite calling himself an aesthete as an undergraduate and continuing to carry this somewhat kitsch appellation for the rest of his life, he's really rather gutsy. Physically he's big and his approach to the world is Machiavellian, not delicate, his taste robust, not effete, his interests mainstream, not esoteric.

'What's that?' I ask.

'It's security.' La Pietra is protected by laser beams. 'It's an awful nuisance because cats and dogs are always setting it off but one has to have it for the insurance people. When my father bought this house it had an English garden because English gardens were all the rage in 19th century Italy. But he turned it back into a formal Italian garden. Most of the statues he bought in Venice.'

'It's in excellent order – unlike the Boboli Gardens.'

'Oh well, that's kept up by the Comunale. All my lady friends tell me that a lot of flashing goes on there. You see a gentleman reading a newspaper – then the newspaper goes up and you see a *cock*.'

Lunch begins with green cannelloni, stuffed with egg and herbs, and a lurid orange-coloured sauce over the top. I explain that my journey to Noto was inspired by a conversation with Sachie Sitwell and Harold says 'We used to correspond until quite recently. He was awfully upset by the death of his wife, although she had numerous affairs. Ada Leverson was in love with *Osbert* Sitwell who was rather embarrassed by her attentions – but amused. Once while she was staying at Montegufoni she peered at him through the bathroom keyhole. What was he like? I asked. Like a wingless swan, she said.' Naughtiness dances in his small brown eyes. 'And Nancy Cunard was an extraordinary woman. She always had to have eno-o-o-ormous black men *plunging* into her morning, noon and night.'

'She must have eased up towards the end.'

'No. It got *worse* towards the end. After the age of 60, she'd accept any colour.'

The butler peeps over the screen to see if we are finished or want more, then in white gloves comes forward with the next course: lamb, potatoes, red peppers, carrots and green salad. He is helped by a young assistant with hangdog face of whom Harold observes 'He's not at all bright. I've often asked him things without eliciting any response whatsoever. But I think he's been taking English lessons on the quiet – in order to eavesdrop on my dinner parties. But my butler is a very good man. He came from the Whitakers of Palermo. Osbert's mother, you know, Lady Ida Sitwell, used to sit in Doney's in the morning. The waiters called her Lady Double Double because she'd have 2 double whiskys before ordering anything, then she would make a play with the menu, but usually order tea and lots more whisky. She was so terrified of her husband finding out about her morning tippling that she made Doney's send the bills to my father. He eventually got fed up with this and went on strike which she thought frightfully unfair . . .'

Letter from D. H. Lawrence to Aldous Huxley – Villa Mirenda, Monday: *Reggie and Orioli and Scott Moncrieff and a young Acton came en quatre – I poured tea, they poured the rest.*

'Lawrence encouraged Frieda to have affairs with young Italians,' says Harold. 'He was so funny. One would see him walking along the via Tornabuoni with his little shopping net. Frieda was very much the hausfrau – always sitting there darning. Unless Lawrence did the darning which he often did. There was something very feminine about him. He had a woman's complexion. Alabaster skin. With sudden colour – that was the TB of course. If it hadn't been for his somewhat potatoey nose, he would've been very good-looking. But you knew he was a genius. The eyes, the intensity, the voice! You felt important things were being uttered – even if they weren't. No, I don't recall any Nottingham accent. That day when I went up there with Reggie Turner and the rest, Lawrence could talk about nothing but his paintings – and there they all were, up on the walls, really ghastly stuff. He had no sense of humour at all, that I could discern. Many people considered him pornographic in those days. Orioli used to publish pornography – as well as some very good books . . . Do you know, John Lehmann had the manuscript of a meticulous pornographic novel by Christopher Isherwood. It was excellent. I wonder what's happened to it.'

Pudding arrives, chocolate sponge topped with fluffy cream, and Harold expatiates on his abiding sadness at having been prevented from leaving La Pietra and its treasures to Oxford University as a study centre.

'They said – we don't maintain properties abroad. And that was that. I tried and tried but it was like trying to interest stones and rocks. Roy Harrod and Maurice Bowra were for it but even they could do nothing.'

The Villa Finale next door was left to the University of Paris by a French Jewish banker. And 21 American universities maintain villas and study centres in and around Florence. Soon it will be 22 because La Pietra has now been left to an extremely grateful New York University. 'Oxford's attitude made me want to *puke*,' he says, 'but I've had to put it out of my mind. Would you like a cigarette? I don't smoke either. Except perhaps if I've spent a long time searching for *le mot juste*, if for 40 minutes I've been looking for it without success, then sometimes I'll have a cigarette and the word often turns up. The only drug I really go in for is a Mogadon at night. If I don't take one, things start going round in my head, all the unpleasant things, never the nice things, all the disasters and mistakes – and of course, you see, one longs for another body to be there and usually there isn't one. Sometimes there is – thank goodness there are gerontophiles around, I never understood it myself, but, yes, there are quite a number of gerontophiles around. Even so, I usually sleep alone and with a Mogadon, sleep comes quickly.'

Over coffee I realise that both he and Sachie are young spirits. In their company there's no sense of being with someone old. Harold waves me off on the steps and says 'You'll discover that the Sicilians are very much more intelligent than the north Italians.'

'I'm looking forward to Pompeii first.'

'O-o-oh, lots of *cocks* at Pompeii! Bon voyage!'

And I head for the motorway. Slot in Ella Fitzgerald singing Cole Porter. *I love the eyes and mouth of you, the east, west, north and south of you*. South is the direction of the genitals. We are driving south, away from the brain and towards the genitals.

I have been to Siena where the best Italian is spoken and the population has sturdy legs from lifelong climbing up and down gradients. The zebra-striped cathedral is unforgettable, especially when floodlit, and has mosaic sibyls on its floor. The panforte is unforgettable too. But there is something bleak about this redbrick town, claustrophobic, perhaps because it is treeless, plantless, greenless. We are not going there. And we are not going to Rome. I do love Rome and it's a wonderful town for love – sweeter than Paris, freer than London, safer than New York, funkier than Madrid, happier than Berlin, cleaner than Istanbul, more human than Tokyo. But it's bland. All the bars and restaurants are identical because Italians only ever want Italian food. The architecture is magnificent – but entirely uniform in the flavour it imparts to the imagination. All the people look the same. Rome lacks diversity. This uniformity of character is valued in Florence or Naples but in 'the big-big city' a Londoner or New Yorker expects more. Besides, the magnetic force of the south is pulling me further down.

Brief diversion to the Villa Adriana at Tivoli, retreat of the Emperor Hadrian. When I first came here 17 years ago it was an aloof site down a quiet country lane. Now the area is much more built up and the site has been thoroughly *organised*, with a museum and a café and a complicated entrance for cars. But within the perimeter, it retains its dreamy, forgotten, overgrown spaciousness. 150 acres have been revealed but the villa was originally 5 times this. Ruins keep falling down. There are notices saying zona pericolosa every so often, bits of marble steps, pieces of cornice in the grass. Many of the cornices are carved with oakleaves – and a lovely one of cupids riding seahorses. It was in its day a fabulous repository of treasures and, although sacked and looted by the barbarians, an enormous number of artworks from here survives in the museums of the world. Hot peaceful afternoon in the campagna – quiet – bees buzzing – a few birds. Look languidly into my *Baedeker*. The hardcore detail of these old guides is never found in a modern guide. I close the book, lie on my back in the long grass with wild poppies brushing my face, and close my eyes . . . yes, I was here before . . . arrivederci, Villa Adriana, arrivederci, Benedetto Palombo . . .

To-night's bed will be at the Castello Balsorano and I'm presently making my way through the Simbruini Mountains in an attempt to find it. Night is falling. Slot in Szymanowski's Third Symphony and out slithers one of the strangest chords in all music. After this very unusual opening, however, the work becomes increasingly rhetorical. Suddenly up ahead, floodlit on a black mountainside, is the castle. A side road is indicated and this winds up past a tiny silent village and on, as if to Dracula's eyrie. The car squeezes through a narrow gatehouse, badly scraping its paintwork, round another bend, to find itself in a venerable courtyard which is as light as day, floodlit walls rising high on 3 sides and in the centre a small family group sipping aperitifs and playing ball with 2 mighty Alsatians. This is clearly a most remarkable hotel. My pulse has quickened. A pretty young woman, with dark eyes and a face looking leprous white in the unnatural glare, steps forward and says 'Closed until June'. Her English is very precise.

Can't believe it. After so long a drive. At so thrilling a destination. I'm downcast – unlike the castle, looking ever more superb and unattainable as the moments slip away. I stand here, not knowing what to do or say, lost in an unknown region. A voice says 'Try the next town. Sora.'

The car, scraping its sides again, rolls all the way down to the main road and drags itself listlessly along to Sora. Where, after cruising aimlessly about, it judders up outside the Motel Valentino, a masterpiece in the art of anonymity. A wedding reception is taking place inside. Marriages, births, and deaths are the only real events in this sort of place – in the absence of wars.

Room 303, a blank modern hotel room with tiled floor. Molto
zonked. No bath, only a shower with mix tap which renders water
either very hot or very cold, nothing less. Jumping between these
opposites, my shower is perfunctory. Naked I collapse on to the bed,
let it all flop, and the despondency lifts. Because my plans have been
overtaken by chance, by spontaneity, I feel *truly away*. Nobody in
the world knows I'm here – except the check-in man downstairs.
To-morrow we shall drive to the palace at Caserta but to-night . . .
nothing . . . nowhere . . . Moral is: everyone should have their Sora,
their Motel Valentino, the blank space where they can be nothing in
particular, where they can lose their name, not be anybody's son or
father or mother or daughter or wife or husband, not be a writer or
a businessman or a dustman or a fruit-seller from Florence. Where
they are simply themselves. Nobody in particular . . . .

                           Z
                              Z
                                 Z
                                    Z
                                       Z
                                          Z
                                             Z
                                                Z
                                                   Z
                                                      Z

A wonderful night's sleep. Get up *late*, breakfast, pack, fill up at the
garage beside the Motel. Pour a litre of oil into the engine, check
tyres, water, battery. This Capri hasn't let me down – yet (it was
bought second-hand in Reading, after being checked out by my father's
manager Gerald Gore, who knows everything about cars. He drove at
high speed round roundabouts on 2 wheels, jammed to a halt halfway
down steep hills, and finally pronounced it an excellent buy).

The drive down the motorway towards Naples is surprisingly lush,
with very little trashing of the landscape, rough hills covered with
purple, boughs laden with yellow, poppies bleeding in the fields –
but no butterflies apparently. Taking an easy pace, so that by the time
uscita for Caserta shows up, it's well into the afternoon.

The first thing you notice about Caserta is that it's a real southern
town: shabby, dusty, noisy, faded, permanently unfinished, approximate, sexy. It's rush hour and traffic approximately 4 abreast drives
down a one-way street with approximate pavements and traffic signals
which are ignored. Then perversely a lone car battles against the

oncoming clog – this is us – because it's not a one-way street at all, just one subject to spontaneous tideflow every rush hour. Unexpectedly the palace trembles on the left, massive, tinted the powdery pastels of the sunfaded south. The tawdriness of the public area in front of it comes as a shock – this could be India or Latin America. The elephantine palace of the King of the Two Sicilies – what a ridiculous title! I suspect there's only one Sicily – and that ungovernable too! We'll go round the thing to-morrow. Sunset is turning the façade candy pink and grey. The fore wing on the left has been restored but the one on the right is in deplorable condition with thick plants growing on the roofline.

Book into the oddly named Jolly Hotel (there is no J in the Italian language), a small modern monstrosity of cement and plastic, because it's there and I can't be bothered to look for anything amusing or funky. The view from my room has to be seen to be believed: a cement building fills the window, with piles of scaffolding, disused railings and rubble on the ground. The room itself (No. 137) is tiny, a back room and not cheap. But the bathroom is the same size which means *large*, all gleaming white and chrome, with mountains of fresh white towels, vast wash basin and bath, torrents of hot water pumping forcefully from big taps. It's the most magnificent modern bathroom I've ever had.

Throw up legs onto bed and turn on radio. I hear the name Duncan . . . then gibberish. Is that Duncan again? More gibberish. Going to be murdered? Weird . . . Roll over, bringing my ear closer to the speaker. With much difficulty, it's discovered to be a radio performance of *Macbeth*. In English! Lady Macbeth is in full swing now – but she's gabbling so fast, it's very hard to follow. To the Italians it must be absolutely incomprehensible. Why do the modern Shakespearean actors rush their words so? *Please go slower*. So we can understand.

I turn off this preposterous splutter and occupy the remaining night by drawing up a provisional list of differences between the French and the Italians as follows:

French	*Italians*
System	Family
Cerebrum	Soul
Politeness	Familiarity
Organised	Anarchic
Hysterical drivers	Good drivers
Desire to complicate	Desire
Sexually individualistic	Sexually warm and simple
Not guilty	Guilty

Distrust intuition	Intuitive
Trust letters, not phonecalls	Trust phonecalls, not letters
Brittle to hard	Soft to mawkish
Self-conscious	Louche
Fear of appearing foolish	Fear of appearing foolish
Poseurs	Strutters
Conceited	Proud
Impatient	Lazy
Don't blush	Blush easily
Never like to appear impressed	Like to show enthusiasm
Great sense of occasion	Great sense of party
Intellectually emotional	Emotionally intellectual

The afternoon of the next day. Well, I've now done Caserta. It takes it out of the feet so I'm going to put them up on the bed again, open an Orangina from the fridge, eat a torta alla corte di Gonzaga, while I mention a few things about the palace.

The first thing to be said is that this Gonzaga cake is disappointing, like Scotch shortbread (which is delicious) but too much sugar and minus the butter. In other words, sickly cardboard. The second thing is that the 1200-room royal home is surpassingly lavish within, though severe and neo-classical without (designed and begun by Vanvitelli, a Dutchman trained in Rome, in 1751 and finished over 20 years later by his son).

You enter through a tunnel opening in the centre of the main façade. This pierces, front to back, the whole building which externally is perfectly symmetrical, ranged round 4 brick and stone courtyards of rectangular shape and equal size. The tunnel is cool, massively marbled, and placed on a major axis which is the governing principle of the entire creation, shooting ahead through the park and halfway up a small mountain and shooting backwards to Naples. At the entrance are supports for statues of Justice, Magnificence, Clemency and Peace, which were never done.

In the centre, where the 4 courtyards meet, you turn right through a tall arch and find yourself at the foot of a long flight of shallow steps. This rises beneath a great dome to a pair of open-mouthed lions with lugubrious eyes and furrowed, worried brows, at which point the staircase divides into 2 and flows up and back on itself, carrying one into a second domed chamber supported on a controlled but complex arrangement of arcades and vaults. Sunlight streams into this sprung space seemingly from all sides, with an empyrean effect. The whole exalting system is known, rather cheaply, as the Staircase of Honour. The shallowness of the steps means you can ascend only slowly – it takes time to approach the king and the time is likely to be occupied by a gathering nervousness and sense of inferiority. During World War II, when the palace was the headquarters of the Anglo-American command, George VI is said to have fallen down these stairs on an official visit.

From the upper domed vestibule opens a sequence of 3 immense halls, leading through to the main front along which runs the enfilade of principal state rooms. These begin with 4 named and decorated after the 4 seasons. All the rooms have very high painted ceilings, floors in rich mosaic, and walls encrusted with pilasters, marble and gilt fittings, and painted panels or brocades: each is a colourful and seductively elegant creation. But as spaces they are very simple, empty rectangular volumes with no free-standing pillars or other architectural features – just one vast, hollow box after another after another, glimpsed through successive doorways and vanishing in a misty golden distance. The only spatial intrusions are supplied by chandeliers which fall from some of the ceilings. And of course, as in most southern houses, there's very little furniture and no carpets. The interplay between opulence of adornment and purity of space creates an operatic levity in defiance of the building's overall bulk.

The front enfilade climaxes at the Throne Room, with throne of winged lions. There are 2 guidebooks on sale, both poor, neither with a ground-plan. The one with an English text says of the Throne Room *The lightnings of this room is phantastic.* A delightful ante-room is adjacent, with an unusual colour scheme, mostly lemon and gold, but details picked out in lavender, green, orange and maroon.

Eventually you reach the end of the main front, pause, turn your head and there, at a right angle to the first, is a second string of decorated boxes receding to infinity. You swim through these, sliding under ceiling after painted ceiling, breasting room after fabulous room, any one of which could reward an hour's contemplation, until eventually at the end of the second string you pause, turn to your right, and gasp – a third string disappearing to a point. I can't remember the precise route round the block but it seems this turn & gasp manoeuvre occurred several more times before one arrived back at the domed vestibule above the Staircase of Honour in a somewhat numb condition – to be told by an attendant that one had traversed but a portion of the palace's glories and that although most of the main rooms were open there were many, many more suites, hardly less splendid, which were permanently closed. Was he exaggerating? But Caserta itself is an incomparable exaggeration.

En route, there was a beautiful portrait of King Ferdinand and his family playing, 1820, very large. And a shrunken Italian guide of about

60 years, escorting an English party and using the hectoring tone of a rigorous but good-natured schoolmaster. In a royal bathroom, beside a solid gold bath, he said 'And this is a special window so that the Queen could see her husband returning from Naples if she was with a lover. Oh yes, I know what you women are!' The ladies titter in cotton prints.

These royal apartments are truly spectacular but after a dozen or so a kind of nausea overtakes one at the relentless application of a single idea, at the lack of sculptural variation. Like the institution it housed, Caserta is tense with an unyielding lack of imagination – apart from the opening brilliance of the staircase and the verve of the horseshoe-shaped theatre. One leaves with the impression that the monarchy of the Two Sicilies was a witless affair. And yet the glittering spaciousness remains in the memory, the incomparable *amount*, and the perfection of colour and detail. I want to return some day, to go deeper into this magnificent sarcophagus which, despite everything I've said, is one of the wonders of Europe.

After the palace, it was time to do the park which is designed as a single vista rising slowly through distinct phases of lawn, water and statuary, with woods either side, terminating in what appears to be a whitish column but is actually a cascade down a hill. So as not to block the view, the fountains are low but in full squirt. House and park together present a simple-minded stupendousness I've not encountered since Teotihuacan in the Mexican scrub (though Teo' is more subtle in its use of gradients and planes along a main axis).

The earlier sunshine had gone. The sky was hazily overcast, the air warm, thick and humid. Nonetheless, having seen horses pulling carriage-loads of self-conscious tourists, having noticed the risible manner in which these trotting dobbins threw out their legs, I decided *to walk up the vista*.

It is exceedingly long – 2 miles, I think I read somewhere – and looked it, viewed through the central tunnel from which one emerged at first on to a great lawn of rough grass planted with 4 circles of trees. On the left is a zona militare and from it came the sound of a brass band playing Rossini. Desultory gardeners ambled around with picksticks, spearing litter and filling black dustbinliners, reserves of which were tucked into their waistbands at the back. Then the lawn narrowed to an avenue between thick trees which continued to the very end but led initially to a small fountain in a round pond encircled by herms. These statues were covered with graffiti (applied to marble, graffiti are very difficult to clean off). Just beyond, a main road passes under the vista but it was scarcely visible because of trees, which also muffled Rossini, and one was directly upon the next event, La

Grande Peschiera, a long body of littered water with crude railings round it.

Despite the haze, the sun felt strong on the head, so I decided to walk under a line of trees on the left side. Lizards scattered into the undergrowth ahead of my steps and cobwebs broke constantly against my face – everyone else was using the central open-air route. The long water was closed at its far end by the Fountain of Dolphins, dominated by 3 pugnacious stone fish from whose jaws gushed waterfalls. Boys were playing football on the platform above it where the railings are more graceful.

There followed an oblong of lawn – and it had been *cut*, raising a delicious scent. I was enchanted, not expecting this particular delicacy so far south. Continuing under the trees, I looked down at my white ducks and they were speckled with dozens of caterpillars. Under the trees, deeper in, embracing on a chunk of stone, were 2 lovers and they stopped, looked at me coyly but full-faced, full-eyed as the Italians do, then continued kissing. The girl was about 14. Her fingernails as she rubbed the boy's neck were bitten and the nail-varnish chipped. He was about 15 in a short-sleeved shirt and had very white scrawny forearms covered with black hair. These trees are perfect for assignations – except the bugs gather beneath them and midges whizz in tight circles. A little further on, arranged in the undergrowth like a Still Life, was a group of empty Coca Cola tins standing upright, and a foot or 2 beyond them a crushed Pepsi Cola tin on its side as if the Coca Cola tins had beaten it up and left it there for dead . . . birdsong . . . and from over a wall flowed the heartening smell of cow dung.

After the long lawn came the Eolo Fountain with waterfall, jets and grottoes, and another transverse road hidden by it. There was plenty of activity here, with many writhing statues, but the genitals were concealed by twists of cloth and even the bottoms were covered by draperies spouting ridiculously from between the buttocks. One small boy was pulling a fishtail through his crotch, a blissful expression on his face – presumably the sculptor was here taking unobtrusive revenge on his commissioners. The bed of the pool was packed with plants resembling coils of rope and carp cruised over them.

There followed a short water, then a series of broad steps in the stream which, by being tilted back, created the illusion of water flowing upwards. This device occurred again after the interval of the Ceres Fountain and a short lawn. By now I was almost there. The second water staircase was finished by the Fountain of Venus, then after came a terrace, a wide flight of steps, and the groups of Actaeon and Diana in a pool beneath the cascade itself.

The statuary at Caserta is much admired but lacks vitality. The poses are stiff and made more so by a prudery which forces drapes over groins and breasts against the laws of gravity and motion. The outcome is a lasciviousness at once titillating and ashamed of itself in the way that Alma-Tadema can be. Never before have I associated this uneasy prurience with Italy. Yet it is a fine walk for a king who eats too much and sits too long on the throne or beside his despatches.

The palace looks even more enormous at a distance than close to, because it dwarfs its surroundings, a high-shouldered block with hipped roof of red tiles, its outline echoing that of a typical Ancient Roman villa. In its day it was held to be the greatest work of building since the Romans, and was made possible by the exertions of Moorish and African slave gangs. But apart from its gargantuan scale, Caserta is just an Italian house with a front door onto the main road and a back door into the garden – even here the intensely bourgeois tone of Italian life holds firm. A factory chimney was discharging smoke behind it. I could see the smoke but not the chimney so it appeared as if the palace were on fire. All hovered quietly in hazy warmth, until 5 Italian Air Force jets screamed low over the scene . . .

I bought a small plastic ashtray from the souvenir shop to the left of Actaeon, then had to walk *back*, having missed the little bus which I'd discovered also plies the route. The park was busier at 4 p.m., populated by parties of schoolchildren. The younger ones wore blue or red tunics over their normal clothes, tied at the neck with floppy bows. Some had white spotted bows, some had rosettes pinned to their breasts, others did not wear tunics at all – all the arcane insignia of an enclosed institution. But each had been freshly scrubbed and dressed by an adoring mama and as these young groups passed, chattering sweetly and holding hands, so did wonderful clouds of soap aroma.

The older schoolchildren walked in groups of either boys or girls, constant banter and coquetry being launched across the invisible canyon separating them. Pre-marital sex diminishes as you travel south and this frustration is released vocally.

On approaching the palace, I saw that a number of beggars had taken up positions on the lawn for the post-siesta trade. A young boy with no arms was sitting beside a square of cardboard on to which coins were being thrown. I threw one too.

8

Naples

Last night my car was parked in the unprotected forecourt of the Jolly Hotel. I had emptied it of all luggage but didn't think of taking out the petrol too and this was removed during the night; not all of it – sufficient was left for me to reach the nearest petrol station. Petty crime is a problem in the south. So is major crime. But the criminals are thoughtful. There is usually a rationale to their behaviour. In Great Britain the problem is irrational violence.

Now I've overshot the uscita for Naples and ended up at Nola where the Emperor Augustus died in AD 14 and the magus Giordano Bruno was born in 1548. Bruno, who was obliged to live abroad for much of his life and first published many of his works in London, was burned by the Inquisition in Rome, 1600, for saying such things as the cross pre-dated Christ and was an Egyptian sacred sign fixed to the bosom of Serapis. While I turn the car round a group of young boys throw several snakes under my tyres. Is this just for splat pleasure? (Later I discover that the serpent was Bruno's personal emblem.)

It's beginning to smell . . . whiffs of rich sewagey mud from the outlying fields and suddenly we're in it! Funnelled down off the motorway into a seething dump – it's midday, one of their rush hours (they have 4) – what a hellhole! Well, I'm ready for them – no shitty little mugger from the backstreets is going to screw up my trip by getting his filthy paws on my money and passport – the south Italians are possessions *mad* – of course it's volcano territory *and* hairpin bend territory – where's Vesuvius? I demand to see Vesuvius! Oh my God, cool it, Duncan, please but yes here we are, yes, workers' blocks, miles and miles of them, the familiar modern Mediterranean horror show: industry, flats, rocks, shit in the eye.

Flapping white washing really doesn't make it more charming until we get further in where the streets are cobbled and it's shudder shudder shudder – flying towards me on the wrong side of the road, a bus! – alleys of quaint slums shoot off left and right – what's going on? –

but have discovered there's one rule: FIRST COME FIRST SERVED –
arrrgh! my traffic lane has vanished – what do I do? drive on! –
drive on! – I can't go on I go on! – traffic police are frantic with
batons and whistles – a second rule may now be added: IGNORE
TRAFFIC LIGHTS – bus lanes, taxi lanes, they've been painted in as a
joke – in fact let me correct that second rule to IGNORE EVERYTHING
except the need to go on, ever onwards through the swirl, and the
logistics of this forward movement absorb all one's problem-solving
faculties so that it is not possible to think *where* one is going or in
what direction. The road rule in Italy is: in case of accident the one
in front is in the right, even if it's by only a couple of inches – hence
the scramble to get ahead of the next driver. Canoeing down rapids
must be like this, the only thought to stay upright and avoid hitting
anything too hard – American sailors look bewildered on a corner –
shudder shudder shudder – narrow alleys shoot up on left with
masses of washing – Italian democracy is fresh laundry for all! People
thronging, jaywalking, chaos – and the sea! No, it's gone again and
there's a young man driving an ice-cream van looking *haggard* with
terror so immediately I feel much better because one always imagines
it's only *one* who is suffering but this is NOT true, many locals are
also terrified and I'm being swept round onto a promenade but maybe
this is the wrong direction and there's nothing I can do about it, yes,
the sea, the sea! Well, that's something, and the whole river of traffic
swerves right past the Castel Nuovo with its wonderful skirt of pleated
stone – oops, right turn, why? Oh God, ah! . . . mmmm . . . . . oh , , ,
wrong gear , , , , , oh . . . .

Now that is the most extraordinary thing. The traffic has simply
vomited me up outside the Hotel Majestic which is where I want to
be. Heaven knows how – one second all is chaos, the next I'm delivered.
It's hardly less than an act of God. And here's a second act of God: a
parking space outside, probably the only parking space in Naples. This
is the time to spray some soldi about in gratitude – a few thousand for
the attendant who transfers my car to the hotel's underground garage
(£7 per night for the metal beast!), a few thousand for the porter with
my bags. When in doubt, tip. Money does not embarrass them. Room
309, small and dull but spotless, with the usual blazing white towels
and sheets. On the wall is an engraving of Solfatara by Pouncey.

The Rev. Peter Blackburn is in when I phone and invites me over for
tea which is easily accomplished since – third act of God – his church
is about 6 inches from the hotel – 'and hard by the finest cakeshop in
Naples,' he adds down the blower. Let's hope he's a rosy-cheeked 18th
century pastor, interested in fine wine and architecture and human
nature.

Christ Church is quite an eyeful in the via San Pasquale a Chiaia (which is quite a mouthful), sinewy gothic revival surrounded by blowsy southern classicism. Above the entrance: *Redemptori Sacrum*. And on a tablet fixed to the outside front: *In grateful memory of Giuseppe Garibaldi who on October 3rd 1860 in the name of the Italian nation gave the British community the land for this church dedicated to Our Lord Jesus Christ.*

Inside the first thing you notice is a huge Union Jack and a huge Stars & Stripes hanging in the nave (American Episcopalians being part of the Anglican Community + all others welcome). These flags look disgusting. And you realise that what keeps the thing going is not local piety but NATO. There is fine Victorian stained glass.

Notices are pinned everywhere. *Ladies & Babies – we meet in the Church Hall alternate Wednesdays 10 a.m. – noon. Chief Mum: Clare Cricelli.* A woman stops polishing the lectern and says 'The vicar's through that door there.' *Close door to keep the cats out.* There is a yard where a group of men are hoisting palms in pots on to a roof ledge. It's obvious which one is the Rev. Blackburn. He's big and gentle with fair features, a soft, slightly Australian voice and his face is beaming like an overgrown putto. A number of Americans are with him, huffing and puffing away, 'and this is Michael Rae, the last British merchant in Naples. Michael, could you turn on the gas? Then she'll make us some tea.'

The plain 19th century gothic of the Church Hall makes one feel back at school – surrealistically un-Naples. 'It's hot to-day. My collar's quite limp,' he says. 'They all have to be sent back to England to be laundered.'

Italian laundry is like Italian sex – they do it splendidly so long as no unusual variations are introduced.

'Michael's family owns the Harrods of Naples, a big old-fashioned British shop called Gutteridge's on the via Toledo. It's set up with beautiful curved blondwood furniture, the smart decoration of the 30s, and huge space in comparison to other Neapolitan shops which are very crowded. By the way, HMS *Cardiff* arrived this morning to a 21 gun salute. I have to go to a cocktail party on board to-night. Last year we had HMS *Invincible* – oh, that was won-derful!'

'I remember meeting some American sailors in Saint Tropez – they were very fat. I asked them why in a polite way and they said "There's nothing to do on board. We just eat and read. On a modern ship, it's only when something goes wrong that there's work." Does the church take up all your time?'

'I teach at the British school here. It's the Forces school, an infants school. 2 classrooms were burnt down recently by the camorra, the local mafia. We'd been warned several times with little fires. I think our landlord hadn't paid his dues or something.'

'But that's terrible, a school being set on fire.'

'That sort of thing happens all the time – but the Neapolitans are wonderful, family people, vulgar and earthy and affectionate.'

In the loo it says *All our drains get blocked if nappies etc, are flushed down this lavatory. Please use bin. Thank you.*

When I return he says 'Parts of Naples are like India. And the last earthquake didn't help. The epicentre was at Pozzuoli only 5 miles away where Sophia Loren was born. Pozzuoli is a ghost town now. No one is allowed to live there. They are mostly rehoused at Monte Ruscello. A lot of the money given for rebuilding was of course "lost" in inverted commas.'

The last earthquake was only the most recent earthquake. The city shifts, slides, crumbles – always has done, always will do. Doorways and windows often carry cross-beam props to prevent collapse. Many buildings have slips of glass fixed across cracks in their fabric. When the glass breaks you know the building is moving again.

'Let me take you out to dinner on Saturday. Are you doing anything in the meantime?' he asks.

'The main thing I want to do is go to the opera as part of this music festival. But there were no tickets, programmes, invitations, bumf, nothing waiting for me. I expected a Festival Pack sort of thing. There's a woman I must contact, Ritzy Accardo, who should know all about it. I'm frightened I'll not get the tickets in time.' Specifically required are tickets for *The Barber of Seville* to-night and for the forgotten opera by Liszt, *Don Sanchez*, to-morrow (this is its first 20th century performance).

'That's very Anglo-Saxon of you, wanting everything organised. Going to the opera is amazing here. Incredible costume jewellery and pearls. You can wear pearls in Naples because they can't be stolen. If someone rips them off your neck, they fly everywhere. And look for the big clock above the proscenium – that's so the Neapolitans can tell the time if they're getting bored. And after we've eaten I'll take you up to Capo Posillipo on Saturday evening. It's something you *have* to see. They all go up there at weekends and put newspapers up at the car windows and get down to it. And afterwards they just throw the newspapers out of the car and so by Monday the whole park, which is an attractive spot with a lovely view, is ankle-deep in a sea of newspapers because of fornication. You see, they have nowhere else to go.'

Peter talks on all subjects with well informed gusto.

'I'm told,' I say, 'that a car will not sell in Italy unless it has fully reclining seats.'

'Exactly so. Lust wagons. Strangers wouldn't believe the rows and rows of bouncing cars. The greatest character in all Naples is Humpty Dumpty who's this fat old granny who's been sitting on this wall for *years*, catering to generations of British and American servicemen. She is repulsive beyond belief. In winter she occasionally wears a woollie but in the summer she wears this thing which is more like a belt into which she tucks her nipples. Until Saturday, then.'

It's hot. Back at the hotel, the windowless gloom of the reception area is very welcome – gloomy characterless marble cool in the heart of throbbing Naples. Upstairs my bed has been covered with music festival paraphernalia as if Santa Claus had dropped by. Thick elegant programmes. A box of chocolates from Mr & Mrs Alberti. Welcomes and invitations – when Italians address an envelope they put the surname first, followed by the Christian name. Tickets for the Villa Acton and the Liszt opera – but no *Barber of Seville*. I'm searching for it when the phone goes.

'Is that Duncan Fallowell?'

'Yes. Is that Ritzy Accardo?'

'Rezi Accardo.'

'Oh, I am sorry.'

'Did you receive everything?'

'Lots of things, yes. But I can't find *The Barber of Seville* ticket.'

'It's sad. It's cancelled. The orchestra is on strike.'

'Oh, why?'

'I'm not sure. It often happens.'

'They're highly strung.' The joke misses.

'The concert to-night at the Villa Acton will be very good.'

I say I'll look out for her, then after putting down the phone, sigh with a smile, select a chocolate and open the large bedroom window. 2 boys are playing football on the roof terrace of a block of flats opposite, one about 10, the other about 16. My God, these people are alert to the world about them – the elder boy has caught sight of me *at once*. The moment I went to the window he knew I was there. So now he's stopped playing with the younger and is knocking the ball into the air with his knees and feet, showing off his skills for my benefit. And there goes his red tracksuit top, pulling it off to show how fine he is. Ah! he almost knocked the ball over the parapet, growing too cocky, not concentrating on the ball, allowing the active idea to be weakened by the passive, i.e. showing off.

The Villa Acton is a short and pleasant walk from the hotel. I stretch it by walking down to the sea and along the promenade of the Villa Comunale. There are joggers and scooters and motorists,

browsing individuals and snogging couples. The Villa Acton is small
but beautiful, in the style of a Greek temple with Doric columns. At last
I meet Rezi Accardo. She has a cheeky sunburnt face with pixie hair
and rushes round trying to keep everything sweet while her husband
adopts a more noble stance. He is an Italian violinist but his fair, severe
features and gold-rimmed spectacles make him look like a Hollywood
Nazi. For a violinist he has remarkably good tailoring. His pinstripe
suit encases him with pressed perfection, apart from a light spray of
dandruff across the collar.

Rezi asks 'How's Gabriella?'

'Who?'

'Gabriella Abbado.'

'Oh, yes, um . . .' This is why I'm here. Because I'm a friend of
Gabriella's. But I've never met her. 'She's having a wonderful time.
Claudio's in Vienna. I mean – '

'Yes, we heard. Is Gabriella happy about that?'

'Oh – I'm sure she's *heartbroken*.'

For the concert the open loggia of the villa has been *closed in*
with transparent polythene panels between the columns. The heat
is horrific. I stand to one side and survey the shiny incandescent
faces and wet necks of the audience as Dvořak's whining String
Quintet gets under way. Their stoicism is remarkable. Open to the
evening sea air this would be a divine place for a concert but to
close it in with plastic sheets drives up the heat and humidity to
danger level. To follow is Debussy's String Quartet and although
I love dearly everything he wrote I also recall that he once said in
an interview that his definition of unhappiness was 'Being too hot',
so I run away after about 12 bars of Dvořak and breeze down to
the prom.

After a good night's sleep I'm more orientated and to-night is the
Night of the Opera Critics. It has been communicated to me by subtle
means that I am to meet a Mr Robert Leslie who used to edit *Records
and Recording* and whose title at this beanfeast is International Artistic
Consultant. Bully for Bob. Apparently it means that he's responsible
for a small group of British opera critics staying at one of Naples's
more hideous hotels – the Jolly (yes, there's a chain of them). He will
be my liaison with events and will also be at the San Carlo Theatre this
evening. I'm late and I've made the mistake of telling the taxi driver –
his driving is berserk because one thing they do understand in Naples
is that it's OK to miss the end of an opera but you mustn't miss the
overture. He drives with hand continuously depressing the horn – even
the Neapolitans think something is up and the traffic parts before us like
the Red Sea. Along the seafront snogging couples are already gathering

for an evening's juicy conjunction. The most popular position is for the
boy to relax his head in the girl's lap while she strokes and pecks his
face. The machismo of the south is heavily tempered by the way boys
are idolised by their mothers. The males respond to the same idolatry
in later life and although they can be active, they subside more readily
than northern males into narcissistic passivity. So often when you see
couples walking together it is the male who is receiving the entreaties
and attentions from the female.

Naples is not a planned town. The San Carlo Theatre is jammed at
a crude angle to the Galleria Umberto opposite. The traffic is gluelike
here. Thin boys move among the cars trying to sell cigarettes and
packets of tissue paper. Because of the demonic drive I'm actually
a few minutes early and so briefly explore the Galleria which has
a glass roof with ornate walls and shops in a circular arrangement,
and resembles a honey-coloured wedding-cake turned inside out. It
resonates with talk like a booming beehive.

The foyer of the opera house is packed with young soldiers and
not much else. Some wear khaki uniforms and caps with feathers in
them. Others are in full Ruritanian rig: blue jackets with purple trim,
stick-up collars with no butterfly turn-down, trousers buckled to the
boots, bucket helmets with heavy chinstraps. The Ruritanians hold
their helmets under their arms and have cropped heads which bob
like a sea of black thistles.

No sign of Mr Leslie and the Opera Critics, so I go to my seat.
The theatre is enchanting, with comfortable stalls in red plush, 4
palci and 2 balconetti. All the boxes are fitted with large mirrors.
The upper balcony is finished off with a pelmet and tassels as if we
were in a grand marquee, except that the ceiling is not tented but the
realm of gods and goddesses swirling against a blue sky (painted by a
son of Luigi 'Caserta' Vanvitelli). There are more godly goings-on in
gilt panels round the walls. The proscenium is supported by 4 giant
Corinthian columns, 2 either side, and between each pair rise 4 full
boxes. Above the proscenium is the arms of the Kings of Naples,
topped by a crown, and set a little behind it, a clock of semi-circular
shape.

The theatre is only ½ full and without the soldiers would be ½ that.
Opera is sex. Grand opera is externalised orgasm. The occasion
is sexual. Everybody looks at everybody in the theatre, a pulsating
generalised want expressing itself in specific eyes and turns of the
head. Everybody wanting – even when they already have someone. A
young Italian girl, very beautiful, with a symmetrical open face and
a long shaggy mane of hair, walks down the shallow decline of an
aisle. Several times she tosses back her hair, not in the hard French

way but in the softer Neapolitan way which has something drunken about it. Her body is not being ordered about by the mind and has already gone a little way into the serenity of abandon. At the same time she is upright and aware of the effect she is having, so there is hauteur too. A soldier turns his head and his brown bovine eyes express the awful pain of yearning – the clenching pain – as if one's interior is contracting with a tension prior to springing forward. But it stays contracted, unreleased, painful, under the ancient pressures of inhibition and taboo.

At the last moment a loving couple dash to their seats in front of me, then there is an announcement over a crackly loudspeaker of what we are about to hear. *Don Sanchez* is to be performed by an opera company from Budapest. The band strikes up, the curtain goes back, and – they're all in rows, orchestra, chorus, soloists. It's a concert performance – how maddening. The Hungarian conductor has a gauche mop of Afro wuzz – behind the Iron Curtain, long hair still has a whiff of Bohemian defiance. The playing has energy, though the strings sound thin. Weber, Rossini – it sounds anything but Liszt and not very remarkable. A strangled tenor jerks into an aria, giving the impression that all his singing takes place above the shoulders. A woman, majestic and immobile, sits in white drapes while this dreadful noise has its moment.

The loving couple in front are restless. The girl has put her arm round the boyfriend who rests his head on her shoulder, happy for a while, then he shifts away with a nervous movement and props his head on his right hand. Her arm is thereby stretched too much across his back. She allows it to slip from him and looks peeved. After a minute of assertive independence he looks at her, makes a decision, and put his left arm unemphatically round her shoulders. She gives him a brief conspiratorial smile and goes to snuggle against him, with her head on his shoulder. But he then removes his arm from her. She turns away and stares stiffly ahead at the raucous stage. Unable to maintain this alienation, she touches the back of his hair with her fingertips, leans across, he turns to look at her and she gives him a quick kiss on the nose. His head falls on to her shoulder. She enfolds him with her arm. Directly she does this, he sits up again. Withdrawing her arm, she tries once again to rest her head on his shoulder. This position never settles – he keeps moving his head about because her hair tickles his face, he looks at the ceiling, looks at a girl on his right in the same row, squares his shoulders. The first girl leans forward to glance at the second girl and then relaxes back in her seat. On and on it goes until eventually he snuggles back with his head on her shoulder which is the only position he feels easy in. She accepts that it must be like this, coddles him, they rest thus, perhaps they even listen to some music. The woman in the white Greek drapes, a contralto, is the Hungarians' most passionate and confident singer. Her big number ends the first half.

During the interval the main resort is a long marble crush bar. It is sparsely populated, because the soldiers are not permitted to use it, but Rezi and Salvatore Accardo are here. They seem uptight, and it's with great pleasure that I espy at the far end Frank Granville-Barker, editor of *Books and Bookmen* when I contributed to it in the addled 1970s.

'I heard you were coming,' he says laconically, dressed in blue suit and reddish damask tie, 'but I thought you were coming later.' Frank is petit, the only grey-haired faun in captivity, with a round sweet face made from pink velveteen, and curved lips over which a naughty smile usually plays.

'It's not very full,' I observe.

'They've papered the house with soldiers. The Italians only come if it's Italian opera. And the Neapolitans are not interested in new things, not even in new old things. It's the first 20th century performance.'

'I keep hearing that and honestly I'm not surprised. So you're an opera critic now?'

'I always was. There's not one bar in it one would recognise as Liszt, is there? Weber, Rossini, Auber – but not Liszt. He wrote it when he was 13. It's what is known as a curiosity.'

'Yes – and it's interesting to hear Hungarian *sung*.'

Opening his blue pixie eyes wider than usual, he says 'They're singing French. The libretto's in French.'

'What? But it sounds exactly like sung Hungarian.'

'Yes, that's the way they sing French in Hungary. I'm being dragged off somewhere afterwards by the Accardos.'

'Me too I think – I'm never certain of my status on these occasions. Is one or is one not wanted? That is the question. Where's the International Artistic Consultant? He used to edit *Records and Recording*.'

'Yes, we're all here. I'm a guest of the organisation. They're paying for *everything*. See you after the show then. We've been given peculiar seats, over to one side. Can't think why.'

As the second half begins I see that the loving couple have gone. 2 teenage soldiers are in front now. It's very hot to-night and one can smell them sweating in their khaki uniforms. They keep looking at each other and giggling. The stage lights illuminate the fine downy hair which fringes their ears. End. Polite applause.

In the foyer Frank introduces me to Robert Leslie, a large flushed man also wearing a blue suit and reddish tie – presumably opera critics have developed this uniform by a kind of osmosis (rather as women working in the same office eventually develop a uniform menstrual cycle). Robert says 'Sorry, it was too late to get you full accreditation, the free hotel and all that, but you can come to everything. Who will you write it up for?'

'I don't know.'

'Oh, I see. Er, anyway come to this big meal. This is Conrad Wilson. He's opera critic of *The Scotsman*.'

Mr Wilson nods dourly and says nothing. He looks like a cross between a bank clerk and a hippy – he wears a dark grey suit and carries a shoulder bag with *Penguin Books* stamped loudly across it.

'I'm selling my flat in W1 and moving to Kennington,' says Frank. 'But it's got to be near the Tube so I can get back quickly and phone through my reviews. Are we going to this dinner, Robert?'

'Yes, at Umberto's. We can walk. It's not far. I know the way.'

He strides manfully into the night like the Chief Scout but is brought up short by a wide road boiling with traffic. It's no good waiting for them to stop or for a gap. You have to barge across. You have to *join* the traffic – in Naples, people on foot and people in cars are not distinct categories. Frank screams and clings to me like a panicked monkey as we wade in.

'This must be like Lima!' I shout above the circumambient horse power, because I know he's a Peru wallah.

'No!' he shrieks in terror, yelping and prancing among the cars but managing to hold on to me. 'This is civilised – agh! Lima's much worse because – oh God help me!' He almost disappears under a bus but I fish him up before he drags me down.

'Why?!'

'Because in Lima the cars don't have lights!'

Lights are flying at us from every direction. Can't see Robert, but Conrad Wilson is using his Penguin bag very effectively to part the traffic – vehicles veer away from it as if by reverse magnetism. We wade on and at last make the far bank which is the Piazza del Plebiscito where Robert Leslie is already waiting for us, adjusting his toggle, upright, full-bellied, rubescent of face and smiling.

'I love Naples,' he says. 'Follow me. It's this way.' He points across the square with a sheaf of papers he's carrying.

'I'm exhausted,' murmurs Frank.

'Have you got Neapolitan Thigh?' I ask.

'What's that?'

'It's like Roman Foot, but higher up. From walking the slopes.'

'Oh, we've been walking *everywhere*. Robert likes walking,' says

Frank with an expression of mournful fatigue in the ice-blue lamplight. 'Robert, are we nearly there?'

'Not far now. This way.'

We are among intricate backstreets of uneven buildings and slouching people. Robert, ever upright, pauses, looks left and right, then takes the left with purpose.

'Why Kennington?'

'It's cheap. Are you hungry? I'm losing my appetite.'

'I was very disappointed,' says Conrad Wilson, 'about *The Barber of Seville* being cancelled. I was really looking forward to seeing a Roberto de Simone production. I've not yet seen one.'

This statement from Mr Wilson, who has until now not said a word, strikes a distracted note since it is very clear that the Opera Critics are lost in the labyrinth of one of Europe's most notorious cities whose atmosphere has reached that point where the picturesque tenses with menace. It is hot, and uncool English voices, in quest of the mythical Umberto's, cut the dark and sultry alleyways with 'Is that the right direction?', 'We've been here before', 'I don't remember this bit', 'Let's ask someone'.

Robert insists it's not necessary to ask anyone anything but I do anyway – 'ris-tor-an-tum-ber-toze' – and discover a widespread ignorance.

'We're going round in circles. Please let's find a main road,' says Frank and his voice cracks.

The locals sense we are without bearings and make sarcastic remarks. Boys whistle leaning against scooters, old men grunt, women moon at us in listless curiosity. Togged up in opera dress we look ripe for mugging, confused aliens making too much fuss.

'Let's ask a policeman.'

There are no policemen.

'Let's get a taxi.'

There are no taxis.

Eyes flash in our direction. Low conversation in Neapolitan dialect breaks into sinister laughter. Conrad Wilson hugs his Penguin bag with both arms. 'Oh yes, let's get a taxi!' he says, repeating the idea.

Robert, emboldened by the need to eat, strikes out again. We walk towards a burgeoning brightness – and arrive in the Piazza del Plebiscito once more, back where we started.

'I can't think what I did wrong,' reflects Robert. His bald pate rising domelike is beaded with sweat and resembles a Russian crown covered with pearls.

'I'm all in,' says Frank. 'I'm going back to the Jolly. Yes I am. I can't take any more.'

The Scotsman looks white and says 'I don't want a large dinner. All I wanted was a small pizza in that place next door to our hotel.'

But Robert is sticking out for the big one at Umberto's and I too feel it churlish not to go along. We bid adieu to the others – Frank says 'By the way, thank you for saving my life. That bus was going to kill me' – and try again. 'I know where I went wrong,' says Robert – and by Jove he does. We reach the restaurant in 3 minutes flat.

Like many establishments in Old Naples, Umberto's has a narrow frontage on to the lane but goes back a good way. Inside about 50 musicians and festivalites are sitting at one long table, all ordering and eating different things. Despite our delay, they are not much ahead of us. Robert and I are swallowed up at separate ends – a woman opposite me says 'I don't want anything to eat. Just a Pizza Margherita. And afterwards some veal.'

I order the same. Everyone is talking very quickly. The woman next to me is Naples born and bred and says that the North has sucked the South dry and that Italian unity originated with the Kingdom of Naples. I say but it was ruled by Spanish viceroys for hundreds of years and a Spanish puppet monarchy after that and she asks me where *I'm* from and I reply born in Middlesex but family live in Berkshire and she says she spent a long time in Wembley (for a reason I cannot grasp despite several explanations) and that, before studying English and German Literature at Naples University, she was au pair to an Orthodox Jewish family in Berkshire when she was 17 and *loved* it because of unusual things like the women had to have their heads covered *all* the time, even in labour because she saw photographs and the woman was wearing a headscarf in the hospital bed, since only the husbands are allowed to see their hair but that the woman of the house would get round it when going out by wearing a wog on her head and –

'A what on her head?'

'A wog? No. A wok on her head?'

'That's a thing the Chinese cook with.'

'What's that on the head? A wag?'

'Oh, a wig!'

'Yes, a wig, a wig! The women wore wigs on their tops.' She is elated to retrieve this word from her English past, smiles up at the ceiling, and then breaks forth afresh 'And I knew this Jewish boy there but when I saw him again I did not recognise because he looked like an old man with beard – '

'Yes, a Pizza Margherita here too, yes, waiter, *here!* . . . Thanks, it looks delicious.'

'Naples invented the pizza. And he said don't you recognise me?

And I said oh, it's you and he said yes, I'm not allowed to shave for
1 year after my father died, that's the rule. What will you eat after
the pizza? Some meat? Eat some meat.'

'Why did the orchestra go on strike?'

'Ugh!' she says. 'Ugh!' and as her eyes rake the ceiling again, her
hands wave in the air either side of her head. 'Roberto de Simone
asked the orchestra for 2 extra rehearsals because he said the opera
wasn't ready – and they went on strike. They'd been offended.'

One of the musicians sitting opposite us overhears this and they
have a long clash in rapid Italian during which my veal arrives.

At 2 a.m., after much food and wine, the party breaks up. The
musician is going to a club and wants me to accompany him. There
are a few transvestites at this club and he says that most of the
over-the-top prostitutes in Naples are transvestites or transsexuals
'because they have a greater sense of sex fantasy than real women'.

I suggest that women have just as great a sense of sex or any
other fantasy as men have, but women rarely *act it out*. It is a male
characteristic to act out fantasy. Women dream it.

The musician makes a joke I don't understand and asks 'Would
you like to go to bordello?'

'What sort?'

'Any sort. We have every sort in Naples. I would like you to be my
guest and take you to . . . young girl.'

A reference flashes into my mind. In 1943 Maurice Richardson
met Norman Douglas who was in London for the duration of the
war. Richardson recalled 'It was all right at first. But by the end of
lunch Norman was enthusing about the smell of children's armpits
and I got faintly embarrassed.'

'How young? Not 8 or anything?' A slight tremble is agitating my
thighs.

'No, no. Maybe 13. You English like the youngs. So do Italians.'

'So do the French. Look, there *must* be pubic hair.'

'Of course, Whatever you want. You are in Naples. You are my
guest. You cannot refuse my hospitality. OK?'

*After much deliberation, I have decided to omit the passage which was to
follow here.*

The next day I am in excellent spirits, feeling connected and centred,
and decide to search out the cloister of Santa Chiara over which Harold

Acton enthused. Walking across town, a number of observations may be made about Naples:

(1) The town is covered with posters and graffiti. Viva Russi! Europa Libra. Diana e Charlie. Many in English, e.g. KILLERS.

(2) For chaos it doesn't equal Calcutta and for beauty of location it doesn't equal Rio de Janeiro but for a queasy volcanic combination of the two, it can't be equalled. It feels unstable, alive. At any moment the ground beneath could lurch and the whole bloody shebang avalanche down into the sea.

(3) Blond and ginger complexions are not rare here.

(4) It's a very provincial town which I didn't think it would be.

(5) But it's racy. Neither it nor its people are particularly lovely but the climate and the temperament make for an unbuttoned physicality. The Neapolitans are succulent. One is aware of breasts and penises straining against thin cotton.

The French and Italians get their priorities right: good art, good love, good sex, good food – in any order, as it comes. This is what they want – which isn't the same as this is what they get. The French and Italians love to communicate, love to live on the outside. They are fearless in pleasure. They enjoy a greater freedom in their bodies and emotions than do the British. Art is freedom; sex and touch are freedom. The British distrust all that: art is high-falutin, sex is smut.

The French especially love to live in the spaces between individuals, hence the arts and institutions of love and sodality which they have elaborated: the hotel, the restaurant, the café, the nightclub, the brothel. Italians rely more on the sloshing backwards and forwards of emotion wherever they happen to be, the British on strapping people up in rules. I love the French because they put you on your mettle, they dare you to live, to have no shyness; they draw you out, want to know your story, though they won't necessarily tell you theirs. In Italy it is enough to participate but in France you must contribute – or they will ignore you. They are mean in that sense. The French weakness in all this splendid life-enhancing organisation is – vanity. Their intense self-consciousness weakens them. One never encounters among the French the pure emanation-of-being from the centre. There is always somewhere the back-curling self-regard, the calculation of the effect they're having – which reduces the effect greatly. Unlike the British and the Italians, the French find it almost impossible to subside into dreamy self-forgetful states. Eye contact + mental sharpness = showing-off + paranoia. The French are trapped in a condition of uninterrupted vigilance. When a Frenchman reflects he becomes panicky. They are the world's greatest consumers of tranquillisers. 165 million per annum, according to a recent survey – and rising.

The per capita figure for the British is half – and falling. For the USA, a quarter – and falling.

The average Italian uses fewer words than the average Frenchman who uses fewer words than the average Englishman (who, I suspect, uses fewer words than the average Irishman). The number of words used by the average Italian is decreasing. Italian has a complex grammar which most people ignore – in practice it is a plastic do-it-yourself language. It contains many glories (one of them is the verb 'godere': to enjoy). But Italians do not respond to strictly verbal ideas. Their philosophy is vapid. When an Italian reflects he sighs and falls asleep, though the noise may continue. Verbally he needs disputation to stay conscious – preferably with another human being. Italians respond to body movements. Underline an idea with a gesture and they light up.

For these reasons Italians talk about *love* so well – not necessarily seriously or lightly – but with a natural understanding – better than any other race, I think, and better than the French who tend to intellectualise or construct. The Italians have a gift for the *ethos* of love. It commands their curiosity, intelligence and compassionate respect, no matter how eccentric its manifestations. Italian innocence and directness help them here. When the Italian says love must be full of fantasy, he doesn't mean full of pretence but that it should be imaginatively alive, that it should be creative. The British can't talk love. It embarrasses them.

Girls shouldn't get too uptight about the Italians. They should take it all with a pinch of bottom. Although the Italians talk love well, they do not talk *sex* well, because they are frightened to reveal quirks, of being thought 'weird' – and the revealed quirk is the essence of good sex talk. The French talk sex well. They pick up on the verbal fantasy very quickly. The British talk sex well – if you can get them started – and if you can prevent them getting bogged down in that filth/dirt/smut number (the idea that sex is permissible, let alone healthy, is foreign to the British mind). But once started, the problem is getting the British to stop – they make extensive and often very amusing use of the double entendre to sexualise everything.

Sexual love is the best way to explore yourself, to explore someone else, because you can't hide. It depends on a continuous and actual, not theoretical, process of psychological as well as physical stripping/exposure/nakedness. It is also very good for the posture.

Sexually the French suffer from knowingness, the English from awkwardness, the Italians from guilt: 3 varieties of hiding. French matter-of-factness linked to French ingenuity can be sexy – for a few days. But sex is not merely a game. English awkwardness can be exciting. But sex should not be an obstacle course. At least the Italians have the decency to be guilty *afterwards* and they do have better posture than the English (although this could be because a warm climate obliges them to clench less against the elements). But guilt, unlike awkwardness, is corrosive and never goes away. It derives of course from the Roman Catholic Church, guardian of the unbroken Christian tradition of the human as a defiled and defiling thing. A recent survey has revealed that the sexiest class of Italian male, those with the most expressive libidos, are butchers.

Which brings us to *food*. Although the British invented the sandwich and have the finest cuisine of puddings in the world, they do not have a food culture the way the French and Italians do. The British do not *talk* food with the passion and commitment of those Europeans. They do not *live* food in the manner of French and Italian shopkeepers and restaurateurs whose establishments are frequently small family businesses and therefore a matter of pride. One of the most appealing things about a French or Italian restaurant is that they appreciate the customer. If they have misunderstood your order, they do not mind taking it back and correcting it, whereas British waiters always try to make out it's your fault, grow petulant and correct an order only by creating such bad odour that the rest of the meal becomes uncomfortable. Therefore on the whole the British do not eat as well as the French or Italians. The British diet has too much sugar, too much fat, too much processed food. Most British children have food from boxes, tins and packets. The British also have some disgusting food habits – for example they use boxed pre-grated Parmesan cheese which tastes like dried vomit. Parmesan must always be freshly grated.

Pasta is a perfect food for a warm climate. It keeps virtually forever without refrigeration. An unpleasant development is wholemeal pasta: foul colour, lumpy texture. And unnecessary since pasta is already made from hard durum wheat which is excellent for the bowels. By law all Italian pasta must be made from this wheat. Pasta producers in West Germany and France make an inferior product, an amalgam of hard and soft wheat which is cheaper and requires less cooking time but results in a slimy mush. The Italians are fighting for pasta purity against the EEC commissioners who are for degradation. There is a precedent in the West Germans' campaign for beer purity – the Germans lost. The pizza is also made from this hard wheat and in Italy is never junk food. The Americans have 'improved' the pizza, as they have the sandwich, into a rich pulpy experience. In Italy and Britain the originals remain relatively simple. Out of these and other ambulatory cogitations, 3 provisional columns appear in my head, as follows:

French	Italians	British
Centripetal	Regional	Centrifugal
Bourgeois public life	Anarchic public life	Regulated public life
No private life	Bourgeois private life	Multiracial private life
Moderate variety of type	Small variety of type	Great variety of type
Not spotless in anything	Spotless in home	Semi-spotless in home
	Spotless in body/clothes	Semi-spotless in body/clothes
	Filthy in street	Semi-spotless in street
	Only rich have gardens	Spotless in garden
Balanced society	Heterosocial/matriarchal	Homosocial/patriarchal
Freedom	Repressive customs	Repressive laws
Fear of irrational	Fear of exceptional	Fear of spontaneity
Snobs	Status obsessed	Class ridden
Age doesn't matter	Age doesn't matter	Distinct youth culture
Social	Gregarious	Individual
Nationalist	Local	Post-imperial
Arty	Artistic	Philistine
Witty	Lively	Witty & humorous

The cloister of Santa Chiara is dedicated to the grape. The garth is large and laid out as a pergola for vines. The pergola pillars are encased in majolica tiles which depict coiling plants heavy with flowers and purple grapes. Between the pillars are seats and low string walls similarly covered with tiles and bearing idyllic secular scenes painted in yellow, blue, orange and green. Poppies, roses and flowering shrubs also find a home here. It is a most alluring spot, not too tidy: cool and green and quiet in the very throat of this noisily coughing town. Franciscans in brown habits shuffle among the handful of Neapolitans who are reading newspapers on the seats.

The sun now feels hot on the back of my neck and I go for lunch near a wig shop also selling facial wigs for men. The restaurant is empty. The waiter is old and dirty with gigantic belly, black cummerbund awry, and thick gold bracelet. I order spaghetti bolognese and beer. The pasta comes with a rich and ancient tomato sauce on to which are sprinkled chopped spinach, onion, and a few pieces of gristly meat. The bread is grey, very salty and greasy, with rock hard, dark brown crust as if boxed in wood. It is dumped near me in a manner which suggests I'm seriously disrupting his day. The food tastes horrible. I am overcharged. So much for food culture.

When I emerge from the restaurant at 2 p.m. the terrific DIN of Naples – car horns, car alarms being set off, police sirens, unsuppressed scooters, loudspeakers, loud people – has melted into a dazzling silence. The sun is high. The streets are empty. 2 p.m. is the hour when the day breaks in half. Everybody is back at home eating. Then they will rest. The siesta grows longer as the summer deepens. In Naples, the month of May is summer. All garages close at 2 p.m. for long lunchtimes. Museums close at 2 p.m. and usually don't open again. 2 p.m. is the check-out time in Italian hotels. The heat is fierce and with it comes a blurring of perception. I sit on a bench under a tree. How many benches have I sat on in how many hot foreign cities, staring out at the world?

Dinner with the Rev. Peter Blackburn. Saturday night at the Pizzeria. The place is simple, full but not overpoweringly so.

ME: Do you remember the Famous Parmesan Cheese Scandal? They were selling it in drums in England and it turned out to be ground-up cricket bats.

PETER: Mozzarella's the great cheese of Naples. It should be made from buffalo milk.

ME: I don't see many buffaloes around.

PETER: No, that's one of the great mysteries.

ME: This pasta's very good. (*Waiter arrives to take plate.*) Er – un momento, signor . . . Did you see that? The waiter tried to whisk my plate away while I'm still eating!

PETER: Yes, the service here is strange. And your beer will take an hour to arrive.

ME: You've finished before me. Do you want some meat? Eat some meat. I'm paying. Do.

PETER: Some veal perhaps.

ME: Perversely I find this Neapolitan turbulence rather relaxing. It's when an atmosphere is formal and respectable that I start to get twitchy.

PETER: I am by nature an insomniac – but I sleep very well in Naples.

ME: I'm losing a few skins of prissiness on this trip and that always improves one's sleep.

PETER: What happened to you – parking in the market in Florence – happened to me in Bruges. There was a warning sign there, clear as day, saying Thursday is market day. But in Flemish.

ME: Is Bruges wonderful? Oh, the waiter's brought my beer. But not your wine.

PETER: I told you the service was strange. I think I'll have salad as well. Here's the waiter again . . . oh, there's no salad. Because of the Russian fall-out.

ME: That's heartening. That they bother.

WAITER: Carote. Funghi.

PETER: I see, yes, but no leaf vegetables. I'm not really worried about fall-out.

ME: I wouldn't insist on the salad if they said it was alive with fall-out. Why isn't he bringing your red wine? I keep asking him.

PETER: It's always like this with that chap. Did you notice his eyelids? The Neapolitans have very heavy eyelids which is why they look sad sometimes. And if you look them in the eye, they often have white underneath the iris.

ME: The Japanese call that sanpaku and say it denotes criminal tendencies or mental disturbance.

PETER: You try it. You can look people in the eye in Naples, it's allowed.

ME: It's allowed in Wales too – and in Scotland – and in Ireland. But it's not allowed in England. Sod the English. And it's not allowed in Japan. Sod the Japanese. Did you say a prayer in your church at the time of the nuclear explosion?

PETER: I prayed for the victims of it.

ME: You didn't beseech God not to let it happen again?

PETER: It's man's fault this.

ME: You don't believe in Divine Intervention?

PETER: I believe in God's sovereignty. If he chooses for us to be wiped out, that's fine by me. I'm *terribly* fatalistic.

ME: I have fatalism at the 12th hour. But not at the 11th. I get very annoyed by overpopulation, acid rain, destruction of the planet through greed and stupidity.

PETER: You'll see a lot of that round here.

ME: How amazing – it's your red wine.

PETER: Now that I've finished my veal. I'm also a Romantic Tory. I was very amused to read the other day that the son of the Earl of Derby was going to be offered the throne of Greece in the 19th century and he said 'What can they be thinking of? Don't they realise I'm going to be the Earl of Derby one day?' I just saw the pineapple and it looks so good . . .

ME: Too late. He's brought us both the fraises.

PETER: When people who've been living in Naples go back to England –

ME: They drive through the red lights!

PETER: No. That they can adjust to. But they stop at green lights because they can't believe that the people in the other direction are stopping for the red lights.

ME: Are you sure these fraises aren't radioactive?

PETER: I'm not sure of anything.

ME: Can one taste radioaction?

PETER: I don't think so. Where are you going after Naples?

ME: I'm doing the Amalfi Drive and staying at a place recommended by my mother.

PETER: What's that, the Hotel Palumbo? Oh, you'll love it. It's fabulous.

ME: Then south to the Sila Mountains because I want to look at San Giovanni in Fiore. Then Sicily of course.

PETER: I think your story about the Black Lake of the Gods very fascinating. Let me know if you find it and I'll go and have a look. Gods are always fascinating, aren't they, whatever form they take.

ME: I'm not sure about the ones which eat you alive. I love that kid over there, don't you?

PETER: Incredible. Operatic. (*A young boy about 8 years old is dining with his parents. He is short, tough, and wearing a denim suit and mirrored sunglasses with hair greased back. The party leaves.*)

ME: In France he would've had a bow-tie and the shades wouldn't've been mirrored – the effect would've been classier but more effete. Did you notice that extraordinary swagger as he left? It was for real. At 8 years old. Like a baby Al Capone.

PETER: His parents no doubt expect great things from him.

ME: Family life is *very* strong here. And crime is *very* high. This is the great argument against the idea that crime results from the breakdown of traditional family life.

PETER: I'm going to take you up to Capo Posillipo to see the newspaper park.

As we drive along the promenade, through low-key night revels, he supplies a commentary.

'Look at that shrine – so tinselly, so Bombay – and behind it there's a little card room where they play cards . . . See this Greek Doric temple on the left? That's the gatehouse of the Raes' villa. It's fabulous, with 5 acres of garden going down to the sea. It was built for one of the Bourbon kings' mistresses. The Raes have Scottish dancing in the winter and a big feast on Saint Andrew's Day – the haggis is flown in . . . the Villa Rosebery is down there. Lord Rosebery gave it to the Italians as the Neapolitan home of the Italian head of state . . . Here we are. The newspaper's beginning now. This is the Parco della Remembranza. Mussolini landscaped it rather beautifully. You can see the fasces on the entrance. He wanted that villa up there but the Neapolitans wouldn't give it to him. Look at all the rubbish. See what I mean?'

It is absolutely astonishing, unbelievable. The park is covered with an almost uninterrupted carpet of paleness stretching far into the dark. It would appear concreted over, did not some of the surface stir in the soft breeze.

'Don't they ever clean it up?'

'Yes, every Monday. This is only Saturday. You should see it after tomorrow. I once saw a little cinquecento car humping up and down so much I thought it was going to fall over the edge onto Brutus's villa. Let's get out of the car. The view's so good . . . Because he couldn't get the villa up there, to spite them, Mussolini built those steel works down there, on the edge of the Neapolitans' favourite bay.'

'What a shit.'

'Well – yes. This is Bagnoli here. That is Baia over there, the Brighton of Ancient Rome – it's all under water now. And that bit there is boarded off, a dead part of the city because of earthquake damage . . . Cuma is just beyond, where the Sibyl came from . . . and that's part of NATO there . . . People bathe just here – by the steelworks.'

'. . . What a wonderful mess . . .'

'Yes. Exactly . . .'

I leave the hotel at 2 p.m. next day. Left 10,000 lire on the dressing-table for the chamber maid whom I glimpsed for the first time – a tough little man of about 50 in a jacket of narrow red and black stripes which buttoned up to the neck.

9

Ravello, then the Deep South

Leaving Naples, travelling east alongside the docks, shaking over blocks of volcanic stone – the town grows slummier and slummier. Ah Vesuvius! It looks a *brute*, as though it could blow all Naples to kingdom come if it chose. Endless cement towers of various heights covered with washing. Where's Vesuvius gone? Oh there! Even when veiled in a pollution haze, its earthy brownish form still overshadows the city like a morose beast, a hostile dream, a superior being. It is older by far than anything else around here. The squatting presence of Death looks eternally down on Naples and this must have been the key to the formation of the Neapolitan character, of their vitality and lushness. And lushness grows up the volcano's slopes, then stops decisively, not daring to presume further.

. . . Tiddley-tum, tiddley-tum, we are bowling along the road to Sorrento and at 3 p.m. it has become less quiet. A view north across the Bay of Naples abruptly thrashes out, giving me a twinge. The road keeps exploding into spectacular views and cliffs drop sheer into bluish water, but glare and haze impair visibility. Olive trees, fig trees, cactuses, wild flowers, pines, grasses: south Italy is much greener than I envisaged. Lots of advertisements for Permaflex whatever that is . . . Sorrento went by . . . grey 3-wheeler pick-up stacked with tomatoes and the vendor hailing through a husky loudspeaker. After Sorrento the landscape becomes prettier. The road goes up and down, round and about, shoots out into blue voids, back into rockfaces. There's a man having a pee by the roadside but curiously he's peeing into the road, so as I come round the bend his urine splashes the car.

Now the Amalfi Drive proper, with the road clamped on to vertical rockfaces by the brilliant Italian engineers (I suppose the world's greatest engineers were the Incas. It took runners 8 days to convey a message from Cuzco to Santiago, a distance of 1,700 miles). The Italians play dice-with-death overtaking games along here. The views distract, but you need all your concentration for the road flicking back and forth. This produces an exhilarating anxiety . . . Positano went by, very cramped, with coach-loads of German trippers ploughing their way through, forcing cars onto the narrow pavements . . . Beware rocce sporgenti . . . and there is the road to Ravello winding up up up up up trees wires Moorish palaces churches a few clouds . . .

The hotel people tell you to bring the car right up but they shouldn't. It's another tight squeeze through another small archway and again I scratch the bodypaint badly. The Hotel Palumbo is housed in a small medieval palace whose Arabo-Gothic style of architecture is a piquant foretaste of Sicilian masterpieces. The entrance hall, full of plants, has a blue, red and yellow tiled floor in circles and lozenges, worn Corinthian columns supporting pointed arches, and a staircase with unglazed arcades opening on to a blue sky and pots of red geraniums on ledges.

Signor Vuilleumier, the owner, is sitting in the hall with a walking cane and introduces himself in excellent English. 'I lived in Yorkshire during the war,' he says. White hair, charming manners, rapacious. I say I don't want the most expensive room and he says 'We have a beautiful penthouse for you.' I clamber up to the attics and can't believe it – a sweaty little hole with small round window through which nothing but sky can be seen. 140,000 lire per night! No thanks. He tries again. Still small but bright and extremely pretty. 180,000 lire per night! By this stage Signor has disappeared and a woman is left to negotiate. She explains that if I were 2 it would only be 200,000 per night. But I'm not 2. 'OK, we do special price just for you' – and doesn't alter the price but throws in dinner for free.

Room 62 (but there can't be more than 15 rooms in the whole place) is done up in pale blue and white. The walls curve, the ceilings curve, arches curve, the bathroom incorporates curved lancets. Sheets, pillow-cases, towels, blue damask counterpane, all are woven with the hotel's name and crest. Curtains are heavy and *lined* so that they properly shut out the light. Few hotels have proper curtains. Mostly it's warped shutters. In the Mezzogiorno (as the deep south is known) bedrooms have thick fitted blinds in wood or plastic slats to keep out the fierce light. But not here, because the glory of the room is a full-length panoramic bay window let into a, yes, of course, a head-spinning view collapsing downwards in terraces to the sea 1200 feet below. I could never write with a view like this. It blocks your mind with the authority of a supreme cliché realised. The only thing to do with a view like this is *screw*.

The bathroom is Moorish. Large white bath and basin with chunky taps manufactured by Ideal Standard (as was my bathroom at Caserta). The Atkinson's soap has the hotel's name on it. So does the sachet of foam bath which is put to immediate use. Hanging over one corner of the bath is a long cord. *Allarme* it says in red. There's a great temptation to give it a yank and have a chambermaid rush in, boobs a-wobble, all concern, but I meekly suds my private parts instead.

One of the games to be played in these sooper-dooper hotels is fault-finding – the French do it with haute cuisine too. The proprietor goes to such lengths to get it perfect, to pre-empt every need, that one tries to catch him out. It's not mean-mindedness, just playing the game that he's playing. I've found a couple of faults. The wash-basin in the bathroom is built against a lancet recess and the mirror which backs the recess is too far away for shaving. Also, for obvious reasons, floors in the Mezzogiorno are usually marble, stone or tile. Even with a rug on, this makes them too hard for exercises such as standing on one's head. That's not a fault but a cultural difference. The fault is that, coming out of the bathroom, I discover this tiled floor to be extremely slippery and dangerous when wet. I collide with an antique bureau and hurt my elbow. Earlier I even saw the woman who runs the place go for a burton on dry tiles in the hall. I ring her now, to see if she has Gore Vidal's number which she has and he's in.

'You're lucky,' he says. 'I'm leaving for Rome to-morrow.' And we arrange to meet after dinner.

The church bell is tolling 7.30 p.m. As the sun declines, the sunlight shrinks from rockface to rockface. The air is of misty pastels, especially peach. Having recently come from the bath, I realise I am presenting my nakedness to the giant window and that a woman is staring up at me from the garden below with an absorbed look. I wave and withdraw and sort out my money. There are wodges of Italian banknotes all over the place not because I'm rich but because the currency is bulky. Caravaggio sneers on the 100,000 lire note, and Bernini on the 50,000 looks possessed by devils.

As you gaze, the view appears static, but each time you return to it something new has happened. A little boat has anchored in the bay but one didn't see it arrive. A minute later I turn round – and all the lights in Maiori are on. Smoke from a fire is drifting through the mountains. Now the view is all blues, mingling with the blues of the room which becomes disembodied, simply a blue idea suspended among other blue ideas. Put on shoes – and re-encounter the view again. Solidity has returned. The hill in the foreground, with a church on it, has been thrown into prominence, glowing an unnatural chemical green while the rest of the view drowns in indigo.

I dress simply for dinner. I hate eating alone in public dining-rooms. One has to perform to survive and I perform 'the English writer travelling alone'. This gives me something to hide behind when I'm feeling nervous.

Dinner on the terrace over palpitating blackness. Tortellini al brodo: tortellini in a thin clear soup with parmesan. There's a middle-aged English couple on my right. She's rather county, he's more worldly. I try to catch her eye but she's seen me naked and won't be hooked. Confalone al golfo: fish baked in mint served with a single roast potato and cooked peppers. She says to him 'I must eat more mint. Do remind me.'

On the other side an old German professor is talking to a young Japanese professor in English and the old German says 'He uses guinea pig antibodies to inhibit mice.' After which the young Japanese observes 'He has Peter Pan syndrome, I think.' And the old German replies 'Yes, she's much more mature.'

Vanilla ice-cream with candied orange and orange liqueur ends a tasty, simple meal. Ordering coffee the Englishwoman says to the waiter 'Negro' and the man says 'Noire' and the waiter looks blank. Then they both say 'Black' and the waiter says 'Ah, black. Nero, nero.' These days the English, who've been so much attacked in the past for not trying, feel they must make some effort to speak 'foreign', even though they usually have no aptitude for it and English is more widely spoken than ever. The woman is saying 'I do understand how Babs can get into such a state between Italian and Spanish.'

Gore Vidal is finishing his dinner on the terrace at Salvatore's. He's fat, loosely dressed in old summer clothes of various browns, spectacles with TV-shaped frames, unshaven, and in the company of 3 American friends.

'What are you doing in Ravello?'

'I'm on my way to Noto.'

'Well, I suppose that's as good a reason as any.' Then he says out of the blue 'Do you know what the trouble with the British is? They don't like success.' And he starts talking figures, repeating them, turning them this way and that, like prisms, to refract multiple meanings.

I get lost and say 'The 100,000 lire note has a picture of Caravaggio on it and the 50,000 a picture of Bernini.'

The youngest of the Americans, who is very fey, says 'Oh, I like both those men. I must get some of those notes.'

GV looks at me and says 'God, you must've got a good advance.'

And the young American says 'Oh Gore, your timing is *so* good.'

GV beams with pleasure and says 'My timing was *always* good.'

Another American, very ginger, covered in freckles, lumps of gold jewellery, ginger eyelashes, and eyes of brown which make him look very ginger indeed, like Régine, says 'Gore Vidal means protector of life in Italian. Gore means moat as in castle which is protection and Vidal is vitalis.'

Is that Italian? I wonder to myself, and have I stumbled into the AGM of the Gore Vidal Fan Club? Then aloud I venture 'Duncan Fallowell means the brown warrior fell in a well.'

'Were you brown before you fell in or after?' enquires the fourth American who hasn't spoken yet. He is a professor somewhere and 'with' the young American.

'Before.'

'Mr Nabokov told me – not that I ever met him,' begins GV, 'but we used to exchange rather stately insults through various media, *he* told *me* that Gore Vidal in Russian meant – One who has seen suffering.'

'Is that different from one who has suffered?' I ask.

GV blinks and says 'Er . . . I *think* it is, yes. But I can't be sure. Do you know what the trouble with the British is? They don't *read* anything. They don't even read Proust any more.'

'Oh – I haven't read Proust,' I confess.

'Haven't you? . . . Well, you know about him anyway. That's *something*. Not much. But something.'

'Have you heard of the Lago dei Palici?'

He narrows his eyes, as if it's a trick. 'And why should I have heard of something like that?'

GV is a big man whose disproportionately large head sports at regular intervals a fruity, mobile smirk. He likes to wear his learning on both sleeves which suggests he did not attend a university. A senator complex inclines him to orotundity of expression but he is not at all precious, is always ready for a scrap, and has about him a battle-scarred plenitude. His noblest quality is a terrific sense of mischief which is rare in a successful man and very appealing. Despite extravagant, almost 18th century vanities, he is *interested* and wants to be involved.

GV announces in the slow loud senatorial manner 'You can be insufficiently famous. And you can be *so* famous that you become unknown again. I am the latter. They think – ah, another novel by Gore Vidal, yes, we know what that is – and they pass by on the other side. Arthur Miller has this problem. Arthur Miller, oh yeah, he was married to Marilyn Monroe – and that's that. I am now *so famous* in America that I'm not really known at all any more. I'm pocketed.'

'You hate that,' says Ginger, who is waspish and rushes to GV's aid when GV doesn't need it, 'because you like to get a response, don't you?'

'Exactly!' expostulates GV. 'But I'm getting them going again! Now I am accused of being America's greatest anti-Semite because in a polemic I suggested that America cut aid to the Middle East – to Jordan, to Egypt, to Israel – if they wanted to stop terrorism.'

'If the Americans moved out, would the Russians move in?'

'Oh God, the Russians, they can hardly get through the day, let alone rule the world. And so these right-wing fascist Zionists are accusing me of anti-Semitism. It's all linked up with this fundamentalist Christian movement in the United States who want to nuke the reds. Anyway I'm going to sue! . . . But I haven't decided when. Do you write in a different voice for different journals?'

'No, I write what I want to write, that's all.'

'Well, I adopt a different voice for every journal I contribute to. I do it because I want to be *understood*.'

The Professor of Something comes from a part of San Francisco populated by Italians from Lucca. 'I heard this girl talking Italian with a Lucca accent,' he says, 'and I asked her how long she'd been over here and she said for 5 generations. The people from Lucca are very beautiful.'

'Oh yes,' says GV, 'when you go there you'll come across, say, a wonderfully picturesque old man working away on his plot and you go up and talk to him and he turns out to be a retired BBC producer. What do the English say for jerk off?'

'Wank.'

'It's a great word.'

'More churning and self-indulgent than jerk off which is too short, too desperate.'

'I should go back now and make those calls to Los Angeles – we have to do those at night. During the day I write. To write novels it is necessary to have the bovine temperament. I certainly have it. I can sit there for hours munching munching, paragraph after paragraph. I'm the biggest cow in the business.'

'Not me. I agree with Scott Fitzgerald, that writing is like swimming under water holding your breath. A sense of strapped-down panic is with me when I write a book, distant when I'm actually writing, much closer when I interrupt the writing.'

'Oh well, you're just a jittery cow,' he says.

Next morning I arise, approach the curtains to encounter the VIEW. And it's entirely obscured by fog. Wet grey fluff right up to the window. Perfect for a cool drive to Pompeii. Ravello isn't as cut off as it seems. There's a back road through the green mountain which links it to the autostrada at Angri. From here it's a short sprint to, well, the trouble is there's a live Pompeii as well as a dead Pompeii and I came off at the wrong one and got into a jittery-cow-type tangle.

The ruins occupy an enormous site and the entrance fee is 5000 lire which is one of the best deals in the business. The first impression is bleak and disappointing and thousands of screeching schoolkids do nothing for one's sense of history. I decide to put on the Herbert Johnson sunhat which is not pansy affectation – it's midday, the sun is very hot, and there is virtually no shelter at the site. It's a white cotton stetson which I fancy makes me resemble a cruel Brazilian plantation owner but it must look English because schoolchildren repeatedly come up to me saying 'Good morning' or 'What time is it please?' to practise their elementary.

As one meanders along, fascination grows. The air is suffused with the lovely aroma, soft but alert, which pines give off in the heat. Brownish stumps of buildings emerging from long grass begin to cohere and one can be moved to tears because unlike most ruins, where the religious or superstitious element is paramount, here it is the human factor which is so strong. The buildings are small, revealing the diamond brick pattern one saw at the Villa Adriana. The entirely human scale of all the architecture is out of keeping with this place's legendary reputation. These are not ruins which overwhelm the visitor but ones which draw him in with a quiet hand. Vesuvius does all the overwhelming round here. The streets are narrow with one pair of grooves for cartwheels down the centre, so presumably a one-way system operated. The road is recessed below pavement level to a depth of two feet or so to take the rubbish and there are crossing points of raised blocks. Ivor Bartels told me that the Pompeians poisoned themselves with lead plumbing. There are graffiti everywhere – modern ones – and it's about time school teachers and the guardians of monuments took a tougher line with these scrawling brats. A number of paraplegics are bumping round in wheelchairs determined to partake of the legend. Black snakes scuttle out of one's path.

Pulses of eroticism ripple through the site without cease, not least because of the presence of Vesuvian death. One is reduced and switched on by the great pistons of History, Time, Death. But these erotic pulses come too from the natural and unafraid sexuality of the Pompeians themselves. This is the pre-Christian world. Human nature, in both its joyous and cruel aspects, has not yet been twisted into agonised shapes. Desire is not taboo here – but it is organised. There used to be a part of Pompeii where women could not go but now everyone can go everywhere – largely because most of the explicit material has been removed to the National Archaeological Museum in Naples. The most noticeable feature of Pompeian eroticism is that,

although they had places of particular resort (the street of brothels
is closed to-day however), they did not veil their sexuality. Its images
in all its variations were found throughout the city. Recently a series
of orgiastic homosexual wall paintings were found in the House of
Paquius Proculus – there is also a very beautiful portrait of the owner
and his wife. At the entrance to the House of the Vettii is a painting of
Priapus weighing on scales his gigantic phallus and attempts by various
headmistresses from around the world to have this removed have so
far been resisted by the authorities. Passing schoolgirls grow acutely
giggly and unsettled as they chance upon it. They blush, run away,
and push forward their girlfriends to look too. The Vettii were rich
merchants and the image, in the tradition of phallic cults, was placed
here to ward off the evil eye. Can one imagine such a thing in the hall
of Lord Sainsbury or Mr Rockefeller? We can't even cope with an erect
satyr any more (in exhibiting its collection of Greek vases, the British
Museum refuses to show the livelier ones or turns immodest images
to the wall). But it is very healthy for children to become familiar with
human functions at the earliest possible age. Why are adults frightened
to be seen as natural beings by their children? Why do they insist on
transmitting to their offspring by a rigorous censorship this divorce
from the elemental? The Christians told us that the way to surmount
our animality was to reject it. How wrong they proved to be. The
only aesthetic prudery I can ascribe to the Greeks and Romans is the
convention in sculpture and painting of never representing the pubic
hair of women. I believe the complete woman wasn't portrayed in art
until Gauguin.

Of course it is not only erotic art which has been removed to
Naples. Almost all the other wall paintings and objets d'art have
gone too, for protection against weather and thieves. Even the Villa
of the Mysteries, which according to the guidebook purchased at
the main gate should still be resplendent with frescoes depicting
the initiation of a bride into the Dionysiac mysteries, now has plain
brown walls, so presumably the villa was stripped only recently. The
Pompeian style of wall painting is fantastically attractive and colourful – black, green, purple, yellow, an unforgettably rich vermilion – and
I count it the greatest mistake of my journey so far to have missed
the National Archaeological Museum in Naples, the price I've paid
for travelling 'clean' as it were, with very little advance research and
no back-tracking. Not only is it stuffed with marvels from Pompeii
but possesses, I also woefully discover, the Farnese collection of
classical statues. It has been suggested that a museum should be
built at the site for the Pompeii collection, and clearly this makes
sense, but I think it understandable that the authorities have used

this lure to draw visitors into Naples since without it few would wish
to go there.

By 2.30 p.m. itinerants are sitting about in doorways, under arches,
on knobs of stone, whacked and dusty. There's a thing called Pompeian
Ankle – a twist in the ankle from the hard uneven surfaces across which
one constantly scrambles. I don't have that one. I have Pompeian Toe –
the small toe on the left foot is developing a blister from the
constant twisting of the shoe over these irregularities. I started out
in black suèdes – now they're brown all over. I hear a girl say in
deep Cockney 'Aw, tonight I'm gonna have a great shower.' Turn
round but can't recognise her. Voices differ but all tourists look the
same. Tourists have no identity.

There is a café in the Forum, full of steaming, mildly disgruntled
Germans. In this café I have my first salad since arriving on mainland
Europe. At the scene of one major disaster I am eating food radioac-
tivated by another. The first was as act of nature. The second was
an act of man. This is called progress.

Don't try to see everything. The ruins are by definition incomplete,
so one's experience will be incomplete, open-ended. Back in the
car park the tourist coaches are arriving in great numbers – it is
approaching 4 p.m., the heavy influx hour. Do try to park your car
in the shade. After a slog round Pompeii, nothing is more dispiriting
than having to drive off in an oven. Mine was left in the shade. By
the time I return, the sun having not remained still, the car is in
broiling heat.

If I came back to Ravello I'd stay at the Hotel Caruso Belvedere, also
an old palace but half the price of the Palumbo and more relaxing,
down-at-heel, with mellow bookish rooms and faded painted ceilings,
and a garden of rioting verdure. There is something sterile about
the Palumbo. Their ability to pre-empt *stops things happening*. One
is cocooned. And the staff are deflected from intimacies by what
they imagine to be the grandeur of the clientele. The hush over all
parties at dinner, including the staff, is unpleasant. In fact deluxe hotels
almost everywhere have this contraceptive effect – except in Calcutta.
Nothing can keep Calcutta out. I remember having an ice-cream with
Sarah (Moffett) Gilbert-Rolfe by the pool of the Oberoi Grand on
Chowringhee. The hotel is built round a court, inward looking like
all the posh Calcutta hotels. Rich Bengalis disported under coloured
umbrellas. And down on to the topmost boule of Sarah's vanilla
ice-cream floated a flake of soot.

Night. The view from the window is pitch black speckled with lights. Half way down the mountainside, a swimming-pool glows a lurid blue. Dogs bark erratically. There is a great sense of liberty, of space, of peacefulness, no sense of living in the head or of tightness, and I'm drifting off to sleep, being gently embosomed in sleep. Then a humming noise starts up, originating in the region beneath my bed but vibrating through the whole room. What on earth is it? The hum resonates out of all proportion to its actual loudness and plays on the nerves in a most appalling way. What can I do? This is ghastly. I switch on the light, sit up, and decide to read, hoping it will eventually stop. Pushkin's short stories. *The Queen of Spades. Torture in the old days formed so integral a part of judicial procedure that the humane edict abolishing it for long remained a dead letter . . . Young man, if these lines of mine ever fall into your hands, remember that the best and most enduring of transformations are those which proceed from an improvement in morals and customs and not from any violent upheaval.*

At 12.40 a.m. the humming stops. Oh, bliss. Relief – release – relax – return to sleep, drifting snugly off . . . At 12.55 the humming comes back on. It's horribly insidious! and takes over the whole room! I'm in the mood for violent upheaval, throw the book at the wall with a coarse imprecation. There's no chance of sleep. Maybe we are as obsessional about regular sleep as the Victorians were about regular bowel movements – but I'm no good if underslept – this is because a writer has to be a self-winder – with insufficient sleep this is difficult – solitary work is the pits from this point of view – I hate working alone, I hate living alone too – it's too much alone – I'm sure that's why – please stop humming! – I'm sure that's why so many writers take to drink or marry capable down-to-earth women who keep them properly orientated to the external world and – the humming shuts off! . . . Silence . . . peace . . . sleep at last? . . . then the humming comes back on again. It must be a sort of generator, one which hums for 20 minutes, switches off for 15. Yesterday it can't've been operating. Can you imagine a more cruel thing to put under a bedroom?

I had a bad night, then the toast at breakfast was so hard it was like trying to crunch diamonds, then the fucking hotel told me they didn't accept credit cards so I had to hang around in a sweltering bank cashing cheques – nearly £100 per night and they demand payment in *cash*, they're not right in the bloody head, oh let's get out of here – scrape the car again – now I'm speeding along the motorway, free once more, wearing the blue cotton shorts from Saint Tropez, cool and comfortable because they don't pull too tight across the crotch in the driving position. South of the Villa Adriana I've seen only one

other British driver which is surprising since this time of the year is
the best for driving south. Later it will become intolerably hot. It's
already hot. The window is down for breeze. When you slow down the
breeze slackens and the heat rises enormously. Then as you pick up
speed, the heat falls as the breeze rises. A big machine is clipping the
oleanders down the centre of the motorway and the traffic is shunted
into one lane for a couple of miles.

Past the uscita for Pagani. The word 'pagan' does not mean 'nasty
sinful beast' as the Church would have us believe, but 'country
dweller'. Either side of the road the landscape is fertile and the flora
abundant. Hills entirely covered with trees resemble gigantic lettuces
and cabbages. Past the uscita for Paestum which Harold Acton said
is pronounced 'pestum'. Apparently it's a superb site for old temples
and does have that elating fresco 'The Diver' (470 BC) but I'm saving
all the Greek stuff for Sicily and besides I've had enough ruins for
the moment. Past the uscita for Taranto and Lecce which the Rev.
Gerard Irvine so adores – he goes there in August, at its hottest.
Lakes of green water . . .

The route becomes more dramatic as we leave Basilicata and
enter Calabria. A quarry on the left is extending with mustard-
yellow scoopers its scar into a full-breasted range of hills. Carried
on blue-painted viaducts, the motorway runs through capriciously
formed upland. We are in a subsidised region because there are
no longer motorway tolls. A stupendous vista opens to Castrovillari
on the left – agh!!! not concentrating – adrenalin spurts through me
as I swerve away from the edge and the whole body clenches in a
tingling spasm.

Sibari 12 kms. Ancient Sybaris. Shall I turn off there? The adjective
sybaritic comes from it, as the adjective luxurious comes from Luxor.
In one of the histories of the Roman Aelianus (d. AD 140), the Sybarite
Smindyrides complains of spending a sleepless night because one of
the rose petals strewn on his bed was folded in two.

I want to go there not because I want to go there but because
I'd like to say I've been there. Indecision, indecision – a Libran
characteristic (but of course astrology is rot). What did *Baedeker* say
of Sibari? I looked it up . . . formerly *Buffaloria* . . . *Malarious district*
. . . Doesn't sound very adorable. Indecision produces a shiver all
down my arms. I can hear myself 'When I was in Sibari, formerly
Buffaloria, and long before that, the ancient Sybaris renowned for
the refined sensibility of its inhabitants . . .' The point *is* – I know
that nothing remains of the ancient city. It was thrown down by the
Crotonians in 510 BC. What will it be to-day? Sora – with a past.
Another appealing, messy, pointless southern town. No, stay on the

motorway, stay focused – the immediate objective is to find a bed in the Sila Mountains before nightfall. As always, a correct decision depends on ascertaining the fundamental need.

. . . . . We are entering the National Park of Calabria, a land flowing with milk, honey, wheat, trees, not at all bleak, nor does it feel Mediterranean. But what's this? Suddenly the landscape is speckled with numerous unfinished breezeblock buildings. Hundreds of them. Is this really a national park? And if so, what does that mean down here? Desecration increases until one finds oneself at Cosenza which is the place for striking inland to the Sila. And the reason for going to the Sila is that it's supposed to be even less Mediterranean than the rest of Calabria. Some say it is like Scotland and since I don't know Scotland this would be an opportunity for finding out what Scotland's like. Furthermore I wish to visit San Giovanni in Fiore, the principal village of the Sila, because I know Edward Lear was unable quite to reach it in his peregrinations. Saint John among the Flowers. In my imagination it is a sunny Shangri-la where the forests part onto dewy Alpine meadow and toy battlements.

Having missed the main road, I find myself circling up on side roads through unkempt villages where widows in black uniformly turn their heads to follow the car as if directed by Busby Berkeley. Is this the Cimigliatello road? A labourer with orange face says yes, yes, keep going, sopra, sopra. The landscape is indeed developing a more northern character with oaks and ferns of luminescent green. Suddenly I connect with the main road to Crotone (where Pythagoras established his brotherhood) which leaps up into the Sila on a series of bravura viaducts. They give one the sense of driving on air, mile after mile, and some have high sides of wire fencing to prevent lorries from being blown over or lorry drivers from experiencing vertigo. Broadcasting masts painted red and white spike the tops of the mountains and still the road climbs.

Cimigliatello is an untidy ski resort, with chalet style buildings of corrugated iron distributed among pine trees. After it the mountains flatten out somewhat and mix with verdant plateaux. Here conifers, deciduous trees, wild flowers and dairy pasture all intermingle to the sound of crickets. The smell of vegetable moisture which is so rare in the south flows through the open windows of the car and it is indeed as if we have climbed up and dropped over the lip into a secret land of perfect climate, warm but away from the roar of heat. Only on entering Montenegro have I encountered something similar. My body recognises its temperate home. I am comfortable and clear-headed.

But there are no charming old inns here such as you find everywhere in France and England. Eventually in the middle of nowhere I come to a weird hotel called the Albergo Lo Zampillo (the gush, the spurt), 20,000 lire per night, and decide to drop my bags. It is very new, a tourist development hotel, and I'm the only guest. But it's surrounded by hills and fields and trees in which sit unfamiliar birds. The sun goes rosily down and diametrically opposite rises the ghostly fluff of a moon in a fading blue sky.

The place is run for the moment by the cook and his wife. He wears all-white overalls and apron and for dinner cooked me an unpleasant pasta tasting of cardboard with sawdust sauce. For 7 years he lived in America but had an allergy to it – red eyes. The doctors could do nothing. He thought maybe it was the water. I say maybe it was homesickness. Anyway he returned to the Sila in 1983 and his eyes are now fine. He says that the reason he hasn't given me a salad with the pasta is because of the Russian radioactive cloud. 'The Government says it's OK now but we don't believe. And we don't drink the milk yet.'

The people south of Naples are less gushing than the Neapolitans, with a sardonic tone I've not much met with since leaving England. But the Sila is a national park, a department of the civil service, and the local people no longer divide the years into good or bad harvests but good or bad seasons.

I pile all my travelling gear onto one bed (luggage, presents, books, radio, etc) and after a bath in a small tub which forces the knees up under my chin I lie on the other bed and read a little on Sicily from these 2 guidebooks I've already quoted from – *Baedeker's Southern Italy* and *Sicily: the New Winter Resort* by Douglas Sladen, both coincidentally published in 1908. The Oxford ragwort is native to the slopes of Aetna is the sort of thing one discovers. But by far the most thrilling news is gleaned from one of the pamphlets given to me by the girl at the Menton border. It says that there is not a single golf course on the island. I can't think of anything more promising.

Breakfast. The butter and jam come in miniature parcels – these are universal in Italy, even at the Hotel Palumbo – and so does the toast, more cardboard in a cellophane wrapper.

The cook follows me out and eyes the car. 'Expensive?' he asks.

'No.'

'It looks expensive.'

'No it doesn't.'

But first to Saint John among the Flowers. It's delightful to be driving off into sunny freshness instead of heat but I notice that the local building lacks distinction. The few farms and settlements appear to be built from prefabricated parts and all of recent date. Hoardings advertising holiday villages crop up every half mile or so.

Then almost before realising it, you are in San Giovanni in Fiore. And it's a nightmare under the sun.

The first major offence is the gravel works on the outskirts. Then it grows rapidly worse. Uncontrolled building, pylons and wires disfigure every prospect. New road systems, with big-city lights and flyovers, are unfinished and in a terrible mess. Sides of hills have been scraped away into terraces and tower blocks plonked along them with no attempt at harmony and all unfinished, crude, deathly. The town has literally exploded in a random building hysteria. About 50 per cent of the buildings are incomplete and will probably stay that way, with thick rusty steel cords sticking out of the tops and exposed breezeblocks. They are connected in jagged sequences by piles of rubble and junk and gouged earth. The only hotel, Dino's, is a modernistic kennel marooned among half-built blocks of flats. The town's one attractive feature is the used car dump: the cars are pressed into blocks and stacked in colourful rows. The old town on a rising spur is semi-abandoned in the middle of a cement death which abuts it on every side. All this monstrosity in a small town where the men wear berets and the women have moustaches . . .

What's going on? 10 years ago San Giovanni, famous for its crafts and costumes, would still have been wonderful. Now it is utterly utterly destroyed — through some gruesome miscegenation between government subsidy and mafia opportunism? There is madness afoot, an insane lust and active ignorance, a mental cancer externalised. Something loathsome has been allowed — indeed encouraged — to go berserk here. There is not the slightest evidence anywhere of even a vestigial civic pride. All is mutilation, greed, hopelessness. San Giovanni in Fiore is the Devil's Town. We have to get out of it. We have to escape . . . .

. . . . Wild irises and orchids, foxgloves, and a smell of pines so sweet that it could almost be roses. Reduced patches of snow glint on the mountaintops which are not high enough to prevent trees growing right up to the crests. The torrenti are dry but their beds are moist and full of flowers. Between the forests are sweeps of meadow filled with more flowers — pink, white, yellow, blue. Occasionally tough little packhorses can be observed bringing up logs from the steeper gulleys. Pine cones bounce off the roof of the car and a large bird of prey flaps across the scene from right to left.

At Lorica is an artificial lake with straggling tourist installations built from corrugated iron. All are closed and I'm the only car on the road — mercifully this is neither the ski season nor the summer

season. It is surprising that in such a district, whose forests have been
famous ever since the ancients came here for ship-building materials,
there developed no wood-based architecture. Occasionally one finds
a hut with split-trunk walls. Otherwise the only decent buildings
are Mussolini's case cantoniere, government staging posts which are
abandoned now and form ruins in leafy spots. The absence of old
buildings, the sensation of there being nothing here except tourists,
nature and government departments, gives the Sila an oddly unreal
quality. Is this what a national park is in Italy? A rural terrain set aside
for tourist development? Parts of the Sila are truly lovely, with space and
peace and wild hyacinths, but you cannot drive for long without coming
across these gauche holiday developments and hoardings promoting
them. That which is exploited cannot have magic. The precondition
for magic is integrity.

Now descending out of the Sila by a quiet serpentine road – and I
can already feel the heat and pressure of the lowland Mediterranean
rising to meet me. The population thickens, the traffic grows, and one
is aware of space and peace being left behind, of the world crowding
in again. Where we rejoin the motorway at Grimaldi, the landscape
is stunning, soaring erratic hills covered with a variety of trees and a
river looping between. This is a backdrop by Altdorfer. But rapture
dies as we enter another territory of mafia exploitation with its hideous
environmental effects. This is at its worst along the coast where the
beach is sensational and the ribbon development resembles bomb sites.
For some reason nothing is ever finished down here and this, coupled
with the lack of any effective planning laws, gives rise to the visual
equivalent of mafia violence and corruption. It would appear that one
is driving through a society that is preyed upon by a savagery of which
it is both the source and victim.

Pull into a petrol station to fill up and buy a bottle of chilled fruit
juice to wash away the taste of vicious devastation. A few withered
snacks are on sale. A monk in grey habit, duffelbag over his shoulder,
wants to hitch a ride to Sicily. His tonsure needs redoing. It's grown
to crewcut length inside and out. I suppose he is about 25 and speaks
excellent English but his beard is either scurvy or clogged with crumbs,
I can't make out which. He is barefoot, smells, and holds his body
in a vile supplicating posture. I want nothing to do with him, so say
I'm not going to Sicily. In fact I'm heading for Tropea about which
I've heard very little except that it's the end of the line; and passing
one Belsen-on-Sea after another, I wonder what I'm letting myself in
for. Uscita di Tropea. The Calabrian Riviera is a cement disaster,
treeless, unfinished, neglected, uninhabited and desolate in the bright
afternoon sun. Are we supposed to join the travel brochure conspiracy

and pretend all this shit is pure heaven? It's tragic. But the sea is a remarkable, shaming blue.

And Tropea, when finally I reach it, isn't at all tragic. It's captivating, a little Firbankian Mediterranean dream-come-true, the last stop of a single railway line which reaches it via a brick viaduct on high arches. The town is perched operatically on a rock above the sea. Arcaded buttresses run down the rockface, giving Tropea the appearance of flying upwards. My hotel, La Pineta, is beneath the rock, modern, simple, behind pines. It is opposite what used to be described as the whitest beach in Italy, but they are digging up the beach to build a Grade IV port. Then the yachts will arrive and the place will become very modish, sister to Saint Tropez and Marbella. But for the moment it is adorably itself.

The men who run the hotel are noticeably conscious of their dignity. There are no porters and they just sit there as I struggle in with my bags. One of them continues rigidly to watch television, terrified of losing caste by showing me the slightest consideration. Having checked in, I then stagger up to Room 15 which has a view of the town on its rock and overlooks the garden of the art deco town hall, il Preventorio, next door. This cute building has a squat clocktower with stylised gothic arcaded cornice and a small bellcot on top bearing the cross of Lorraine. Purple bougainvillaea surround the gate to the municipal garden and palm trees form a curved lattice of fronds across my window, completing the synthesis of elegance and exoticism. As I look, *Ave Maria* exudes from loudspeakers up in the town which disperse a fine spray of sentiment over the locality. Church bells begin to chime and there is clamour during the sun's final bloodred surge. At night the town is floodlit, but a portion of the floodlights is faulty and flashes on and off at uneven intervals, putting one in mind of Count Dracula's castle.

To-night is a double first on this trip: the first time it has been so hot that I've sweated naked under a single sheet and the first time I've been bothered by the drone of a prowling mosquito. There is a spray-on concoction, bought in France, to keep them off – but it doesn't work. Turn on the bedside light, squirt more repellant on wrists and neck, turn out the light, try sweating to sleep but the mosquito comes screaming back, so I turn on the light, take a deep breath and think. First thought: why does this Italian mosquito so much like this French repellant? A gecko, with blunt head and endearing goggle eyes, adheres to the wall, immobile up near the ceiling. Second thought: how long does it take a gecko to catch a mosquito? Geckos have colossal patience. I haven't and search for the mosquito along the white walls. Nothing. However I'm the only source of hot red blood hereabouts so if I sit still and wait the mosquito will be back. Third and fourth thoughts: does the gecko have blood which the mosquito wants and, if not, how does he catch the insect? . . . . . Yes, here it is. The whining buzz somewhere near. It stops. A black fleck catches the eye, yes, it's landed on the sheet very near, very visible. The mosquito has a beautiful design, graceful curve of legs, back, wings, nozzle. It is like the Concorde but more soigné. Slam *An Unprotected Female at the Pyramids* by Anthony Trollope (from which I have learned that the plural of 'dragoman' is 'dragomans') down on the bed! Which makes a cherry red smear across the sheet. Probably my blood. The gecko is still frozen on the wall in exactly the same position, its tail curved in a poseur's arc.

At 7 a.m. a motor saw outside the window cuts through my brains. They are tidying up the municipal garden. I've hardly slept, look terrible, puffy eyes, creased face, and already the throb of the day's heat is pressing on the temples. After breakfast, swimming seems the only plausible reviver. At 9.30 a.m. the air is sizzling and, walking past the Grade IV port-to-be and a few jocose fishing boats painted green, red, blue, I discover a long beach below shallow cliffs entirely unmolested by developers, with a single wooden shack among the cactus selling soft drinks and beer and the tinkle of goats grazing on the rocky slopes behind. There are several wonky trees for shade. A goatherd squats under one, reading a newspaper, and beyond him along the golden strand there can be no more than half a dozen sun worshippers tucked between rocks. No tar here – very unusual on a Mediterranean beach and this will change when the port opens. The sea is emerald green near the shore where the bed is of white sand, becoming rich blue further out. The water is silky and chill and afterwards I sunbathe – mmm . . . don't have to move, do I? Don't have to go to Sicily, do I? Temples, palaces, the black lake, the golden city lie ahead – but can I not linger here? Tropea is beguiling . . . although the people aren't giving. I haven't made a personal connection, haven't had a good rap since Naples, and to-morrow night I'll be with Von in Taormina, so no, I shan't stay here. Let's briefly look at Tropea town, then be off . . .

At about 4.30 p.m. I leave the hotel and slowly mount the steep staircase up the rock to Tropea proper. The ascent is thickly populated with lizards which are bellicose and cannibalistic and hardly give over fighting each other, eating each other, in order to avoid my tread. At the top, gasping and dripping, one is rewarded by a miniature city overlooked by a miniature cathedral. Small palazzi lining the streets are enhanced by natural decay. Monumental doorways bearing swags, grotesques, lions' heads or conch shells are mostly closed but some lead into secret courtyards. In the via Boiano the smell of soap and ironing perfumes the shade. A woman of extreme corpulence sits outside on a stool, chin propped on palm, knees well apart, exposing her knickers and mega thighs which look as if made from a hanging accumulation of pale uncooked dumpling. Her blue eyes follow me but she doesn't smile. Blue eyes are not uncommon here, a greyish greenish blue but not vague, a sharkskin blue. A group of girls lean from a window in a gothic tower, pointing at me and giggling, and in the Piazza Galluppi old men are already settling into café chairs for a good evening's ogle. From one of these cafés a disco version of *Ave Maria* (Gounod's of course, as was the previous) jumps into the street, Stromboli can be seen from the Belvedere – a boy points in its direction for me but there's nothing, only heat haze. Beneath the Belvedere the sea is a virulent green. I have a sneezing fit and much fluid runs out of my nose. 'Oh, not a bloody cold, please God!', but it's a false alarm, it's trapped seawater from the sinus. One of the disadvantages of travelling alone is that one is more susceptible to false alarms.

Tropea with its dozen churches is built on a very shapely site and its builders have made the most of it, adorning the rock and nearby slopes with uncommon felicity. This dramatic yet casual disposition of buildings is visible because, astonishingly, the enclosing landscape has not been destroyed. Tropea retains an integrity which indeed is strengthened by the few hotels and gentle villas occupying the immediate vicinity, since these express its later function as resort without coarsening it. The new port makes change inevitable but if it's intelligent Tropea could develop from a sleepy gem into a smart gem: Saint Tropea. However the evidence elsewhere in southern Italy suggests this will not happen. The locals are more than eager to offer up their town for immediate profit. The very idea of protecting the coastline is a joke to them and even if it weren't, probably unenforceable in a region where bribery and corruption and violence are the only ways of making things happen. Already, with the sensitivity of a drunken ape, a row of holiday flats has been dumped on the brow of an adjacent hill. Goodbye, Tropea.

Spend the last petrol coupon and meander to motorway – Reggio 93 kilometres but for the ferry across the Straits of Messina we want Villa San Giovanni just before. Orange, lemon and almond groves either side of the road are having jets of water shot through them and hills ripple into the distance. The countryside all the way down Italy has been very green, much lusher than Provence for example, and this southern extremity is no less so. As one approaches the toe of Italy, the route becomes truly a marvel. Viaducts, each as breathtaking as that at Genoa, appear to pierce with a series of tunnels the mountains which drop greenly into the sea. You fly out of a tunnel to overhang the water many hundreds of feet up, Scylla and Charybdis flanking the perilous Straits of Messina, and Sicily opposite like a mountainous dream, girt with a strip of white sand. Then blackout, another tunnel – dazzle, another debouchment into the pellucid empyrean. Despite the almost complete absence of traffic, concentration on the flexing road is essential and close to impossible. The car has been given wings and the soul too soars up in a vigorous euphoria which somehow renders one both disembodied and intensely conscious. Never before have I travelled such a road. The skill of its construction, the sleek ultramodernity of its passage through an immense landscape of ancient myth replete with stories from Greeks and Romans, yet strangely still and untroubled, make this one of the peerless European experiences.

It isn't easy to find the correct channel for the ferry. Confusing signs. The car judders to a halt in a short queue of 3 cars – one of my wheel balances has come off. The port area smells of piss and it's hot on the tarmac. I'm in shorts and loose shirt. How can the Italians wear blue denim jeans – and most of them do – in this heat? The 2 biggest pylons I've ever seen, like a pair of Eiffel Towers painted red and white, carry power across the Straits, but one cannot discern at this distance the cables strung between. Messina on the far side, much earthquaked, much bombarded, much arisen, birthplace of Juvara (who dedicated a book of drawings to Lord Burlington), stretches along a sandspit looking as though it might vanish beneath the waves any second; and behind it on cliffs of rock rises the mass of Sicily. The superbness of it sends a tremor through the limbs.

Eventually we board. The first sign is one which says in 4 languages that locking of cars is forbidden on this ferry. You must be joking, mate – I do as the locals do and ignore the rules in the interests of self-preservation. The second sign reads *To the lifeboats*. Useful. The Straits of Messina is the most accident-prone waterway in the world. Many small craft plough back and forth and the currents are devilish. As the engines shudder into life my excitement becomes tinged with apprehension. A Sicilian is asking me to swop cigarettes – my English for his local – but I don't have any. On the deck below, an old man is playing on a peasant flute. Already on this boat I'm aware of a more far-flung racial mix than on the mainland, and of an alive chemistry and intelligence after the dourness, the dullness of the Calabrians. A couple of Sicilian boys say hullo. The bigger boy asks me where I'm going.

'Taormina.'

'Oh, that's easy. Just turn left when you land. Ciao.'

He gives me a small hug with one arm and they both disappear. How sweet. In this more alert milieu even my Italian seems better. Yes, I'm excited! Dying to see Von and talk about everything! But more – something strange, intoxicating, ancient is bearing me away.

Messina slowly, hoveringly, approaches like a prehistoric space city, and behind it row upon row of pastel-coloured mountains. They rise very rapidly from the coast with a billowing movement and seem as high as the Andes. The ferry crashes into the wharf.

10
Taormina

One's first impression of Sicily was the lack of roadsigns, so I aimed to the left as the boys had advised and arrived in Taormina quite quickly. Now I am sitting on a large double bed in one of the most beautiful rooms in the world, chuckling away.

The drive from Messina was via a new motorway with mountains up on right so there wasn't much to see except prickly pears along the roadside and down on the left water which wasn't blue but the colour of fog. Taormina is built high above the Ionian Sea on mountain ledges, Inca-style, and the motorway delivered the car right into the centre of it via twirling viaducts on concrete posts sullied with large spray-can graffiti, at which point the feed road contracted abruptly into narrow toytown streets and I went completely wrong.

The plan was to head for the Timeo, then contact Von whom I'm dying to see – probably said that before. Back in London Keith Raffan had said 'You must stay at the Timeo because it's the old hotel of Taormina and hasn't been done up and is wonderfully pretty and cheap and there's a super garden with views, well, everything in Taormina has views, but you can get a room with a balcony and the food's quite good, not sensational but hotel food never is usually, but there are lots of restaurants and the thing I like about it is the peeling paint is pink and very 20s, you'll see what I mean, but now I've got to go the House and vote!' Then he repeated everything he'd said but in a different order. Like all good modern MPs, Keith can run on empty when he gets going.

The Timeo it transpired was almost inaccessible to motor vehicles but the car just managed it, knocking a plate which I had to pay for off the outside wall of a souvenir shop, only to discover that the hotel was closed – for renovations and general tarting up. Goodbye, Timeo. So the car reversed, tremulously avoiding those plates, and took the via Circonvallazione to allow for an interval of brow mopping. Yes, the ring road, which sounded quite large but was tiny like everything else here. But it could be driven along without plates being struck off walls and sometimes one even got up into third gear – which was the gear I was moving into when a 19th century gothic fantasy swooned into view. It was too batty to pass, so pulling over I investigated and discovered it was an hotel of sorts, more a boarding house. I struck the desk bell and eventually there was the muffled sound of several doors being opened in sequence, each nearer than the last, until a door at the back of the hall opened and there was – Aurora.

She clacked in on high mules, coughing, spluttering, smoking, gasping, small and slight, with pale brown skin, brownish eyes, hair and teeth the colour of tobacco juice. No, she didn't have a single room – and gave the sweetest smile. Cough splutter. Yes, there was a double room. Wheeze. She smelt of cologne and grappa. 40,000 lire per night. As usual in France and Italy, the price of the room stays the same no matter how many use it. She must've been about 60. Colazione 3000 lire extra. But if I wanted breakfast I had to say so the day before.

Could I see the room?

She unhooked a key and clacked coughingly off round a corner. Room Number 6. Double doors into the small hallway of a suite. Turn right into a cream bedroom with fittings and furniture in chocolate wood. It had a high ceiling making it very nearly a cube and was on a corner with lancet windows in 2 directions. Cream muslin curtains, falling almost the height of the room from wooden pelmets, blew softly in the afternoon breeze like the essence of virginity, as if made from pressed hymens. The windows and shutters were open. There was a side view onto the luxuriant garden next door but the main view was over Taormina with its playful gothic turrets, molar-shaped battlements and glass houses on rooftops. The windows in this direction were full-length and opened onto a small balcony of wrought-iron lancets from which Aetna was visible to the right. There was a bad oil painting of this volcano in the room. The other pictures were photographs of marble statues, including one of the Virgin. The coldness of marble extinguished the usual insipidity of this image and almost lent it nobility. In the middle of the room was a very large double bed. Bells came tinkling up from the cathedral on cue.

Back to the hallway and double doors led into the bathroom where all was white and old-fashioned especially the bath which was also very big, permitting a full extension of the legs with water left over.

'I'll take it.'

The place is called the Villa Isadora and looks as though it were once a grand private house. There are only a dozen or so letting rooms and I'm the only guest. I've stretched out on the bed, with hands behind my head, and find the situation so congenial that I keep breaking into chuckles and whoops of delight. I do a bit of unpacking and the coatrail collapses in the wardrobe. I ease off my shoes – tennis boots – hot blisters from driving in pumps. Run a bath and flush the loo, don't know why but a good job I did because all the water has drained out of the apparatus and none has refilled it. I go and find Aurora in the dining-room who buries a fag in the tilth of an ashtray beside the TV set, coughs and comes to the bathroom and says I must treat the mechanism come una vecchia signora because it's very old and she demonstrates and it works now. So after my crap I'm about to step into the bath when I realise there's no soap. I pull on some clothes and pad off to find Aurora but discover that the latch on the double doors out of the suite is stuck and I'm locked inside. So I set up a refined howling, whistling, hallooing, and I hear her clack towards the room and say to her through the door in my pidgin Italian that presumably the door is a vecchia signora too and she says yes, unlatches it somehow, and I ask for soap which she goes in search of and eventually returns with and by the time all this hoo-ha has happened I'm feeling very at home and happy. There's nothing like domestic calamities for getting one on Christian name terms. So I go back into the bathroom where the bath is filling up nicely with scalding water – yes, that's enough scalding water – really that's enough – Christ, the hot water tap has jammed *on*, so I run in cold hoping to cool it down sufficiently to enable me to put my hand in and extract the plug but now I have to turn off the cold because really it's getting too full – what can I do now? It will overflow any second. Calm, calm. Adopt the vecchia signora principle, grasp the burning hot tap with a cold flannel and delicately vary the pressures around it until, moments before disaster . . . I detect a . . . giving, and off, it's turned. Too full to get in, too hot to remove plug, so wander to the window overlooking the garden where a young gardener unzips his fly, pees, looks up perchance and grins in mild embarrassment. Go into the bedroom to sort out money, a necessary and pleasurable task at every major stop. There's Caravaggio with his tremendous, thick-lipped sneer. And Bellini's much less obvious face, a luminous face, childlike, intelligent, feminine, boyish all at once.

The last time I spoke to Von was from France and she said she'd be arriving at the Hotel Villa Kristina about now. I said I'd be arriving about now too but would play the accommodation by ear since the Kristina came as part of a package tour and I didn't. I ring now and discover she's been there for 2 days. What's more, the hotel is only a few hundred yards up the road and round the bend. At the Kristina reception I ask for Miss Whiteman. The manager opens his eyes wide and says 'Oh yes . . .' He contacts the room, handing over the receiver through which a voice says 'Io io Pan! Come up, *do* come up! I want to show you something! Io io Pan!'

She's in one of her excited states. We kiss and embrace with mighty hug, and red of face and arms, dressed in a terracotta shift, she drags me across the room to the balcony, saying 'Look, look, look!' It is Aetna, slopes of, the crest lost in cloud. The crags about us are covered with small square concrete villas and flats from the horizontal railed rooftops of which Alsatian dogs leap up and down, barking frantically at each other, an aerial community of hate.

'Have *you* got a view of Aetna?' she enquires.

'If I crane.'

'And look!' She pushes me into the bathroom, indicating a bottle of Veuve Clicquot wallowing in water in the washbasin. 'We've got a pool. That's where I was when you rang first. Have *you* got a pool?'

'No. It's a sort of private house.'

'You can use ours. We get meals. Do you get meals?'

'No, but I get breakfast if I tell them before.'

'You can eat here if you like. I should eat here because it's all in. I've brought your post from London.'

'Wonderful! I'll take you out for dinner.'

'Oh, jolly japes!' This comes in inverted commas. Oxonians put inverted commas round a great many of their expressions.

Taormina was founded in 396 BC by refugees from the Greek colony of Naxos nearby. The resort prospered on tuberculosis. *The winter, especially on the coast, is very mild, so that the island in general and Palermo in particular are becoming more and more resorted to by delicate persons and phthisis patients. At Taormina the influx of strangers begins as early as the second half of January. The mean temp. of the island in Jan. is 51.4° Fahr.* (from *Baedeker*).

The majority of tourists now are German and Von's tour operator said 'If you wanna job here you gotta speak German.' In the main square, which has one side overlooking a steep drop to the sea, tourists sit around at evening in the cafés, stunned by the day's sun, staring out at the young men of the town who parade up and down singly, in couples or groups, laughing, playing with each other, staring in. This playful strutting curiosity of the male is found here to a greater extent than anywhere else in Italy and is at first rather oppressive and has a counterproductive effect. There seems to be no interaction between foreign tourists and Sicilians. I've never been in a place with so much ostentatious soliciting and so little actually happening. It makes Saint Tropez by comparison a very casual, easy affair.

The best shop in the world is on the Corso Umberto. It's called

Ginger and is located in an ancient and abandoned gothic stone church. Purple, green and red neon pours out into the night through the filigree of windows and door. It sells trendy clothes but what it sells isn't the point. This shop is sculpture, not a place to buy things. Von picks up a top and puts it down. She asks the assistant if there's somewhere she can pee – women always need somewhere to pee – and then we find somewhere to eat, a pretty restaurant in a garden off the main dragette. Seated under a tree with fairy lights I start to open my post.

'That one looks interesting,' she says.

It's from a Welsh transsexual asking me if I can help her get her novel published.

'The local prawns are supposed to be extra sweet because of the special algae in Taormina bay,' Von continues, shaking her mass of long wavy henna-red hair.

'I expect pollution's finished that off.'

'Anyway I don't want prawns to-night. I want something *big*! Did you stop at Paris on the way down? I want to go up Aetna. *Right* up. And we must see the Greek Theatre. And there's a valley of temples at Agri . . . at Agri-gin-whatever the place's called. Tell me about Noto.'

'Later.'

'And about that horrible Black Lake.'

'Later.'

'Noto sounds Japanese.'

'I know. And Taormina sounds Chinese.'

We are pulling in slightly different directions. She's just arrived in the Mediterranean and wants to gorge on food and ruins. I've already done a lot of that and want to gorge on people.

'I think those von Gloeden postcards of naked boys in all the shops are wonderful! Though none with erections,' she adds ruefully. 'I think Greek vases are the only public art to have portrayed the erect penis – not on satyrs or gods or pornography or as phallus cult objects – but on men and boys, on *people*.'

Oh well, perhaps she does want to gorge on people after all.

'Can you imagine the rumpus if someone tried to sell those postcards in Oxford Street? And another thing I want to do is find Aleister Crowley's Abbey of Thelema at Cefalù.'   •

'Yes, for that one, you're on,' I say.

'Oh, JG! *Cefalù* sounds Hawaiian, doesn't it?'

'Perhaps we're not pronouncing it right.'

Throughout the conversation we keep breaking into helpless giggles, accompanied by clinks from the mass of heavy gilt jewellery she's supporting. Great jokes are not being cracked. It must simply be delight in each other's company. There is something ludicrous about our being here.

'Do you think it's a good idea to move into my hotel?'

'No. Because I've fallen in love with the Villa Isadora.'

'Try some of this *heavenly* goo,' she commands, pushing a spoonful of her pudding into my mouth.

Normally my orientation is good but for the first few days higgledy-piggledy Taormina confounds it. But one morning we do reach the Greek Theatre which is red brick with plenty of reconstruction, graffiti cut into the cactuses and hairnets round the rocks. The view through it is one of the world's most celebrated; a number of hills descend from Aetna on the right to the sea on the left. Whoever contrives these things has placed a string of small pylons across the centre.

At noon there is a terrific racket. Church bells, barking dogs. Not sweet bells but fast furious clangs on 2 notes only. Cannons go off with a flat boom. In the afternoon a number of carved and painted carts, drawn by fantastically caparisoned horses, parade down the Corso. Tourists gobble their ice-cream cornets in order to take up their cameras. Plumes tremble as with stiffened front legs the horses begin to slide on polished lava down the shallow gradient of the street. In each cart is a band of 3, 4, sometimes 5 players: accordion, flute, tambourine, boom-boom drum. They wear black trousers and waistcoats, white shirt, red scarves, red cummerbunds. The flutes have an especially tender tone of Peruvian character. We applaud with the other tourists, then visit the town library which is housed in a deconsecrated church on the main piazza. Having been based on the old British Subscription Library which existed here until the Second World War, it has mostly English titles. *Through Persia on Sidesaddle* by Ella C. Sykes, *Kashmir in Sunlight and Shade* by C. E. Tindale-Biscoe, M.A. Ah, those were the days, when an author might place 'M.A.' after his name and be not abashed. The British influence was long sustained hereabouts by the Viscounts Bridport, descended from Admiral Nelson's brother. Lord Nelson was given a large estate at Bronte 40 minutes west of Taormina by Ferdinand IV and the family maintained it until 1981 when the current Viscount Bridport, alias Duke of Bronte, sold it to the Italian Government for £2 million. William Sharp, alias Fiona Macleod, is buried at Bronte. Equally surprisingly, Samuel Butler is buried at Calatafimi on the other side of the island. Edmund John, the English poet, is buried in Taormina's protestant cemetery. Dylan Thomas's widow, Caitlin, lives somewhere on the east coast here.

Breakfast, which finally I've got the hang of, is brought to me in

solitary state in the dining-room by Riccardo. He is 24 with round
dark eyes, semi-circular eyebrows which convey an air of bewilderment,
short black curls and a cheeky alertness which is neither Arab nor
Spanish but from the Ancient Greeks, He knows he is handsome but
is prevented from being cocksure by an underlying anxiety expressed
in nervous or aggressive hand movements. He says he is paid very
little for this work 'but my wife works so it's not a problem. Did you
sleep well?'

'No.'

'Neither did I. My little son wouldn't stop crying. So I've learned
to sleep with a pillow over my head and now my wife complains
"But I can't see you, Riccardo!" You have a nice car.' They miss
nothing. Later he surprises me by telling me my age – it dawns on
me that he's memorised every detail in my passport while it was
lodged at the desk for registration. 'How do you find it, driving on
the right-hand side?'

'Fine. Except where a viaduct curves outwards. Then it seems
there's nothing between you and the air.'

'Yes, I know, because I was a passenger when my friend drove on
the viaducts of the Cosenza-Crotone road. I hated it. Do you want
breakfast to-morrow?'

'Yes, every day. I'll pay for it even if sometimes I don't sleep here.
Do you do laundry?'

'No, but there's one in the Piazza del Duomo. By the fountain. I
have to do something downstairs now. See you later.'

Return to room for a bowel movement. I'm gradually becoming
acquainted with the vecchia signora. Occasionally I have to remove
the lid and manipulate the innards to precipitate a flushing. And there
is a knack to the handle which I'm beginning to comprehend. The bidet
however functions like a cool dream. All of which is accomplished, with
hands washed and towelled, by the time Von arrives.

'I'm falling in love with this room too,' she says, spreadeagling
on the bed. 'It reminds me of Oxford. It is like being in a picture
that's on the wall of a room in Oxford. Are you ready for the beach?
Guess what.'

'What?'

'Aetna's making impressive growlings. God, I'd love a blow-off!'

The beaches beneath Taormina are reached by a funicular and are
not very good. The best are at Letoianni where there's also a chiesa
Cristiana Evangelica (one sometimes sees them in Italy; they usually
look like shops). But all the beaches have a road, a railway and now a
motorway along the back of them. Whereas the beach boys in France
are solicitous, agreeable and earn plenty of tips, the beach boys here are

a gloomy lot. They show you to a deckchair, put up your umbrella, and that's it – they sit all day long ignoring the clients. Even creepier – no fee is charged for the use of these items. So what's the form? To get something for nothing in a tourist town gives one a strange sense of unease. Unalloyed jollity quickly becomes inane and one isn't asking for that, but the sullenness among the beach boys amounts almost to resentment of holidaymakers.

'Oh, don't keep on,' says Von, 'I'm sure it's just part of their Sicilian inferiority complex.'

'But we didn't pay to come in and we haven't paid to use these things – I'm sure they'll sting us later.'

'Your shorts are that grey with a bit of green in it.'

'Chewing-gum grey.'

'Some grey has blue in it which is a different sort of grey.'

'Then of course there's grey. Black and white mixed.'

'Oh yes, there's always that,' she says. 'Ennui grey. I haven't done my bikini line. Does it look dreadful?'

'Not absolutely dreadful.'

We move on to hair in armpits. She shaves hers. When she came back from Greece it had grown and her mother told her to get rid of it because it looked like dirt. 'And another thing – when I press my navel I can feel it right down into my vagina. I told my mother about it and she said she could too. This is the sort of thing that's never mentioned in books. Do you know what's best for sunburnt skin? Bleach. Heinz dabbed it on me – and I didn't feel a thing. This sun isn't hot enough for me.'

'The sea's cold.'

'It's a funny colour. Ash grey, tin grey, cadaver grey. It's a very *arcane* sea, don't you think?'

But the sky is blue and out of it large heavy drops of rain begin to fall. Where is the rain coming from? Verily a mystery. It falls faster and faster, vertically, and all the Italians stream for cover in the café, aghast at the merest touch of rain. But the weather clears later for the Assumption of the Virgin Festival in Taormina where a waiter picks up a chair and pushes it up under an awning to shift the water which has collected in a deep sag. A blue virgin is paraded through the streets on a large ball of pink roses to the accompaniment of brass bands. Schoolchildren in black smocks hold gladioli and lilies. At night shells explode in the sky and many firecrackers are thrown sputting down the stepped alleyways. In the Piazza del Duomo I say 'That laundry over there is bloody expensive,' and she asks 'When can we go to the Abbey of Thelema?'

I'm up early, having slept well, and surprise Aurora in the dining-room desperately screwing the top back on a gin bottle, looking round

at me with mouth full and a drop of spirit on her lip. Bosford Extra
Dry Gin. Prodotto Italiano.

She swallows – and sings 'Buon giorno! I get Riccardo.' Cough
splutter.

Who saunters in wearing a freshly ironed salmon shirt. 'Gin gin
gin,' he mutters up at the ceiling.

'I hope you slept better.'

'No,' he replies. 'I had terrible toothache. I took many pills but
they don't help. I often get it.' His beautiful face is creased.

'Why don't you have the tooth out?'

'I'm frightened of the injection. I faint with fear. And the pain has
now spread to 3 teeth. I take Novagin. You mustn't take too much
because it's bad for the heart but I took more than twice the maximum
dose yesterday.'

'But you look marvellous this morning.'

'I feel terrible.'

'Is there anything round here I should see?'

'The rocks of Alcantara are very beautiful. I show you if you like.'

'Let's go to-morrow if the weather doesn't clear up.'

Aurora clacks back in, her coughing calmer and more regular, her
sweet smile working to perfection and without a trace of irony. She
wants to show me her drawing-room, the salone. It is large and divided
from the dining-room by a brown wood screen incorporating coloured
glass panels of flowers in vases. Without this screen the huge pillared
salone of the original house would be restored. Aurora's half contains
bizarre and flimsy ornaments in pewter and silver plate, reproduction
antique furniture, and delicate gold lace curtains the height of the
room. Against the screen stands a black upright piano in the Art
Nouveau style with a pair of candelabra holding 4 red candles fixed
to its front and a faded album of old songs written by her father
propped above the open, waiting keyboard. Despite a patterned 50s
carpet, the atmosphere is 1920. Pre-Mussolini. I stand there repeating
'bellissimo' while Aurora purrs.

The sirocco brings stodgy, oppressive weather, with bursts of torrential rain clearing into misty heat. Von has found a cheaper, friendlier
laundry, the Lavanderia Primavera, near her hotel. Antonio who runs
it gave us aperitifs before lunch and Von did the splits on the floor.
She says it's the first time she's ever done the splits in a laundry.
Antonio can't speak English but his uncle lives in Staffordshire.
Another load of banging: dogs, church bells, cannon fire. At the
beach the steam rising off the lava rocks has a pungent metallic and
vegetable smell. A violent storm finally breaks, the sky collapses on
to roads made for maximum puddlisation and we return to the Villa

Isadora where multiple thunderclaps mix with the sound of church bells. The storm-over-the-bay electrifies the blood and irritates the nerves. I play the *Gurrelieder* very loudly on the radio cassette machine and cry. There is something about Sicily which works directly on the emotions. Early impression of Sicilians: they're crazy. This is an enormous relief. They could've been horribly straight and severe. They live closely together, always communicating with each other – but from their surfaces only, rarely committing themselves from their depths. In this, not in a reticence of behaviour, lies their reserve. They love to play games and derive a tremendous kick from successfully hoodwinking another.

Riccardo has recommended a restaurant, the Papyrus, run by a friend of his. 'You get special deal if you go.' I don't see why we should and am prepared for a dead-end experience but the food is delicious, simple but prepared to perfection, and one recipe is sensational: pasta alla Papyrus: sauce of olives, tomatoes, basil, coriander. The pasta is in the form of large short tubes known as rigatoni.

'I'm glad it wasn't spaghetti, I can't eat spaghetti,' confides Von who has quite a collection of these little rules. 'Go on, tell me how stupid I am, but I think of *worms*. Have you seen any snakes? I've been dying to see one – but haven't been vouchsafed the pleasure.' With inverted commas.

'Is that a serpent's head on your chain?' Von has a number of metal talismans hanging round her neck, as well as heavy bangles on her arm.

'No, it's a penis. Are you hoping to find anything at Noto?'

'One's always hoping. Hoping is a kind of disease. But in a sense, it's just an excuse for this drive, isn't it? Do you know *Ithaca* by Cavafy?'

'Noto is such a weird name.'

'There's lots of weird names in Sicily. Gangi for example. One I found on the map the other day – Rampingalotto.'

'Oh, I'd love to go there!'

That night Von suffered an excess of vibrations so I gave her an all-over massage, returning to the Villa Isadora very late. Aurora watches endless television in the dining-room, plays endless Patience, endlessly smokes cigarettes and endlessly tipples – she's never drunk, only a little high – never moves from the villa but prowls smilingly and dazedly about it, full of the past, sustained by memory. To-night she has fallen asleep with her head on the dining-table and the television-set utters an end-of-transmission roar. I have asked for a key but she says it's not a problem. Scop's owl in the vicinity adds its odd whirring call. At least, I've been told by a resident of Fentiman Road, Vauxhall, that this uncanny Mediterranean nightnoise is attributable to the Scop's owl, but have been unable to verify it.

In the morning there is high-tech luggage in the hall, grips of ribbed rubber, and I say 'I'm not the only guest now.'

'It's a couple from Turin,' says Riccardo, 'but they stay only 1 night.'

'Shall we go to the rocks to-day?'

The original intention was to go during bad weather but in fact it's a fine day after the storm and Aetna, whose upper parts are normally concealed by cloud and smoke, exposes her snow-smeared crown. At lunchtime I collect Riccardo who is scarcely recognisable since the shorts and sunglasses into which he's changed have altered his entire aspect. The rocks line the gorge of the Alcantara river with sculpturesque formations at a location 15 minutes inland. We bolt a lunch there, buy tickets, choose waders and take the lift down to the river. The river is high but after a moment's consideration, during which Riccardo worries about the consequences of getting the tummy cold and wet so soon after eating, we pull off our waders and trousers and plunge forward against the stream, barefoot and in underpants. For 10 minutes we make slow but creditable headway until the rain-swollen torrent and the rockiness of the riverbed make further advance inadvisable at a point just short of the bend round which the sculpturesque formations begin; and so, having seen nothing phenomenal, though well exercised, we return to the car parked above in a secluded spot and remove all our clothes, setting them to dry in the sun. I notice that Riccardo has slightly fleshy nipples. It is a Sicilian characteristic, he says, for men to put on weight first at the breasts. Sometimes he breast-feeds his son with one to keep him quiet. He shows me his knife which slides horizontally into his belt and is thus hidden. It has no blade, only a sharp steel point a few inches long.

'You have to be careful in Sicily,' he says. 'The latest trick in Catania is for some scooter boys to make a little accident in front of your car and when you stop to help they rob you.'

We pull over at a café in Giardini Naxos and whenever a girl walks past it's incumbent on Riccardo to cluck or coo or hiss or whistle or yell or make any of a number of other non-verbal noises at her, whereupon he turns back to our conversation as if there'd been no interruption, as if nothing had happened – and of course nothing has happened. He polishes off my flask of whisky and I say 'Let's go.'

At the villa, Aurora asks 'Un buon bagno?' which is invariably her greeting regardless of where I've been. A wheeze and a cough collide in her fragile torso and while she's involved in a minor paroxysm I notice over her shoulder David Niven's typical expression on the TV, a combination of superciliousness and surprise. His voice is dubbed into Italian with a marked English accent, a form of pronunciation known as 'Stan & Olly' (from the Laurel & Hardy films which are immensely popular here) and which causes all Italians to die of mirth.

At night I tell Von of my trip to the rocks and she says, vis-à-vis nothing I can discern, 'You have a profound contempt for women.'

What have I done now?

First Sunday after Trinity, June 1st. Corpus Domini Parade. Everyone very dressed up, even the Chief of Police who wears a comic-opera tailcoat with epaulettes, pavement-scraping sword, and all the trimmings. At night Castel Mola explodes with aerial bombs and star shells. My stool was very together when I arrived in Taormina. This is no longer the case.

Riccardo is strange with me too.

'Riccardo?'

'Yes?'

'You know that drug and sex fiend I was telling you about? The Englishman?'

'Yes.' He tucks one foot behind the other and nervously rubs the knob of a chairback.

'Well, can you help me find his abbey at Cefalù? My Italian's not up to it.'

'Maybe.'

'To-morrow?'

'No.'

'Dopo domani?'

'Maybe.'

This simple outing grows complicated. When on the following day I explain that I'm bringing Von he looks down in the mouth; and on the day of departure he refuses to come unless he's allowed to bring along a Norwegian piece he's managed to find. 'It would be OK the 2 of us,' he explains, 'but you have someone, so I must have someone also. Otherwise we are not equal.'

Sicilians can make a drama out of anything – this is exciting or draining according to your mood.

Von has discovered from Nicky Hall, her tour operator, that a Professore Pietro Saia has written a book about Aleister Crowley's period in Cefalù and she has his phone number. With much gesticulation and pleading Riccardo is persuaded to try the number but the professore isn't at home – his wife explains he's a schoolmaster at the local school and will be back later. We decide to drive to Cefalù and hunt.

His 'Abbey of Thelema' idea (and name) Crowley took from Rabelais, likewise his motto: Do what thou wilt shall be the whole of the law. Is there *anything* original in Crowley? No, he's a genuine charlatan, and a remarkable character. His ostentations are irresistible, indeed courageous when set against the attitudes of his time. Having dressed up and invoked various gods and goddesses in London, he went to Cefalù, took a cottage overlooking the town and founded his 'abbey' therein in 1919. He wrote a fictional account of it in *The Diary of a Drug Fiend*. The titles of his books are always more promising than their contents are rewarding, e.g. *Of Eroto-Comatose Lucidity*. The activities at the abbey, including many varieties of sex-magic and inebriation, became notorious and in 1924 he was expelled by Mussolini.

Riccardo suggests we go to Cefalù via the motorway as this will be quicker, thus affording our first experience of the Sicilian interior which stuns us with its gyrating beauty. A want of trees is noticeable, as are the peculiar shapes of hills and crags and the absence of inhabitation. Furry heat flows in through the open windows. In the back Riccardo and his Norwegian, Odrun, are snorting powder – he becomes a little loud while she remains red, chubby and tranquil. 'I am a student,' she says, 'and I begin my studies in October at Oslo University. I am happy to come with you to-day.'

Von turns round and explains with painstaking care why this fun pilgrimage is very much part of her Sicilian experience, how life is a kind of stenography which only some can read, how Crowley had a lot of things against him but probably even more things going for him, after which Odrun, clearly nonplussed, repeats 'Yes, I am happy to come with you to-day.'

On the outskirts of Cefalù we halt at the Bar Galizzi for coffee and arancini (savoury rice balls, a toothsome speciality of the island), and after a double whisky Riccardo once more phones the professore who is now at home. The professore, not at all convinced of our good intentions, reluctantly explains that the abbey is a small cottage in the Portera district up the hill, owned by a woman from Palermo who rarely uses it. Riccardo rapidly absorbs another double whisky and we motor off to the Portera district, drive around in several circles, and stop outside a police station. Riccardo, now quite voluble, chats them up. They are most amused, say yes, they've heard something about this mad and beastly Englishman, and think it's *that* way. Odrun smiles and Von looks aroused. 'Yes, I'm *sure* it's *that* way,' she affirms, having sniffed the air and checked out the psychic data.

We continue up a hill of modern villas with the great rock to our left and stop the car at a small rudimentary stadium on the edge of town with a view north across the sea.

'I'm sure . . . we're close . . .' divines Von, after scanning several directions – her voice has acquired a hierophantic tone and she now looks decidedly hormonal. Followed by chubby Odrun, she makes off along a mudpacked path and disappears among wild shrubbery, in search of something, someone, a clue, a revelation, while Riccardo and I lean against the car, staring out to sea.

'Odrun has clearly come to Sicily to lose her virginity,' I say. 'Many girls don't want to begin university as virgins. It's too much of a weight.'

'She won't lose it with me,' he says to my surprise. 'Last night she begins to suck me, it's OK – then I lose the force. This happens these days. I used to have many girls. Now only with my wife. With her I can always make love. But with other girls I lose it. I wish it wasn't so.'

Although he demands fidelity from everyone else, the male finds his own fidelity shocking, upsetting, sinful, a trap to be fought against.

'It sounds as if you really love your wife.'

'Is that it?' He looks shy, thoughtful, amazed. 'But I'd like to be able to have others. I used to like older women because you can do different things with them, in the ear, in the trees, everything. You know, I'm very nervous to-day. This is the reason I have the whisky and the drug. I wanted it to be only the two of us, you and me.'

I'm touched by these confessions and give him a hug.

The girls trudge back. 'No luck,' says Von. 'It would help if we knew what we were looking for.'

'That's not a very occult remark. Can't you feel your way by vibration?'

'It's too hot. Is there any water left in the car?'

Odrun says 'We are looking for an old church, yes?' She's very red.

Riccardo boldly suggests knocking on the door of a nearby peasant dwelling but an old woman, bent at the waist, is already shuffling towards us across its garden and she asks 'Why have you come looking for this place? It's terrible. We hear ghosts at night. He took a local virgin and tortured her to death, a dreadful murder in the woods. At night sometimes we hear her screams. He was an *evil* man. Those 2 girls,' and she indicates Von and Odrun who have their heads cocked to one side, 'they could've been killed.'

'She says you could've been killed,' explains Riccardo.

'Why?'

'Because,' continues the crone through her several teeth, 'they went up that path. There's a mad dog up there. Very big.'

Despite all this discouragement, the hag points an accusing finger at the Abbey of Thelema which turns out to be a small traditional Sicilian cottage not far away in a large overgrown garden. Only its reddish rooftiles can be seen above the leaves. We turn back to thank her but she is already retreating. Von, flushed and enthralled, throws a loud British 'thank you' after her. The old gammer pauses, half turns as if she might've heard something, vanishes indoors.

The gate into Crowley's erstwhile garden is locked but the cottage nestles against a low ridge and perimeter wall by which access may be had. 'Coming in?' asks Von with a most unnerving leer and slips over the wall and down into undergrowth. Odrun and Riccardo won't follow. They return to the car, perhaps to essay another suck, although by this time Riccardo has very likely been discouraged from everything by the possibility of evil spirits. Like all bright cynical grown-up Sicilian boys he's extremely superstitious. But I follow and descending the wall find myself in a thorny thicket which breaks into long grass, rampant vines and gnarled olive trees. Below is the sea and the old town with the duomo sheltering beneath the great rock on which there is said to be a prehistoric house that the wandering Ulysses would've seen with his own eyes. And then of course the unsightly postwar accretions. If you can subtract these in your mind's eye, you will be able to grasp how sublime it was in 1919 – the magic of that.

The cottage is one storey with closed green shutters along the garden side, whitewashed walls, terrace with no porch, 3 steps down from a double front door, pink and red geraniums running wild. In a copse there is a tilted plinth of maroon, blue and white diamond tiles. Nothing stands on it. A battered suitcase and broken-down gas oven are sunk in grass. By the back entrance is an old door painted with a ghoulish grimace, perhaps one of the survivors of Crowley's invocatory decorations.

'Must have a photo of *that*,' declares Von, levelling her camera.

'It's the only Crowleyish relic.'

'There may be others. *Inside.*'

'No, Von.'

She tries a few shutters but they are secure and impenetrable.

'I don't feel at all threatened by anything, do you?'

'No,' she agrees, taking more photographs. 'The place has a good feeling.'

'Very good.'

Indeed it does. We sit in the bee-loud sunshine awhile, enjoying the secret sweetness and solace of the Abbey of Thelema.

Suddenly Von jumps to her feet, clenches her face, shouts 'Io io Pan! Io io Pan!' and laughs long in a high trailing ribbon of heartfelt gold.

We buy cherries and grapes before returning to the motorway and on the drive home the conversation grows ribald. We learn:

(1) The different words in Norwegian, English and Italian for fuck, penis, vagina. Sicilian for cock is 'ciolla' or something very like it. I commend the English slang 'to shag' – truly pagan and slightly horrible.

(2) How in my visits to straight saunas I have noticed that the Italians are less hypocritical than the English and will more freely look at one's body, whereas British men stare rigidly into one's eyes as if saying 'I'm not remotely interested in the rest of you. Not remotely.' It's normal, especially in a clothed society, to check out the genitals of a naked human being. Men's sauna in corpore sano. Von says 'They did a test about what women really look at when they see a naked man, as opposed to what they think they look at. They look at the penis first and the face second.'

(3) That Riccardo has 'a friend with a very big cock. He was leaving a garage to go and jump on his scooter when the attendant stopped him because he thought he'd stolen something and stuffed it down his trousers. He wouldn't believe it was his cock until he'd felt it. We Sicilians can be very suspicious.'

Riccardo is lolling in the back with Odrun who is feeding him grapes. I notice his face in the rearview mirror. He's swigging from the flask – black curls, he's placed cherries over his ears, Greek ogling eyes, being larky. He IS Dionysus. I catch his eye and he opens in a huge relaxed smile.

'Von, you didn't raise Pan – you raised Dionysus.'

She turns round and exclaims 'My God!' Von also looks relaxed, happy, fulfilled by the day, free to do the next thing.

Odrun remains Odrun, unflappable, heavy-titted, tethered to the earth by her warm wide rump; lovable sanity, Norwegian style. We drop her off at her self-catering flat in Giardini Naxos and she says 'Have a happy voyage!'

We ask Dionysus to join us for a meal but he and his wife are going to the house of Argentine friends for a football dinner. With great approval he describes one of the English footballers as 'very bastard'.

Back at the villa, Aurora asks 'Un buon bagno?'

I give her a peck, have a bath, dress, and walk up to Von's where at last we open her bottle of champagne, then have during dinner plenty of Corvo red on top of it. I have something to say.

'What does Syracuse convey to you?'

'Nothing,' she says.

'Doesn't it convey something fabulous and uncertain to your imagination? It does to mine.'

'Yes, that's what I meant. Something fabulous. And uncertain. Look,

I know it's your next stop and I've got to go back to London, and shan't be able to see Noto, so don't taunt. Let's have some more wine.'

'OK. Now listen. Just before I left England I received a freebie in the post from Island Sun – a week for 2 in Sicily, everything paid for. Just like that. Don't ask me why – I don't have to write anything in return. And sheer coincidence that I was coming anyway. But I've been chatting to them and they will commute it to a free week for 2 in Syracuse at the Grand Hotel Villa Politi, half board, which means breakfast and one other meal per day. So what I'm saying is – come along.'

'But . . . let me think. I was all geared up for being back in the office on Monday morning and someone's just thrown a free week in Syracuse at me and I'm not sure that – but what am I saying *I'd love it!* Oh God . . .'

'What?'

'I don't think I can change my ticket.'

'Try. Nicky Hall will help you.'

'I've gone all doo-lally . . .'

11
Syracuse

Aurora wanted cash. So I had to go down to a bank in the town to change money. I dread going to an Italian bank. They are always minding each other's business, which means a clerk does 3 things at once; he attends to you and also to what each of his colleagues is doing either side of him. And should he take it into his head to start walking about, then you'll never be through. It's the same with a waiter – he is involved with the business of all waiters. Southern Italians can't get on with one thing. They are overlapping all the time. So nothing is ever finished.

Von had already gone down to the town and I passed her coming up again. 'God, I feel dreadful,' she said, pushing back the damp prune mane. 'Hot, hung over, and I've got the shits.' I thought 'Silly Von' and proceeded down to the bank where a twinge asserted itself in my stomach and the room began to rotate. As the clerk set about the extensive process of form-filling, I came over all sweaty and thought 'Shall I faint before he completes this cruel business?' The French are so fast and efficient at cashing money – but the Italians, one bloody form after another, go to this desk, go to that desk, and they repeatedly stop to chat or confer, then you have to join the queue for the cashier to whom all the forms have finally been delivered . . . Periodically I was asked to sign somewhere and this sufficiently focused my senses to prevent collapse. Picking up a fat bunch of lire, I stumbled out, haggard and tense, the effect of that champagne with red wine having hit me – hit me in an especially unpleasant way as a result of the caffeine from the strong breakfast coffee coming on in the bank with a pitiless pounding of the blood in the early morning heat. Climbing back up the Taormina terraces to the Villa Isadora my heart started racing and I had to sit down. There was a lorry jammed in one of the narrow streets, so I rested while it unstuck itself, and on regaining the villa drank much water and swallowed 3 tablets of Brewer's Yeast as a restorative, and soon righted.

We loaded the car and put in travelling fuel (large tin peanuts, bottle water, pear juice, chocolate biscuits). Taking photographs of the send-off party wasn't easy. Anna the chambermaid didn't want to be snapped with mop in hand. Aurora ran screaming and peered round a corner with one brownish eye. Riccardo covered his face with both hands and made scissors with 2 of his fingers to let vision through. This is how they are on the 3 photographs. Kissing them good-bye – Anna tasted of face cream, Aurora of powder and tobacco, Riccardo of shaving-cream and tobacco.

'Take care, Riccardo.'

'And you take care – maybe you need to more than me.'

'Oh yes, definitely.'

There was a traffic jam outside – perhaps the lorry had restuck. But Aurora waved us off as we inched away on the road to Syracuse, her thin arms going backwards and forwards for an infinity of time until we were out of sight.

Motorway to Catania passes Acireale, famous for its carnival (Sicilians make much of carnival, dressing up as figures from the Commedia dell' Arte, and young children are allowed to throw eggs at unsuspecting visitors). Snarl-up at Catania where Frank Sinatra's father was born. A by-pass is to be built but for the moment the motorway ends here and you have to scramble through the town. In London Clarissa Baring said 'Catania's cool' – nothing could be further from the truth. The city holds the heat record for Italy, 109.4°Fahr. in the shade, and to-day it must be twice that. Appalling crime record as well, not a place to get lost in, so of course we do. There are times when driving through a conurbation, with all the pedalwork and gear-changing, is like playing an organ symphony.

Oil tankers off the coast, harsh odour in the nostrils, and we are upon the petro-chemical works at Augusta which grew up in the 50s, the largest such works in Europe, covering the earth for miles with a skein of pipes, cables, valves and drums. Sea pollution has killed marine life. Air pollution necessitated the evacuation of Marina di Mellini in 1979 and the houses were razed to the ground. Just past Augusta, blood flicks on to the windscreen out of a clear sky. Very odd. Could it be a bird haemorrhaging in the polluted air? And blood suddenly manifests on Von's calf. Odder still. We solve neither mystery.

Sicily doesn't feel Italian. Here it feels Greek with a splash of Africa. The island is full of detritus, ruins, remains of things, often of very recent date, and has quite as many unfinished buildings as Calabria. Typical Sicilian sign at the garage: *Please do not walk on the cement*. First impressions of Syracuse are sleazy, not what one was expecting. First impressions of the Villa Politi are sleazy, with faded pink façade, ugly flats nearby and sinister men in the foyer. By sleaziness I don't mean squalor. I don't even mean faded grandeur. I mean a state in which something superb and something bestial are blended, a state of decay and growth, well-used yet not fatigued, full of possibility and aliveness. I do not mean it as an insult. It is difficult to tell who are staff and who are not. Most of the men wear dark glasses and keep drawing each other into corners or round pillars. Little deals are taking place everywhere. Sicilians seem pathologically secretive. The simplest transaction becomes nefarious and controversial. Sicilian men seem quite a nervous breed – perhaps this is connected to their immoderate consumption of very strong coffee. A party of French can be heard – otherwise the hotel is virtually empty. They say it fills up in late June. So we have the pool to ourselves once the French woman has breaststroked her 6 or 7 circles while maintaining a perfectly dry chignon. Churchill stayed here.

A porter takes our luggage and we order tea at the bar before going up. The barman looks very unhealthy. His teeth are yellow and his skin is grey with a green tinge. His hair is the colour of dead mouse with a hint of ginger and more than a hint of dandruff. He is about 35. The tea is excellent and comes with cold milk even though we forgot to specify. Taylor's of Harrogate it says on the teabag tab. Blissful imbibition restores clarity to the brain . . . Von says that the barman whom I so cruelly described a moment ago has one of the sweetest faces she's ever seen.

Our room, No. 222, is fine, twin-bedded, with green shutters and view over the garden. 15 years ago we would've seen all the way to the island of Ortygia (Old Syracuse) but the view is blocked by flats. The garden is thickly planted and holds shaggy-necked palm trees and waterfalls of purple bougainvillaea. In the grounds is one of the quarries in which thousands of Athenian prisoners, would-be conquerors of Syracuse, were imprisoned and slaughtered. The site is confusedly overgrown. The song of birds is very noticeable in the garden. One often misses it in this country because birds are slaughtered in their millions in Italy. Despite laws to the contrary, Sicilians have killed the rare honey buzzard almost to extinction – its migratory route alas is over the island.

In the bathroom the loo pan is one I've encountered a great deal in south Italy. The back curve of the bowl intrudes in such a way as to prevent the evacuation falling directly into the water. It is not as unsavoury as the German model which has a porcelain platform for a detailed Teutonic examination of the product. None the less with this Italian model the evacuation has to ski down a porcelain slope into the water, With even a slightly loose stool, this produces heavy smearing. But Von and I are old friends.

The TV is black & white. On it Gina Lollobrigida advertises the Moulinex Microwave. Long may the magnificent all-ingredients-fresh south Italian kitchen be spared this barbaric monstrosity.

Going down in the lift I goose Von, and in the foyer, and lark along to the dining-room and since she's been talking a fair bit this holiday about her schooldays at Wycombe Abbey, I say I bet they didn't teach her about unacceptable gooseing. And sitting down at our table, she says 'Oh yes they did! Canon Brian Greene came into the Sixth Form to talk about the facts of life. Which were largely, it turned out, about going to church. But when he'd finished, the Headmistress, all 6' 3" of her, Miss Fisher, niece of the Archbishop of Canterbury (Miss Fisher had come from a school in East Africa where during Mau Mau she'd manned a machine-gun at the intersection of 2 corridors and armed all the girls with pepperpots), she loomed up after Canon Greene had finished and said "I have just one thing to add. When in doubt, cross your legs and say No Thank-you." And that,' Von says, 'is why I am sitting here with my legs splayed.'

The dining 'terrace' is formed by a glassed-in verandah along 2 sides of the ballroom from which it is separated by screens. The ballroom is very grand, whitewashed, with a giant order of Corinthian columns in pairs and enormous chandeliers like inverted wedding cakes. So one eats in a situation that is both intimate and magnificent. Cena:

First Course. Fettucine alla something or other. With basil and tomato. Delicious. Von says 'What you told me about that young girl in Naples – I found it very sexy. The three of you.'

Second Course. Von has a hunk of meat alla something else or other. She says that what's remarkable is its blueness as a matter of course. I say my father wouldn't touch it because, though a heavy meat eater, he can't abide it when food reminds him of living animals. She says she tried to be a vegetarian once and failed – she came over faint. I say I've never seen a vegetarian who's struck me as vivacious. She says 'You're right. Vegetarians are not sexual people.' But she's more right – Krishnamurti was vegetarian and had vivacity but was not a sexual being. I once asked him if he'd known sexual love and he said 'Little bit'. This means no because it is possible to have a little bit of sex but not a little bit of sexual love. Sexual love consumes. We drink Corvo red which is typically Sicilian: dark, warm, lively, with a sullen weight; the heat brings out its peppery abundance. People who won't drink red wine are not to be trusted. People who drink only white wine (excepting champagne) get pissed without getting jolly. An example of this is James Joyce who did not care for red wine which he called 'beefsteak', much preferring white wine which he called 'electricity'. There is an excellent Sicilian mineral water, Pozillo: carbonated, soft taste but not too creamy.

Third Course. Von has a local melon for pudding or, let us say, dessert. The English think it rather common to order melon, especially for a first course. But the English also think it rather common to drink rosé wine or pink champagne. This is because the English, shut away up there, place far too much importance on 'getting it right' and far too little on enjoying themselves. Anyone who imagines there is anything socially to be said, either positively or negatively, on the subject of ordering melon, rosé wine or pink champagne, is clearly of very limited experience. Sicilian melons are superb. Italy has no rosé wines. And *I am disappointed not to find upon this boat the variety of puddings to which I had looked forward* (Harold Nicolson, *Journey to Java*). So order no third course.

'Shall we take a closer look at the old town?'

'Oh, JG!'

There is a heavy aroma of jasmin and honeysuckle as we pass through the garden but no sound of cicadas or crickets.

'The air is cloudy with myth,' Von observes. 'Can't you feel it all about us?'

'*You* are cloudy with myth.'

'There is something very strange about the sea.'

'You said that at Taormina. What do you mean by it?'

'I don't know. Just – something.'

'But it's dark now.'

'I can feel it.'

'Hocus pocus.' (Which is a term of Protestant scorn, a contraction of *Hoc est corpus meum* by which Roman Catholics understood a literal transubstantiation.) She looks at me, pitying my lack of . . . whatever.

In a maritime world of swishing waves and flickering lights, a stately bridge connects the mainland to Ortygia which is the heart of old (as opposed to ancient) Syracuse, built in ramps on an island. For the first time we are in a truly famous and beautiful southern town that is not a tourist town. There is no commercialisation of the Taormina sort, no coaches, no foreign voices, no cheap cement hotels. I also realise that we are golden people in a dark paradise, not only because we've gone gold in the sun but also because Von's clanked up with the stuff.

'Von, you're wearing too much gold.'

'It's not real.'

'They don't know that. I wear nothing, not even a watch. I was mugged in Acapulco. The Latins are particularly drawn by gold.'

She huffs and takes off a couple of rings and puts them in her handbag.

'You're still showing too much.'

'For God's sake, don't be ridiculous.'

She really is quite shirty with me for daring to suggest she might tone herself down – Von likes to go out looking vivid. And as if on cue, a boy riding pillion on his friend's scooter makes a playful grab for her silvery dangling evening bag as he speeds by. Unsuccessful, he waves and laughs as the pair pop-pop past the remains of the Temple of Apollo and are lost in the night. This shocks her and she declanks.

Ortygia seethes around us magically yet is uncannily quiet, rising on its low sea-girt hill in the cobalt blue night. The streets are shadowy and amber, the air balmy and freshened by subtle breezes. Drifting moonstruck up a stone alleyway lined with bouffant wrought-iron balconies, we are none the less not quite prepared for the vision into which we ascend – the Piazza del Duomo. We pause on the threshold of this dramatically lit square, arrested in a transport of disbelief. The piazza declares itself the most beautiful urban space in the world, with a golden light, red-gold after dark and, as is to be discovered, lemon-gold by day. Here too, it is exceptionally quiet, with only 3 Greek-faced boys chatting on the cathedral steps, and there are no cars. One of the remarkable features of the piazza is therefore doubly apparent, that its floor is convex and on a tilt; which gives a careen to perception and also a physical opening out, as if the façades are tilting back to welcome down the sky. We drift across it like 2 solitary stars on a stage, through a slow swirl of baroque shapes, balustrades, and palm trees, taking possession of it as it takes possession of us. Cutting down a side street, the reason for depopulation is made clear. Doors are open to cool and in ground-floor rooms small groups are huddled round the abstract glare from black & white television sets: Argentina versus Italy – Riccardo will be having another of his football dinners. And now we are at the sea parapet, breathing deeply from the inky void.

Next day is hot and we go to the beach which sparkles. Syracuse doesn't have a beach. The spiaggia (strange word for a beach. How did it evolve in the consciousness of Italians? Surely it means 'omelette') is a 20 minute drive through orange groves and scrub countryside dotted with new cement villas trailing bougainvillaea, to Fontane Bianche, a pretty little resort with all the amenities, but thankfully not overdeveloped or fashionable. We drive into the Lido Sayonara on a rocky whitesand bay, with wooden bathing huts painted in primary colours and a few rocks scenically disposed in the water. There is an admission fee which includes an umbrella.

'We don't need a cabin,' says Von.

Yes we do. The sun to-day is fiendishly bright, brighter even than India, perhaps because the air is so clear. Von snoozes on the ovenplate of the sand, baring her boobs to the flogging sun. There are 2 or 3 dozen holidaymakers in all, with a variety of complexions. Several other girls, none of whom looks Sicilian, are topless but there is no nudity. Sicilians on the whole are rather prudish about actual nudity, though unperturbed by its representations. We bathe in the blue blue blue blue and I blurt out 'The Stygian flood shot forth its frothy stew!'

'Whimsy whimsy,' shouts Von kicking up a foam. 'Who warned me against whimsy *just last week?*'

To which I reply 'And having shot, it then shot forth anew!'

Von goes for a walk while I languish in the sun, then languish in the cabin and think it would be a good idea to ask the Manager of the hotel for a guide to accompany us to Noto. One hour later she returns saying the perambulation was made hell by boys yelling cheap unpleasant things.

'Don't they realise that to treat women in this way is incredibly insulting?' she enquires of the immediate vicinity. 'Why doesn't some-one teach them some manners? They're so *fucking* rude. But what's especially interesting is their hostility. I know it's all supposed to be unbuttoned amorous display and bravura but the actual fact of the matter is that their behaviour is very *aggressive* towards women – as if they were angry with us for something we did to them a long time ago. Incidentally, all the ladies' loos are utterly disgusting in Italy – they don't seem capable of aiming straight. Shit smeared on the seat.'

That night there's sand in the bath. And I have Beach Eye – that twinkly drunken effect from a day beside the sea. We try the pizzeria opposite the hotel for a change. At 10 p.m. there are kids in there, the wine is strong, and the mood semi-delirious.

'I seem to have been complaining a lot,' says Von, 'but actually I'm having a marvellous time. In fact, I'm having a religious experience, did you know that?'

I look up from my burdened plate, see not the slightest self-mockery in her, and before I can prevent it, say 'Oh, for God's sake, come down to earth.'

One thing one mustn't do is belittle Von's relationship with the higher pneuma and, looking fiercely at her equally burdened plate, she replies, in the enraged sotto voce of one not only helplessly taking a great step but paradoxically having to force herself to do so, 'Stop getting at me! Do you have to be such a bloody know-all? You treat me like a silly kid. Do you have to be so bloody patronising and facetious? I feel . . . I feel *squashed!*'

And I am shocked and intensely peeved at this outburst. One wants to be thought perfect. 'The reason you feel squashed is, er ... because you've expanded.' But it comes out in that awful absolutist tone which drives her mad.

'Oh, shut up! I mean, the way you went on and on about the gold!'

'Yes. I did! Can't you be practical and realistic for once? You are always trying to deflect attention from the real to the fanciful, from the specific to the vague, from the consequential to the lateral.'

'Stop listening to the sound of your own voice!'

Ouch. 'And you stop sloshing about in a dream!'

'I'm clumsy, so what?'

'Look ... I apologise if I've been putting you down. Is that what you meant when you referred to my profound contempt for women?'

'Ah! Has that been bothering you?'

'Yes.'

'I can't remember what I meant by that. Oh God, I don't know. Does it matter? Just don't be so ... patronising to me ...'

'I'm sorry.'

'Oh God, what've I said? I didn't mean to hurt you ... I ... Forget I said anything.'

'Forget?'

'I daresay it's all my fault.'

'No, it isn't.'

I'm chastened.

The following day some nagging tension between us has gone. Von cleared it. We are closer. She said I snored in the night. Across the table her face is pillar-box red. I don't mean to be patronising or facetious. OK, so I'm facetious – but she looks the picture of health among the parchment faces of the indoor-working Sicilian staff. I've had longer to acclimatise to the sun and didn't overdo it yesterday like she did – but my hair has gone White Man's Burden yellow. It's a breezy day with patchy cloud so we decide to stroll in Ortygia.

Syracuse is a true port, small but active, with merchant ships and genuine sailors and fishermen. The boat from Naples to Malta, in smart blue and white, anchors alongside the very broad esplanade of the Foro Italico or marine parade which is overlooked by a glorious stretch of buildings on high ground with a double row of pom-pom trees beneath. Almost anywhere else these noble edifices would have become deluxe flats but here some of them are barely standing, The old Hotel des Etrangers at the southern, Aretusa Fountain end, is completely derelict with cornices dropping into the streets. Throughout Ortygia one comes across buildings in varying degrees of dereliction, their doors and windows propped up by joists made on the plan of the true crucifix, thus:

The Piazza del Duomo looks sensational in the pure morning light. Unlike the piazza at Siena it isn't at all claustrophobic but laid at the highest point of the island and one is aware of the sea. The sense of levity, almost of levitation, is enhanced by its convex tilt. The shape is that of a long loaf, straight on one side, unevenly curved on the other, a natural, biological shape. The atmosphere is bubbly and easygoing, whereas at Taormina there was something unkind in the air. All piazzas but especially this one deliberately encourage interaction and chance meetings – in contrast to Britain where such activity is distrusted and where a series of laws against obstruction, loitering with intent, soliciting, etc. attempt to eliminate it. This endless opportunity for the off-the-cuff encounter is what one most misses in British life. The equivalent of the piazza in Britain is the pub and the dance hall but already these involve decision-making whereas the piazza does not.

The buildings are in honey, white, cream or glucose stone. The most remarkable of them is the cathedral, built from the Temple of Pallas Athene with original Doric columns in almost perfect condition. An ancient Greek temple and a Norman church are folded into each other and in the early 18th century an exuberant baroque façade with bulging meaty columns and shuddering entablatures was grafted on to this already unique organism. The result is neither hybrid nor uncomfortable but a wise and venerable friend, the ultimate European religious building in which all our history, art, myth and spiritual aspirations are embodied. Continuous worship has gone on here for more than 2500 years, surely longer than at any other place in Europe. The interior is hushed – dark – simple – intimate. The stone of the Doric columns, polished by time, heavy and floating, muscle without mass, glimmers in the candlelight. Here there is nothing exotic or theatrical, nothing declamatory, formulated or proselytising, nothing mean, ungracious, gaudy or intense, nothing cruel or enfeebled. We are not in a Catholic place or a Christian or a pagan place. We are not partial or self-conscious here. An uttered phrase echoes, is batted amiably back to us but in unrecognisable form. At a few places on the planet there are trapdoors to infinity. This is one of them.

Opposite the cathedral is the Archaeological Museum. It is closed while the august contents are removed to a glassy purpose-built museum in the Archaeological Zone, the district of extensive Greek remains on the mainland. The new museum has not yet opened because interested parties cannot agree on how best to arrange the collection therein. This typically Sicilian impasse has endured for several years.

On the south side of the piazza is the church of Santa Lucia, a fine example of the 'furry' character of southern baroque when it decays. Royal crowns crumble like cake either side of the main door. Saint Lucy died at Syracuse in AD 304 during the persecution of Diocletian. Her eyes were torn out but are said, according to the Vatican guardians of truth, to have been returned to their sockets by a miracle, so her emblem is 2 eyes on a dish. She is invoked by suppliants with eye problems. Another minor deity from east Sicily, Saint Agatha, who died at Catania in the 3rd century AD after torture, has as her emblem 2 breasts on a plate. She is invoked against eruptions of Mount Aetna and breast problems.

At the northern end is the original Municipio, recently restored prior to becoming once again local government offices after a long interval. This is quoted as an example of the revitalisation of Ortygia after years of neglect during which much was siphoned off to the tacky modern town around the Corso Gelone. Wandering the side streets and being dripped on by washing from hundreds of writhing iron balconies, we discover the Opera House, enormous, fine, and tucked away, also undergoing renovation. And a Gilbert and Sullivan fortress on the sea – real guardsmen, no admittance. A number of judo and body-building establishments are scattered through dim gothic palaces and mouldy baroque courtyards. It is all so bewitching and perfect. There is even a porn cinema called the Ariston (whither I took myself one evening. Unlike such cinemas in north Italy, there are no women in this one. Below Rome, indulgence is a male preserve. In porn films, the women always keep on their ear-rings and high heels: it's all throat, ear-rings, hair, tits, fica and high heels).

There are more people out of doors to-day. In the piazza groups of men and boys hang around, women scuttle through on errands. The Tony Curtis look from the 50s never went out of fashion here. Some of the men have Piazza Hip – pelvis at a permanent angle from many hours' standing. A lone souvenir stallholder tries to attract my attention with a small papyrus painting of Nefertiti. He has dozens of them and although papyrus does grow in a local river, anything less of a Syracusan memento I can't imagine. He is also proffering gimcrack copies of Greek vases on which the naked male figures have acquired cumbersome breechclouts. Oh, the prudery of internationalism . . .

Von says 'I keep seeing faces that were on pots thousands of years ago.'

'Was my face ever on a pot?'

'You have 2 faces. And neither was on a pot.'

Which are the great cities? Vienna, Oxford, Syracuse ... the southern town of one's dreams become reality, ravishingly built, mellow, maritime, flirtatious, ancient. Theocritus, inventor of bucolic poetry, was born here. Plato taught here. Aeschylus lived here. Archimedes was born and died here. The population of this island municipality rids itself of rubbish – everything from old mattresses to vegetable peelings and Fanta tins – by throwing it over the parapets onto the rocks and sand below where, failing to be removed by the sea whose cleansing powers have limits, it forms an unsightly and pestiferous girdle. At present, they have little civic pride.

A wedding is taking place in the ballroom adjacent to the screened-off terrace where lunch is being served to us and the few other hotel residents. The bride and groom look happy and carefree, not at all put out by this day. They move separately among the 300 guests chatting, being charming. A rather trendy crowd. Unlike at an English wedding where the men adopt antique clothes, the men here are in blue or grey suits with box jackets and padded shoulders, fancy bow ties, pistachio green or strawberry pink shirts. The women dress more coolly in smart light cottons – and not one hat to be seen despite the sunny weather. Every Sicilian boy can turn his hand to being a waiter on Saturday afternoon and all those not at the wedding are serving them. Food isn't good at weddings – even here, I can tell, although the food generally at the Villa Politi is excellent – and it's thrown at them. Worst wedding food I ever had was at Claridge's, which goes to show.

On the other hand our lunch is delicious – castor and pollux, i.e. pasta and pollo. The pasta is Fettuccine Nelson. Base: aglio, acciughe. Then: pomodoro, panna, basilico, oregano. Then: zucchini, melanzane. Then: combine sauce and fettuccine, with mozzarella on top, put under grill to melt cheese, serve. All this appetising pasta does keep one regular – and keeps faeces firm. Von interposes here and says she's got the shits, no doubt about it. All I can say is she's kept bloody quiet about it – and what's more, *tight*, since we walked all round Syracuse this morning without a squitter.

'Oh, no,' she interposes again, 'I haven't got funny tummy. It's just that when I do go, which is 5 times a day, I don't have ... nice firm ones. It's like black lava.'

'This bread's awfully good.'

She tugs my sleeve. 'Black lava – black with all the iron I've taken in.'

'Yes, dear, I hear you. I'm eating my chicken.'

'Red wine has a lot of iron in it, did you know?'

'I didn't know. I've had a fair bit of red wine – but, well, when I go, mine's yellow. The colour I imagine Noto stone to be.'

'Have more of this spinach then. It'll blacken it up. In England we have neat bowel movements. But abroad – '

'Oh, I don't know about that, Von. I've had some corkers in England. That is to say, some uncorkers.'

When the wedding cake is paraded in, it turns out to be exactly the same size and shape as the chandeliers, only the other way up. Von is of the opinion that it's mostly cardboard with only the top tier real, like the wedding cakes in wartime England. 'It's darkening over,' she adds, looking out from the table. ' 'Twill be a louring *Antigone*.' (We are going to see this play at the Greek theatre to-night.)

'I must ask the Manager about getting us a guide for Noto.'

'Oh, JG! Is it far away?'

'Not at all. But I'm staving it off a little bit. Do you understand?'

'Oh yes. Foreplay.'

'And we've been invited to dinner by these university people in Catania. Tuesday 8.30.'

'JG, JG!' The cake isn't cardboard, Chunks of white stuff are circulating round the room on small plates.

'What is this JG you keep saying?'

'Jolly good. It comes from school. Didn't you have that one?'

'No. We had "fabulous".'

'Yes, well, I've been reading, in that *fabulous* old book of yours, about the Necropolis of Pantalica. *The most famous city of the dead in Sicily, a wild gorge full of tombs and troglodytes' dwellings* . . . (Douglas Sladen). That gets my vote for an outing.'

'JG . . . Do you really go 5 times a day?'

'I do here.'

The Manager is tall and brown-haired, with the unemphatic good manners of a successful London doctor. For Noto he will arrange something.

'Will it rain to-day?' I ask as of a remote but exceedingly pleasant oracle.

'No, it will not rain to-day,' he replies softly, at which point the grey sludge sweeping slowly across the sky begins to micturate. Large raindrops cause wide rings which intersect with each other on the surface of the swimming-pool. Von and I swim in circles, giggling.

In the evening Von clanks forth from the bathroom in gold amulets

and rings, bangles of glittering metal, several brooches which are
actually breastpieces of beaten alloy, ear-rings which would not be
out of place strapped to the thighs of an Assyrian war god, and various
belts, chokers, collars and necklaces of primitive but expensive aspect,
saying 'I'm ready'. It's as if the British Museum had decided to go
walkies.

'Oh God . . .' I murmur.

'What?' She bites her lower lip.

'That . . . schmuk. I thought I'd *explained*.'

'But we're going to the theatre!' she yelps, tossing the prune-
coloured mane.

'It's not fucking Covent Garden! And I'll be the one who has to
defend all that . . . stuff.'

'Are you afraid you might have to be physically courageous?'

Ouch. 'Yes. I don't want to be attacked. Kinky, isn't it. Are you
afraid that without all this adornment you won't exist?'

'It looks good with my tan.' But there is chagrin and submission
in her voice.

'And you better have your fifth shit of the day.'

'Already have. OK, you're right and I'm wrong,' and while removing
portions of her refulgent armour she hits herself quite hard saying
'Silly Von, silly Von!' She's really getting quite mad. We both howl
with laughter.

Now we are sitting on stones at the back of the Greek theatre,
the most impressive monument in the Archaeological Zone, the rest
being mostly rubble, stumps of pillars, broken platforms. View flawed –
pine and cypress screens have been planted behind the stage to hide
the rows of pylons and industrial mess. Wind blowing and sky layered
different greys by the sirocco, slanted greys like the folded wings of
giant pigeons. The hills to the right are a flatter, slatier grey. The
auditorium is packed and I notice that the stone tiers are alive
with millions of ants. The grey theme is continued in the set,
contrived from grey blocks which slide about the stage. Half the
chorus is in grey, half in black, while Creon wears royal blue
and Antigone wears, Von says, Tyrian purple (from shellfish).

Don't understand a word. But the acoustics are famous. A light
crunching sound can be heard throughout the performance as theatre-
goers shell peanuts, sweets being unavailable due to the ants; the
bleep-bleep of digital watches is also audible, like mice calling to each
other. The lover Haemon wears cobalt blue and dashes about the stage
in the hammiest manner – a fulsome Italian rendition does nothing for
the nobility of Greek tragedy. The members of the chorus wearing
black are also wearing, Von says, Phrygian caps. There is a creaky

instrumental and vocal accompaniment, presumably very authentic. Plonk plonk wail . . . A rumpus breaks out at the back of the auditorium where an old loony starts raving atop a rock. Since he is no more comprehensible than anyone else, I momentarily assume that this is theatre-in-the-round or at least in-the-audience and that this is some soothsayer telling of terrible portents. These plays usually contain such a figure. However, carabinieri and ushers stream towards the poor sod whose wild vocalese is beginning to disturb the players as well as the audience, and he's hustled away over the brow of the hill, protesting loudly.

As the play enters its fifth episode, a few lights twinkle behind the pylons and Alsatians bark. Ants are crawling in my pants, and, judging by the expression on Von's face, she has a similar problem. The blind Tiresias, a memorable figure with lank hair and blacked-out face, makes his entrance foretelling a ghastly future. At the climax of Tiresias' speech a young boy very thoroughly blows his nose and the famous acoustics do their job. The stage is unlit. As the cloud-hidden sun declines, events are subsumed in deepening greynesses and the vivid, painted darkness of cypresses. After the final clutch of suicides, the audience files happily into the night.

We go into Ortygia – the passeggiata is very late here. At 10.30 p.m. it begins to become crowded along the Foro Italico. Nearly every group has someone carrying a slip-out car stereo, which indicates that many have driven here from other parts of town. Von says that the arms and legs of Sicilian men are stunted, that they are too short from shoulder to elbow, from hip to knee. We pass the Fontana di Aretusa where Nelson watered his fleet before destroying Napoleon's navy at the Battle of Aboukir Bay, and find ourselves at a madly fashionable bar called Lungo La Notte. It's done up in beatnik décor and has an extraordinary collection of high-backed wrought-iron 'Picasso' chairs + an unbeatable location in a cosy part of town overlooking the Bay of Syracuse. It's the best café I've ever come across and is full of breathlessly smart and beautiful young people, tuned up to the gills but with none of the hardness or anonymity which one finds in such places in big cities.

'Can I have an orange juice?' Often in Sicily you don't get real orange juice when you order it but a horribly sweet sherbet concoction. But it's fresh here. The waitress has a perfectly symmetrical face which could've been on a pot thousands of years ago and I tell her so.

'Thank you,' she says in excellent English, 'but I'm from Brazil.'

On the Tuesday, after Von has tried to tone down her complexion which is now an electric scarlet (I'm amazed she hasn't burst into flames but she swears it doesn't hurt), we drive up to Catania for dinner with the university people. As we pass through the Augusta chemical works a variety of acrid smells succeed each other inside the car and Von says she has a headache. Tankers slumber on the dead polluted sea.

They live in the old part of Catania, up a lift to a top floor flat. There are only women when we arrive – all the men are watching football in another room. Ersilia is the head of the household. We have a friend in common, Marie Curry, and on the strength of a phone-call, Ersilia has produced a spectacular dinner for 2 strangers. The men arrive and we all move on to a large terrace to eat al fresco. The women – Ersilia, Lisetta, Ingrid – speak English but the men don't.

First course is prosciutto and melon. Lisetta, who is slim, coquettish and very alert, says how amazing it is that the English can combine great rationality and control without loss of emotional content in their life. 'We have the emotional,' she says, 'but it destroys completely the rational.' I thank them and suggest that the English can combine the rational with the emotional because they do not venerate the intellect. Their compliment turns out to be the overture to a sustained frontal attack on England by these 2 Sicilian English teachers, Lisetta and Ersilia. Lisetta continues 'The English are deeply disturbed and neurotic of course in their relationships. It all comes from this chasm between the child and its mother. This chasm does not exist in Italy where all love comes from the pure love of the mother.'

I say that in my limited experience the Sicilians (as opposed to the Italians) were very neurotic too and that this is one of the reasons I find them so attractive. Lisetta replies, flashing her eyes impishly, that you can find the key to the Sicilian character – how something can so easily turn into its opposite – in Pirandello. A sweet little old lady called Graziella says 'It is impossible to be sad when there is sun.' This is the sort of thing you might get away with on Cap Ferrat but it doesn't wash in the heart of Europe's most violent society.

Ersilia is an unusually fine-looking woman who presides goddesslike. Her head is large and rendered more so by a swept-back hairdo. Her nose is prominent and from its top the eyes, immense but feline, swerve up and away. In fact her face resembles the front of a sports car. Its centrepiece is an immense radiator smile which she turns on like 1000 seraphic trumpets. I ask her why she chose to study and teach English and she replies 'We could choose either English or French. I chose English. It's just something to teach. But I didn't like the misty north, the pastel colours, the dreaminess, the gothic. I was so happy to return to the richness and roundness of baroque and the warm colours, blue, red, yellow.'

Second course. Maccheroni alla Norma. A great roar goes up from the rooftops of Catania. One of the men, who has a greenish Arab complexion, says Italy must've scored a goal. Ersilia says that when Italy won the World Cup the whole town went crazy and she was frightened to go out.

Von asks 'Is it safe to walk round at night?'

'Not in Catania. But I think in Syracuse it's no problem – so long as you're not wearing gold.'

Von gives me a little smile, a flash of white in the midst of her facial conflagration. Ersilia I find very difficult to engage in conversation, largely because she's not remotely interested in anything I am, say or do, or in anything English at all. Her attention is wholly taken up by what her immediate group of friends are gossiping about.

Third course. Involtini (small meat rolls) with a salad which is said to be typically Sicilian but which as far as I can discern is simply sliced tomatoes and onions. Lisetta is altogether easier to talk to and I say 'If the central fact of Italian life is the mother's love for the son, this will have bad as well as good consequences. The failure of rationality in Italian society – this comes from the indulgence of the mother too.'

Lisetta, with much flashing of eyes and smiles and shimmying of shoulders, says 'Italian men can love women better than Englishmen because this memory of the mother, this warmth resurfaces. To have many women is no problem for the Italian man [flash, shimmy, smile] because it is this constant return to the warmth of the mother. He is not guilty.'

I think she's day-dreaming here. Sicilians are many wonderful things but they have, in addition to this earth-mother paganism, the contrary heritage of sin and guilt from the Church. As always, we fantasise about love.

Turning to Ersilia I say 'So here I am, driving south to Noto and writing about it. Can you imagine a Sicilian driving to Scotland and writing about his journey?'

'This is unthinkable,' she says. 'And why Noto?'

'Because it's as far south as you can get without Europe turning into something else.'

'And you're in love with the south?'

'I'm in love with the *idea* of it.'

The men crack some jokes among each other, but otherwise do not shine. The women are in control here. The men seem curiously shrunken.

Von, whose face is now once again the full beaming scarlet, having dissolved its tone-down, is far from shrunken. She is sister indeed to the other female deities here and says 'Ersilia, you are Sicily's answer to Silvana Mangano.'

And Ingrid, who is 150% Sicilian because she's a German from Munich who's married into the island, replies 'Ah, but Silvana Mangano lives by herself and has a very unhappy life and hasn't much money.' To live by oneself is staggeringly eccentric to the Sicilian mind.

Ersilia smiles the *smile* and enfolds and subdues the table with her spirit. I ask them to suggest a small country town or village untouched by coarse modern development. One of the men suggests Centuripe. It is near Catania. All the towns they suggest are near Catania. They are eastern Sicilians and the west of the island is another country for them. Then Lisetta comes up with Assoro. It sounds promising.

'There's nothing there. *Nothing,*' she assures me.

'Are you certain?'

'Yes, yes. *Absolutely* NOTHING.'

'Excellent. Where is it?'

'Near Enna. They'll be very surprised, very suspicious of you. They'll wonder – What does he want? What is his game?'

Fourth course. A delightfully silly pudding – translucent pink watermelon jelly with chocolate flakes, cinnamon and jasmin flowers on top. When I was at the university, I once ate a whole white arum lily, pistil and all, washed down with Green Chartreuse – my mouth stung terrifically and though I wasn't ill, I've not liked to eat flowers since. And there's a lemon jelly. Both these dishes, Von says, remind one of Sicily's Arab heritage. They were made by Ingrid.

'I now feel completely Sicilian at heart,' says Ingrid. She's dead wrong there. Her straightforward enthusiasm is very noticeable among the slipping and sliding of the others.

Lisetta says 'The thing I hate about England [flash, smile, shoulder shimmy] is the class system. In Sicily everyone mixes.'

And I say [flash, smile, shoulder shimmy] 'I don't know about that – but in Sicily I find a veneration of status symbols greater than in any place I've ever visited, *including* India.'

'Let me tell you!' she replies 'I've just discovered Krishnamurti!'

On the way back to Syracuse, Von and I conduct a post mortem.

ME: Lisetta likes men.

VON: That's very clear.

ME: She's very pretty and a nice figure for her age. What would you say was her age?

VON: Mid-forties. They were all mid-forties.

ME: She has a child. She was flirting with me. She said 'I bet you went to Oxford University,' and I said 'How on earth?' and she said 'Aha . . .' I was amazed.

VON: It's not amazing at all. It's your manner.

ME: What do you mean?

VON: But I don't want to go into your manner.

ME: She said she really hated the class thing in England while working *very* hard to project a classy image herself – as all Sicilians do.

VON: You see, she's an Anglophile, she can't help it. When I said she sounded Hungarian that was very near the mark because all the Hungarians I've met are great Anglophiles.

ME: Yes, but that's because you only ever meet them in England. You've never been to Hungary.

VON: She hated the class thing because she couldn't break it.

ME: Who's that standing in the road?

Some character in a funny costume is standing in the road waving at us. We're in the middle of nowhere but I'm not going to drive on because it's a policeman. In fact there are 2 and they're both saying 'Documenti, documenti, documenti!' So I get out and rummage in the boot where all relevant documents are kept, except the passport which is back at the hotel. I find the driving licence and hand it to the bigger of the 2. He scrutinises it in torchlight, turning it this way and that as if it's a shard from a Pharaoh's tomb. His expression is half blank, half bemused; at no time does it reveal that a connection has been made between his intelligence and the thing in his hand; and there are wine fumes on his breath. Eventually he returns it with a contrived look of authoritarian languor, says 'OK', and waves the car on with his torch.

VON: What was that all about?

ME: I think they were a bit drunk. They were certainly bored.

VON: Ersilia is a queen bee. She's a royal jelly person – with drones. That smile, so luscious.

ME: There is no way you can get past that smile. She is closed by it. But compared to the men, the women were very secure.

VON: Did you notice that too?

ME: I thought it the most obvious thing of all. There's a kind of pathos in Sicilian men, even when they're being aggressive and macho. The women know exactly who they are. But the men – machismo is a manifestation of insecurity, the male's attempt to convince himself and others that he's somebody.

VON: Yes, even the mafia can be seen as the aggressive compensatory behaviour of men who feel they are excluded from the *real*. Sicily is a land of goddesses and men. Worship of Demeter and Venus and the Virgin Mary.

ME: What about the Temple of Apollo at Syracuse?

VON: But the main temple, which is now the cathedral, was to Pallas Athene or Minerva. And I expect there was more veneration of Adonis than of Apollo. Adonis was a man – he turned into Saint John.

ME: So Sicily eschews God worship. Male authority is rejected by the males.

VON and ME together: Oh God! This is AMAZING! What *is* it? It's just oh God A-M-A-Z-I-N-G . . .

Space city, stretching for miles – towers of red lights, some topped by torches of flame – windless, therefore hundred of columns of pale grey smoke, made fluorescent by the moonlight, rise vertically into the night – metallic silvery pipes glitter and convolute – the installations are illuminated not in a glare but in a delicate tracery of red and white lights – tower tops burst into flame, throwing up a hellfire orange against the black sky, then die down – incisive, chemical smell – this is Augusta *at night*. The beauty is prodigious and unearthly and the extent of the site, stretching to the horizon on all sides, creates an overwhelming impression.

'This is much more exciting than the Greek theatre,' says Von.

'Yes. Because it is alive.'

We drive on in silence.

Von jumps into bed, saying 'Bedfordshire!'

'Do you want some of this red wine.'

'No. It'll make me all doo-lally – in Bedfordshire!'

'We opened it at lunch, so we should finish it to-night. The thing I've noticed about Corvo is that it doesn't keep even for a day. It degenerates immediately.'

'Can we look for the Necropolis of Pantalica to-morrow?'

'OK, if you do the navigating.'

'Let's wallop off that wine.'

I guard myself from temperance, as I formerly did from volupté, because temperance draws us too far back, even to dullness (Montaigne).

The following morning the Manager beckons me across in his svelte, agreeable bedside manner (so that even if one hasn't been ill, one immediately feels better from the mere proximity) and reveals in an affable voice that 'If you ring Professore Rosario Tinè on this number he will escort you round Noto at a time suitable to both of you.'

The very notion sets me buzzing. But instead of rushing to the phone, I decide to extend the foreplay by going on this jaunt to the

City of the Dead over which Von has already worked herself into a
skull-rattling stew of anticipation . . .

Von studies the map with professional zeal and announces
'Thattaway.'

Though intensely cultivated, the countryside as a place to live has
largely been abandoned for the towns and the coast, and this has saved
it from desecration. The river gorges are fertile at bottom, stuffed with
green trees and plants, bleaker higher up but never cold or impersonal.
But the stone walls in the fields are collapsing and all the old cottages
too. The traditional rural homestead is usually 1 storey with a rosy tiled
roof of shallow pitch and shuttered windows. These cottages hunker
down beautifully in the landscape, but the majority have fallen into
ruin, as have the elegant Deposito buildings.

Stop to determine our position. We are lost. The gnarled trunks
of olive trees are like old friends. Concrete pillboxes are scattered
over the hills from World War II. Von says 'Thissaway' and we soon
find ourselves in a small town called Ferla, full of baroque churches
and appearing very monumental for its size. A sign for a club called
Boy Music adds piquancy to the main street. Old gentlemen in caps,
black trousers, black waistcoats, with walking sticks, sit outside the
cafés on bentwood chairs at 5 p.m. A few black widows shuffle along
with shopping bags. A noisy gang of children harass us to take a
photograph and they compose themselves into a perfect Victorian
group in front of a florid church door. To our astonishment they
don't ask for money and so the verdict is – Ferla has retained its
integrity.

The town climbs a hillside and at the top I show indecision. Von,
after diligent examination of the map, commands 'Thattaway' and we
move on to a country road. After several minutes she exclaims 'Look,
there's a ravine!' In the setting sun, the limestone has turned rose pink
on one side of it and lavender grey on the other. It's transcendentally
lovely – but the wrong ravine. The sunset also hits Von's face which,
defying all possible laws, continues to become redder and redder and
redder.

'But I've kept out of the sun all day,' she protests.

'Then it must've crept up your legs. You could fry a couple of eggs
on your face.'

'Yes, well, it's a happy face.'

'We're lost.'

'I know.'

We find ourselves in a very natural stretch of countryside where
the farming is not greatly mechanised. The stone walls are intact
but overgrown with plants. Trees and wild flowers grow out of the

wheatfields which also contain the occasional boulder. The variety
of trees and shrubs is considerable and higher up there's a velvety
green scrub on the limestone terraces. Von says that parts of it are
pure Gainsborough and curiously she's right, since there is that
same quality of collusion with nature, not nature controlled, tailored,
trimmed back to the bone, subdued. Birds sing and a sunset pans out
across the fields.

'Let's forget about the dead,' says Von.

12

The Golden City

It is Sunday and quiet. We have arranged to meet Professore Tinè beside the statue of San Corrado at the edge of Noto. The road south passes large banks of red or purple bougainvillaea and pink oleanders, limestone ridges with vivid green citrus groves, more muted orchards of almond and apricot. The grass is beginning to turn yellow.

This is it. The big moment. With a thrill and quickening of heartbeat, Noto is seen up on its escarpment, grandiose but contained, fascinating, oriental – then is lost behind a bluff. The approach is closed-in, unrevealing and tidy, apart from a pillar on the left bearing its graffito *Baby, you are my destiny*, and unlike any other Sicilian town I've yet seen, the flats on the outskirts appear to have been controlled in height and finished off with trees round them. It is entirely different from what I'd expected. One had imagined dust tracks and donkeys but this is a new road with cars more up-to-date than mine.

Second-gearing up a moderately steep hill we reach the Largo Marconi and the approach to the town proper – one should correctly say 'city' – and the statue of San Corrado (its patron saint) erected in 1955 on a belvedere with a view of terraces falling in an immense, natural amphitheatre facing the sea and the Gulf of Noto. Standing here is our guide who teaches English at the local secondary school, Professore Tinè, small, fair-haired, chubby, very serious and well intentioned, and sweating – at 10 a.m. it is already hot.

We shake hands and he leads us along a promenade towards the ceremonial entrance to the town. This walk is planted with a thick double row of ficus trees whose interlocking branches form a green and dark brown tunnel of shade. On the left are public gardens and already Noto has demonstrated a special quality, of being *cared for*. It isn't spruce; it has the softness of the south. But clearly the inhabitants look after it and do not allow it to be crudely wrecked. I may be wrong but it feels like a place into which mafia viciousness has not progressed very far. Ortygia is very captivating of course but ruinous in parts and all its approaches on the Syracusan mainland have been devastated. This sense at Noto of a gross destructive appetite successfully kept at bay is unique in Sicily in my experience, for a settlement of this size.

As we walk Professore Tinè explains that Noto traces its ancestry back to a prehistoric inhabitation, 900 BC. The Sikels built a city here which was then conquered by the Greeks. Later it came under the protection of Rome. In AD 864 it was conquered by the Arabs who made it capital of one of their 3 administrative divisions of the island; in 1090 it was the last citadel in Sicily to surrender to the Normans. Throughout the Middle Ages and up to modern times it remained the provincial capital but was in constant threat of being overshadowed by Syracuse. When in the 19th century the provincial capital was transferred to Syracuse, Noto entered its forgotten era. Meanwhile in 1693 eastern Sicily had been shaken by an earthquake. Noto was destroyed and the present town built about 10 miles away from the previous site which is now known as Noto Antica. It was planned as a total environment in the baroque manner. And that is what it is.

You enter through a triumphal arch, the Porta Reale, that would look at home in Berlin − it was erected for the visit of Ferdinand II in 1838 − and the first thing you notice is the colour of Noto. Built from the limestone of the region, in bright daylight it is basically giallo pagliarino or straw yellow, though much mottled and varied by the weather. The Porta Reale has telephone wires attached to either side and is surmounted by a tower, a pelican and a cat. The tower symbolises the strength of the city, the pelican symbolises 'abnegazione − what is the English word?' asks Professore Tinè, nervously rubbing a hand across his beaded brow.

'Abnegation? Self denial?'

'Si . . . and the other is not a cat but a dog.' It is a greyhound which represents fidelity. But the most exciting aspect of this arch is that you can see clearly through it along the main east−west axis (the Corso Vittorio Emmanuele which divides the city into Noto Alta and Noto Bassa) to the countryside beyond.

After these few minutes of speaking English, Professore Tinè asks 'Don't you speak Italian?' with a beseeching look in his eyes.

'Not enough, I'm afraid.' There's an inane grin on my face.

'Yes, OK then,' he says and takes a deep breath, mindful of the dignity of the situation. '. . . The town was built in the first ½ of the 18th century by . . . scapolini . . . What is this in English?'

'Masons? Keith would love this, wouldn't he?'

'Oh, he would! Master-builders?' suggests Von.

We can't find it in the dictionary. 'Scapola' − shoulder blade. 'Scapolo' − bachelor. Small bachelors?

The first architectural extravaganza we come across is a most peculiar grouping – the Church of the Immacolata with a precipitous staircase in front, and next door the Monastery of the Holy Saviour which incorporates a queer pyramid-topped tower and along the Corso a string of fancy windows closed by bulging ironwork grilles. This wall and another have nothing behind them which is either a theatrical feint or the result of a fire in 1934. Communication breaks down over this point.

'Compare the pyramid tower to those in Salamanca, Spain,' he says.

'I've not been there.'

'Ecco – OK then.'

Bells clang. A tall, gangling priest greets us on the street with a huge key. His manner is gentle and he is introduced as Padre Caruso who as a special favour will let us into the small church of Santa Chiara. The interior is oval, articulated by 12 columns on which stand the 2 apostles. The oval vault springs from these to gather in a sculptured cluster of angelic heads peeping from clouds and surrounded by sunrays.

'The floor tiles come from Valencia.'

The colour scheme is simple, basically white with detail picked out in chocolate and dark gold, but the whole has a rippling delicacy and freshness which is rococo. Perhaps we shouldn't talk so much of baroque in this town but of rococo because there is an enchanting lightness of touch to Noto's splendours.

Padre Caruso indicates the Madonna con Bambino brought from Noto Antica and attributed to Antonello Gaggini (late 15th century). Professore Tinè draws our attention to the beauty of the Madonna's expression but privately I do not think it beautiful. She looks rather drunk – an expression of woe partly cancelled by wine – or simply ga-ga. But the child is arrestingly alive, with a face full of tension, intelligence and a frowning brow.

Padre Caruso says 'Yes, he's a Sicilian child.'

I want to leave a few coins but Professore Tinè says 'No, the Church is very rich in Noto.' Padre Caruso nods, laughs and wishes us well.

Next we come to the main town square or rather space because it is composed of several interlocking squares, esplanades, gardens, groups of trees, a bandstand (the only one I've met with since leaving England) where you can hear selections from the operas, statues, memorials, and fountains. The precinct is grand but personal and inviting too. On the left is the self-possessed, free-standing Town Hall which has a Palladian character. (The main saloon of it was decorated in 1932. One of the most appealing aspects of Noto is that the original plan is still being realised and that embellishment has gone on slowly and harmoniously ever since the first stone was laid.) On the right is the most majestically sited building in the town, the Cathedral. It is like a small, yellow stone version of St Paul's in London, but softer, simpler. The principal reason for its majestic effect is that it is reached up 4 flights of steps with 3 intervening landings and instead of being folded into some clever arrangement, the whole lot (except the last brief flight immediately beneath the façade) runs the width of the building and ascends parallel to the road. In fact all the buildings on the upper side of the Corso are impressive in their situation because the road subsided in the late 18th century and extra flights of stairs were required in order to reach them. Inside, the Cathedral is sombre. Its frescoes were painted in the 1950s. One of the side chapels houses the Ark of San Corrado containing his remains and supported on 4 silver gryphons. This is paraded round the town 4 times a year by associations especially constituted for this purpose. Corrado Confalonieri was a nobleman from Piacenza who after an accident while hunting withdrew to a cave a few miles from Noto and became a hermit renowned for his piety, dying in 1351.

'Is there a society to protect the buildings of Noto?'

'There are 2 societies but they have not much money. There's Pro Noto – we fight very much for improvements and restoration. I am vice-president. And there is ISVNA for Noto Antica.'

'One of the reasons Noto is so beautiful is that it's a real town, not full of tourists.'

'Yes, but we have some tourist. We would like more,'

'Oh dear, what a shame.' We're all hot.

'All the churches and palaces were built by craftsmen from Noto itself. But to-day there are very little craftsmen here. Perhaps nobody. There is a man, 85 years old. He makes some carvings in stone for the old villas nearby.'

Rosario as we now call him is 41, Noto born and bred. He takes us down into the narrower streets of Noto Bassa behind the Municipio. Though this is the 'poor' area there is nothing poor about it. Its houses are pretty and well built in the same straw stone. At the corner of via Ducezio and via Salvatore La Rosa is a good example of Noto Art Nouveau, complete with sunflowers and ivy relief. (There is also a decidedly weird 'Aztec' shopfront on the Corso near the Royal Gate. It has that LSD nightmare quality which you find only in the 19th century and in some pre-Columbian American architecture.)

'The quartieri are very special here. These small vicoli are particular to Arabian towns – so in Noto we have this Arab inheritance. Would you like ice-cream?'

Not half. He takes us down another street and through the beaded curtain of what appears to be the front door of an ordinary house. But we find ourselves in a small emporium filled with ice-cream, cakes, biscuits, crackers, bottles, sweets, framed diplomas and silver cups. Rosario says many shops in Noto are inside houses and have no commercial signs outside.

We are introduced to Signor Corrado Costanzo, artigiano del dolce, burly, moustached, who offers us tastes with delicate hands – rose ice-cream, jasmin ice-cream . . . I have strawberry with tiny wild strawberries and juice on top. Von has jasmin. Rosario refuses to join us. 'Aqua, aqua!' he implores the padrone and downs several glasses. Signor Costanzo looks for our reaction and Von and I beam back flamboyantly. To confirm this good judgement, he proffers cuttings from the *New York Times* and the Italian edition of the *Reader's Digest* wherein his prowess has featured, which is mildly vexing though we don't let on. It was through Sicily and the Arabs that ice-cream came to Europe, employing the snow and ice from Aetna (once the monopoly of the Archbishop of Catania).

From here we enter the Piazza XVI Maggio, with evergreens and palms, whose principal joy is the town theatre, a delectable mid-19th century creation with giant Corinthian pilasters on the front, festooned with musical instruments, open books, and theatrical masks. It is undergoing restoration, so we can't go in. There is statuary on the skyline, the Lyric Muse flanked by trophies. Opposite is the Fountain of Hercules rescued from Noto Antica and above hangs the bulging façade of Saint Dominic's (very Borromini), a building that is perfectly poised between extravagance and elegance. The interior apparently is high and domed but it is locked and no padre with a key presents himself.

The slope on which Noto is built, with the main routes running at right angles to the gradient, makes the town a marvel of changing vistas. It alters significantly the higher you climb and it is into Noto Alta that we now go, the district of private palaces. Tiled rooftops interlock at different planes and angles, adorned by aerial statues, capitals and peeping pediments, domes, cupolas, volutes. The stone, which first seemed uniform, in fact varies enormously in colour: custard, peach, pink, grey, yellow, gold, orange. In general the buildings are low and the streets wide for an Italian town so that no part of it is oppressive.

We come to the Palazzo Nicolaci, sometimes called the Palazzo Villadorata and perhaps the most famous building in Noto, largely on account of its balconies with their heavily carved supports in the form of grotesque creatures. It is strange to chance upon such memorable sculpture in a side street, serving only to support iron balconies, and the effect is quasimedieval.

'The Prince Nicolaci is in his 70s and is the last of his line,' explains Rosario. He never married and lives by himself in this palace of 95 rooms. He also spends time at his palace in Catania and at the Villa Dorata, a big farm with vineyards not far from here. This is the last palace in Noto still inhabited by its prince – although one wing of the Palazzo Trigona is still inhabited by a descendant of the original family. Prince Nicolaci – his name is Corrado Villadorata – is a dynamic person.'

'A playboy?'

'No, no! He works very hard. He is donating the palace to the town.'

We pass several other palaces, including the Trigona which faces north and has wavy decorations producing an underwater effect. Indeed the whole of Noto has a wavy, underwater look, enhanced by the midday sun.

'This is a very beautiful palace too,' I say a little further on.

'Yes, it's the prison. One of them. We have 2 prisons.'

Poor Rosario is exhausted, from having to sustain his English as much as from anything else, and with a weary smile of relief brings us finally to his school on a terrace above the centre of town, built in 1953 in a neo-classical style so as not to offend. Attached to it is a priests' seminary and the Basilica of the Holy Saviour which is just above where we came in. The basilica is large and oval inside, very cool, painted in pale blue, pink and chocolate, with a dancing rococo movement, incorporating many cherubim and grotesques. It is an uplifting place to end.

'Rosario, you live in an incredible town.'

'Yes, Noto has starred in plenty of films. But you should visit Noto Antica too. That is very wonderful ruins.'

'Incidentally, have you heard of the Lago dei Palici?'

'No.'

'I rather suspected that.'

'He asks everybody,' pipes Von. 'It's an ancient sanctuary.'

'Is it important?' enquires Rosario.

'I think it probably is,' I reply.

We press on him a donation to the Noto preservation society which he is extremely reluctant to accept and then say good-bye. At his recommendation, we have lunch at the Trattoria del Carmine, a real trattoria, a cool room in an old house, very simple and clean, with deliciously wholesome home cooking for a few thousand lire.

'This bread,' says Von, 'is just like the buildings. Yellow, sweet, with a slightly cakey texture. Very very good.'

'So what did you think of that?'

'It's like a smaller, quieter, fruitier, *hotter* Bath – which makes it almost perfect in my book. Except – did you notice? – even this most civilised Sicilian town is not civilised like an English town. I mean – there are no antique shops, no secondhand bookshops. You always get that in England. It's because Sicily doesn't have a proper middle class. Did you find what you were looking for?'

'Ha . . .' A wicked question. It's too soon to draw conclusions. First, let it sink in. 'I haven't the faintest idea. What *was* I looking for?'

'Don't ask me. You often seem to be looking for something – but I don't know what it is.'

Noto is as far south as Tunis. On the great spinal road south, down through the heart of Europe, Noto is the very last ebullition of the European genius, the last radiant explosion of light before the sea . . . and the seething darkness of Africa . . .

We continue driving south, towards the sea, to find a pleasant spot for bathing. The road from Noto to Pachino is through neat farms and stone-walled fields. The earth has been dried by the sun to a pale brown. Every so often a derelict railway station strikes a nostalgic note on the closed railway line. But at Pachino everything disintegrates. The town is ghostly but prosperous oddly enough. The rusty railway lines, goods yards and old depots collapse silently in the afternoon heat. Dust, dust. Very siestaesque. Everything is beaten up, warped, broken. Between Pachino and the sea the fields are untidy, covered with plastic cloches and greenhouses. This gives them several crops a year and plenty of cash but the soil is being exhausted. It will be desert down here before long. At the coast are lighthouses, a 19th century mock-Saracenic castle falling down, a tunny station falling down, and much random uglification. After the joy of Noto, it feels really peculiar to be here – depressing and cold despite the burning sun.

Von says 'Lots of armpit and groin down here.'

She's being polite. It's a windswept wasteland. So the very last stop on the spine of Europe is not Noto but, of course, the arsehole. Rubble, brown grass, broken fences, derelict cottages, abandoned cars, and out of the shambles rise shabby cement blocks, half built, presumably paid for with new tomato money. Portopalo it's called.

'I don't want to swim here,' says Von solemnly.

'Neither do I. Someone said Marzamemi is a pretty fishing village. It's a mile or 2 up the coast. Let's go there.'

Marzamemi is worse because one can see that once it was indeed a pretty fishing village with lava rock falling into the sea. But now it's abandoned and so totally a wreck that it acquires a sickening fascination of its own. Lady Macbeth, Queen Mab and Hecate might holiday here at the one small hotel on a road of potholes. All the old stone cottages, with shuttered windows, redtiled roofs and beautiful proportions, have been left to collapse, as have all the quaint port buildings, and there's been a macabre attempt to build a new cement village beside them. The will to complete it gave out after a few streets were put up. These are inhabited but already look like a bomb site, with blistered paintwork, busted fences, broken balconies, and cracked walls. Chunks of rubble lie about in the roads – lamp-posts falling over – rubbish everywhere – melancholy pulverisation of place in heat. Someone has put up a few dirty cement holiday huts but whatever idea was behind them has faded away on a beach carpeted with brown and black seaweed and litter. The sea too is full of this weed which traps rubbish, and the combined unsightly mess throbs against the shore in a way which turns the stomach. A relentless buffeting wind harasses the place. A lone wind-surfer skims over the choppy weed-clogged water, a line of oil tankers on the horizon behind him. This is the end of the line, where Europe peters out in trash. The most God-forsaken place I've ever been in for the simple reason that this tragic state of affairs has nothing to do with poverty and everything to do with savagery and moronic indifference. If the nuclear bomb went off, this is how every place would look about 25 years afterwards. But they didn't need a bomb down here. They did it all by themselves. As we leave, we see a motor car wrapped round a lamp-post. Very appropriate. A number of fat Sicilians stare gloomily at it.

We are silent on the way back to Syracuse. To be hit with Noto, then Marzamemi, on the same day shocks one into silence. This must be the famous Sicilian contradiction.

Von has to fly back to England the day after to-morrow. It suddenly dawns on both of us.

'What are you looking forward to most about going home?'

'Nothing,' she says.

'At least you won't find carbuncles like Marzamemi.'

'Lizzy had one in her back.'

'A carbuncle? On her back?'

'No. *In* it. It was so big that when finally it broke and drained away, you could see the bone of her spine.'

'I had one in the neck which prevented me from going to Cleone Askew's Coming Out.'

'I had one which broke at Dartmouth,' she says.

'Mine broke at Folly Bridge. Oh God, exposing her spine to daylight?'

'Yes, some things are best hidden . . . Will you stay on at the Villa Politi?'

'No, I'll move to the Grand Hotel.'

'Yes, it looked very . . . louche.'

'And cheap. I'm paying again after to-morrow.'

'I feel quite different,' she says.

'So do I. Very open.'

'I feel I've said what I've wanted to say over this past week. Normally I filter out a great deal. I mustn't say this because, I mustn't say that because.'

And the next day she says 'To-morrow night I'll be back in London. How weird.'

'Yes, that's the curious thing about modern travel. Different cultures, different lives, slammed against each other. My mother often says "Where will you be this time to-morrow so I can think of you?" or "This time next week you'll be at so-and-so."'

'Yes, so does mine. And "I can't go. You enjoy it for me." Did your mother hold your head when you were sick?'

'Yes.'

'So did mine. I don't think I could hold a child's head while it was being sick.'

'Oh, I could.' I'm obviously more maternal than Von.

Her muff glints in the light of the setting sun. She says it's a happy muff. I say it's a hungry muff.

'You'll meet more Sicilians when I've gone,' she says.

'Oh yes . . . certainly . . . I'll meet more Sicilians . . .'

'Here,' she says and presses her Swiss Army Knife into my hand. 'Now you've got one. And I hope when you get to the Black Lake it's not too black.'

At the airport she passes through the aperture, turns back, shouts 'Io io Pan!' but not too loudly, and is gone . . .

The Grand Hotel, Ortygia, on the viale Mazzini which is the northern extension of the marine esplanade, is the place I return to. There's hardly anyone there. It's a grave. Look at *The Times* which I bought at the airport because they didn't have *The Independent*. The world of course is in terrible shape . . . The age of the Andes, according to the Science Report, has been reduced by 50 million years . . . Case before Justice Stuart-Smith. I wonder if he's a relation of Julian Stuart-Smith who committed suicide at Magdalene College, Cambridge, when I was visiting Jo Morgan there . . . Reuters report from Messina. *Signor Calogero Lo Ricco, a wartime airman who was given a suspended 3 month jail* [sic] *sentence for 'indecency in a public place' for kissing his future wife in 1941, now stands to lose his veteran's pension because of his conviction. The Treasury wants him to repay the 5,700 he has already drawn.*

Who said the Italians loved love? But one mustn't confuse the Italians with the Sicilians. They are different. God, I feel awful. We're not supposed to be alone. So . . . what am I supposed to do now?

The Grand Hotel, a felicitous essay in Venetian gothic, is one of the great hang-out hotels. It has a superb location, romantic and civilised, on the waterfront. But like all great hang-out hotels (Christina – Mexico City; Petit Hotel – Berlin; Malaysia Hotel – Bankok; Carlton – Calcutta; etc.) there's something slightly off-beam about it too. When I came and said I wanted a room overlooking the sea the receptionist said no, these rooms were booked for the whole summer. When I came back a different person said I couldn't have any room at all because they were full up! But it was clear they were almost empty. I badgered. I said I really wanted to stay there and I really wanted a front room overlooking the sea, that I'd been coming past for a week now and the shutters of these rooms were always closed and anyone could tell they were unoccupied so what was the problem? He realised I'd come prepared, his lips unglued in a sickly smile, and he said OK but all these rooms were senza bagno. I said fine, I never minded wandering the corridors in a bath robe, and with great relief booked in. I was quite unable to grasp the rationale behind his attitude.

The room is narrow, simple and clean, i.e. rude and sexy. If a hang-out hotel is not sexy, it's nothing. The entrance door is very big and the ceiling very high. Why is it that as people have grown larger, doors have shrunk and ceilings have lowered? In one corner is a wash-basin and portable bidet like a baby bath. There's one shuttered lancet window almost the height of the room, with red, blue and yellow glass filling the point. If you close the shutters for a siesta, the coloured glass remains uncovered and the room is filled with a seductive light. Looking out of the casement, to the right is the real port with ships; to the left is the marine parade of the town; below are pom-pom ficus and an oleander tree; ahead the Bay of Syracuse and a shocking pink, blue and electric peach sunset; and above a saracen moon and star appear. A sailor walks beneath the window, cracking his fingers, alone in port and slightly nervous perhaps, white cap under his arm. All this in one lancet window in Syracuse, £9 per night.

Suspiciousness breeds the desire for intimacy. The staff, having overcome their reluctance, display a wry good humour. One of them is overtly gay and follows me around making lubricious suggestions under his breath. On my way to the bathroom he mimics the action of soaping the body which I take to imply he'd adore to wash me. The principle is reasonable enough but there's something slobbery about him which is off-putting.

Next morning I open my eyes and sense a faint disturbance in the room. On opening the shutters I see there's a real gale blowing out there. The water is green and whipped up. On the esplanade a British yachtsman from Malta tells me that Syracuse harbour is well known for its winds. 'If you think it's falling down now, you should've seen it when I first came here in 1951. We like to come up to Syracuse because it's civilised. We avoid north Africa.'

I want to return to Noto and also visit Noto Antica. Driving out of town, I feel hot and bothered, lump in throat, breathless, but the countryside soothes a jittery cow. Writing makes countryboys of us all. At the Agip petrol station I'm cheated. He put in 38,000 lire and charged me 48,000. I realise it on checking my change. When I turn to show him the price on the petrol pump it's too late – another attendant is using it to fill another car. There's nothing I can do. It dawns on me that I'm by myself – meaning that there's no one else around to help out with perception. So I must wake up. If I become broody and inward-turning, I'll be ripped off again or worse. But it's tiresome always having to be vigilant, never taking anything on trust; and worst of all, it makes one suspicious of people whose behaviour is exemplary. And in fact in my personal dealings with Sicilians I have found them, despite all the warnings, to be trustworthy and helpful. This morning was the first deceit. I look at him with his silly Tony Curtis quiff and yellow t-shirt rolled up to reveal mean little bicepettes, and tell him he's overcharged me. He makes that irritating Sicilian gesture – a sharp backward movement of the head accompanied by a frown which is feigned surprise mixed with hostility. If I had persisted he might have gone into Gesture No. 2 in which surprise is replaced by exaggerated bewilderment – the arms thrown wide, the head sunk into raised shoulders and turning to left and right in appeal. Who me, steal? My God, what a thought! But I can't be bothered to get into all that for £5. We both know he's ripped me off; it's in our eyes. Thanks mate, a right ol' kick in the culo. I leave.

Because I am this time concentrating on my surroundings and not talking to Von, I notice with a stab that the first sign of Noto is a large grey high-tech building up on the left with terracotta-coloured blinds. Now, this is the first *grey* modern block I've seen in Sicily and where do they choose to put it? On the edge of Noto, the Golden City, and up on a treeless bluff so everyone can see it. This wilful destructiveness is mindblowing.

In Noto I visit the Civic Museum which contains very beautiful fragments and a partially reconstructed Sanctuary of Demeter. Many small terracotta figures of women whose faces are earthy, unearthly, alive, impassive, all at once. And prancing grotesques with exorbitant members. On this island one is never far from the penis, the breast, the womb. At 12.30 p.m. I feel the need for meat and cutting short the museum visit, walk to the Trattoria del Carmine where I ask for pasta followed by lamb and beans – a girl pops out to buy the cutlet. It's served with ½ a lemon to cut the oil and fat, and more of that delicious yellow bread.

Leaving the town for Noto Antica I pass a new hospital of aggressive rectilinear design and great size which sends a shudder through my body. The glory of Sicily now is its countryside, mysterious, extraordinary, moving. Over a bridge with 4 obelisks and showing on the left, a rare sight, a grand country villa. A limestone gorge whose river makes the bottom thick with trees like a winding secret garden. Then a twist in the road, over a bridge, and hanging above is the Sanctuary of Santa Maria della Scala, growing out of the stone on which it stands, established by Fratello Terzi in the first ½ of the 18th century. He liked to whip himself as a penance and in one of the cells here you can view the bloodstains.

A few kilometres on and the fortress of the old town greets you with ruined bastions. It is the most substantial survival at the site and hereafter the road becomes rubble. Leaving the car, I walk. The rest is mostly remnants of house walls, not very high and heavily overgrown in an arcadian wilderness of ivy, low trees, stones and bushes. Occasionally a tumbled block is carved with a cornice. Small brown animals elude the glance, vanish behind rocks. There is no one up here – and it feels as if there hasn't been for many years. Not a speck of litter, not one empty tin. It is warm and quiet, birds sing, and the countryside reveals itself between trees and recedes into poetical panoramas. Here and there in Europe you may still find something cultivated but absolute in landscape, something which is perfectly beautiful because man is there and yet his parasitism and greed and ignorance are not. The borders of England and Wales between Hay-on-Wye and Montgomery. The landscape from Lacoste to Bonnieux. And here too. Everything balanced, connected, functioning, harmonious, belonging. I am in a glade full of birds, take off all my clothes and become elemental. The sun is hot across the shoulders and my shadow is strong upon the earth. Only in the north are shadows weak. In the south shadows are jet black and sharp-edged and if you here describe someone as being like a shadow you do not mean a feeble quantity but one more sinister and decisive. The body breathes. The blood slows. A few old buildings snuggle in the hills. And a breeze sends gusts of warm air into the nostrils and the perfume is like incense, not in a vague metaphorical way but exactly like that. I sit on a fallen tree attracting brown and yellow butterflies. A brimstone yellow variety bears large orange blotches on its wings like a Rothko. A profound composure settles in me. Perhaps it is only for some minutes but this is the moment of perfect peace at the end of the trail, the idyllic point beyond which it is impossible to travel, about which it is difficult to speak. If all travel is the pursuit of magic, and the purpose of the pursuit of magic is to get one's rocks off, what is the purpose of getting one's rocks off? . . . To exalt oneself . . . And the purpose of exaltation? . . . To find oneself . . . Which is to say, to lose oneself . . . And the purpose of losing oneself is happiness . . .

I dress, return to the car, drive along the rubble road and in due course spot a broken wooden sign, hanging down and blowing in the breeze, with 'Museo di Noto Antica' daubed on it. It points in no particular direction but there's another rubble track leading off this one, so I take it and it becomes rougher and rougher. This must be wrong. There can't be a museum up a track with boulders in it. But there can . . . and eventually a small group of dilapidated structures comes into view . . . and eventually an ancient codger, with weathered nutbrown skin, cloth cap and jolly smile whose centrepiece is a single tooth with ½ tooth adjacent, shows up on a path and drags open an iron gate into a grassy courtyard. He wears a pair of threadbare orange canvas shoes held together by wish fulfilment but his manners are sanguine.

This is the monastery of Santa Maria della Provvidènza, derelict of course, built after the earthquake to celebrate deliverance, although since the entire city was thrown down and many killed this might be said to be stretching a point about God's kindness. The last monks left in 1929 or 1959 – he has a thick accent difficult to penetrate – but it looks as if it were 100 years ago. The vacant cells upstairs have a view of the sea, a slice of brilliant blue through a fissure in the hills. Outside the upper windows, fig, pistachio and olive trees poke up their arms from the monastery garden run wild. The inside of the tiled roof is lined with bamboo and reeds. He takes me up again to a roof terrace and asks if I'm cold because of the wind blowing up here. I say no, because I'm from London and he laughs showing all his gums and 1½ teeth. I ask about a small villa over there. 'Vacuo,' he says. And that one? 'Vacuo. Vacuo. Tutti vacui . . .' he says, twinkling, chuckling. They are marvellous old houses, quite large, all empty because the owner does not want them but refuses to sell any land. You never sell land in Sicily if you can help it, not even the small squares on which the cottages sit, so they rot.

He wants to know why I am by myself. I feel a faint stab and say because my friend had to return to London to work. He said he had a visit yesterday too, a couple from Argentina.

Taking off his cap he leads the way into the chapel, disintegrating baroque stucco painted over with an ivy motif, painted vault falling down, floor of cracked majolica tiles, rickety chandelier holding stumps of candles hanging lopsided in the nave. He takes me up to the gallery. The windows are broken and open to the weather. Swifts swoop up and down the nave, chasing each other at high speed, then zip out of the window then zip back again. The vestry has a vivid ceiling of blue, mauve and orange. The 'body' of the museum is on the ground floor, odds and ends, fascinating, slight, as though ornamental stonework had been propped up where it fell. Round the back is half the skeleton of an 18th century coach, bits of carved and painted doors splitting in the sun. This place should not be restored. It is a true museum, a living, decaying relic from the past, returning in tranquillity to nature . . .

I shrug my shoulders and grin and give him 3000 lire which he accepts gracefully with a little lift of his cap and smiling eyes. It is 4.40 p.m. The heat of the day has matured. That vicious edge has been worn off it. The day is in its democratic prime, a time when all its aspects can comfortably coexist without any one dominating.

Taking another road back, one sees Noto from a different position, from *the* position, the one which encompasses the whole in its setting. But wholeness alas is destroyed by the new hospital which is the largest building in the town, a chunk of Brasilia with hard corners and sharp lines completely out of character and slapped down without a thought on one of the most sensitive sites in Sicily. Until the hospital came a few years ago, Noto had preserved its drama and integrity from all assault.

I move along to a point where by shuffling round a bit I can entirely mask the hospital with the trunk of a tree – and the result is *unbelievable*. Noto becomes once again a regal city, the seat of potentates, utterly fabulous, rising in palatial terraces softened by palm and pine, rich gold with the mature sunshine of afternoon streaming on to it. Having recourse to this optical trick, by moving not an inch forwards or backwards or to left or right, I find myself gazing at last upon the shitless city of my dreams.

Friday 13th. A low day. Von gone. Post Noto anti-climax. Earlier I sorted through all the bumf accumulated on this journey – catalogues, programmes, guides, maps, postcards, brochures – and decided to post back to England everything not immediately required. Quite an amount of feuilleton. Purchased brown paper and sellotape and did up a fat

parcel and went off to the Post Office which is to Syracuse what the
Liver Building is to Liverpool, an unmistakable lump down on the
water which is rather appealing. I queued for a long time. When I
reached the girl behind the grille, she said I was in the wrong queue
and should go to Counter 1. So I went to Counter 1 where in front
of me a man was choosing various stamps to start off his son's stamp
collection. This took a long time, involving thoughtful discussion of
the respective merits of various packets on offer. Eventually he paid
up and left and I proffered my fat parcel. The man behind the counter
said I was at the wrong place. Very disgruntled, I asked why. He said I
should be at Counter 7, so I went to 7. Which was unattended. I waited.
No one appeared. I tapped and coughed. A twisted bloke with ginger
freckles shambled out of a hole at the back, a cigarette hanging from
his mouth. He took one look at my parcel, shook his head and spoke
at length. I didn't understand. He demonstrated slowly. There is a
standard procedure for wrapping parcels which I had not observed.
The brown paper was fine. But it had to be sealed *completely* with
wide brown tape, wound about with string, and a special soft metal
clip fastened to the knot. Discouraged, I withdrew to the cartelleria
to purchase this solemn kit, only to discover – wonder of wonders –
that the cartelleria will do it all for you! Can you imagine a stationery
shop in England wrapping your parcels? It cost a mille, as these
things do. Suddenly I was buoyant and returned to the Post Office,
Counter 7, glad of eye, springy of step. After a little hectoring from
me, twisted-with-freckles laboriously worked his way out of the hole,
another fag hanging off his lip, and squared himself up behind the
grille. He presented me with a form in duplicate and with another
form in triplicate, the indications in Italian and French. Anything
I didn't understand I left blank – which appeared not to matter at
all. We were breezing through now. He took the forms and began to
write. His writing went on and on and on, a smooth act of inscription
with ballpoint in an elegant script. He then weighed the monster.
Over 4 kilos and expensive but by this stage I didn't care a hoot.
Anything to get shot of the bugger. Airmail? Yes, airmail please. *Very*
expensive. But I felt it would never arrive if sent any other way. So he
started writing again. On and on. Followed by stamping – stamping –
stamping – glueing insignia on to forms – glueing insignia and forms
on to the parcel which he stamped and wrote upon as well. He gave
me one of the forms back, asked for 40,000 lire, and said Ecco. By
this time a faintly fascinated crowd had gathered at my back and was
craning over my shoulders. I turned, smiled at them all, walked out
and kissed the sky.

To-night I go to the Vagabonda for Maccheroni alla Vagabonda –

spinach, ham, cheese, peas, herbs. They turn on the television for me to watch. It is a programme about AIDS. The whole family watches it while I eat.

The Malta Express is in, a large blue and white ship moored near my hotel. And suddenly Syracuse reminds me of Penang.

Sunday 9.30 a.m., Foro Italico. A canoeist in the bay, a hang glider above him, 2 cyclists, and on the seat next to me is a man in a tracksuit reading the Bible. Then hundreds of roller skaters enter from the right with a heavy drone. There is to be a rally here. They will race in a loop and at the end an enormous number of long-stemmed cups will be borne away by the victorious. I have spent hours on the marine parade, looking around. No one talks to me. I'm beginning to feel invisible.

A beautiful yacht called *Queenie* is to-night moored opposite my window and lit up with lights. I can't connect here now. It's like a pane of glass separates me from the place. Even the gay porter has disappeared. I've become like a shark. Unless I move forward, I sink. I must move deeper in. Deeper into Sicily. I must find that Black Lake. By morning *Queenie* has gone – and so have I.

13

The Black Lake

Bowling along on the Great High Way – unstructured, swimming – or rather, the structure is the line – the line of time, of movement, which is not an intellectual structure but the line of life, that is to say, the line of *a* life (and which can therefore be rendered only in the present tense) – past Canicattini the landscape bleakens – a floating limestone horizon spotted with trees – the cemetery at Palazzolo Acreide is a miniature baroque city of domes and turrets and pediments, about 8 feet high among dark cypresses. The inland people are noticeably more curious about me than the coastal people, but they are also more relaxed. The road is serpentine, bordered by yellowing grass and red poppies. Here is a fine group of buildings half-abandoned, with several farms beyond totally abandoned. On the road from Buccheri to Vizzini this abandonment of the oceanic, wheat-gold countryside is very strange but not mournful . . . aroma of rosemary and animal shit blowing in through the window . . .

Vizzini presents a piebald cataract of old tiled roofs tumbling down the hillside, spoiled by several mini skyscrapers dumped in the middle. No undamaged hill town so far in Sicily. Many of the hill towns of Provence are undamaged – I don't mean unmodern – just that the French have in many places demanded that new buildings respect the visual coherence of the whole. But it is beginning to dawn on me that Sicilians actually *want* to destroy that visual coherence. For them the mini skyscraper is a signal of success and the past means inferiority.

A pitched roof reflects the shape of a hillside, the irregularity of landscape. But blocks of flats with flat roofs have a cruel, incisive effect, comprising an act of aggression against the terrain. A mass of pitched tiled roofs at different levels ripples in the eye. That's almost all it takes to preserve the beauty of these old towns – pitched tiled roofs and blocks which are not too big. But it is too much to ask. It's a curious paradox that randomness en masse produces harmony but regularity en masse produces cacophony. Pico della Mirandola thought that the essence of beauty was 'harmony in discord'.

I've been looking for a country hotel but this is not a Sicilian concept at all. Sicilians need people around them, the reassurance of noise. Animals live in the countryside. People live in the town. And another curious thing – most towns are divided into the old town (pre-war) and the new town (post-war), and the new town feels itself superior to the old town which in turn feels inferior. In Britain it's the other way round.

Mirabella, silent as death at 1.50 p.m. – dead dog in the road – very steep wheatfields – they can plough up to 45° – now a thick woodland runs beside the road, gorgeous and unfamiliar because trees cover only 0.75% of Sicily. Pull over onto a sidetrack in a deciduous valley with stream, so fresh and reviving that it's impossible to believe one is only 150 miles from Africa. This is Berkshire. Now don't start getting homesick . . .

Sign to Piazza Armerina. Riccardo spoke of the Villa Imperiale here, with lavish Roman mosaic floors. Better check it out but the signs are confusing and I get coiled up in the town. Stop to ask for help and a man, with extraordinary consideration, offers to lead me there in his car since the villa is some way into the countryside. My goodness, I can't imagine an Englishman or Frenchman being so chivalrous to a stranger. I follow the obliging car down steep streets of lava cobbles, juddering terribly. Currently a by-pass is being built, since the mosaics have become one of the biggest attractions on the island. The great concrete piers are already up. Workmen smoke, after lunch, lolling against the massive bases.

The mosaics were discovered in 1716, having been buried by a landslide, but systematic excavation did not begin until 1950. One enters the villa via the ancient lavatories, and of the villa itself, which is thought to have been built by a late Roman Emperor as a hunting lodge, virtually nothing remains above floor level. But what floors. They lie beneath a mauve perspex roof shaped to reproduce the villa's original outline. It's *hot* under this perspex; in fact it's suffocating; but I move, dripping, valiant, agape, through the circuit of walkways suspended above the pictorial mosaics (of the North African School) which have sagged in waves. The temperature makes it impossible to look at leisure, but I am held nonetheless by the expression of a figure labelled 'Ambrosia' on the postcard. Ambrosia was the food, sometimes the drink, of the gods but was not to my knowledge personified in mythology. Here she is however, Michelangelesque, with the breasts of a woman but the massiveness of a man and a face which is both powerful and androgynous, fruits and leaves twisted into the hair. Why is the expression so affecting, so restful and sublime? As though recognised by the heart from long long ago, recognised but not remembered. Its power is sensitive. Its androgyny is not ambiguity. Its emotion is loving but with a strength that reassures. The face has good bone structure, is generously made, without excess, sensual but not self-indulgent and on the verge of a smile, sweetly ironical. The eyes are wide apart under firm and gentle eyebrows, alive to laughter and tears but for this eternal moment steady, clear. Many contradictions are resolved in this face. Most androgynous figures are boyish, of pretty males, but this is of a vastly handsome woman, young and wise, empresslike, solitary, never alone.

The absence of rustic accommodation forces me on to Enna, passing Lake Pergusa, a once-holy spot and locus of the chthonic dieties: Demeter (Ceres), Persephone (Proserpine), Hades (Pluto). This is the larger of Sicily's 2 'mystery' lakes, Palici being quite small according to my information. Pergusa has been turned into a holiday centre, with a racetrack built round the circular sandy shore of the lake. It's shabby and downcast. Maybe it comes to life when there's a race. Nobility bestialised and vice versa is coming to be part of Sicily's awesome, awful fascination. In minutes we've passed from bestiality to bliss. The thrusts and posturing of the Sicilian landscape whip themselves up at its exact centre into a craggy flourish on top of which Enna plonks itself. My room at the Hotel Belvedere here has the most staggering view of any room I've known. Can you bear to have another view verbally communicated? What *is* the point? Here it comes anyway, disjointedly because it is too big to encompass in a glance. The reason why this view is so staggering is that it isn't just staggering. This one is *unusual*. A view's view. It is a landscape painted by Cranach or Altdorfer. It does not exist in the 20th century but is medieval which, to the civilised mind, makes it seem much older than say a classical view. It is phantasmagorical, suggestive of a tale by the Brothers Grimm. There are modern things in it but not many and nothing which interferes with this sense of being in a different time zone. It is a view north, rain right, sunshine left, mountains in background. It contains everything light can do. The colours – blue, grey, green, gold. Some clouds move at eye level like absent-minded ships, contributing much to the rippling play of light. There is a lake; and a million fields, each a different colour. And in the centre middleground is Calascibetta the Impossible, at long last a perfectly whole hill town unafflicted by blocks, a knight errant's dream, impenetrably old, dreamily alive. The landscape is brooding, as if there's to be a storm, but there is a coolness in the room which I haven't felt since the Sila.

The hotel is Vicwardian without, Art Deco within. Old men sit outside and stand along the Belvedere and in the small adjacent piazza with its fine statue of Hades raping Persephone. The lamps in the centre of the piazza are tall and the lights are in globes of milk-white glass which are held in nets of wire. The old men are dressed in the clothes of the 1940s, of their youth – wide ties, passegiata suits, some cloth caps, the occasional 'Sinatra' hat. Many carry walking sticks and all have moustaches and totter about like a crowd of ancient Clark Gables. Men and boys, but few women, come up here and gaze over the parapet for hours, hypnotised. The men at the tables outside the hotel are in conspiracy – put 3 or more Sicilian males round a table and they at once acquire a look of devilry. Take any Sicilian male and make him stand up on his own and he either becomes ludicrously inflated or squirmy, vulnerable, interesting, revealing.

As Mahler's 6th Symphony begins to turn on the cassette player there's an almighty crack of thunder! It echoes right across the view, that is, right across the island. Then silence. Smoke from far-off stubble burning drifts slowly across the scene from right to left. Then – I don't believe it, dead centre – a fork of lightning, off-white, attacks the earth from clouds of Biblical purple rolling biliously. Silence. Birdsong . . . Crack of thunder . . . The gathering storm seems fantasy made palpable, mythology in action. Another fork of lightning, orange . . . Boom . . . My skin is crawling with goose pimples. Need a groin to earth this growing intensity. Comes over one the absolute necessity to fuck. Don't know what to say about this – I feel most peculiar . . . Here comes the rain, fierce rain echoing in the room . . . My mind goes back to when I was in prison.

In the evening a well-dressed little boy comes up to me in the street and shows me his fluffy pink bunny. His grandmother, one of those dear old ladies in black with a bun, smiles and prompts the young boy to ask me for lire which he does. Repelled by this coarseness, I glare at the old bat and shout 'Non!' and walk away. I'll never be sentimental about black widows again. Continuing up to the cathedral I notice a fair bit of fascist architecture and surmise there must be an election going on because everything is covered with posters, even church walls. Though getting dark the cathedral is open and lit up but difficult to appreciate because the nave is filled with scaffolding for renovations. The interior has that brazen weirdness one associates with the Victorians but it is much older than that. The Rev. Gerard Irvine told me that someone told him that in the cathedral at Enna is a statue of the Virgin marked as holding the *santissima bambina*. 'Which is Persephone of course,' he said. But he told me this next year at the Chittys' midsummer garden party in Sussex. I do not know it yet so cannot look for it. One thing I do want to look for is the church of Santo Spirito. Douglas Sladen says though built only in 1817, *the date does not prevent the hermit who shows you over the church pointing out the spot where Our Lady received the Annunciation and the stove at which she was cooking, and the nine green tiles on which she was standing. You are also shown the crown of thorns.*

A man flicks through a great number of television channels in the Art Deco TV room. Reception is very good because Enna is the transmitting point for a large area. He stops at a film set in London – London looks very smart, clean and bracing, a highly wrought, playful environment. In fact it looks bizarre. Red telephone boxes figure greatly in the film whose heroine keeps pulling up outside them in a white Mini. An old Sicilian gent is utterly absorbed, rapt, but breaks off from time to time to make dirty remarks in a guttural voice to anyone who cares to listen. The end credits announce Monica Vitti in *La Ragazza Con La Pistola* with Stanley Baker, Corin Redgrave, Anthony Booth. Stylish 1968 lunacy.

Awake to a view smeared with mist, cloud, rain. Thick scarves of cloud twirl round Calascibetta. My whole body responds to this sensual coolness and moisture flowing in through the window.

'Piove, piove! Fantastico,' I say to the waiter at breakfast.

He pulls a scowl and says 'Bruto tempo. Non normale.'

2 German tourists at the next table. Men. I ask if they speak English and one of them, fat, distinguished, with grey hair, says 'Yes I do, as it happens.'

They are from Munich. I say what an amazing hotel this is for its view and Distinguished Grey Hair replies 'We have found one that is even better. At Cortona. With a view over Lake Trasimene.'

These Modern Germans always know of 'a better one'. Whatever you mention – hotel, wine, method of cooking pork, leather shop – they always know of 'a better one'.

They are going on to Syracuse and want an hotel at this price in the old town. I suggest the Grand. 'It's a bargain.' Nobody loves a bargain more than the Modern German. 'But it's slightly worn.' The Modern German doesn't make the mistake of equating 'new' with 'quality'. In fact the Modern German's world is so new, so managed, so product-based, that shabbiness, decrepitude, decadence have an irresistible fascination for him.

'There are lots of Germans at Taormina,' I say.

'We've not been there yet,' says Undistinguished & Quiet.

'You must stay at the Villa Is – I mean, I don't know anywhere to stay there. There are busloads of French at Piazza Armerina.'

'Those mosaic girls in bikinis,' wonders Distinguished Grey Hair, 'do you think they are fake? I think they are.'

'I assumed they weren't fake. When could it've been faked?'

'In the 1950s, when they were beginning to uncover it. A good idea to promote tourism. You notice that it is laid upon another floor.'

'Yes, but this is not uncommon, one floor laid over another.'

'None the less it would have been a good opportunity for a fake.'

He chuckles, looks into his newspaper and tells me that it's 28°C in London. Undistinguished & Quiet complains about how all the towns of Sicily have been destroyed by terribly ugly concrete buildings. 'How can they dissociate so completely from the reality of the place?' he asks, which is certainly one way of putting it.

'Yes,' I say, 'the towns have grown cancers, cellular rebellions of the body. But funnily enough, Calascibetta looks untouched. But I shan't visit it in case I discover I'm wrong.'

The waiter, delivering more cups of very strong, corrosive and lethal morning coffee, says that the people of Calascibetta are unpleasant, 'Arabico.' I look out of the window into the little dripping square. The streets are deserted. Sicilians hate the rain. It interferes with their clothes and hair-dos. But in 30 minutes the mist and rain have cleared to bands of low cloud strung between the world and the heaven. A powerful odour like wet woollens rises from the vegetation. The sun comes out. The heat switches on.

I walk up to the Castle of the Lombards and the Rock of Demeter beyond. The view is astonishing but the usual blight prevents Aetna from being seen. Up at the Rock, ornate lamps are smashed to pieces; graffiti and broken glass bottles everywhere. When it comes to abuse of the environment the contemporary Italian is the most unrestrained barbarian in Europe. What is the significance of leaving one's initials over everything? It must be thwarted egoism, the need to be individually significant. This need is checked in Italy by the presence of church and family and expresses itself in these puerile ways. And the amount of broken glass is startling. It must be the thing to do, to come up here and shatter bottles against the Rock of Demeter.

The church of Santo Spirito is the other end of town and by the time I reach it, it's a ruin. Perched on a cliff edge in a forgotten plot overlooked by flats and tall radio towers is this tiny neo-classical shell with dead belltower. The vestry looks inhabited as 'a house'. Long grass grows round the church. I peer between the doors padlocked with rusty chains. The roof's down. Grass and small bushes grow in the nave. The arches are flaking. So much for that. Behind the church a tethered orange dog begins to bark and wag his tail. I rub him behind the ears and look out from the weed-grown precipice edge to the unfolded countryside which begins to swoon and hiss in the morning heat. Somewhere out there is the Lago dei Palici. OK, let's go and find it.

The land is made more vivid by recent rain. Leonforte presents a fine rooftop pattern above prickly pears and olives, and beyond I glimpse Assoro of which Lisetta spoke. It looks quite large and when I reach it, the inhabitants do indeed treat me with unconcealed astonishment. Many of them have blond or ginger complexions. Ruined fortress above the town, a ruined church, splendid views, and poor modern building. But it doesn't feel isolated. All these small towns regard themselves as party to the latest goings-on in urban civilisation, largely through the TV culture which has strong international characteristics. If a common pool of understanding comes from a common pool of experience, perhaps TV will save the world. Cultural distinctions these days are valued for tourism, sexual excitement, and as raw material for TV programmes, that's all.

Road N. 121 . . . Aetna appears ahead looking huge, and below it the town of Agira, wildly romantic on its hill which echoes the shape of the volcano. It's almost approaching midday and I'd like to stop the car for a while in order to contemplate the scene but I need a tree to shelter under and there are none; both myself and the car would burn up without the breeze of movement. Petrol at Agira, then the road south enters a region of wheat Sahara, seas of gold stretching to the horizon and *no trees*. You don't want to blow a tyre in country like this. The flaring fields sport rocky outcrops like fluffs of ice-cream. Not a tree, not a town, not an inhabited cottage to be seen anywhere. But instead of being bleak the effect is thought-provoking. A herd of cattle comes bounding down a hill like puppies, churning up the brown earth with their hooves. Unlike the landscapes of Tuscany, Provence, England, Switzerland, even Australia, the Sicilian landscape has not been painted and exported into general awareness. Driving south from Agira, an autostrada crosses my line of vision and before I know it I'm thrown helplessly on to the motorway. I don't want this. Plunging towards Catania in the fierce heat but I don't want this. Look, I'm flying towards Catania, help, let me off! – A sign says: Fango. What an attractive word. It suggests something lilting and festive. (Later I look it up; it means *mud*.)

I fly off the motorway at the first opportunity, take the road south and find miraculously a grove of eucalyptus beside a spring to park under while I have my orange, but eucalyptus trees do not have dense foliage so there is only partial shade. It's the old hairdryer story now. Any breeze is like a hairdryer in the face but the heat makes my balls loose. So l-o-o-s-e . . . Tootling along – lavoro in progresso –

oh hell, this road is blocked too – will they dump me back on to the motorway? Look, I have to get down to the area between Mineo and Palagonia. That much I've divined from *Baedeker* (because the Lago dei Palici is not marked on my otherwise extremely detailed Touring Club Italiano Grande Carta Stradale di Sicilia) . . . What are we doing in a tunnel for God's sake? I'm driving in a tunnel. Ugh, out the other side and on the right is a lake of *turquoise* water set in *gold* hills . . . Oh God, the road's being ploughed up. Have to go all the way back! This is the *third* fucking road to die out on me. The turquoise lake is very pretty but it's not the fucking black lake! Cool it, cool it, less bad language, but honestly, all 3 cross-country routes are being modernised simultaneously – why don't they do one at a time? Now there's a question you're not supposed to ask. Backtrack and pick up the main routes – Aidone – Piazza Armerina – Caltagirone – then along the N.417 northeast. So l-o-o-s-e. Short cut to the left – strada discsstata. Procedere con prudenza. No, no, I've had enough of these ruined roads. We'll stick to the main one . . . well, the road I'm sticking to is pretty ruinous too. Another strada disesstata. Oh fuck this. Car dump as you enter Aidone and the town slides by like a heap of rubble.

Now we are on a road. I suppose we were on roads before but it didn't feel like it. N.117. Leave Piazza Armerina in the Gela direction. Turning off at San Michele I see the first punk in Sicily – diffident mohican haircut and rather foppish attire but what courage to declare himself thus where the forces of social conformity are the strongest in western Europe. Haven't seen any tattoos in Sicily . . . I'm thirsty. I'd love to find a bar where I shan't have to be either an entertainment for the locals or hold myself tensely aloof. There's aqua minerale in the car of course – I'm not an idiot. But it's 2 days old. And it's hot. Still, when you're sweating and thirsty, hot water 2 days old is not to be sniffed at. Actually, I ought perhaps to give it a sniff, to make sure . . . It's taking me hours to get to this lake. 5½ hours so far. And another of the wheel balances has come off during all that jolting over ruinous roads.

Palagonia 6 kms – turn off right here. Sinister outcrop of rocks covered with cactuses and filthy turf. Could this be it? Ah! A powerful, perhaps even godlike odour emanates from a line of cypresses on the right. It has a musky, animal quality, which seems apt for a god. Suddenly the entire vicinity seems possessed by a supernatural power. Shaggy. Pagan. It is impossible to say why, because the area is basically a fertile plain of citrus and olive groves surrounded by scrubby hills, but nothing looks normal round here. Those piles of rock have strange smooth shapes. *Slimy*. Oozing with occult meaning, as if they are trying and failing to communicate with me. There is a sign. *Feta dei Palici Stabilimento*. I don't understand. According to the 1908 map, the lake is somewhere here. Yet not the slightest evidence of it.

. . . as soon as they enter the water. The ancients regarded the spot as sacred and the peculiar resort of the gods. The Dii Palici were believed to be sons of Zeus and the nymph Thalia. A sumptuous temple was accordingly erected here, to which the pious flocked from all quarters, but every vestige of it has now disappeared. Fugitive slaves found an asylum in this temple. An oath sworn by the Dii Palici was deemed peculiarly solemn. (Baedeker's Southern Italy and Sicily, 1908.)

But nothing . . . nothing . . . Here is a T junction on to the main road between Palagonia and Mineo. Is it along here? Nothing . . . No. . . . The village marked on the Baedeker map as Fondacazzo has entirely disappeared. A few derelict huts over there, presumably that's Fondacazzo . . . Better turn round because I'll soon be in Mineo and it's definitely not there. This is creepy. I stop and ask a farmer spraying his trees and he hasn't a clue what I'm on about. I see a group of field labourers standing by the road and ask them. They tell me to ask at a house about a kilometre further along the road. Well, that's where we came in, so I drive back towards the funny cactus-covered rocks and opposite I see a house with a small factory behind it, corresponding to the sign which I had previously misread. *Mefeta dei Palici Stabilimento*.

A man is asleep on the front porch. I spy him through railings and pink oleanders. I call, explain myself and he opens a pair of green iron gates. 'Come in, come in. I'll show you the lake.' This is very rum. He's got it wrong. He doesn't realise. But he is charming and courteous.

'No, no, the Lago dei Palici,' I protest.

'Sì, sì. Qui, qui.'

What is going on?

I park the car and 2 big dogs rub against me. He takes me round the side of the house to the small factory where men are working. Iron canisters of gas are stacked against walls. We pass through the hissing factory and out the other side into a citrus grove and I think 'Yes, he's going to take me through the citrus groves to this extraordinary, secret place that I've come across all Europe to see.'

We walk past several low sheds, a few trees, the dogs disappear, and suddenly he stops.

'Questo,' he says. 'Il lago dei Palici.'

There is a pungent odour in the air, reminiscent of the flanks of hyaenas or of the blood-matted hair of Aztec priests. And in front of us, surrounded by a vivid green pool of slimy bubbling water, is a tall metal shaft like a silver rocket.

'What?'

'Sì. Il lago dei Palici.'

I can't believe it. This? Which is to say – that? The oldest religious sanctuary in Sicily? A weird slimy pond, muddy, weedy, grassy round its edge. And from its centre rising to perhaps 20 feet is a silver rocket. A silvery pipe extends from the top of the rocket and disappears through undergrowth towards the factory.

'Gas!' he proclaims in English. 'Gas!'

I look around. Another strange device, a silvery dome, is embedded in the ground beyond the pool. And beyond this dome, the groves.

I'm confounded. He slaps his thighs laughing. I think maybe he's having me on, enjoying a practical joke to enliven a soporific afternoon. He makes the motion of hurling a stone to the ground and howls with laughter. 'Gas! Gas! Gas!' He has a mass of silvery alloy in his teeth.

But it's not a joke. This is the Black Lake. 10 or 12 feet across. He says it used to be much bigger but it's getting smaller all the time. And that the water used to be very dark but the slime has turned it bright green. Bubbling green slime with a rocket emerging from its centre.

They have trapped the subterranean gas source which produced the curious phenomena and turned it to a commercial purpose. CO_2 for beer, Coca Cola, water, etc. And they make dry ice from it too. He shows me all this on a guided tour of the factory. The dry ice is beautiful, like steaming marble. 'Dal lago,' he says. He approaches a large metal cylinder, twists a knob on the top, and it hisses furiously with concentrated power, like a genie outraged by its imprisonment. 'Dal lago,' he says, 'gas naturale.'

He tells the great joke to one of the workers, about how an Englishman, overcoming all manner of impediments and distractions, travelled the whole length of Europe at great expense in order to view a small gas plant.

'A fine subject for a book,' I say, feeling gormless – morose – angry.

'It's been like this for 50 years,' says the worker as he screws up something with a spanner.

But the mystery is solved. They've fucked Pergusa. And they've fucked Palici. They don't care. I tell him the story of the lake as best I can in pidgin Italian. 'Very old story. From before Greeks.'

'Yes, I know,' he says. 'Now it's a very modern story!' And he breaks into more laughter and slaps his thighs as he escorts me back to the car. He waves me off with a broad grin of silvery teeth and the

2 dogs wag their tails, seeming to smile too. And I drive back past the cypresses with their heady, groiny odour, and past the sinister greasy rocks covered with prickly pears, and up to the main road. A little way along I stop at a garage and bar and order cappuccino, a panino prosciutto e formaggio, and a cold pear juice. The boy serving has a long fingernail on his little finger to prove he's not a labourer and expresses great interest in my sunglasses. I'm wearing the blue shorts of course and flies repeatedly bite my legs.

Well, I found it anyway. Play the Blow Monkeys *loudly*.

But back at Enna in the Hotel Belvedere I go into a dive. Disappointed, depressed, homesick, lonely. I'm hungry for human contact which I mistake as hunger for food, cross the road to the nearest restaurant and order a huge meal. Maccheroni followed by fegato. The maccheroni I manage to get down but the liver – 3 great flaps of it each the size of my hand plus a mountain of beans – I simply can't swallow. When your throat closes on liver, it *really* closes. I feel completely choked. A panic of loneliness sweeps over me. I ask for the bill, explaining that I'm a bit bad in the stomach from too much red wine. It's a lie of course and they are offended all the same but I've got to get *out* of this restaurant and get my head down on the bed, and have a good cry.

The vagabond state which was so sweet at Sora has here turned sour, ugly. My balls which were this morning so loose and free are now pulled up tight with anxiety. Tight in the balls and tight in the head. I'm hot and I'm sweating. And I'm unhappy and worried. I'm unhappy because I'm alone. Am I looking for love? Of course. OK, let's think about love for a moment. Unhappiness shared is unhappiness halved. But that's negative and selfish and the difficulties of life hardly end there and love itself is an action, not a palliative. Love is a need. The need to give. And the reassurance of receiving. Love is an art, the communication of the true self, and therefore it is difficult. It is growth and therefore painful as well as joyous. Love has fullness – and emptiness too. One can be open to love or closed to love but one cannot plan for it. Many people don't like it because they consider it an invasion of privacy. Fear and habit are deadly to love – not so much physical fear as emotional fear, not so much physical habit as mental habit. All travel is the search for love, or the exploration of love.

And I'm unhappy because this journey to the south, so full of wonders, has also been acutely chastening. Travel is escape – which is the abstraction of love and love's precondition. I use here the word 'escape' and not 'freedom' because it is more dynamic, has that sense of a resistance overcome. Freedom becomes significant only in so far as it is exercised. The act of escape is always magical. Translocation becomes transformation. Becomes discovery. Not all discoveries are pleasant. So many magical names on the map – and so often when you reach them, such a mess! In the future people will stay at home and dream.

The world was contained on a human scale until 1914 – after which technology permitted us to create on a scale which overwhelms us. Technology replaced man as the measure of capability and the world became jagged, sudden, gigantic, crazy, alien, unexpected, irrational, explosive, electric, zig-zagging, ruthless, ugly, sexy, astonishing. And so populations became more passive. The book remains significant because it is the only art form or medium in which mechanisation increases opportunity without increasing passivity. Music, cinema, theatre, painting, television – the audience can loll before these and often does. But without the *active* participation of the *individual*, the book does not happen. For this reason, most people prefer to read pictures and images and sounds rather than language.

The media work on a passive population to sell them faraway places. Brochures, television programmes, pictorial articles in the press and the cinema, feed us images of a dream world. As I have discovered on this journey, it is extremely difficult when driving to find yourself *in* beauty for more than a few minutes at a time. There are pockets of it, always shrinking. You can look at a picture of it, framed, cropped, misleading. The implication is that the image extends beyond the frame but move the camera or the eye to the right and you encounter a power station spilling out lines of pylons, to the left and you hit a cement holiday development of great ugliness and closed for the greater part of the year, or blocks of flats, or a car dump. We are bombarded with these selected, idealised, perfected images and come to believe that they are representative samples from the matrix of reality. But they are not. The world they represent does not exist.

The fact that these images are lies does not prevent them from being very powerful. The lie ennobled is the dream, and dreams are frequently more powerful than reality – for a while. This means that tourism is the opposite of experience. It becomes a mute and questing voyeurism, permanently dissatisfied. Perhaps next year the dream place will be found. Perhaps next year the dream connection will occur. Perhaps next year *something* will happen. But the tourist tunnel is designed to prevent things happening. What did Von expect to happen at the Abbey of Thelema? What did I expect to happen at Noto? What are we all looking for? A consecration of experience. A magical connection between experience and our deepest needs. But the events at Thelema are over. At best one can wallow in nostalgia. The Black Lake has been deconsecrated by a commercial plug which is sucking it out and will eventually erase it. One may be inspired by the past or by beautiful images but one cannot live by proxy. One discovers nothing by following or by expecting. You must make your own abbey. And if they have deconsecrated your lake, you must consecrate another. If you can find one, if they'll allow you the time. Life now is a race against time. Perhaps the images are all we have left. Perhaps now the only undefiled spaces are in the inner landscape. They are condemning us to live in our heads. This is madness,

What *was* I expecting to happen at Noto? I had amorphous hopes, dreams, expectations that something important would happen, thoughts in which decaying porticoes, laughter, sexual organs, plants, sunshine and poetry vaguely moved. But here I am alone on a bed in Enna, filled with dismay and insecurity, stripped of a protective idea. Having reached the destination, I have lost my focus, purpose. Vertiginous energy drop. Certainly I am no tourist. A tourist would've been happy with a few weeks' break. Not me. I've got to be fucking *transformed*.

What was I expecting from the Black Lake? To chance upon a forgotten curiosity and make a very private connection with the remote past? What did I find? That nothing is sacred? That all is economics? And that the relentless advance of this ethic will probably kill us?

I feel frightened. I reach out to touch someone – and no one is there . . . So what happens now? I'm trembling. My only hope is that, though uncomfortable, at least insecurity is fertile. It leads to things. Whereas security is static and leads nowhere. That is why people who are too secure are unattractive. Complacency is unattractive because it is the other shoe to ignorance. But power is attractive, indeed is aphrodisiac. Power and security are not the same; they are opposites. So I'm a romantic traveller. What could be more romantic than to search for love? What could be more romantic than to search for the reality behind the image? I detest the image! Anxiety rolls through me in tingling waves.

There seems no end to this process of destruction. The entire world aspires to a standard of material well-being that is characterised by artificiality of experience and represented by the covering and buttoning up of the body. And long before this aspiration can be universally gratified, the Earth will be dust. What wildlife does man encourage? Flies, cockroaches, rats and human beings. We have created huge cement cities which are factories for the mass-production of flesh and its parasites. The particles of this flesh aspire to self-realisation. People look to their governments for food, shelter, a job, and a reason for living (in the past the reason was usually supplied by religion or war but neither will do any longer). Few governments can even partially satisfy these demands and even where they can, the demands only redouble – as the history of the developed world demonstrates. None the less in their ever more frantic attempts to keep abreast of human appetites, governments preside over the destruction of the world. I do not want to return to the past. The present is always the most fascinating period of human history. It is the past which has brought us here, to the very brink of nuclear, ecological and social disaster. And it is the past, with its beliefs and religions, its taboos and rewards, which prevents us from making the vital responses. So at the end of the journey, we come to this cliché of horror which numbs us.

Our planet has cancer and we've just caught wind of it. Greenhouse effect, ozone destruction, poisoned water, poisoned food, you can complete the list yourself. Is cancer a parasite or an expression of the actual character of the system in which it arises? In other words, is the destruction of the planet by man inevitable? How long until the next Death Cloud? Or can we delay Earth's demise by a few hundred thousand years and allow it to die of natural causes? This is only a relative question of course because eventually all journeys end in death.

Death. A very Sicilian subject. Oh, bleak, bleak, bleak ceiling! Here on the bed, paralysed in the face of impending disaster, impotent in despair, what remains but to await the final embrace? And what more appropriate place for its contemplation than Enna, suspended at the very heart of this deadly isle? Paralysed, impotent, and therefore preyed upon by panic, that awful terror and confusion of impulses which engulfs us when we feel we can do nothing and feel we must do something.

Sicilians are pessimists. They expect the worst in an attempt to cheat disappointment. They see the end of things too readily, the death of things, and in this way they kill things. They do not trust life. They trust only death. They reach for death as the only solid fact. There is a short poem by Quasimodo:

Ed è subito sera	*And suddenly it's evening*
Ognuno sta solo sul cuor della terra	*Each of us is alone on the heart of the earth*
trafitto da un raggio di sole:	*pierced by a ray of sun:*
ed è subito sera.	*and suddenly it's evening.*

The Sicilians see life as raw material for death. This living relationship with death gives life here an intensity and drama greater than elsewhere in Italy – other Italians can seem munchy and dull in the comparison. The sense of panic until death makes Sicilians desperately symbiotic and lonely. They make much of November 2nd, All Soul's Day, the

Day of the Dead, when it is the custom to eat no meat, to eat corn cooked with cream, or peas & beans mixed together. This is eaten at a picnic in the graveyard and is the closest the Sicilian comes to peace of mind: eating lots of *food* with the *family* in the park of *death*.

I get off the bed and walk to the window, breathing deeply. The light-catching surface of the landscape is very irregular and the inter-mittent passage of clouds across a Schinkel sunset operates like a kaleidoscope of inexhaustible invention, to which are added the prismatic coruscations of my moist and uneasy eye. Yes, it's a great poem, but I shan't be sucked down by Sicilian death! Few trees in the view. Trees are too slow for the panic life. The Sicilian forest which survives is sometimes legally protected, which means that it is often set on fire by interested parties to release it for exploitation. Another law needs to be enacted which demands that legally protected forest be replanted after fires. The landscape here evokes *Anabase* by Saint John Perse. I play Handel's *Ode to Saint Cecilia*.

'Women are more at home in the universe than men,' I once said to Von – it wasn't a good time to mention it, she was in one of her alienated moods. 'Women are circular. They abide,' I went on, 'but men are nervous, restless, incomplete, active, pathetic.'

'How do you know this?' she asked.

'It's what I feel.'

'I certainly agree that men are more pathetic than women.'

'It's this pathetic quality in men which I find so attractive,' I said.

'Men are also more cruel and more childlike than women,' she said, 'and it's masculinity, not femininity, that's destroying the world.'

Cosmology. The Steady State theory, now discounted, is female. The Big Bang theory, currently in fashion, is male. I favour the hermaphroditic system, the Oscillating Universe.

We romanticise the South as the region of physical expression, of life touched by a divine warmth. They romanticise the North as the place where important things happen; success cannot occur in the South. There is a proverb for this: the grass is always greener on the other side of the hill.

But all that I now discard. And the process of destruction continues inside. I've lost my companion, my golden city, my black lake. What to do now? To drift? Why the hell not! To float, yes, because floating is a precondition for learning how to swim and play. To loose oneself from moorings and drift will snap a 1000 addictions because one ceases to depend on external points and the inner resource is emboldened. You can float! You can trust life! OK, from now on I don't expect *anything*. I make no demands whatsoever. I shall free myself even from hope, especially from hope, and I shall surrender to the fecund moment, to the Mother, to this syrupy Carlo Dolci madonna worship, this queasy rocking softness, this whining pig-stuck emotional softness, and be infused by it, as a dry teabag sinks into the warm water which alone can soften and release its particular tang, its enlivening properties. And as this process of inner disintegration and abandon continues, a hard and resistant cyst at the very centre, in which I reserve the sacrament of my identity, my unique separation, the source of ego and endeavour, the walls of this dissolve and liquefy as though made from sugar and I cry and cry and cry . . .

After this sobbing fit – which went on for a while – I search my papers for the 3 Palermo contact numbers which I have:

(1) Arthur Oliver's and Kris Mancùso's, both from Maria Colonna via James Ruscoe.

(2) The Principessa Costanza Camporeale's from Julia Stonor via Bunny Dexter.

I don't know them but call the first, Arthur Oliver's, because I want to hear an English voice. His wife answers in a gentle Italian accent.

'We're both terribly old,' says Fiammetta Oliver. 'Is that a problem for you?'

'No,' I reply. 'I'm quite old myself.'

'Not like us,' she says. 'Nobody's old like us. My husband's British. Well, Welsh actually. Is that British?'

'Yes, the Welsh are very British.'

'I thought so. He's not here, otherwise you could speak to him. But we'd love to see you.'

I pack my bags, sleep with interruptions, and first thing in the morning, set out for Palermo, Europe's most violent city. I shall abandon myself. I shall ramble and discover. I don't know what to expect. Therefore what follows may not cohere. Or it may. I don't care. Why should I destroy my composure, just so that *it* can have composure?

14
Palermo

I espied in the distance a fantastic tower of rock out of Hieronymus Bosch. One uses the northern reference because the Mediterranean remains resolutely religious or classical in its iconography. Even Mediterranean gothic architecture, which is plentiful, is shot through with classical or saracenic elements. But this soaring plug was not religious, classical or saracenic, but medieval, fairytale, romantic, Tennyson meets Dürer, Richard Dadd in the sun, Gormenghast with apricots. Truly allucinante, as the Italians say. It was the town of Sutera, the most astonishing citadel in Sicily when seen from the Mussomeli road, whose amiable population pointed me with smiles and courtesy in the direction of the metropolis.

A couple of hours later the car flew into Palermo and whirled round and round, notwithstanding the fact that Palermo's main streets are famously long and straight. This was the first of many paradoxes. Hitting a new city in the car is always uncomfortable but also stimulating because one must function 100% externally. Buses – commuters – political speeches – palm trees, collapsing buildings, traffic, dust. The only clear image salvaged from this abrupt insertion into chaos was the barbaric splendour of the Porta Nuova like something strayed from a Mayan city, its lower part reinforced with 4 herm pilasters resembling Easter Island idols, its upper part graciously arcaded with pyramidal roof topped by a lantern: that throbbing combination of savagery and refinement which is Sicily.

None the less it was a fleeting image. The bloodstream swept me on and I might have circulated indefinitely had I not at one point found myself chugging past the only Palermo hotel I'd heard of, the Hotel des Palmes where Wagner worked on *Parsifal* and Raymond Roussel played silly buggers. Its foyer was spacious, pillared, gilded – and silent. At reception a man in black jacket, striped trousers and dark glasses summoned a porter who complained bitterly that my bags were parked round the corner, all of 15 seconds away. He condescended to carry 2 while I staggered behind with the rest. My father always says 'Be generous with the porter who brings in your bags. It can't do any harm and it might do some good – you may need him.' But the extra lire just stuck in my throat.

The place seemed empty but there were 3 big blokes in their 30s hanging about my landing for no apparent reason. One wore dark glasses and they all looked dangerous. The deluge of light in this country is such that many ordinary people wear sunglasses throughout the day (the Mezzogiorno has a higher incidence of eye disease than the north) but indoors this always looks shifty and weird. I passed the entrance of the suite to which they seemed vaguely attached, saw black suits and heard impassioned talk within. Obviously a mafia syndicate.

My room (No. 350) is small, inward facing, and recently refurbished in a style best described as an International American version of European. After unpacking I went down for a pot of tea in the bar – they do it here – and the 3 heavies poked their heads out of 3 doors and I, the solitary guest, had to run the gauntlet of their suspicion. At reception I asked the man in dark glasses if anything important were happening on my floor and he said yes, the leader of the Italian Communist Party was staying on it and since he's anti-mafia . . . He shrugged his shoulders, assuming that I'd understand the rest, and of course I did. The immediate prospect of violence in the best hotel in town did not dissuade me from using what remained of the daylight to explore a little. Anyway it is physically impossible to stay in one's room for more than a few minutes after arriving in a new city, whatever the time of day.

Palermo, like Naples and Nice, is in 4 parts: old town, port, 19th century town, modern town (the Hotel des Palmes is in the 19th century town). It has that entrancing port characteristic, which Penang and Syracuse have but which has gone from London, namely ships blocking the ends of streets. There are many palm trees and much noise. Boys sell cassettes from street trolleys, playing samples through harsh loudspeakers. Men sell goods from open trucklets, howling through similar speakers. The badly amplified voice in church, street or arena is one of the characteristic sounds of the Italian south. What has happened to the tiny Sardinian asses which were said to have been such a feature of this town? But the most immediate and unsettling impression of Palermo is its shattered, ruinous state. Cornices drop to the ground as you survey a façade behind which, you realise with a shock, there is only rubble – waist-high walls are built every so often along the pavement to prevent pedestrians walking directly beneath dangerous structures. Extensive bomb sites remain from the bombardments of World War II while furious towerblock construction takes place elsewhere. Rubbish spills out of skips and stacked plastic bags.

However, this degradation of what was undoubtedly one of the most beautiful cities in Europe (in the 18th century Palermo was the greatest Italian city after Naples) does not beget a melancholy air. The atmosphere is aggressive and infernal. This is the capital of an uncontrolled society. For an Englishman, whose society is minutely regulated in law (there may be even more regulations in Sicily for all I know but they are obviously unobserved – custom is far more important), it is a thrilling encounter.

I was stared at a great deal which was rather unnerving. By the time I returned to the hotel it was dark and Palermo was quite suddenly deserted. I am to discover that the emptiness of Palermo is its most striking characteristic after dark; that perhaps uniquely for a southern town it has *no nightlife*. When the working day is over, that's it, everything retreats behind doors. There's not even a passegiata. Some restaurants stay open but the bars and cafés start to close at 8 p.m. and by 8.30 the city is locked up and mute. Quite simply the Palermitans are too frightened to go out at night.

So now I'm watching TV – Samantha Fox, the Cockney girl with big tits, is wowing them in Siena. 'Touch me! I want to feel your body!' she implores with fine lungs above the disco beat as mighty bosom, cute face, ragged mane and skintight trews go stamping across the stage on high sharp heels and the Sienese bellow, clap and cream. In an advertisement a loo roll is described as having 'morbidezza'. I look it up and am relieved to discover it means 'softness'.

Next morning I smile at one of the bodyguards and to my amazement receive a smile in return. Breakfast (self-service from a buffet) takes place at one end of a grand dining-room. The coffee, which stews in a samovar contraption 3 feet high, plunges impossible depths of vileness and is absolutely undrinkable. There was a further contact which I overlooked, one of the Bishop of Gibraltar's lieutenants, the Rev. Harper, whom I now ring. He says that his church here, the Holy Cross, which is almost opposite the hotel, is now closed for the hot season and he's 'about to open up shop in Taormina'. He advises me to ring a man called Toby Moore who used to be vice-consul and is still very much au courant. Mr Moore invites me for a drink this evening (JG). Then I ring Kris Mancuso, the foreign editor of *L'Ora* newspaper. He turns out to be a woman.

'How long are you here for?'

'Well, I've just driven from London so I'm not planning to dash away.'

'Good, good, you're on Arab time.'

'I'm going to look at the Palazzo Reale to-day.'

'Then come to my office afterwards.'

There's not much to see at the Palazzo Reale, seat of the Sicilian government, because it's undergoing heavy restoration, but the Cappella Palatina is open, a jewelled mosaic interior, dim and gold, in the gorgeously chromatic Arabo-Norman style, illegitimate love child of illustrious but improbable parents.

L'Ora is owned collectively by its journalists and is the only independent newspaper in Sicily. Kris is tall with an oval face, warm dark eyes and chunky jewellery. She smokes like a factory.

'I thought you were a man.'

'Lots of people think I'm a man. Kris is short for Kristel. My mother is German. My father is Sicilian.'

A diminutive 8 or 9 year old enters with coffee from a nearby bar. He's very young to be working.

'Oh, they can start much younger than that,' she says, sipping and puffing. 'I'm a bit women's lib but I say first we must liberate the children. No, no, that's wrong!' She laughs huskily and raises her hands. '*First* we must liberate the men! Children must go to school until 11 years. Then after that – whatever. Be careful by the way in Palermo. Don't carry anything.'

'If I do it's in this plastic bag.'

'Oh, they know all about plastic bags! You see, you don't look at all Sicilian. And you shouldn't wear those shorts.'

'But I don't see the point of dressing like a banker when it's so hot.' This insistence on formal dress among the bourgeoisie of the south is almost Third World, the desire never to be mistaken at any time for a member of the peasant class.

'Can you keep Saturday evening free?' she asks. We've hit it off immediately – it happens with some people.

Drinks, Toby Moore's modern flat near the Politeama, 'colonial' inside. He's fat, rosy and good-natured and I present him with a jar of Sir Nigel's Marmalade from Fortnum & Mason. A couple of English from the University are here and a Barone Pucci who invites me up to his farm 'where the bees are very wild'.

'By the time the Queen came in 1981 the Consulate had been closed down' says Toby, 'and so the British community had to produce someone to escort the royal party round Monreale and the choice fell on Olly, Fiammetta's husband, Oliver Onions's son. But the problem was – could he stay sober until 10 in the morning to do it? I had the casting vote and said yes and indeed it all went terribly well. Then everyone went for lunch to the Gangi Palace which is very splendid and they used it for the ballroom scenes in *The Leopard* film. The Princess of Gangi lets it out for *enormous* sums, wedding receptions and so on.'

Apparently she's really the head of the family since her brother committed suicide by taking an overdose.

'Is there no son?'

'Oh yes. One of the heirs was in the bush.'

'In the bush?'

'Yes, he went into hiding. But they arrested him eventually. The problem was he owned a castello and turned it into a nightclub which they said was used as a mafia meeting place for drug deals.'

'Everything is politics, everything is mafia,' says Barone Pucci with a long face.

One of the University teachers says 'It's exam time next week. I dread it. There's so much backdoor pressure to give particular students high marks.'

All agree that Palermo is a very violent town.

'Because,' says Toby, ventilating with a deep breath and wiping his flushed brow, 'you can get away with violence. Violence pays. It even boosts a man's reputation. The Mafia Trials are on. Have you been?'

'Sounds like a new play. But I shall go.'

'It's taking place inside the prison so that they don't have to move the prisoners. You'll recognise the prison because there are tanks outside it. Whether it will lead to any long-term improvement I don't know. The mafia is hand-in-glove with the powers-that-be. It's like trying to separate the left hand from the right.'

'But surely,' I venture into the quagmire, 'the heroin business will lead eventually to the isolation of the mafia because it attacks the family?'

All agree that heroin has made the mafia entrepreneurs *hugely* rich 'and that counts for everything down here. Who else do you have introductions to?'

'The Camporeales.'

'Not rich. But well-connected.'

'Who are rich?'

'The Bordonaros. The Tascas.'

'I heard that a Bordonaro had his legs cut off.'

'Yes,' says one. 'Bricciola Bordonaro's husband. Diabetes. Stroke. Wheelchair. Terrible state, terribly rich – amazing art collection and no one to safely leave it to.'

As I'm leaving, the Englishman from the University says 'Can we give you a lift?'

'I thought I'd walk.'

'I wouldn't do that.'

'No, I wouldn't do that!' chorus the others.

'You'll be stopped by someone with a knife. Or a gun.'

Everyone keeps telling me I'm a *target*. It's making me uneasy. On the short hop from car to hotel doorway there's a twinge between my shoulderblades. There's a phone message from Kris: meet her if I can at the *L'Ora* office, 1.15 p.m. to-morrow, to go sailing. On the landing a bodyguard says goodnight and I return the greeting. Very reassuring.

9.30 a.m., Toby phones and kindly offers me a bedroom for the rest of my stay, an offer I'd very much like to accept, but already it's clear that this is a town of many factions and that I'll see most by preserving my independence.

'Well, if you change your mind, just give me the nod. And you must come to lunch. I have a Singhalese servant who cooks me a curry lunch every day.'

'That's unusual.'

'No, it isn't. There are about 1500 Singhalese servants in Palermo.'

Kris is sailing with a Miss Hugony whose family owns the Harrods of Palermo. Skimming across the Bay is wondrously cool after the heat and battle of the town. Seen from the sea the city presents a forest of sand-coloured tower blocks stretching away to left and right but at the centre the original skyline just survives, an exotic cluster of domes and spires glowing in a yellow haze of pollution. Especially visible is the Teatro Massimo, the greatest 19th century building in Palermo and for long the largest theatre in the world.

'It's been closed for 9 years,' says Kris. 'It's falling down. They can't agree on who should have the contracts for repairs.'

'No, it's not falling down,' says Miss Hugony at the tiller. 'It is only that the roof is falling in.'

'Isn't that what falling down means?'

'No,' says Kris. 'In Palermo when you say something is falling down, you mean everything is literally crashing to the ground. So Iole is right really. But it's true to say that the Old Town, the centro storico, is *falling down*.'

'Don't they have a plan to save it?'

'Oh, they have many plans! But nothing ever gets done. Perhaps a little bit here, a little there.'

A great deal of money has been allocated by the Government in Rome for the restoration of the historical centre but the building industry is mafia controlled and mafioso influence paralyses with relentless lobbying the decision-making powers of the committees set up to supervise the work. The money continues to sit in banks. Sometimes it 'disappears'. Building scandals are common in this town. Vicious rivalry is the core of Sicilian destructiveness.

Kris says 'If you live in Palermo you have to escape.' She inhales the rich air and coughs. 'So I escape to the sea. Once I escaped to Bonn and it was snowing and I thought what am I doing here? Shall I stay or return to Sicily? I couldn't decide, so I put 2 pieces of paper in a hat and the one I picked out said Palermo. So here I am.'

In the evening we visit Duca Gioacchino Lanza Tomasi di Lampedusa, adopted son of the man who wrote *The Leopard*. We drive down to the Marina by the sea, once the grandest promenade of the town, but it received maximum carpet bombing prior to the wartime Allied Landings and now presents a disconcerting mix of grandeur, ruins and bomb sites, all variously inhabited. Someone also decided to build the town gasworks here, overlooking the Villa Giulia and the Botanical Gardens. On the Marina itself, the cultivation of yesteryear has been replaced by packed mud with fairground and market. At the north end beside the Porta Felice is the Palazzo Butera, previously the grandest of the private palaces, half bombed away; the other half is occupied but vanishes into overgrown rubble, torn stonework and jagged roofbeams obtruding into the sunshine. The Buteras still exist but in much reduced circumstances – one of the princes committed suicide not long ago by jumping out of a window.

Duke Gioacchino has rebuilt the Palazzo Lampedusa almost from scratch and it now sports a cream neo-classical façade above a terrace facing the sea (this is not however the true Palazzo Lampedusa which was deeper in the city, much larger and destroyed during the war). He is tall with brown hair and a languid manner that belies his vigour, for among other things he runs a Roman symphony orchestra and the Taormina arts festival. His wife is small, young and chic in dungarees. She is from Venice and has recently translated a biography of Beethoven from English to Italian. The locals consider her a northerner – certainly no Palermitan would have the up-to-date style to wear dungarees when receiving a stranger. They inhabit the undercroft where the ceilings are low, while the staterooms above are shut and used only a few times a year. Pride of place among their beautiful possessions goes to his 'n' hers word processors humming side by side in the study.

The staterooms are almost empty. All the ceilings and furniture and decorations were destroyed. The praiseworthy reconstruction restores their proportions but only a little of their savour. However a superb pink marble staircase, salvaged from a church, asserts the ducal style.

It is now dark and, framed in the windows at the end of the

dining-room, the funfair switches its rainbow lights through staccato sequences to the accompaniment of ferocious pop music, screams of machinery and people: dust, lights, pleasure and villainy.

'It's illegal!' exclaims the Duchess. 'It turned up 12 years ago and stayed. There is nothing we can do about it because there would be vendetta.'

As we are leaving Gioacchino says 'These might interest you,' indicating with a slight gesture a collection of small portraits – those of his ancestors who were saints. 'We've just added *him* to the group because he is to be canonised next month . . . And this one received a letter from the Devil.' He chuckles knowingly.

Dinner at 9.30 p.m. is in the opposite but connected world: the high bourgeoisie, very high, a large penthouse on top of a new block beyond the via della Libertà and the Giardino Inglese, an area where many beautiful 19th century villas have been demolished and replaced by flats and shops. This is the penthouse of Miss Hugony II, Iole's sister, and it is to her that I present the Sir Nigel's Marmalade. At a long table on the terrazza among small trees and soft breezes, a servant passes round a huge fish.

Kris is fully rigged in bangles and necklaces that remind me of Von. A sad look comes over her features and she asks 'Why won't the British give Ulster independence?'

'Because it would become Lebanon.'

'Occasionally terrorism is justified,' she says.

I turn on her with bulging eyes. 'You mustn't say that. The most you can say is that in this particular place, in these circumstances, I can understand why this is happening.' But is she right? Is it *occasionally* justified? Should one suffer Hitlers for example just because their authority is legitimate?

The man opposite is an architect and I enquire about the Palazzo Bonagia whose sepia photograph had mesmerised me in Florence. He says 'It has gone. It was falling down and now the site is cleared – except for part of the outdoor staircase.' Then he asks if I'm interested in football.

I say 'Maradona very bastard.' All the talk is of how brilliant Maradona is for scoring a goal by punching it with his fist but disguising it as a header – everyone saw the deception except the referee.

Kris says 'Can you keep to-morrow night available? Dinner at Toti's.'

The Italian Communist leader has departed the hotel, taking his henchmen, and the landing has a forlorn look . . .

This afternoon a man struck up a conversation at the bar of the sex cinema in via Mariano Stabile. He was a finance lawyer from Rome, married with children, involved in the prosecution of the mafia here, and he asked me for sex. I didn't find him attractive and said I wasn't in the mood to which he replied that one of the reasons he asked was that he could see I was a foreigner and therefore safe. He was very open and pleasant.

'There's another sex cinema in the older, rougher part of town, the Orfeo,' he said, 'which is better for pick-ups but I can't go there. The mafia is very strong in that part. Someone might recognise me and blackmail me.' Then a dolorous look came over his features, rather in the manner of Kris questioning me on Ulster, and he asked 'Why are there no sex cinemas in London? I was there and I couldn't find anything. These films are such a pleasure to watch.'

'Yes, exactly. That's why they are forbidden in England. The British consider pleasure the opposite of virtue.'

'Really? That's a strange philosophy.'

'Yes, it is. And this separation of virtue and pleasure is the separation of beauty and eroticism. Very unhealthy. The Roman Catholic Church started it off.'

'No, before that, there was Stoicism – and Judaism. You see, it is an old story, that you must not enjoy the here-and-now, that you must suffer for the promised land. But Romans do not believe this. Other people believe this.'

Toti's turns out not to be a restaurant or nightclub but Salvatore's, another leafy penthouse under a warm night sky, belonging to a banker friend of Kris's. Salvatore, alias Toti, receives his jar of marmalade (what a godsend Sir Nigel is turning out to be) with the sort of smile that's described as 'winning' (wide and white with a teasing ripple in it). While Kris gets to grips with cigarette packet and lighter, he introduces me to a boisterously charming woman called Renata who loves the English language, who tastes it as it leaves her tongue, who flirts, who says 'Why need you never starve in the desert? Because you can eat the sand which is there,' who swallows me alive but spits me out again so that I can be introduced to the Baronessa Anna Bordonaro, a rather different type. The BAB is a platinum blonde who enters on an aluminium crutch. She is about 60, short, stout, and her face slopes forward to the tip of her chin. Out of it comes a low harsh voice and a *very* dirty laugh. Her manner is jolly, even outrageous, and she speaks to me in French. The only English she utters is 'I love to drink', after which she cackles and grabs my thigh with a glittering claw. On the polite subject of pictures the BAB says 'We have a Cranach, a David, a Rubens, a Rembrandt, a Botticelli – San Giovanni as a boy . . . a Tiepolo. We're having something done to the house, so they're all lying on the floor.'

'Isn't security a problem?'

'No, because you see we also have something called the mafia.'
She makes a long shshsh noise with a finger to her lips, then burst
into another cackle.

'I've heard of someone called Bricciola Bordonaro.'

'She is married to Gabriele's brother.'

Gabriele is the BAB's husband, the Barone. He has nothing in
common with her, being tall, thin, with a straggly beard and pedantic
manner. Until recently he owned a small coffee plantation in Kenya.

'It was an enviable existence. I have written a book about it. What
am I doing in Palermo?'

At dinner, which is inside, the BAB describes me as 'un amorino'
and the others begin to joke about my name. Phallo-bene . . . The
Barone Bordonaro interrupts the ribaldry to declare that Corvo is
the best, most reliable wine in Sicily. Toti's manservant, a handsome
young African boy, brings round the dishes which, to judge from the
abrupt way in which Toti's wide winning smile appears and disappears,
causes our host some anguish.

Renata gives vent to an audible sigh and says 'Borges is dead. He
was coming to Palermo to present the Golden Rose to Cartier-Bresson
on Tuesday. Now Madame Borges is coming instead. Did you say you
were at the National Gallery to-day?'

The National Gallery of Sicily is near the Piazza Marina, the most
beautiful and one of the most ancient piazzas in the city and which is
being s-l-o-w-l-y restored after terrible bombing (there is an immense,
convoluted fig tree in the centre of it). Half the Gallery was closed for,
that's right, restoration and only religious art was on show: an endless
number of Madonnas and Bleeding Christs and Books being held up to
people as Truth. The art of superstition, unleavened by anything else,
produced a choking oppressiveness and disgust before long. And the
great many representations of books being forced into people's faces
were especially repulsive, because literal-mindedness is the enemy of
truth. In addition, groups of custodians and workers shouted at each
other the entire time, and the building, which is stone, vibrated to the
din of hammers. I was glad to escape this grating uproar and the ugly
Christian art of blood and freakish women.

'Did you see the *wonderful* Virgin of the Annunciation by Antonello
da Messina?' asks Renata on megawatt twinkle.

'Probably.'

'But you cannot forget her. She is loooooooooooo-minous,' she
intones with a seraphic ululation and eyes closed in bliss. Then the
eyes snap open. 'You must be careful coming out! The street outside
is a favourite for attacks on tourists.'

'And outside the Archaeological Museum too, that's popular for attacks,' adds Kris, rapidly turning the stem of her wineglass with 2 fingers, longing for a puff between courses.

I stare at the black boy who nervously executes his duties in a white jacket and feel rather uneasy on his behalf. Toti doesn't even *talk* to him which is perhaps not so much from disdain as from the nervous hope that if he absolutely ignores the boy then nothing will be perceived to go wrong.

'He's just arrived from Africa,' whispers Kris. 'This is his first dinner party.'

It is a cruel induction.

Gabriele Bordonaro says 'There are still plenty of animals in Africa. It's ridiculous that one is not allowed to shoot them!'

'That of course is why there is no wild life left in Sicily,' I say (and want to add 'apart from the people' but cannot). 'Although I met someone called Pucci who said he had very wild bees.'

'Goodness gracious,' says Renata, who has a hint of tongue-in-cheek when she comes out with these phrases, 'he's my brother! Now where is my handbag? I had it a moment ago. I've lost my handbag. Oh, oh, oh!' She trots round the table and goes into a wail which lasts until she's found the article under a chair in the sitting-room. She has eaten virtually nothing.

In the course of dinner the BAB has used the word 'stronzo' a great deal. Stronzo this, stronzo that. I know it means 'shit' and that she's splendidly abandoned for a Palermitan lady but I'm surprised she keeps saying it. Renata, sotto voce, explains that to call something 'stronzo' in this way means that it is 'pretentious and silly'. Well, we use 'shit' in a similar sense but, prude that I am, I'm still surprised to find it resorted to so often. Renata then invites me to accompany her to the Golden Rose presentation.

Watermelon jelly again. Toti smiles and says 'Typical Sicilian' in unsteady English, adding 'Signor Phallo Bene' and beams generously. He's a right tease. Some jelly slithers over the rim of my plate. Toti says that his office is in the Palazzo Reale and that if it would be of interest he'd be happy to take me into the closed parts.

Current reading is *Little Dorrit* which I purchased in the bookshop at the Quattro Canti, the heart of Old Palermo where the long straight axes of the via Maqueda and the Corso intersect at right angles. Coming out of the bookshop, I saw a woman on the opposite side of the road pushed into a doorway and her bag snatched. A boy ran off. Immediately the woman was comforted by 2 other women but no attempt was made to intercept the ruffian who was still to be seen running along the via Maqueda until he darted left and was gone.

Next day when Kris collects me to visit Toti at the Palazzo Reale
I am wearing shorts and she's angry.

'We are to visit the President of Sicily's private apartments!'

'Are we? Sorry, I didn't know.'

'Please change to trousers. You wearing shorts is imperialist!'

'No, no, I'm hot, that's all. Now you have a cigarette, I'll go and
change, and everything will be fine.' While changing I try to work
out what she meant by 'imperialist' and conclude that she must
mean expressing contempt for local convention – which is not true.
In Sicily every act is so consciously motivated that they find it difficult
to understand that it's possible simply to be oneself. She thought I was
playing a power game.

In the presidential apartments, restorations are nearly complete.
Workmen are on their hands and knees laying new carpets and I'm
the first foreign guest to walk on them. Virtually none of the furniture
is original. Certain presidents have had expert copies made and on
resignation taken the originals out with them. I'm told you see these
originals at dinner parties all over Palermo. In the dining-room where
the parliamentarians eat hangs a large, appropriate painting of dogs
fighting each other; and in the parliamentary chamber itself, Toti tells
me that the Sicilian Parliament is the oldest in Europe, older even than
the British he emphasises with pride, and was founded AD 1130. That
Sicily has Europe's oldest parliament and no parliamentary tradition
whatsoever is another Sicilian caprice. Sicilians never developed a
tradition of *public* irreverence. Insubordination is always underhand.
(Subsequent reading tells me that Iceland's Thing is the first European
parliament, c. AD 930.)

Afterwards I go off alone to visit the corpses in the famous Capuchin
Tombs, where an extraordinary event takes place. It's not far from
the Palazzo Reale but in an off-centre district. Having entered the
portals of the monastery and bought a ticket from a dirty, smelly
monk, one descends a stone staircase out of the brilliance of
afternoon into the cool steady stare of death. But steadiness is
not immediately apparent. In fact there's a riot going on – terrific
animation – but frozen, silent. Rank upon rank of carcasses are propped
upright in their Sunday best, sagging, disintegrating. Drying of the
facial skin has created vivid expressions. Some are withdrawn, caving
inwards; others bear aggressive or absurdly outgoing demeanours:
hundreds of men and women immobilised in the act of snarling,
joking, crying, growling, gazing (glass eyes), forgetting, dreaming,
chatting, complaining, laughing. Often the skin adheres only to one
side of the head while the other is bone or has retracted into lunatic
grimace, twisted leer or dry sobbing. There is even, though this is

extremely rare, repose. And on the maintained and painted visage of
the little bambina there is bewilderment. She is known as the Sleeping
Beauty and through a grating above her may be seen blue sky, palm
fronds, sunshine.

Not all are upright. Some are stacked horizontally in niches. A few
are in open caskets. Many are little more than skeletons in clothes
or bags of sackcloth. Some are named, most are not. All are small –
the men have tiny fingernails, although most hands are gloved. The
Church would separate us even in death and there are distinct locations
for priests, the professions, virgins, soldiers, etc. The priests look portly
in comparison to the others and are covered in threadbare vestments.
The virgins wear rusty coronets. The expressions of the children are
very very old and some, like the Sleeping Beauty, have been artificially
sweetened. The oldest of the inmates is Brother Silvester of Gubbio
who died in 1599 but most belong to the 19th century (towards the
end of which this form of burial was prohibited by government) and
if you go up close the beauty of woven silk, velvet or embroidered
fabric emerges from the dust. They've now put up metal grilles to
prevent vandals from poking the corpses or drawing graffiti on the
skulls (there are a few of these). It's a demented party they're having.
But there is no smell. And there are no ghosts because the spirits still
inhabit the bodies.

The only other living visitors are 3 French tourists, a man and 2
women. They arrived with much chatter in loud holiday clothes but
have been rendered quiet and pensive by the spectacle. The man,
who wears shorts, has been taking many photographs with a flashy
camera – I wish I'd risked it and brought mine. Their cogitations
are broken from time to time by bursts of French vivacity. This is an
articulate, analytical liveliness, quite different from the Italians' loose,
emotional style. I get an erection. Death often does that. The situation
has certain parallels to, say, visiting an exhibition of Francis Bacon
paintings in that you wish to leave the moment you arrive; the visceral
hits, the bottomline truths, are too much; but after a while you adjust
and the adjustment is to the cool steadiness of death in which all fears
are earthed and which thereby becomes a physical liberation. All this
death in Palermo. Horrible and sexy. I return Death's stare, sweeping
my eyes slowly across its preposterous and pulverulent residuum, and
bid adieu.

The 3 French have already departed but I pause at the monastery
entrance to select from a gallery of gruesome postcards. A group of
Italian schoolchildren come tripping raucously in. Having made my
choice of cards, I become sensible of an insistent whooping noise,
seemingly a few latecomers from the school party larking in the piazza

outside. But before long it is obvious that these are not whoops of jollification but screams of distress. I put my head round the door and there, in the middle of the piazza, witness a most shocking incident. An old blue Citroën with Palermo numberplate has arrived to collect the 3 French tourists. The driver is paralysed inside while without, the 2 women and man are being attacked by 6 young boys who've swept in on scooters. The boys are about 11 or 12, cleanly dressed. Baring their sharp little teeth, they are going at the tourists with such fury that the French haven't a chance. One of the women holds tenaciously to her bag but a knife flashes, the strap is slit, and she's lost it. They are picked clean – bags, camera, watches, everything – as by piranhas and the boys zip off at high speed. It's all over in seconds. Everyone who has emerged from cafés, shops, doorways and stood round the rim of the square to be diverted now returns to his business full of conversation. The French party is stunned. They climb into the car, lock it and hug each other in silence. I am stunned. Their host drives them out of the square at funeral pace. I turn to the monk and shall never forget his expression: indifference bordering on the comatose. 'Banditi . . .' he mumbles.

I gaze at him. What is the Capuchin Order? What is it to be a Capuchin to-day? The monks here are . . . nothing. This one is about 50, with crusts of sleep on his eyelids, meagre beard, dirty habit, dirty fingernails, a sweet-sour unwashed smell, and insensate. I've yet to encounter a monk in Italy who isn't halfway to cretinism. He asks 'How many postcards?'

'25.'

'Due mille cinquecento.'

'And the catalogue.'

'Quattro mille.'

I receive my change in a dream. What to do now? There are no taxis here, so I set off on foot, a plastic bag in hand and sunbleached hair a beacon to banditi. 'They know all about plastic bags.' Moving down the street, louring natives on either side, my legs tremble. Any second now – clunk! attack! And I feel humiliated, ashamed at having stood by, watched with all the wretched rest as the assault proceeded. I can make excuses – that I should've been knifed, that other Sicilians from among the onlookers would've joined in against me – but in the end I have to face it: I was terrified, pathetic, a coward. And this is very difficult for the *amour propre* to cope with. When I was mugged in Acapulco it was different – at night, I unshod on a rocky beach, 3 boys with broken bottles. I played it cool, gave them what they demanded, and escaped. OK, I felt pathetic then too but I was alone and had to go for survival. But here it's in daylight, someone *else* is in trouble, and I do nothing to help . . . The plastic bag burns in my hand. Transferring the contents to a large shirt pocket, I throw the bag onto a pile of rubbish. Every group of kids beside a scooter I give wide berth to.

What had the French lost? Some material possessions. But far more important: the trust without which no society is healthy. The fear of molestation by desperadoes is bad enough but the fear of molestation by children is particularly horrifying because it subverts the natural order. Later Kris tells me that outside the Capuchin Tombs is another popular place for attacks, especially because tourists emerge from the corridors of corpses dazed but relieved, i.e. not vigilant. These places of attack are known – why are policemen not stationed at them? Everyone I ask simply shrugs. Oh Christ, I hate you, Palermo, I hate you! The reason is: the stationing of policemen would infringe traditional criminal rights to tourist pickings. They don't put *that* in the brochure. Besides, any concern for public safety comes only from outside, from Rome or from outraged ambassadors. Even educated Sicilians seem to have not the slightest notion that public safety should be a public responsibility. In this sense Palermo is the most savage town I know. So why doesn't someone organise a bodyguard agency for visitors? There are plenty of bored young men hanging about. Instead of robbing tourists, they would earn more by protecting them. But no, this would be too much like intelligent commercial behaviour. This would be beneath them.

And it is more complicated than that. These people have a mania for status objects. They want *things*, to touch, to possess them. Their eyes focus and glow with a dark lust when observing a fashionable belt or a new cassette player. The scorn of *things* is an aspect of puritanism, rather a congenial one I'm beginning to think. Always to live externally, to judge externally, by visible acts and objects, is to make a fetish of this world. Those boys *grabbed* the fetish objects on the French with an hysterical desire to *take*, to *have*, which north Europeans find hard to understand. And this desire to take is intimately connected with the desire to deprive: envy. In Palermo there is now virtually no membrane of inhibition between these boys and the objects of their desire. The only inhibitory factor is the risk they run – and that risk is negligible. And of course they will steal from other Sicilians as happily as from anyone else. A basic human immunity has gone. Its absence allows a sulphuric vapour to prickle on the skin when one is outdoors, day or night.

Back at the hotel I make phone contact with Costanza and Paolo Camporeale. Costanza seems pleased to be interrupted by a stranger and invites me to lunch at the beach to-morrow. Then I meet Renata Pucci Zanca at her flat before the Cartier-Bresson presentation. Her arms are beating the air like wings and she's squealing 'I've lost my scissors, lost my scissors! You must help me find them! Oh, oh, oh!'

I report the assault upon the French tourists and a friend of Renata's says 'That's nothing. Once those boys hijacked a *whole* Pullman coach carrying the Georgian Society of England who'd come to look at the Serpottas. Shall I tell you a story about the Hotel des Palmes? There is a Barone di Stefano living there. He did something wrong and the mafia said "You must die." He said "Oh, no!" and they said "Oh, yes." And he asked "But what if I die to the world?" And they asked "What do you mean?" He said "What if I go to live in the Hotel des Palmes and *never* come out?" And they thought about it and eventually said "Ecco. But you must *never* come out. Not even to visit the cinema after dark. You must not *exist* outside – or you will die." And so now he lives at your hotel. But he's rarely seen even in the public rooms. He gives extravagant, sepulchrrrrral lunches in his rooms, with the curtains closed, and the women receive beautifully wrapped presents. At night he sometimes walks on the roof terrace but prefers it when there is no moon.'

Madame Borges speaks in Spanish and looks very integrée for a woman who lost her husband only days ago. She quotes a line of German, roughly *For the rose there is no why. It blooms because it blooms*. The Italians – or Sicilians rather – applaud this idea vigorously. Cartier-Bresson replies in French and receives from her hands the Golden Rose of Palermo which is based upon a design by William Morris.

'Renata, do you think of yourself as Sicilian first and Italian second?'

'No, we are Italians. Do the English despise the Italians?'

'No.'

'I know the French do . . . I remember when Harold Pinter came here to receive the Pirandello Prize, I had to telephone them and I said, "Is that Mrs Pinter?" and she said "Just call me Lady Antonia." I have a *wonderful* idea – let us go soon to stay in my country cottage!'

The Principessa Costanza Camporeale is in her 40s, very polite, thoughtful, thin and spaced-out behind huge sun specs in the foyer. She says I must swim but she will not, nor will she sit in the sun. Driving into Mondello, we pass down an avenue lined either side with dozens of red Coca Cola signs and make for her beach club, the Circolo della Vela, which she says I may use when I like because her father, Count Tasca, is president. The water is delicious but full of rocks and I cut my foot. A game old bird staggers out – it's her father. 'You must use the jetty and be careful of sea urchins,' he explains.

Lunch is under a pergola beside the water and we are joined by her husband Paolo, charming, thickset and sensual, whom the waiter addresses as 'Principe', and a man called Wenceslao who seems to be the local expert on families and heredity. Their English is almost flawless. Paolo says he's ¼ American and had an English nanny who now lives in Taunton. They want to know what I've been up to so far, so I begin non-committally with the Archaeological Museum. 'But I was disappointed that the great collection of Greek vases is closed.'

'Is it? Don't be put off by that,' says Paolo. 'Just ask for the Director and say you've come from London and want to see the vases.'

Costanza, who is avoiding food as well as sun and water, says 'The metopes there from Selinunte were discovered by the English who arranged to buy them and take them back to England but the King of Italy stepped in and put his foot down.' She scrutinises her fish as if it were something from another planet.

ME: And I tell you where else I went – to see the man who lives in the Palazzo Lampedusa.

WENCESLAO: He's my brother!

ME: It's marvellous that he's restored the building and lives in the old town.

PAOLO: No one can live in the old town any more. It's so dirty, dangerous and noisy.

ME: But everywhere in Palermo is noisy.

PAOLO: That's true. The carabinieri switch on their sirens to get home quickly for lunch.

WENCESLAO: Our family had a very beautiful palace, the Palazzo Mazzarino, perhaps the most beautiful in Palermo because it has all the original furniture and pictures and very few of them do. And it has a *garden*. But there was a legal dispute 20 years ago and we lost it to another branch. (*He gives a little smile which doesn't reach his eyes.*)

COSTANZA: Wenceslao prefers to live in Rome. He prefers to be not so Sicilian. My sister Rose-Marie lives in Rome.

WENCESLAO: Is she still with Ruffo?

COSTANZA: No. (*And greatly daring, she allows a piece of fish into her mouth.*)

ME: Do you live in the old town?

COSTANZA: No. We have a villa near the via Libertà but we live in a modern house in Mondello, very near here. Have you met Renata Zanca?

ME: I was with her yesterday.

COSTANZA: Her husband designed it. He died of cancer quite recently.

Very sad. It's too expensive to have a house at the sea *and* in the town, so we let the villa – to some very nice people. (*An extremely tall, thin man, about 40, walks up to the table, greets everyone, and like a gallant giraffe, bends low to kiss Costanza's hand. They talk briefly and he gangles off again in his absent-minded looking-all-about-him-from-a-great-height way.*) That was one of the Gangi heirs and –

ME: Isn't his brother –

COSTANZA: Yes, but I didn't say anything about that. I asked him if the palace is open but he said no, it's all closed up because the family is in the country for the wheat harvest.

ME: Have you had to come to terms with the mafia in your life?

PAOLO: Yes, one has to.

ME: I heard about Baron di Stefano.

PAOLO: He's a queer fish. (*I'm amazed at his use of this old-fashioned idiom. He is now smoking a post-prandial pipe of Balkan Sobranie tobacco which his wife detests and she waves the smoke dreamily away when it floats near her.*)

ME: Will these trials break the power of the mafia?

PAOLO: I doubt it. But if I came to London and wanted to be a taxi driver, I'd have to join the union. That's just the mafia of the taxi drivers.

ME: But the union is accountable before the law. And they don't murder people who disagree with them.

PAOLO: Yes, there is that, I suppose (*blowing a gust of Balkan Sobranie towards the sea in a patrician, almost satirical manner*).

ME: Don't you think Palermo's an exceptionally violent town?

WENCESLAO: Yes, but Catania's *much* worse.

ME: Catania says Palermo's worse.

WENCESLAO: Well, they would, wouldn't they, but it's not true.

ME: I witnessed a terrible assault yesterday (*and I describe it*).

COSTANZA: Do please be careful. I never took any of my children there. It's a disgusting place.

PAOLO: Right, I must escape. Will you excuse me?

WENCESLAO: What else is on your list?

ME: I'd like to find the Earl of Newburgh. I believe he's a Sicilian with a British Jacobite title – it can go in the female line which is why it's been passed around in this odd way.

WENCESLAO: I've never heard of him. But I'll look in my books and make some enquiries. But one thing you must see is the Serpottas, especially at the Oratorio del Santissimo Rosario, the Oratorio della Santa Zita – here, let me write it down for you – and at the Oratorio del San Lorenzo. It's difficult getting in – there's always a little old lady in a side street who has the key – but it's worth it.

Costanza and I drop him off and go to her house for a siesta. It is modern, full of fine solid things, lots of big dogs and one little yapper. Driving into Palermo she says 'To-morrow we are going to Pantelleria. The island is very interesting, ½ African, ½ Sicilian. Our daughter lives there all the time with a man she met. If you want to come, just telephone. We have some houses there.'

This Palermo generosity is making me dizzy. Really I don't think I've ever been so taken up by a town . . . At the hotel there's a message to ring Kris.

'It took me ages to find you,' she says. 'The reception insisted there was no one there with your name.'

'I know. What can I do? I keep telling them I'm here and they keep telling people I'm not.'

'You haven't forgotten the reception to-night? You have to wear a jacket. Do you have a little present?'

'Marmalade?'

'Perfect.'

Midsummer Day's Night. The reception is given by a rich builder called Franco Amoroso who lives at the top of a new block in the old part of town near the Porta Felice. He is a subdued man but very friendly and shows me round the flat which has low ceilings but many beautiful pictures and pieces of furniture, including 2 tables and a bed inlaid with lozenges of mirror. They look Art Deco but are in fact 18th century, from the Villa Palagonia, the Villa of Monsters at Bagheria which Goethe describes. Then Franco introduces me to the cook in the kitchen. She is short, fat and high-spirited, and is working on a magnificent fish.

There are about 40 guests but soon I find myself whispering on a balcony with Kris who tells me of the drug problems of some of the children of some of the people I've met (which is 5 'of's in a row). Gossip and conspiracy may not be honourable but they do create a warm feeling of being included. Kris says whispering is unavoidable in Palermo because suspicion is everywhere. Even the little boy who brings coffee to the office – she asked him polite questions about his family and his brow furrowed, wondering what it was she was after, and he closed up like a clam. See nothing, know nothing: omertà. She says Sicilians have a wall. You might think they are open – then you reach the wall. And if you ever get over this wall, there's another wall. Always something held back, a profound assumption that the other person intends to exploit you in some way. There is respect for family and friends but not for someone simply as a fellow human being. And even within family and friendships, there are endless suspicions. The Sicilian is so *uncertain*. Finally he can trust no one but himself. And to this description of hers I would add – even Kris, who is very worldly wise for Palermo, is none the less continually worried by what other people are thinking. 'If I say so and so, they will think that so and so . . .'

As we are leaving, Franco asks if I'd like him to show me Old Palermo on foot – I'd love it. So a couple of days later we take to the byways of the 4 decrepit and fascinating districts about the Quattro Canti – down the street of ironmongery, down the street of leather – 2 young children, about 3 and 4 years old, are letting down car tyres with matchsticks – panneli are made from chick pea flour fried, very good for you, taste awful – much prefer the other local specialities of hot pancreas in a bun and ice-cream in a bun – Palazzo Bonagia: through a chink in the building site wall, we see the outside staircase standing graceful, bereft, alone among the tumbled rubble – Palazzo Trigona: 'The old Contessa Trigona was murdered by her lover Paternò which created a great scandal because she was lady-in-waiting to the Queen' – Franco has a dictionary and with its aid we manage to communicate – down the street of tarts but none there – chatter of women in guttural Sicilian sounds like gravel tipping into a pit – we drink the miraculous water in the crypt of a church at the Quattro Canti itself – through a fruit market to the monastery of the Carmine which seems to be closed but a stocky young man with a studious frown, emerging from a side door, says it's OK to enter. In the cool chapel of curved, shadowy spaces, a visiting French priest mumbles mass all by himself. He makes divers cringes at a shimmering altar, then there's a tap on Franco's shoulder. It's the young man with the studious frown. He has a slight stutter and a request. Would I phone Wisbech in Cambridgeshire for him? He pronounces it 'Vizbeck'. This is a very surreal request in the heart of Albergheria, Palermo's most notorious slum (its reputation is undeserved – the worst slums are in modern blocks), but I find myself standing at a phonebox in the little square outside, surrounded by boxes of oranges and tomatoes, trying to get through to Wisbech – and of course failing. The young man's name is Natale Maganuco, a student of electronic engineering at Palermo University who lives in the monastery. He wants a summer fruit-picking job at Wisbech in order to learn English. This is exceptionally enterprising, so I suggest he come with us to Kris's office and we try from there. I have instant rapport with him and despite relative ignorance of each other's languages there is cheerful conversation. He says he is reading two marvellous books at the moment: *The Confessions of Saint Augustine* and *The Collected Works of Karl Marx*. When finally Wisbech is penetrated to, they say he must send a letter and they will send a form which doesn't sound very promising but Natale is satisfied, his eyes light up with Greek sparks, and he goes round shaking everyone's hand, thanking us for our help.

The day after Franco's walkabout, Toby suggests a country driveabout. Lucinda, an Englishwoman, comes with us. She's small and round and looks very Italian and has recently separated from her Sicilian husband.

'The Circolo della Vela,' explains Toby, 'is the aristocratic beach club. Its great rival – bankers and business – is the Circolo della Lauria next door. The bankers achieved an enormous coup by hooking Prince Andrew for lunch when his ship was here.'

'I was told that Catania's worse than Palermo for violence.'

'I doubt there's much in it,' opines Toby, 'but the Catania mafia are doing frightfully well now because the Palermo lot are lying low while this great trial is on.'

'What about Sicilian poverty?'

'It's a bit of a myth what with all the drug money around and handouts from the Common Market. A group of Labour MPs came down from the UK on a fact-finding mission, looking for Sicilian poverty, and they went back to Liverpool, Newcastle, Glasgow where, they concluded, the slums were worse.'

'Well, that's *cold* poverty, you see, which is always worse than warm poverty.'

'You know you were saying there are no country hotels in Sicily – one's just opened in a lovely old monastery at Gangivecchio. I thought we'd try it for lunch.'

The property comprises ranges of sunfaded stone and plaster and a fine avenue of laurels. They invite us to a party next week, celebrating its being in the family for 130 years.

In the castle at Castelbuono is a remarkable chapel dedicated to Saint Anne. Although the fabric is 14th century the stucco decorations which characterise it are late 17th and were carried out by the famous Serpotta's brother. Hundreds of chimerae, half beautiful, half crazy, devils, putti, fishtails, snakes, skulls, lizards, swirl everywhere in a phantasmagorical dance. The very walls appear made of writhing muscle below a restless entablature. I'd like to describe this interior in greater detail but was without camera and have been unable to find it represented in any books. It is an outstanding masterpiece of mutation, in which everything is capable of becoming something else, and makes one want to know more about the man who created it, the forgotten brother. The Renaissance revived the classical art of stucco grotesquerie and associated it with burial chambers and grottoes. But nowhere have I seen it produced with such effervescent effect.

Motoring through the Madonie Mountains, Toby asks 'Do you know the story of the Whitaker birds? Well, Delia Whitaker's father liked to *do* things. For example he dug up a few Phoenician remains. And he went to Tunis, shot a lot of birds, brought them back and had them stuffed. They ended up in an outhouse and no one really knew what to do with them. Eventually there was a great parley just before the war between Chamberlain, Halifax and Mussolini to try and avert hostilities. I came across a dispatch which had been sent down to Palermo because on the bottom of the conference agenda there'd been: Whitaker Birds and what to do with them. Mussolini said he'd no objection against their being taken to England and Chamberlain said he was a lot easier to talk to than Hitler. But they didn't actually leave Palermo until the late 1960s – at the moment they're at Stormont because the Northern Ireland Prime Minister Terence O'Neill had a relation who was consul at Palermo and O'Neill himself was related by marriage to the Whitaker family.'

We stop briefly at the Sanctuary of the Madonna at Gibilmanna where a priest in jeans, blue cardigan and chasuble is blessing this *object*, a small red Peugeot, by shaking holy water over it and chanting, while a young family – father, mother, little daughter – stand proudly at its side. At Cefalù I take them to the Abbey of Thelema.

'I often wondered where it was,' says Toby, red and puffed.

'Von made everyone say Io io Pan!'

'Well, that sounds like the right thing,' he replies, 'so I'll do it too!' And he does.

Eating a light pasta supper at an open-air café overlooking the sea, I mention the hijack of the Georgian Society in their coach.

'Yes, but they got the rotters in the end. They did a house-to-house search in the Old Town. They were *very* determined because it happened *right* at the beginning of the tourist season. The President or the Mayor or someone sent flowers to the hotel. They got stiff sentences, 7 or 8 years, but they'll only do 2 or 3 of course.'

'But the people are absolutely fantastic,' exclaims Lucinda, 'if you get into any sort of trouble yourself.'

She asks me if I'd like to stay in her flat which is large and overlooks the sea on the via Francesco Crispi. Another friendly offer – but it's better that I keep my own place. However, now that I've decided to stay on in Palermo, because I'm having such a good time, but also to try and plumb this perplexing Sicilian *thing*, I ought to find somewhere cheaper. The Hotel des Palmes at 80,000 lire per night is not expensive by international standards but too much for an extended sojourn. So I move to a pension in a square 19th century building opposite, the Hotel Tonic, very clean, pleasant, cheap – 16,000 lire per night. Besides, I like its name – and its closer to the Sicilians.

I came to Palermo thinking I'd not write about the mafia. Trying to be clever and original, you see. But the subject is inescapable, and it would be self-consciously arch to overlook the Maxi Processi which are currently taking place inside the prison. So passport in hand, I take myself along there to the afternoon session which begins at 4.

The trial came about because increasing mafia violence in Palermo, culminating in the murder of Prefect della Chiesa, appointed by Rome to lead an anti-mafia crusade, made it vital that the central authority should be seen to do something. Kris says that when he was murdered, imprisoned mafiosi had champagne brought in, the best, Cristal. -

'But how?'

'The guard is frightened. If he doesn't turn a blind eye, he thinks maybe he loses his job, or a member of his family is hurt.'

But this trial has been made possible by 2 factors: (1) One of the mafia bosses, Buscetta, after seeing an increasing number of his family murdered by a rival gang, turned 'pentito', repentant. (2) A change in the law now makes it possible to force banks to disclose private accounts. Without this facility, no trial could've proceeded far.

None the less the atmosphere is edgy. There is the constant risk of reprisals. Magistrates are driven to court in police cars at high speed – once a student demonstration was encountered and some students were killed as the car ploughed through. Several times these cars have been hijacked and the magistrates murdered.

The entrance is beside one of the tanks, along a path inside the new high steel fence, through another gate where there's a pair of guards with tommy guns and a passport check, through an X-ray scan, hand over your passport to which something is done, perhaps it's photographed, a final door, and in, along a corridor, up stairs to the public gallery where when I arrive there are only 3 others – an old man, a teenage boy, a mama about 55 – apart from a couple of armed policemen.

The courtroom is more an auditorium and very large, though not as large as it looks on television, basically green with green rubber floors. It is fanshaped and the jury bench is opposite the outside curve. In the pit are ranks of chairs and tables with microphones for the many lawyers. Round the outside curve in rooms behind bars are the prisoners, all male, who look no different from anyone else in Palermo, various ages, nicely dressed. One always expects such people to manifest their viciousness externally but they rarely do. In galleries above the prisoners are seats for the television commentators, press journalists, public. I pop out for a pee in the spotlessly clean, rubbery loo and when I return the courtroom has begun to fill. Dozens of lawyers in black gowns with gold tassels at the shoulder move silently about on the rubber floor like black fish in a green aquarium. I count 22 armed guards down there – but $\frac{1}{3}$ of the hall is hidden from my view. The security is essential. The other day in Rome a man undergoing prosecution simply walked out of court and escaped before anyone realised what was happening. The excuse was it was a hot day and the guards were half asleep. Here they have air-conditioning which is very efficient so that the obvious way the lawyers are fanning themselves with their papers must be due to habit or excitement. And here the guards stand on their feet and change position at regular intervals.

The jury enters wearing sashes of green, white and red stripes. The only women in court, apart from those in the viewing galleries, are on the jury – 6 women, 7 men. Several lawyers approach the bench, talk with the judge, then return to their desks. The teenage boy in our gallery is signalling to various prisoners, conveying silent information. A gold bracelet glints on his wrist. He seems to know a great many of those behind bars. This signalling goes on throughout the trial and must be permissible since he makes no attempt at disguise.

A man in a chair on a podium gives testimony into a microphone in guttural Sicilian. Presumably he's not one of the key witnesses for whom there is another chair surrounded by bulletproof glass. The microphones make it exceptionally difficult to follow what is being said. If the witness isn't speaking it is often impossible to work out who is – all mouths look stilled and the voice is disembodied. None the less the whole business is absolutely riveting. Items of testimony trigger various responses from the men held behind the semi-circle of bars. The press calls these 'cages' in a gesture of perverse sympathy but they aren't cages at all. When the guttural Sicilian has finished his piece, there is a noise from a prisoner. Every armed guard turns to face him. I can't see the man because his cell is sideways-on, only hear him. He is speaking in that whining tone which starts high and slides downwards. Now his hands and arms are extended through the bars in a theatrical gesture of supplication, accompanied by redoubled, whining assertions of innocence. It's so damn phoney. The whole courtroom is clogged with phoneyness.

A number of lawyers form a group in front of the bench and there's a general flapping of heads and tassels. I see Mama making to one of the prisoners that emphatic 'no' gesture of the south – the index finger leans back and moves from side to side. Behind distant bars a young man in blue jeans, green shirt with white t-shirt underneath, signals back to Mama, then leaves the cell by himself. Mama applies a flowered fan. She is sweating. Through the distortion of amplification, I make out that someone has been described as 'mortissimo'. Here and there a nose is being picked by its owner.

A new man under cross-examination, wearing a cream suit, is growing heated. He doesn't look a typical Sicilian. Maybe he's a bank manager. There are quite a few bank managers in this trial. The cream-suited one refers to 'pistole' and 'Agira' and 'Bagheria'. Some rowdiness develops between opposing lawyers. Others fan themselves.

And so it goes on. The entire social history of the island has been concentrated down into this determined and expensive attempt to arrive at something akin to objective truth. Almost every Sicilian sneers at the attempt and undermines it. Kris says how terrible it is that the prisoners should be in cages. Renata says how ridiculous it is to spend all this money. Toti says how silly the tanks are. Another says that Palermo used to be safe until they arrested the mafia bosses – now there is no one to control the street boys. Palermitans are indulging their most unattractive characteristic: to destroy, with destructive criticism, initiative of any sort in any field. Nothing will change, they say – and their persistent attitude ensures that nothing does. If you live here, you participate in the psychological process which allows mafia to prosper. It is obvious why it is essential to bring in outsiders to conduct the trial – thus fuelling Sicilian resentment of interference from overseas. But Sicily's rulers have always come from elsewhere.

What is the mafia? It is not a single secret organisation like Freemasonry but it is a criminal system. It can flourish only in a society both intensely self-focused and at the same time in conflict with itself – and Sicily has this double feature to a marked degree. Anton Blok in *The Mafia of a Sicilian Village 1860–1960* defines its central characteristic as the private use of unlicensed violence as a means of control in the public arena. The 'men of honour' they like to be called. Sicilian honour, then, is a curious thing, based not on justice but on physical prowess and the ability to cheat, steal and punch successfully. Is it honourable to deal massively in heroin? To break arms and legs, to burn cornfields? To use shotguns, with nail shot blasted between 10 and 20 feet from the victim's face to render him unrecognisable? To torture and murder children, anyone, in manic escalations of vendetta? The mafia code permits all forms of deceit

and brutality in the pursuit of self-interest. In the old days there may
have been a brigand philosophy to it, but now it is simply bullying and
greed at their nastiest. Mafia is the extreme example of the consumer
approach to life: exploitation raised to the level of extortion.

Of all west European societies, the Sicilian is the one most condi-
tioned by fear – this we can call 'the mafia effect'. Others would call
it 'the mafia cause'. Nowadays it is often sublimated – as the fear
of social disapproval. They terrorise each other, then cling to each
other out of fear, which is one of the reasons the family is so strong
here. In Sicily there is no objective sphere of operations. Objectivity
is a sin because it is betrayal. Some might even see my writing as
betrayal. A betrayal of hospitality, of friendship. If I keep it general,
that's acceptable, that's philosophy, albeit insolent philosophy. But if
I become specific – no, no, no. Being specific is a private activity.
In public you must be vague, dissembling, flattering, meaningless. In
Sicily *nothing* of importance is done in public. Sicilians equate honesty
with betrayal – or with stupidity. Oxygen makes them writhe.

Mafiology is an absorbing labyrinth and we should not stray too far
into it but I'd like to draw attention to the following:

(1) The New Science Building at Palermo University designed by
Gregotti is the most beautiful modern academic building in Sicily. It
is very large with accommodation and facilities for several thousand
science students, as well as spacious terraces, outdoor lecture theatres,
watercourses and fountains. Finished in the early 1980s. Empty.
Silent. Its terraces are cracking and plants sprout in the cracks.
Mafia interests allowed it to be built, taking their cut, then refused to
allow its occupation since this would involve the transfer of thousands
of students from the old town where mafia interests profit directly
from them.

(2) The best book on the modern mafia is *Mafia Business* (1983) by
Pino Arlacchi. He explains that the idea of a mafia superorganisation is
contrary to the character of Sicily where distrust does not vanish in the
criminal fraternity but increases. There is competition among mafiosi,
leading to mafia wars and murders. Co-operation is restricted to the
family and its clients. At least, this is the traditional picture. However,
the huge amounts of drug money, and the necessity of laundering it,
is spreading criminality through all the classes. *We are now seeing the
formation of mafia confederations far more stable and permanent than any
formerly known*, he writes. Having successfully penetrated the political
world, the mafia system is now stronger than before, fuelled by – in
addition to drug profits – misappropriated grants from the Italian
Government and the EEC.

And yet at heart the mafia remains primitive and volatile. *The*

Weltanschauung *of the modern mafioso, like that of the denizen of Hobbes's 'state of nature', is dominated by an anguished sense of danger. Pessimism, fatalism and a feeling of persecution fill the memoirs, autobiographies and court statements of the mafiosi and their circle*, he writes.

(3) Huge amounts of cash are difficult to launder. One of the obvious ways for the mafiosi to do it is through their own industry, construction. By 1981, the building trade – unproductive, speculative, uglifying – employed over 25% of the industrial workforce in Sicily.

(4) Ordinary Sicilians can take a perverse pride in the mafia and its legends because this makes their life situation appear dramatic instead of paltry and Sicilians love drama.

(5) The success of criminal enterprise in south Italy makes success increasingly difficult to achieve by any other means. Since crime is parasitical, the underlying economy of the south is almost dead,

Message at hotel to ring Costanza. She says 'We are having a party for Michael Cimino – can you come?'

'I'd love to. Who's Michael Cimino?'

'He's a film director. He's been making a film called *The Sicilian*. I think it's a terribly silly book but perhaps it will be a good film and I hope it will be a good party. But don't tell anyone because unfortunately we can't invite everybody.'

I move across the road to the Hotel Tonic, into a noisy room at the front which they promise to change for a quieter one at the back. When? 'Domani.' The cleaner is a foxy young girl of 18 who goes swabbing around on her knees while her fag burns in the ashtray.

Ring Kris with the new number and she invites me to eat at her flat. Her balcony has a fine view of the prison with port and sea beyond. She says 'In the 1950s the prisoners managed to tap an oil line that went underneath the prison and they made a lot of money selling bottles of oil out of the prison.'

I work my way through a small bowl of green almonds. On her desk is a photograph of the Icarus of Mozia, recently found. Man wearing a pleated dress of fine gauze through which his muscular body is revealed. Round alien face, hand on hip. Technically and conceptually a remarkable sculpture, very male, yet androgynous, like Burt Lancaster in drag.

Going into the kitchen where she's rustling up some pasta, I say 'I went to the Archaeological Museum to-day and did what Paolo Camporeale suggested and they opened up the collection of Greek vases. The attendant who showed me round had very long finger-nails, a sheaf on either hand, and told me that England won against France at football.'

A great number of erections are portrayed on the vases. On the same

floor there was also a collection of prehistoric remains, including cave
drawings from the Grotte Addaura. To my eye these looked completely
bogus. I know prehistoric art can have an economical refinement in
the modern way but these seemed to have it in the wrong way. The
line was too knowing. There was an element of kitsch which should
be impossible in prehistoric art. Or is my education in local mores
teaching me to find deception where none exists? Afterwards I went
in pursuit of Serpotta at the nearby oratories of Rosario and Zita. This
Serpotta was *the* Serpotta and much more naturalistic than his brother.
I'd heard so much about him and his fabulous baroque/rococo work
that I was surprised by what I found: pale, realistic statuary with perfect
finish and much levity. The light slanted through high windows on to
the sun-slashed figures, some sitting on window-sills, other chatting
in corners, as if in a theatre waiting for the show to begin.

I notice that Kris has a rug bearing the large head of Colonel
Gaddafi in front of her fridge. Toti arrives with his wide winning
smile and says 'After your weekend with Renata you must tell me
all. *All*.'

'I'm learning that in Sicily it's unwise to tell all.'

'No, you *say* you'll tell all,' explains Kris, 'then you tell only a
little bit.' And she laughs and laughs and laughs. 'I'm sorry I don't
mean to laugh.'

'No, I like it when you laugh. It's when people don't laugh that I
get nervous.'

At the Tonic I say to the desk boy 'You said I could change
room.'

'Sì. Certamente . . . domani, signor.'

'Sempre domani.'

. . . Bad, hot night's sleep. Sticky, close. You should go to the sea, yes,
to the sea, the sea . . . At Trapani in the messed-up, mafia-ridden west
of the island, you drive through the dusty chaos of new construction
on the monstrous exploding outskirts and head for the old port with
palm trees and broken belle époque lamps along the quay. Keep going
until you reach the Traghetti delle Isole ticket office. Which is closed.
It opens at 11 p.m., one hour before the midnight boat. It is warm,
teatime, you've had something to eat and drink but are still spaced out
on erratic sleep, so with 6 or 7 hours to kill, head into the old town with
its straight Corso of waving balconies and porticoes terminated at the
far end by a beautiful baroque façade which made a perfect climax to
the whole until recently a shoddy towerblock was built behind it at a
random angle.

Halfway along the street on the right is an archway into an ancient
courtyard with vaulted staircase up several flights of which are the

narrow passages, beaded curtains, tiled floors and crooked bedrooms
of the Pensione Messina. A thin boy, slumped in front of a black &
white TV, shouts for his mother. The signora quickly makes up a
room with clean, frayed linen and towels. There are 2 single beds.
You and your travelling companion climb into one and careen off into a
fitful, caressing snooze pierced by the abrasive scat of evening scooters
and chance encounters in the side street under the shuttered window
through whose fissures flows the final ghostly light of day which seeps
under closed eyelids arresting you at the threshold of slumber. The
digital travelling alarm clock emits a hard signal and the furry purring
southern form, relaxed against yours, stirs somewhat, releasing the
clean safe smell of the body, and asks if it's time to get up . . .

It is 10.30 p.m. in the Corso which dazzles with white lamps against
golden ripples of carved stone and the sky overhead like a rectangular
roof of jet set on the parapets of the street. Moonless, starless. Turn
down a side street, down another, past a church looking huge in the
narrow street, down another, and opposite the monumental chipped
doorway of a small town palazzo it says Pizzeria Siciliana. A woman
glides by in the back of a tiny car. She is huge, spread out over 2
seats and her head rests on the back of the seat with the long hair
arranged over her shoulders and the inbred mutant doughnut face
tilted upwards.

This pizzeria is very old and very busy – takeaway or eat in small
private rooms done up with 1920s fittings. The pizza will be the best
you've ever had because not only is it perfectly cooked but every
single ingredient is fresh. The takeaways come wrapped like newborn
babies in greaseproof paper through which the bloody contents ooze
and drip.

At last the ticket office is open. A melancholy clerk with long
nose and no hair makes out the tickets and points through romantic
lamplight to where on the other side of the road a yellow tub rides
against the quay with its belly open into which the car is driven.
There are a few cabins to be had for the 6 hour crossing. But not
yet. They cannot be booked for some reason until we've sailed. You
are propped upright, bug-eyed under a cruel glare in the mini-saloon,
blinking at hysterical or catatonic nuns in a TV film made from a
novel by Georges Bernanos. There are only 3 other passengers. One
of them mutters 'bella' at the TV screen.

And some time after midnight the car deck is closed against the
water and engines force the tub away from the magnetic hug of the
land, of the creepy beaten-up southern town, and we slide out beyond
the bar into the swooning, heaving sea which is not rough but undulates
steeply with a calm power. The cabin is cold but the bunk is warm and

2 clothed bodies roll against each other under the blankets with a soft, effortless pressure – each in turn pushing on the other as the bunk tips sleazily from side to side, rolling southward, ever southward through the night whose sky, now way beyond the illuminations of the town, has blossomed with stars and a low brilliant moon. Far off, somewhere on the other side of the boat, is the sound of disco music on a tinny radio. It recedes further and further from the attention until there is silence – an enfolding sense of well-being, a childlike abandon to the rhythms of the sea and unconsciousness.

Then a hand touches your face. A familiar voice says 'Look. Look out of the window.' You raise yourself up on elbows, brain squirming only half alive, and look out of the porthole. A sinister black volcanic mass is approaching slowly. And behind it, so that the threatening mass is outlined in jagged silhouette, rises the sun which cannot be seen but casts an immense fan of orange up into the swarthy sky. All the black waters about the black jagged mass are tinted with flashes of fiery orange and at this early crumpled hour the scene presents an unforgettable vision of dawn in hell. This is the weird island of Pantelleria.

The Tonic doesn't do breakfast, or any other meals, so, bleary and tight, I go to the nearby coffee bar but instead of the usual corno, this morning I buy an appetising pyramid covered with nuts – when I bite into it, a vile sweet green jelly oozes out. Then Renata comes to collect me for the weekend. I pack *Little Dorrit*.

'Have you been having a *wonderful* time?' she asks. 'Was Anna Bordonaro at the Amorosos? Oh, you are being treated like a Spanish peer!'

'Where is your country place?'

'Castellana Sicula. Near Petralia Sottana.'

'Is that near Gangivecchio?'

'Very near.'

'I've been invited to a party there. We can go.'

'What party? Who? Ah, Old Palermo is like a dethroned queen – miserable, penniless, but still superb!' Renata has a rickety Mini Minor and we are shuddering along the Marina. 'Will it be formal?' she asks.

'I don't think so. I believe it's country people getting drunk.'

'Very well, then we shall be the stars!'

Renata calls Castellana Sicula a village but it's a town of 2 thousand people. Her house is at the beginning of the main street with a good garden behind and soothing view of fields, hills, trees.

'This land at the back,' she says, throwing out an arm, 'I want to sell for building – but it isn't easy.'

She isn't poor and it would destroy the view. 'But it's money in the bank!' she replies. There are stacks of rooftiles against a garden wall, weathered into many subtle hues, but again she is dismissive. 'Just old tiles, no use, nobody wants them.' These tiles would be extremely valuable in Provence.

The house curiously has shops underneath on the ground floor at the front. Much of the furniture is covered with newspapers and in the course of the weekend these are not removed. No one apart from the maid Giovanna visits us there. But it's a charming old house with a nursery feel, majolica tiles, sticks of painted furniture, flowered wallpaper.

Renata starts caterwauling. She's lost her weekend bag. Giovanna and I join in the hunt but it becomes clear she's left everything in Palermo. 'I can't go to the party!' she wails, arms zipping up and down.

'You must. Go as you are.'

'As I am? Go *as I* am? It's *impossible* to go as I am! I need clothes, makeup, I have to look elegant. I must borrow. Oh, oh, oh!' And in the car on the way to pick up clothes from a friend, she confides 'Giovanna is *wonderful*. Her son was taken away to a lunatic asylum and she said to me in tears "All he did was ask for a girl's hand." So I decided to investigate. The boy had woken up in the middle of the night with the sudden idea to marry this girl, and gone at once to the father's house and woken him up. But he'd forgotten to put on any clothes. He was entirely naked and the father immediately called the police. Giovanna said "Yes, he was naked. But he was so sincere. He had no thought but his love." See that mountain? Until recently a hermit lived up there. They discovered his body eaten by mice.'

Gangi town looks extraordinary at dusk, like a pink steamed pudding studded with lights, but of the party I remember little except candle-light on old stones, pizzas, salads, wine and being drawn into jolly folk dancing. Next day I sunbathe and read *Little Dorrit*. In my Penguin edition, 'gaol' is spelt 'jail'. Did Dickens really spell it thus?

On the return to Palermo we stop at the *Villa Palagonia* in Bagheria, owned by a Professor of Italian at the University who doesn't have the resources to restore it properly – rooms are fading, stone is decomposing, the monsters along the outside wings are eaten away

by the elements, and the grounds have long been sold off so that the
villa is hemmed on all sides by cement buildings. The owner proudly
shows us his new-born baby onto whose cot descend occasionally fine
flakes of painted ceiling.

A priest called Toti is also there and takes us to his nearby Drug
Rehabilitation Centre for heroin addicts, a few girls but mostly boys.
They are allowed tea, coffee, 10 cigarettes a day, but no other drugs,
including alcohol, no sex, and all must help farm the land attached to
the building. They stand round me in a great semi-circle and shake
my hand, one by one, shy and sweet-natured except 3 or 4 disciples
of the pop guru Bhagwan Rajneesh who are a peculiar mixture of
pushiness and servility. It is reasonable that the centre should be
in Bagheria, once the heart of the mafia heroin trade. Sicily is still
the world's heroin factory, manufacturing it from the raw opium
(although recently this trade has started to move to Hong Kong),
and talking to these soft young people my mind goes back to the
sultry and delectable opium dens of pre-Communist Vientiane and
pre-airport Penang. Renata says that the Centre will probably become
an old people's home because there's more money in it.

'Have you any children, Renata?'

'Yes, I have a daughter. And you must create some children too,
so that there is something for your old age.'

'They don't allow them to have sex or affairs. But do they teach them
to handle rejection? We all have to learn to be alone with ourselves
because only then can we truly love.'

'Do you think so? Sicilian men never talk of amore, of love. Love is
always tragic for them. They are the opposite of the Neeeapolitans.'
She tastes the words like coloured sweets as they leave her mouth.

'Bagheria is different from what I expected. I was expecting
Cheltenham.'

'I don't know Cheltenham. But I know Bagheria and it's a very
mafioso town. They are dangerous *and* frivolous. No sense of loyalty
but a great sense of life and adventure. If someone is like this, we say
he is Bagheriatano. There are 3 great villas here, the Villa Palagonia,
the Villa Valguarnera – and the Villa Trabia Butera which I think I
can take you to' (and a week later she does).

Villa Trabia Butera. The villa is white and approached via tall iron
gates and drive. The mafia are always trying to flush the family off
the site by various intimidations so that they can build in the grounds.
Drinks in garden, bothered by mosquitoes. Motto on the garden front:
Sine sole sileo; Without the sun I am silent. Sun quickens life but slows
the mind. Yeats: *A gaze blank and pitiless as the sun*. Natale Maganuco
tells me that 'When the sunlight is bright the cornea is excited more

and enzymes are created which affect the nervous system and make a good temper.'

The family lives in the undercroft, with the state rooms above closed up. The current reception room is in fact the hall: a low vault supported on 4 square pillars, decorated 1797 in cool blues and greens, dark blue and chocolate. In the corners are Prudence, Fortitude, Beauty and Amity. There is a china fireplace from Austria, some interesting chairs whose backs are intertwined serpents, pieces of carpet laid on top of each other Arab-style, pink hibiscus in vases, and a television set.

Dinner is a buffet, given by Nini Moncada whose mother was the Princess Trabia. Tomato pasta, roast tuna with mint sauce and vegetables, watermelon jelly sprinkled with chocolate and jasmin flowers. Nini is very relaxed, smart, international, with a deep husky voice, and I'm impressed by the way she energetically helps the maid to clear up the plates. At these Sicilian soirées everyone leaves at the same time, so saying good-bye can take anything up to an hour.

Driving back to town, Palermo's 2 superlong, superstraight streets (Maqueda and the Corso) are 2 intersecting tunnels of lights, fixed up for the Feast of Santa Rosalia, the town's patroness. I haven't seen such effective illuminations since Mexico City's Christmas splash. And the tremendous thing is that they don't shut them off at midnight which the niggardly British do in London, even the Regent Street Christmas lights. But here, no, they burn on and on until dawn. Several members of the group Save Palermo have said it's disgraceful for a poor town to burn lights all night. But this form of extravagance is the sort of thing that makes the Sicilians very simpatico. The lights stop at the Politeama, along with Palermo's soul. There are none in the via Libertà.

Villa Valguarnera. Cigarette sticking up from the left hand on the wheel, driving to tea with the Principessa Alliata, Kris sketches the background. 'The Principessa is Alliata only by marriage. She is one of 2 sisters from Reggio di Calabria who married the 2 Alliata brothers. The girls were from a rich family because their father had the world monopoly of bergamot which grows only near Reggio.'

We pass an industrial zone which went bust. 'They couldn't afford to subsidise it any more.' So this enormous project lies ruinous, hideous, useless on the coast. But obviously the massive installations at Augusta make money. 'No. They are subsidised too. And they are always having to pay out because of pollution.' Now this is dementia. Pollution for profit is disgusting but understandable, given the time-honoured ethics of our society. But pollution which has to be *subsidised* is insane.

The villa is the most beautiful in Sicily, built in 1783 at a cost of

180,000 scudi. The entrance front is curved, with statues on the skyline and trophies above the centre, and a double balustraded staircase to the piano nobile. The fabric is plaster, painted a confectioner's lemon-cream, with dressings and Corinthian pilasters in golden wash, and glows warmly in the afternoon sun against a blue sky. The scene, touched here and there with purple bougainvillaea, is the quintessence of the south. The wings are extended in low ranges to form a circular gravelly forecourt. The Principessa says that bamboo was used as a framework for the plaster but that the plaster is very hard.

The interior, which is white, pale blue and faded gold, has superb tiled floors but very little furniture. The salone reaches the height of the house in a vault and is white with delicate, gilded plasterwork into which are set family portraits and tall fogged mirrors. In their reflections one becomes a ghost. Soon after my visit robbers broke in and cut the portraits out of the walls.

The Principessa is of medium height and speaks crackly English. She is covered with large brown freckles, has a nasty maroon scab on her leg, and wears a brownish wig of short, shiny lacquered hair. We sit out on the rear terrace where 6 high-backed cane chairs with pale blue and pale pink cushions have been arranged in a semi-circle facing the sea. The top fronds of palm trees in her garden below rise in a few places above the level of the balustrade. On an outdoor table are bottles of gin, whisky, brandy, and a local almond liqueur which is very sweet. There are conical mountains over to the right, but cement blocks are creeping into view and will one day close over the citrus groves and block out the sea.

'These new buildings are all illegal,' she says, 'but it is still very green. When I first came it was the silvery grey-green of olive trees. Now it is the much richer green of lemon trees, which I prefer.'

A Singhalese maid in a yellow frock brings a giant domed strawberry ice-cream bombe on to the terrace. She withdraws and reappears with a second, a coffee one. The Principessa asks which I'd like and I say strawberry, so the coffee is dismissed and the maid carries it back in out of the annihilating heat. I am also bidden to eat from a plate on which heart-shaped biscuits and chocolate wafers have been formally arranged in circles. She and Kris don't eat anything. They talk. So after a second helping of bombe, I ask if the maid might show me round the garden. The maid, who has large dark eyes with liverish coloration beneath, is pleased to have the opportunity of speaking English and mentions a brother living near Manchester who works for an airline.

'The Principessa manages her properties all alone from her study,' she says, as we pass a gargantuan knotted banyan tree. 'She lives by herself and when she goes away to Rome or Palermo I am the only person here. But the villa is not as big as it looks. If anyone comes to stay, they are given a set of rooms in the circus ring at the front – which is where I live too.'

Later I ask the Principessa about the future, especially about the preservation of the Villa Valguarnera and her Palazzo Villafranca in Palermo, because there are no male heirs and because Sicilians are now generally indifferent to the stones of their past – except in so far as these things can be turned into money.

'I don't know. It's a problem in Italy,' she says, 'because we don't have like your National Trust. And if there is no strong man to take it over, property makes a big fight in the family and in the end it has to be sold and divided up and the mafiosi come in and do what they want and suddenly there is nothing where there was something. So I don't know what is the best thing to do. Maybe to keep the Palazzo and the Villa as beautiful places, I have to leave them to the Church.' As she talks she plucks absently at her wig which shifts in fits and starts about her head without entirely dislodging itself. She looks sad but not melancholy or dispirited.

(In fact when the Principessa died not long after the robbery, she left the Palazzo Villafranca to the Archbishopric of Palermo and the Villa Valguarnera to Opus Dei, and alas they will cease to be personal residences. One of the reasons the Church remains so rich and powerful in the south is that although you can hardly trust the Church, you can't trust anyone else at all.)

Driving back Kris expatiates on Sicilian family life.

'There are 2 kinds of Sicilians. The Sicilian who swims in the sea – these are few. And the Sicilian who clings to the rocks – these are the rest. One of the sights here is to watch aeroplanes arriving from the USA with Sicilians returning to visit home. Sometimes it looks like the whole town has turned out for one man. Many old women in black embracing the sons who drink deep from their roots, then return very gladly to America. The Sicilian mother has a really horrible influence on her son. It begins early, because she is frustrated in her marriage – because the husband does not think of the woman, just uses the woman. These Latin lovers think they are the greatest lovers in the world but Latin women do not think this. The girls from the north come down for a holiday and for some sexual experience, drunk on the sun, on the wine, and then they go back north and get on with the real business of living, having told the Latin man how wonderful he is. He believes this! Even though the northern girl has only used him, never thought of him as a man to take seriously, and has returned to the men of the north – still the Latin man believes her. But he does not know how to satisfy a woman. Worse – he has no rapport with woman. He is so simple. So the women are unsatisfied and transfer all the frustrated love to the child. We are speaking generally now. There are exceptions – there are always *marvellous* exceptions. But the husband is unloving – so the mother adores the son, does everything for the son, brings his shoes, spoils him. So when the boy grows up he looks for another mama to look after him, to adore him, to let him do what he wants and give him no problems. He wants to marry not for love but for comfort. He never thinks of the woman once he has her. But since this woman cannot exist, the adoring mama woman who receives nothing in return, the man is permanently insecure. He is afraid always that his woman is underneath a bitch. This makes him neurotic, jealous, unfaithful, cruel.'

'But marriage is a big event in Sicily.'

Kris is trying to drive and light up at the same time, with cigarette packet, lighter, big rings, and steering wheel all clashing, so I do it for her.

'Thank-you. And you know not to make it wet.'

'I know all about cigarettes. I used to smoke 60 a day.'

'Really? My God. Yes, a big social event. You really make something and invite everyone to an enormous feast. But if you absolutely cannot afford it, you arrange for the 2 lovers to elope – the mother wails from the balcony – the pair are brought back in disgrace – and a marriage must be done quickly, quietly, and with no expense whatsoever. I have a friend, a very good avant-garde composer, you will meet him, Federico Incardona, and he knows a working-class boy, 17 years old, who was engaged at the age of 11. The girl is now in Florence and the boy wished to break off the engagement, so he must send *all* the photographs of the girl back to the family and they must be torn up as if in a rage, saying "She left *me*. How dare she? I am in such rage!" This is so that no dishonour falls on the girl. Even in these days, jilting can lead to murders. Can you imagine anything so . . . so primordial?'

'What about Sicilians who marry north European girls?'

'Generally these work out quite well. Because the Sicilian understands that with a foreigner he must behave better.'

At last I've moved into a quieter room at the Tonic with a bigger bed. But at 3 a.m. I'm prevented from sleeping by cassettes being played loudly in the room next door. Bang on wall. No response. Put on shorts and go into corridor and knock on door. No response. Bang on door. No response. *Hammer* on door. At last it opens. A young man in underpants, rubbing his eyes, apologises and invites me in for a drink. I come out 7 hours later, feeling much more relaxed.

Taxi to lunch at the Circolo della Vela where Costanza introduces me to Arthur Oliver drinking in the bar. He is small and sun-shrivelled and looks like an ancient pharaoh, but is exceedingly amiable. 'Why didn't you ring us up again?' he asks. 'We'd arranged to take you to a wedding.'

I bend with embarrassment and shame and apologise as best I can, explaining how the second I arrived in Palermo I was swept away by a whirlwind.

'Enjoying it?'

'Oh, yes. I feel oddly at home here, which is extraordinary, don't you think? But the heat's getting too hot and my tummy's a bit funny.'

'Lemon juice,' he replies. 'Excellent for the squits. And for sea-sickness too.'

'OK, keep your fingers crossed.'

'Keep your buttocks crossed as well.'

Villa Malfitano with Toby and Lucinda. He looks awfully red in this July heat and I feel awfully faint. 'In the old days,' he says, mopping his brow in a suffocating midday traffic jam, 'there were 4 great Palermo families all trying to outdo each other. The Florios, the Whitakers, the Trabia Buteras, the Lampedusas. The Whitakers had most money but the Trabia Buteras managed to hook the Kaiser, though they ruined themselves entertaining him – and he had such a good time that he came back and ruined them all over again.'

As we escape the choking streets and pass through elaborate gates into the urban park of the Villa Malfitano, I cross my buttocks and hold on. We pull up outside a sturdy 19th century mansion.

'Old Delia Whitaker lived here all alone with her staff and 8 gardeners until her death in 1974. She was very keen to leave the villa to the Foreign Office as the British Consulate but Selwyn Lloyd said no. The British really do want to wash their hands of "abroad", don't they? So she left it to the region of Sicily. Now it's used for a few formal receptions and putting up fancy foreign guests. Sad.' It's true – the British are terrified of thinking 'grand' any more, in case somebody accuses them of being imperialist or pretentious. (Not only have we surrendered for example our embassy in Moscow, the most palatial in that city, but in return we have given the Russians permission to demolish several magnificent Victorian houses near Kensington Palace in London. Who are these dopes, dealing on our behalf?) On the other hand, as Europe's supreme ex-imperial nation, perhaps Britain feels it no longer wants to try.

Inside is a classic Victorian interior on the grand scale, complete down to the last damask napkin, and I ask 'Is there a loo?' One of the curators points me in the right direction but once inside I can't do much. Perhaps I'm suffering from nervous exhaustion or heatstroke or Palermo overload or insufficient sleep or love or hate. I feel very spaced out and vaguely sick. There's a bright unpleasant shimmer in the head and my skin tingles dully. In the distance I hear myself ask 'Why didn't Delia Whitaker marry?'

'It's always pronounced Day-lia. Nobody was quite good enough. The Whitakers were always aiming at minor royalty which was aiming too high. And she'd never have married a Sicilian.'

'I don't blame her,' says Lucinda with a little laugh. 'They never work out. At least, mine didn't. You never hit rock with a Sicilian man. They like to present a moving target.'

'Er, do you think I could have a glass of water?'

But water or no water, I'm all in. I have to go back to the hotel and lie down. I can't absorb any more. Physically I feel like sliced-up blancmange and need to rest; mentally I'm bewildered and need provisionally to order my thoughts after the sustained onslaught of new impressions.

With several nights of good sleep, my constitution recovers; and I decide to begin organising my thoughts by having a chat with the writer Leonardo Sciascia and paying a call on Arthur Oliver. I'd benefit from the proximity of minds such as theirs, minds of intelligent, and in Olly's case comic, irreverence. Look for the boy next door – he's gone.

It's rush hour, Natale is doing his utmost to get me to the office of Sciascia's publisher on time, swerving down bus lanes towards oncoming buses, worming along side streets, cutting across traffic jams loud with horns. We are late. Natale triple parks in the local manner. And inside the office all is literary hush and feminine cool. The publisher is a woman, the strong, the sweet, the so-tired Elvira Sellerio who never knowingly publishes a bad book; and as far as one can see, she is staffed entirely by women.

Renata appears in red and black, arms spread wide. She will act as interpreter, because there must be no misunderstandings. And this, shuffling near a bookcase, must be Mr Sciascia, a slight retiring figure with yellowish wizened skin in a grey suit, looking older than his years (born 1921) and looking Sicilian – very suspicious and at the same time very interested. We exchange greetings, after which he immediately picks up a book and buries his face in it, then looks out sideways with one sharp black eye. If he is worried – and his behaviour suggests that peace of mind does not come easily – it is by something deeper than our late arrival (which doesn't bother him at all, a typically Sicilian courtesy).

'Signor Sciascia, do you like the modern world?'

'No.'

'You're a romantic.'

'No. But perhaps a man of the 18th century.'

'What sort of family do you come from?'

'Small clerks.'

'Petit bourgeois? Or something more?' interpolates Renata.

'Something less. My father was an accountant in a sulphur mine. I know the world of the sulphur mines very well. They don't exist any longer.'

'When did Sicilians, who are spotlessly, even obsessively clean inside their homes and in their persons, cease to regard the external condition of their towns as important?'

'It is a problem of the managing class in Italy which has no taste and consideration for history – because it is not a managing (dirigente) class but a digesting (digerente) class. It is not just a Sicilian phenomenon. You should see the Adriatic coast – devastated. And it is almost the same story in Spain as in Italy – it started under Fascism and continued with this new managing class after the war.'

The tradition of violent abuse of people, which the mafia represents, also explains why few are tempted by the idea of returning to the countryside to reconstruct picturesque cottages (an activity in France and England since the 18th century). Sicilians huddle together in towns in flats as a way of overcoming their sense of vulnerability which goes very deep. Sciascia is famously anti-mafia. In 1961, when the existence of mafia was still officially denied, he published a short novel *The Day of the Owl*, the first book to give the true now-you-see-it-now-you-don't picture of mafia.

'Since then I have been condemned to speak about this subject on every occasion,' he remarks with a grim smile.

Sicilians don't always use the phrase 'the mafia' and prefer 'mafia' without any article, indicating something less specific, more pervasive.

'At this moment in Calabria,' he says, 'there are more mafia murders than in Sicily. But one talks always of the Sicilian mafia – especially because it was this form which was exported to America. Also the rest of Italy takes a sort of Stendhalian pleasure in the image of a violent, outlaw island.'

To those unfamiliar with the problem of massive corruption in public life, it is hard to understand how a so-called civilised society can continue to allow itself to be terrorised by illegality on this scale.

'What is the connection between mafia and national Italian politics?'

'Votes. The mafia controls blocks of votes and politicians need votes, especially in an unstable democracy like ours. Fascism was able to beat mafia simply because there were no elections. Here we are, idly talking about the mafia problem. But we all know that the problem of mafia lies in the fact that the Christian Democrat Party has had the power in Italy since the war. Nothing can really be done about mafia until the power changes hands. Because the connection between mafia groups and the Christian Democrats is too well established. In Italy we had great men – but nobody listened to them. One was Gaetano Salvemini. He was an historian who was an exile in England during Fascism, living in London. And he warned the Italian people that they should never give power to a Catholic party.'

(The Roman Catholic Church of course has been in the business longer than anybody else and although it doesn't go in for physical violence itself any more, its representatives are often involved with those who do.)

'Has the mafia ever threatened you?'

'Once. But you must not have fear, otherwise you'll never do anything. They wrote a threatening letter against me to the editor of *Il Mondo*. It was easily recognisable as a mafioso letter. But I didn't care about it – and I'm still alive.'

He chuckles like an affable gecko, the tension lines in his face doubling with mirth. Sciascia's expression can change from 'amused' to 'grim' to 'sad' very quickly. Sicilian mercuriality is not mere caprice but a readiness to express the contradictions in experience.

Amused. Sicilian humour has a dry irony and a subtle, often masked playfulness which are familiar to me from English life. I don't find it elsewhere in Italy.

'That's true,' he says, offering around cigarettes (no takers) and lighting up. 'There's an Italian writer, Giovanni Maria Cecchi' – a Florentine wool merchant who wrote 50 plays – 'who in the 16th century refers to the Sicilians' dry intellect. And our poet Quasimodo thanks his mother for the irony she gave him. But we have to divide Sicily into 2 parts. Western Sicily has, I would say, a great lack of "sense of humour" [Italian likes to borrow the English phrase here] but the eastern, more Greek part has a great "sense of humour" which topples over into comedy, fun. The great players were always born in east Sicily. And the great writers, Brancati for example.'

'He was born at Caltanissetta, wasn't he?' asks Renata.

'No,' replies Sciascia, 'at Pachino. I believe he lived for a short time at Caltanissetta.' And Sciascia was born at Racalmuto – in the middle.

Like Ireland, Sicily has produced a far greater number of major writers than its location or size of population would suggest. The Italian language began here, in the school of lyric poetry at the court

of Frederick II. It is truly a place for writers and esteems them –
which may explain why Sciascia isn't dead.

Grim. Northerners tend to confuse an emotional nature with an
open, honest one, but Sicilians often hide their true selves behind
outbursts of emotion. Trust is very hard won – only after repeated
testing – and even then there is doubt.

'Yes, yes, this is our uncertainty. We have no inner security, no
self-assurance.'

And this uncertainty takes the edge off southern machismo, making
the Sicilian a more complex and wily quantity than the Neapolitan.
Sicilian uncertainty is maddening and very appealing.

'What is truth in Sicily?' continues Sciascia. 'Pirandello speaks about
truth as changeable, impossible to seize.'

'Subjective?'

'It also changes objectively.'

'So there can be no honesty here? Sicilians don't believe in objective
truth? Very convenient.'

'But Sicilians don't believe in anything! *Cicero* said of us: people of
very keen mind but suspicious, people born for controversy. This is
because of our history as an island, the keystone of the Mediterranean.
Everybody wanted it. And everybody has had it.'

Sad. In his life what has been the chief cause of unhappiness?

'Many things – as well as the domestic unhappinesses. The strongest
has been the suicide of a brother of mine. In public matters, I was very
unhappy when Stalin signed the Non-Aggression Pact with Hitler,
because I thought then that Fascism would never end. I am unhappy
to-day in seeing how badly Italy is governed, especially Sicily.'

What does he think of the English? He tilts his head to one side, eyes
narrowing to slits, and speaks in a series of soft, descending curves.

'Borges used to say that the world is divided into those who consider
Waterloo a victory and those who consider it a defeat. I consider it a
defeat. Because Italy must always be obliged to France and Napoleon
for bringing us out of the feudal world.'

It's warm and I drink water. Natale offers Sciascia some water but
he wants only his cigarettes. He reacts to water not with distaste, simply
as if the stuff were alien to him – which somehow it seems to be.

Usually Sciascia writes about crime but this does not make him
a crime writer. In Italy, above all in Sicily, crime is not so much
an exceptional event as the touchstone for looking at the operations
of society as a whole. This is not necessarily because the society of
south Italy is more vicious than elsewhere (when I ask Sciascia if he
thinks Sicilian society more cruel than other European societies, after
a long pause he says no) but that there is this sense of Italian society

being a brilliant improvisation upon the spiritual verities of life and death (and their earthly embodiments of Family and Church) rather than functioning within the verbal verities of laws. In its disregard for the law, Italian society is the freest in Europe – but this brings its own form of oppression. Life in Sicily is a matter of intensity, not of justice. Sciascia protests against injustice, against the rule of fear, in documentary works as well as in fiction, but does writing achieve anything?

'In improving our writing, we improve ourselves. But as far as external effects are concerned, I'm doubtful. Because there are so many different ways of reading the same book.'

'If you understand that, then you are not a Catholic. And certainly not a Moslem.'

'I've been baptised – but I have no Catholic feelings.'

'Is Sicily a religious place?'

'No, no, absolutely not! It's pagan. You only have to look at our religious festivals which are very important here. But they are explosions of vitality, pretexts for riots, quarrelling, drunkenness.'

'Yes, especially at Caltanissetta,' exclaims Renata. She seems to have a thing about Caltanissetta. Maybe she loves to pronounce its beautiful name.

'But everywhere. And the cursing you hear during the religious festivals! Yes, there is an underground pagan feeling here. I'm attracted by it. A religion which is not a religion. This god living at 3000 metres above our heads. It's fine by me. There is a short story by Verga, *War of Saints*. The saints make war on each other through their followers. It's been translated into English. But . . . translation is not always satisfactory. The best thing on the subject of translation was said by Cervantes: translation is the other side of a tapestry. Perfect.'

Despite his slow and quiet manner of speaking, Sciascia's face has a tight look. The mouth is thin-lipped and the words emerge as if from stiff jaws. The brow is creased by a permanent frown. The eyes are held in a squint, half shut as if against the glare of the sun. But there is no sense of weariness and his brain is nimble.

'What is the Sicilian concept of love?'

'It spreads always over a small circle of people. We cannot talk of love for the universe, for humanity. The family, friends – this is where all possible love is poured.'

'What qualities do you admire in a man?'

'Loyalty. Tenacity.'

'And in a woman?'

'The same.'

'And what makes you happy to be a Sicilian living in Sicily?'

'Happy? I'm not happy about it! Another Sicilian writer, Borgese, quoting the Latin poet, said of Sicily "I cannot live with you, nor without you." That's the general feeling of Sicilians. A good Sicilian detests and loves Sicily. A bad Sicilian loves Sicily.'

Then I must be a good Sicilian, loving and abhorring this land named after the sickle with which Cronus castrated his father Uranus (Sicilian men, like Arab men, suffer from a castration complex, a belief that the world is out to unman them and that this must at all costs be prevented); a land of horror and beauty, these 2 qualities deeply interpenetrating to the perplexity of both travellers and the indigenous population. In the circumstances, all Sicilians try desperately hard to be normal. But they're a pretty crazy crowd. Why are they crazy? The climate: loving the sun, needing to hide from it: light and dark: orange, gold, green, blue and black black black. The history: wave after wave of conquerors bringing with them cultures which had little connection with previous or subsequent ones but representing an alien authority. This has left the Sicilians a mass of pieces, conflicts, uncertainties, hopes, fears, magnificent moments, and cynically aloof from destiny. It explains Sicily's 'jangling' effect, which is what happens when the traveller and Sicilian alike fail to assimilate and redispose these various ingredients in a conceptually satisfying way.

Sicilians hate making decisions because decision is commitment is entrapment. They need to keep their options open. This can become paralysis of the will – and unable to act themselves, they undermine the acts of others. They see the possibility of betrayal everywhere and seek to pre-empt this with a prior betrayal of their own. This, they believe, will spare them the hurt, the blow.

Embedded in families, they do not let the bonds of family touch their soul which cherishes its silent freedom. Sicilians are capable of violent, impulsive acts but disinclined to hold to a task for long because it is who you are, not what you do, that is important. Most of all they hold to the self, and this clinging to the self is like a man grasping at paper in a storm.

The Sicilian world is a world of dreams. Its great modern novel, *The Leopard*, is elegant, historical, turned backwards, embodying a fatalism that is narcissistic in its impotence and regret. And of course its susceptibility to the idea of a benign, aristocratic golden age corrupted by the arrival of mafiosi and nouveau riche entrepreneurs, is a dreamer's delusion, a superb lie. The Sicilian aristocracy was always notorious for caring about nothing except its own dignity. Sicilians are dreamers – but they also are busy. They often try to put their dreams into practice. This gets them into trouble, There's wildness and indulgence in fantasy. Sicily is a world of wrecked dreams, an island of ruins, of enterprises begun but not sustained, because the Sicilian is frightened to lose himself, i.e. to expose himself. He is frightened of losing his precious red velvet soul.

When happiness or fulfilment loom, the Sicilian commits a destructive act to prevent it, because in unhappiness he knows where he is, can be certain of himself, whereas happiness obliterates the self and a Sicilian without a self, without a vividly palpitating ego, is a man lost. Unhappiness, bigotry, violence, pain, despair, these are safe because they are negative, finite; they say *stop* to growth, to becoming more than you are, other than you are. Unhappiness is safe. Happiness is unsafe. Love is unsafe. Love obliterates. Death is safe. But death is also obliteration. The idea that Love = Death is very strong here.

Embedded in families, Sicilians have a weak sense of self-possession. Therefore they are very concerned about who they are, especially that aspect of identity which is reflected off those around them, their standing in the community, their dignity. They are prone to upwardly misrepresent their achievements: boastfulness. They are rarely humorous or ironical about their dignity, whereas the British, being more individualised, are nearly always jokey on the subject of dignity – the very word has a ludicrous ring for them – and are far less susceptible to slights on this account. For a Sicilian, to be individually centred is to present a fixed target, and as Lucinda said, they are happier presenting a moving one. But ceaseless vigilance is required to avoid entanglement and the crossing of wires, and this can be a major source of neurosis. Sicilians are neurotic.

Like Japan's and Britain's, Sicily's society has strict codes – and therefore emotional secretiveness. This strictness is softened in Britain by the cult of eccentricity and humour, and in Britain and Japan by the tradition of solitude. Solitariness is a permitted escape. There is no tradition of solitude in Sicily – there is aloneness in the midst of people. Japanese and British hypocrisy become, in Sicily, deceit. Here the excesses of family oppression (emotional blackmail), Catholic oppression (guilt) and mafia oppression (violence) make deceit essential to survival. All 3 strands of oppression say you are *not* entitled to be yourself, you may *not* proceed according to your wishes, you must be this, you must be that. Constantly this is heard in Sicily – what you must be! what you must not be! what's done, what's not done!

It's a bore, this appalling social fascism. Even the young ones are often so dreadfully uptight and choked with the business of projecting a 'correct' image. Appearances are everything. But since appearances clearly aren't everything, appearances are often the opposite, charades to be maintained while the real activity goes on behind. The Sicilian language has no word for 'privacy' – neither has Italian. 'Solitude' and 'intimacy' yes, but not 'privacy'.

Lisetta in Catania said 'Everyone mixes in Sicily.' This is not so. Outside the Third World, you'll not meet an upper class more mindful of its status. I've never been to a place where position is more obsessively calibrated than Palermo. The British aristocracy is far looser (and therefore more prosperous) than the Sicilian which takes intermarrying to an extreme. Since they could all fit into a medium-sized ballroom this has weakened them psychologically. Suicide and drug addiction are common. There are 2 aristocracies in Sicily – pre-1860 (Spanish) and post-1860 (Italian). It is possible to buy a title from someone by arranging the appropriate adjustments in an office in Madrid or at the office of the Italian pretender (whoever that is). This is because titles are things, not functions, and Sicilians are passionate about the trinketry of status. One of my hosts purchased his and is very touchy about it. However, within the borders of Italy, titles have no legality. They cannot be used in any official transactions or in newspaper reports. But they have social significance.

Because Sicilians spend so much time and energy in concealment, they are very interested in the truth. The amount of snooping and gossip is phenomenal, though usually they do not pry directly but through other people. If a Sicilian asks and you say 'I was with someone', he will accept it. Whereas the French will poke: Do I know them? The German will say: Some beautiful girl? The American will say: Who? And the English will say: Oh, I see . . .

They are capable of devastating insincerity but living under such pressure means that they are capable of devastating sincerity too. Yet carrying this sincerity from the intimate moment to the outer world is virtually impossible for them. Americans are the opposite. Americans find great difficulty in bringing the sincerity of public expression to the intimate encounter. For Americans, life is deeply felt show business. As a result, the inner life of Americans is curiously flat. The inner life of Sicilians is like the birth and death of the entire universe. It is volcanic, alive, murderous, illuminating. The blast of heat which hits you coming off the lava flow of Sicilian life is something you can't prepare for.

Sicilians are hopeless at organising but brilliant at improvising. They are versatile – and changeable. They long to make contact, do so, distrust it. They are melancholy and destructive, animated and creative, warm and cold. This is because Sicilians are worried. For them nothing is simple. If they can't make a problem from something – they are worried by that too, they think they must've miscalculated and look everywhere for the trick. And if they haven't miscalculated, if the situation remains simple, then they feel threatened by this simplicity.

The Sicilian disease: deviousness. From A to B must never be a straight line. They invent, mislead and dodge in their boxing-match with truth. For them, truth is confession. It weakens. It is going out on a limb, which they do not like to do because everywhere they see nemesis. Cleverness is saying one thing while doing another. They may begin with a small lie which then has to be supported by greater lies until a colossal deception has been created, wobbling balloonlike and precariously in the air. From time to time these collapse, making assorted messes. The gulf between the real and the professed is enormous. This discrepancy is illustrated at the practical level by the fact that Palermo is 70th Italian city per capita income and 7th per capita consumption, thanks to the hidden economy. At the psychological level it makes for a life as performance, as a game of one-step-aheadship, i.e. for a life of anxiety.

Truth is too readily considered fluid here. The title of one of Pirandello's plays is *It Is So! (If You Think So)*. Which is rubbish. If you have a car accident the other side will make a huge fuss, regardless of events, in order to put the blame on you. It is infuriating after a while, this insistence that what actually happens is unimportant, that what one wishes and feels is all-important. Everything dissolving into appetite and emotion is quicksand. They give themselves too much licence to distort. They know the difference between a truth and a lie as well as anyone but they jump at this foolish idea of Pirandello's because it allows them to get away with . . . murder. But truth is not simply desire, language is not merely rhetoric. Truth involves overcoming the limitations of personality, and ultimately of course that limitation of collective personality we call culture, wouldn't you agree? And yet both approaches to truth, the liar's and the honest man's, have their particular efflorescence of freedoms.

I'm observing, marvelling, loving, hating, approving, disapproving, but I am not *complaining*. Which means really that I'm in love with this Sicily. Love includes the negative. Mere devotion fails to embrace the whole. Which doesn't mean that love is blind, simply that love is not rejecting. Devotion and faith – these are blind – and deaf. Do they love me in return? Perhaps my being a foreigner helps. Foreigners allow them to breathe a little more easily, bring oxygen to this suffocating austral wardrobe. On the other hand, Sicilians do not like to be alone in foreign places. They are not at all equipped for such an ordeal. One of the reasons for mafia success in the USA was that half the family was imported and connections maintained between old and new worlds. *Little Dorrit*: Dickens characterises a certain type

of continental rudeness: . . . *making himself too much at home by half.*
This is very French. But not at all Sicilian. Sicilians are nervous and
extremely polite on other people's territory.

All Sicilians want the same thing: power. Therefore they cannot
co-operate. Therefore they sometimes confuse power with force. They
are very hard on each other. They give everything to a member of
the family or to a friend or to a foreigner. But they give nothing to
a fellow Sicilian. Him they try to cheat. It is a land at odds with
itself where a peculiar form of savagery has taken root: mafia. One
of the Sicilian paradoxes: although they cannot co-operate, Sicilians
collectively generate a tremendously strong magnetic field which holds
each individual in a state of great tension and fixedness. Hence their
secretive natures. Secrecy does not make a man more powerful.
Secrecy makes a man more vulnerable. The equation will balance
only by the introduction of violence. Secrecy + Violence = Power.

As a psychological case, Sicily is a sado-masochistic manic-
depressive. Its own torturer and victim. Up and down, up and
down. Sicilians feel exposed and claustrophobic simultaneously. Their
exposure inclines them to machismo, i.e. overt power signalling, and
their claustrophobia induces a rich vein of melancholy. Nothing
moderate can survive here. They are alive to the immediate and they
distrust the immediate. They are tough, put their backs into work as
if their very soul depended on it. Then they drop it and do something
else, distracted from their purpose by what someone else is doing –
or thought to be doing. They cannot concentrate because they cannot
abstract themselves. Life adheres round personalities, not ideas.

Sicilians love food, money, death and sex in that order. Their diet,
though under pressure of debasement from international consumerism,
is the most intelligent and nutritious in the world. They love to eat food
in gangs. Money and death have been dealt with. Sex – by which I
mean sex and sexual love, all the paraphernalia of physical congress.
For Sicilians, chaste love is something to do with priests, Church,
Virgin Mary, not anything to do with reality. For Sicilians, love is
always erotic – is sexual love, even though the sexual expression
may often be – usually is – thwarted. They like to make love and
to talk love but to fall in love, oh dear, this is a problem for the men
because to fall in love is to leak power. The enclosed self is strong,
they believe. The revealed self is weak. Christians believe this too –
that sexual love reduces one's ability to love God. In Sicily, God is
the Self.

For women the supreme insult is 'puttana' meaning prostitute, bitch.
For men the supreme insult is 'cornuto' meaning cuckold, which has
hardly been used in Britain since the 18th century. If you make the

cornuto sign (index and little fingers raised, others held down), there
will be fighting.

For a Sicilian man the pain of love is the panic at the loss of
loneliness, whereas the Sicilian woman must give all of herself in
love. Her reservation should not be in love but in sex. She should
not enjoy sex too much. The Arab and Catholic traditions combine
to deny her. The Sicilian man is a prude and demands the woman
be one too. His prudishness lies in finding something demeaning in
giving himself in love, whereas sexual indulgence is respectable (for
a woman this is reversed). He may give his courtship, his body and
his life but he withholds, in the end, himself. The woman must none
the less wait for him. His passion can be intense because desire exists
where there is unfulfillment and the Sicilian is restless and unfulfilled
by nature.

They talk about love so well – oscillating between involvement and
cynicism. This is how they keep abreast of the flux. They like to
describe its various stages. 'I love you because . . .' one day; 'I don't
love you because . . .' the next. This is not hypocrisy or lying but the
articulation of panic.

Sicilians, like the English, are helplessly fascinated by sexual non-
conformity. Male bonds can be very close, therefore the taboo against
homosexuality is strong. Bisexuality is widespread but must not be
mentioned. Social oppression tends to displace the homosexual either
into effeminate transvestism or denial. There are many transvestites
in Palermo. Many young homosexuals pose as heterosexuals – since
most girls don't permit sex before marriage, this is easily done. The
insensitivity of the strutting macho male can make women turn to each
other for mental and physical rapport.

Since the Sicilian is terrified of anything which limits his room
for manoeuvre, it is important to his self-respect that he avoid any
imputation of sexual fidelity. In practice he is no naughtier than males
elsewhere and the pressure on him to be a rampant genital performer
can be the cause of impotence. But he must *appear* to be unfaithful. If
the partner yearns for him, he is happy. If the partner looks elsewhere,
he is angry and jealous. The partner must be faithful even when he is
unfaithful. Most men in every culture are like this.

The woman must not theorise about her role. She has 3 to choose
from: wife-mother, nun, prostitute. There is a qualification to this in
the tradition of the noblewoman taking a lover but it is a violent and
unhappy one. Women like Kris and Elvira Sellerio who make their
own decisions are rare – but on the increase.

Kris said 'What I like about the British is that they still have in them
a drop of foolishness. This is something all other Europeans have lost.'

Sicilian outrageousness usually comes alas in the negative form but they can wallow in the comic and grotesque aspects of their existence. Like the English, they confess with a swagger the shortcomings of their society. They are the best talkers of any Mediterranean people because they have such cultural variety to draw on. Their conversation has point, daring, expressiveness and subtlety. Their land is a surreal circus of high-wire improvisations where a restless intelligence sharpens perception and upsets generalities in its ingenious pursuit of what is possible in an impossible world. They are all acrobats. They are all misfits. And being rather a misfit myself, I am drawn to this.

Empedocles, born at Agrigento c. 490 BC, is the characteristic Sicilian philosopher. His central idea was that there are 4 fundamental elements – air, fire, earth, water – which are eternally united and eternally divided by 2 forces which he called love and strife. Philosopher, man of politics, scientist, magician, and trickster, he is said to have jumped into the crater of Mount Aetna in order that his sudden disappearance might cause him to be thought a god. But the volcano threw up one of his sandals and thus revealed the manner of his passing.

Renata rings to say that she's going to *The Sicilian* party too and will give me a lift. The Villa Tasca is neo-classical and hidden among trees off a busy road. It was established in the 19th century as an experimental agricultural station, a function it still performs having been modernised into a garden centre by the present Count Tasca who is a successful businessman in his own right (other aristocrats often sneer at him for this). Tables and chairs are laid out on the lower terrace, drinks are being served on the upper terrace, and the outdoor scene is lit by candles and flambeaux flickering in the arboreal night. The 3 daughters of the house – Costanza Camporeale, Rose-Marie Ruffo, Anna Lanza di Mazzarino – greet the guests while the Count himself paddles round in a white suit, looking very festive in contrast to his wife. The other Sicilian men are in the usual bourgeois dinge (dark suit and tie), except for Paolo Camporeale whose savoir faire permits him the liberty and coolness of a white open-necked shirt. To-night the Sicilian women and girls are noticeably more beautiful, more lively in behaviour and chic in appearance than the men, and many of them seem to spend a lot of time in Rome. The film people can be recognised by their casual, often crumpled variety, and loose, up-tempo manners. I present a jar of Sir Nigel's Marmalade to Costanza, quite inappropriate to the occasion, but it has become a habit.

A buffet is served. Fish. 'We caught the fish when we were in Pantelleria,' says Costanza, adding non-committally 'Perhaps I'll have some.' And there is an octopus cooked in its own ink. Rose-Marie, who is also at our table, works for a jeweller in Rome but has ambitions — she wants to write her autobiography, a revolutionary idea for a woman of the Sicilian upper class. Costanza's son, Filiberto, apologises for not coming to Regaleali 'but I had economics exams. Did you have a good time?'

'Yes. Luigi Albano took me. He's the fastest, most brilliantly hair-raising driver I've ever known.'

(It was a truly skull-stripping drive, during which Luigi said 'Motorways have taken the mystery out of Sicily and made it very small.'

'How did you learn such good English?'

'I spent many months in England at a college near Reading.'

'Goodness me. My father has a wire factory at Reading. There is nowhere to eat in that town.'

'You're not joking!'

Regaleali sometimes has winter snow, so there are machines for blowing warm air over the vines. I asked the Count if the mafia were involved in the wine trade and he said 'Not here as far as we are concerned. But I can't speak for elsewhere. But at dinner at this very table in 1953 my son Lucio, then 13 years old, and my father were both kidnapped. Men broke in with machine guns. But no money was paid — and the police broke the kidnap.')

Regaleali has supplied to-night's meat: lamb. Costanza calls it 'mutton' and doesn't look interested but it's very good, as is the special wine Rosso del Conte (although the ordinary Regaleali red is not to my taste). A taciturn black-haired man is masticating on my right and I ask 'Are you connected with the film?'

The Sicilian is about Salvatore Giuliano, a good-looking and still admired bandit from the 1940s, who robbed and murdered the rich and gave to the poor until, in 1950 at the age of 27, he was shot by a turncoat friend who was later poisoned in prison.

'Sort of,' says the taciturn one.

Rose-Marie giggles and introduces us — it's Michael Cimino, the director. He's cold, dull, and unmarried, with that solemn, self-conscious New York artiness which is the hallmark of the second-rate.

The Marchese Wenceslao Lanza di Mazzarino comes across and says with relish 'The Earl of Newburgh — I found out. He's a phoney.' He also tells me why but it's too complicated to remember.

The dolce is a mille feuilles 4 feet across + bowls of fruit. 'I want to buy a flat in London,' says Costanza, squaring up to a bowl of cherries, 'but Italians are not allowed to buy a house abroad. Have you been to Segesta yet?'

The finest temple in Sicily, yes, it used to be at an isolated site but a motorway has been built beneath. A notice read *Non scribere sul agave*. The theatre was absolutely silent. Goats ran down a hill opposite and their bells made a rippling sound like water over rocks.

Christopher Lambert, the French actor who plays Giuliano, is growing restless and actorly. 'I want to go to Brazil!' he declares. 'Who wants to go to Brazil? We're going to Brazil! Hey, Mike, are you coming to Brazil?' There's no response from Cimino. Brazil is the best Palermo nightclub, out of town, in an old house among trees on Monte Pellegrino looking down on the lights of the city. You dance on the roof.

I go in search of Renata from whom I was separated soon after arrival and catch up with her in the saloon off the upper terrace, talking to Lucio Tasca. He says he's arranged for me to visit the Palazzo Gangi and all that's necessary is to go there and ask for Mr Cucchiara. It's said to be the most splendid private residence in Palermo. Mind you, this saloon is very striking too, on account of its trompe l'oeil décor which imagines it as a ruin being reclaimed by Nature: the walls have tumbled, disclosing rustic vistas; the simulated stone dressings round the doorways are broken and chipped; collapsed masonry painted on the ceiling reveals gods and goddesses gambolling in the sky.

Renata, wearing her favourite red, is likewise in heaven – grandees *and* film stars – and when Lucio passes on, she looks up at the gods, wringing her hands. 'He is so handsome! Such green eyes! . . . Shall I tell you a story about the filming of *The Leopard*? Visconti wanted a Russian to play the lead but the money men wanted an American and booked Burt Lancaster. Visconti was *furious*. He directed everyone, even the leeeeeeeeeeeast important extra, but ignored Lancaster. I was teaching Burt Lancaster Italian – he couldn't concentrate on his lessons for raging at Visconti. Eventually he exploded on the set, calling Visconti every name under the sun. At this point Visconti made a curious wailing noise in his throat and changed his attitude completely. They became good friends and at the end of the film Visconti gave him a head by Serpotta and Burt Lancaster gave Visconti a painting by Picasso.'

'But why did the outburst cause Visconti to change his attitude?'

'I think because he had forced Burt Lancaster to break out of his skin and make the real contact.'

'And do you think Lancaster was good in the film?'

'He was *wonderful* in the film!'

She really is a life-enhancer and I've grown very fond of her megawatt twinkle.

The make-up boy, who is from Guildford says 'Michael Cimino won't tell me what he wants. I need directing too. But he won't talk to anyone. It's dreadful. Everyone's complaining about it. I really loved Saint Paul de Vence. Wendy and I worked there on *The Pink Panther*, didn't we, Wend, and we both really loved it.'

The buffet tables, laid with white tablecloths down to the ground, are cleared of all food and a bowl of flowers set on each. Approaching these tables I discover them to be crawling with millions of tiny ants.

'We saw Michael Cimino on television,' says Fiammetta, delicately sipping her drink. She is gentle, girlish, and seems spun from chiffon.

'He was going on about the lush Sicilian countryside,' says Olly, 'but the only lush thing in Sicily is me! We've been ticking over on Ben Moor whisky for 10 years. It's bloody good and bloody cheap. My son, who lives as a fisherman on Pantelleria, bought me a t-shirt which said "I don't drink any more" and underneath in small print "and I don't drink any less".'

'Where did he get it?'

'Luton Airport.'

Kris and I are dining with Arthur (Olly) and Fiammetta Oliver at their house by the sea on the road to Mondello. At long last. They are both delightful and I much regret not having done this before. Fiammetta, whose claims to antiquity are belied by agility, keeps sliding out to the kitchen while Arthur sinks further into his chair, tumbler in hand, blowing smoke like a genial Komodo dragon.

'My mother was a writer too,' he says, clacking his teeth. The centre tooth of the bottom row slips up and down in a curious way. 'She wrote 147 novels, all of them the most God Almighty crap!'

'What was her name?'

'Ruck! . . . Miss Berta Ruck! And she lived to be 104!' He lights a cigarette with the butt of the previous one. Kris and he between them have rendered the atmosphere foggy and denlike, so that when Fiammetta switches on the lamps after the final daylight has gone, we could be in pre-airport Penang. The room is exotic, dimly colourful and psychically very comfortable.

'I chain smoke, chain drink, and during the day I chain coffee,' he asserts with pride. 'My father was a wonderful old alcoholic on 60 cigarettes a day and he scored 88 years. He wrote ghost stories.'

'Have you ever had a supernatural experience in Sicily?'

'Only once. We were driving into the Villa Valguarnera one day, going under that arch where you turn left, and I *felt* something there. They were cousins of Fiammetta's, you know, and when I visited the Villa for the first time it was lived in by 3 sisters and the terrace to the sea was divided into 3 portions by *barbed wire*. Why did you choose Sicily of all the God forsaken places?' Formalities over, he removes the centre tooth of the bottom row and pops it into his pocket.

'Well, Sacheverell Sitwell talked to me about it in such a way that it really took my fancy. And it is amazing, I mean, there's not one golf course on the whole island and that's absolutely fabulous, don't you think?'

'There used to be one in the Favorita Park. Major Dodds looked after it but it fell to bits after the war because the Americans used it as an army dump. I have a great deal of affection for the Sicilians but the women are streets ahead of the men. We don't go much into Palermo now. Don't you find the jay-walking terrible there?'

'It doesn't bother me very much because I've been letting other people do most of the driving.'

'There should be a competition for jay-walking between Palermo and Tunis. I think Fiammetta's getting us something to eat by the way. Tunis used to be great fun when the French were there. Now it's deadly dull. And I'm not awfully keen on Arabs. They're the most dreadful thieves. During the war, after we'd buried our dead, they used to dig them up again to steal the blankets the bodies were wrapped in. It was really very distressing. So we thought about this and decided to mine the bodies with the German mines we collected which really did make a violent explosion. After a few bangs, the thieves learned their lesson.' His head moves forward out of a swirling cloud of smoke and he observes, 'You're not drinking very fast'.

'It's the heat.'

'I never let that stop me. Look, my mother had a few letters from one of the Sitwells. Osbert, I think. Hang on, I'll go and root them out.'

Fiammetta and Kris emerge from the kitchen carrying large bowls which they place on the dining-table at the other end of the room.

'It's not much,' says Fiammetta, 'but it's traditional Sicilian.'

Pasta con sarde: fresh sardines, pine nuts, fronds of wild fennel, raisins, onions (if I make it now, I add garlic, coriander, capers and — instead of wild fennel fronds which are rarely available in England,

I use the body of the fennel, softened with the onions in a pan over a low heat using a little olive oil – then lightly fry all the ingredients together in the minimum olive oil – avoid breaking up the sardines too much – toss into al dente tagliatelle or rigatoni).

Olly emerges from the study and replenishes the drinks. 'I could only find one. Here.'

Castello di Montegufoni, 4th April, 1962. My dear Miss Berta Ruck, I do think it annoying of Hatchards to have kept you waiting. I don't know what has happened to them lately . . . Here things haven't been going well. David Horner, who lives with me, took a header down a flight of stone stairs here and fractured his skull, as well as causing himself numerous other injuries. He wasn't found until the next morning. He is still in a nursing home . . . I am fascinated by what you say about the song 'The Gypsies in the Wood'. The next time we meet, I hope you will sing it for me . . . Yours ever, Osbert Sitwell.

'Not very earth-shattering,' says Olly.

The letter is passed round the table.

'Strange though,' I say. 'It's almost where I came in.' It does feel strange, and yet oddly reassuring, after so much driving and talking and looking, to find oneself back at the beginning again.

'We have a daughter who lives in London,' says Fiammetta, touching Olly's elbow but looking at me.

'She makes films,' he says. 'She's done this terrific one for TV about the dogshit problem in London. It went down so well that she got the wherewithal to review the dogshit problem in Paris and New York too.' As I help myself to more pasta con sarde, Olly smooths back his grey hair and leans forward conspiratorially, clacking his teeth. 'One of the problems was to get the shit to *steam* for the cameras. So she bought plastic turds from a joke shop and put them in hot water and dumped them on the grass.'

'That's clever.'

'It *is* clever, isn't it,' says Fiammetta.

'She worked hard on that film,' continues Olly. 'She spent an awful lot of time wandering round London with her zoom at the ready. The moment she saw a dog about to squat she'd zoom in on it to catch the turd as it came out.'

'You're not eating enough, Olly,' says Fiammetta who then looks helplessly at us. 'He never eats.'

'They had beating at my school. Did they at yours?'

'Yes. But it was going out.'

'The secret is to get the cane to fall in the same place every time. So the prefects would mark a line on the seat of your trousers with a shaving stick. Then you had to say "Thank-you, sir" afterwards.'

'Toby Moore tells me you showed the Queen round Monreale.'

'No, no, no – I showed the *others*. She'd gone on ahead with the experts. I got the staff. I had to go aboard *Britannia* one morning, where I was given the worst coffee I've tasted in my life, and the Admiral said to me, because you know *Britannia's* always skippered by an admiral, could you take some of my yachtsmen, because they're always called yachtsmen on *Britannia*, along to Monreale with you? And I said the bus will hold 55 and there are only 32 so far, so the more the merrier. When I got to Monreale I asked the Queen's Secretary "Do you want it gay or serious?" and he said "Oh *gay. Every* time." So I gave them the dirty version and they *loved* it. Do you know, the following week I got 12 letters of thanks from the sailors which I think is marvellous. Guess where my daughter's working now. The Ministry of Rubbish. She works from Shepherd's Bush – where I worked with Gaumont British before the war.'

'You were in the film business?'

Fiammetta pushes the bowls in my direction with a beatific smile.

'Yes, 8½ years of it – the most horrible gang of crooks in those days. Of course it's much worse now. Guess what – I was Alfred Hitchcock's assistant for the last film he made in England before going to Hollywood. It was by accident because his previous assistant got a carbuncle on his chin and died and Hitch said "Can you take over from Dickie?" and I said I'd try. It was *Secret Agent*, from one of the Ashenden stories by Somerset Maugham. Our first location was in an hotel room and Hitch directed it from the lavatory seat in the bathroom because it was the most convenient spot. But he so liked it that he insisted on directing the entire film from a lavatory seat which was carried round from place to place.'

'So at what point did you come to Sicily?'

'The War. I was the British Intelligence officer for Sicily. And believe me, I know a few things. Do you know what we did at the end of the war? We burnt the Fascist files in Palermo with all the details of which Sicilians did what with the Fascists or with the Germans. I arranged it with the US man here, General Nestor, who said he'd take responsibility if it got out. So I said "Here you are then, take them all away and burn them." Because you see, we thought that if ever these Fascist files were read, it would be *terrible*. The Sicilians would be blackmailing each other to death for ever more. Really there would be no end to it and I think we saved a lot of lives by what we did. Nestor organised some lorries which were loaded up from the archives in Palermo and we burnt the lot. It took us 15 days to do it. But my *God*, this is red hot. If ever it got out, the War Office – I'd be deported from Italy and imprisoned in England.'

I record it now because Olly has since died (General Nestor is also dead).

Shan't be driving all the way back to England – have booked passage on the ship to Genoa which takes cars.

Natale, whose studies are intermittent at this time of year, invites me to stay for a few days with his family at Gela on the south coast. Though the site of the second Greek Colony in Sicily, after Naxos, Gela is almost entirely modern, founded on the offshore oil business. There are sad polluted remains of the old pre-oil lido but on the whole the town has a good open atmosphere, (However, since my visit a war has broken out among the local mafiosi and Gela currently has the highest murder rate in Sicily! All very sudden and unexpected. Typically Sicilian.)

I present whisky to the father, bath oil to the mother, tea to the kitchen and am made most welcome, although conversation is decidedly a problem. Natale's sister Isabella is studying English at Catania University but is too shy to try it out. There is a second sister, married, and endless aunts, uncles, cousins who arrive to view me and to whom I'm taken in an endless round of introductions. The extended family is almost self-sufficient – one uncle is a dentist, another a doctor, another a baker, and so on. I feel somewhat like a circus animal at times, especially as they observe me closely and frequently laugh at my outlandish ways, but there is warmth and unstinting hospitality (I recall asking if they had any Fernet Branca. They said of course. Natale dashed to the shops in secret, came back with a bottle, and a glass of the nourishing beverage was set before me within 5 minutes).

Natale himself I like more and more and, as with Kris, I feel I've known him for years. His intelligence, and mixture of mischief and seriousness, are very fascinating and the range of his knowledge surprises me. I suppose I suffer from the common prejudice that scientists know little of the humanities but I am quite wrong in this case. His scientific background, however, can explain things to me in entirely new ways. He is also a very sympathetic host. Not once do I feel abandoned in this unfamiliar world.

Mrs Maganuco is a strong woman and not one of those indulgent mothers whom Kris described. All 3 children are excellent cooks and were taught to clean their rooms from the age of 10. Preparing tea from the new box, she explains that this is the first time the teapot has been used since she and her husband received it as a wedding present 28 years ago.

Mr Maganuco, who used to work at the oil refinery (which Natale calls 'the cathedral of Gela'), has a bucolic cast of mind. The contiguities of urban life have become increasingly intolerable to him and he prefers to go off alone and sit on a rustic knoll surrounded by birds, plants and rocks, or cultivate the strips of land he has inherited from his father. Though not rich, the family have vines from which they make their own wine, wheat fields from which they make their own bread and pasta, and various other plots for fresh fruit and vegetables. Mr Maganuco has a special fire insurance against malicious wheat burning. This connection which survives between ordinary townspeople and their rural past is still widespread but on the wane alas. It explains why they have such an excellent diet: food freshly prepared from fresh ingredients. They have an instinct for nutritional balance and healthy cooking that is more marked than anywhere I've known and long may they reject the processed shit which is swallowed in Britain and the USA. I have only 2 reservations:

(1) Sicilian cheese, apart from ricotta, is hard and bitter.

(2) They do not keep leftover pasta to reheat or eat cold. It's always thrown away. This presumably is an automatic precaution in a hot climate.

We spend the day at their small cottage in the country ½ an hour away (they never sleep there). Basically it's all eating. Snacks when we arrive and more snacks as various relations turn up and join the party, then the main meal at lunchtime, pasta, steak, salad, bread, wine, cannoli Siciliani (delicious sweet pastries filled with ricotta very fresh from the shepherd up the road), then a walk to some caves and when we return there's coffee and small cakes stuffed with figs, plus lemon and almond biscuits, all fresh from the oven, which is followed by washing up and conversation while cooking in the ovens is a light supper of pastry torpedoes filled with minced meat, spinach and wild asparagus, and finally before departure another snack ('Oh yes, make a space, just a little something before we drive home') of pizza topped with tomato, cheese, fresh herbs, etc. They tell me I should be here for the Feast of San Giuseppe, March 19th, a showcase for Sicilian food when all the traditional recipes are prepared and you go among the houses of friends eating eating eating, and at the end of 3 days what's left is given to charity. A blood-red segment of setting sun throbs between 2 clouds on the horizon and the cloud edge is fired a brilliant gold-red as if a volcano sat there issuing hot lava.

During my stay with the Maganucos I also learn that:

(1) They use Saint Martin's summer for late summer heat (in early November here). We say Indian summer which is an Americanism. Previously the English used Saint Luke's summer.

(2) We say someone is talking about you if your ears go red. In Sicily it's if your ears ring.

(3) Natale will have to do National Service soon. He says that they are frightened to abolish it because the threat of a colpo di stato would be greater from a full-time, professional army. But it is a barren intrusion into many young lives.

(4) Palermo Football Club is not allowed to play elsewhere in Italy for 5 years because of the bad behaviour of its supporters. When the ban was announced the town's football fraternity made an affray, throwing rubbish into the streets and setting it alight.

(5) An Italian scientist has come up with a plan for a safe nuclear generator by reversing the current method from fission to fusion which would produce no radioactive waste.

(6) Re my detestation of pylons, Natale said 'In the future it should be possible to have small local generators so that power doesn't have to travel overland by these big lines. Or waves up into the sky.' Quite what he means by the latter option is not clear to me.

(7) On New Year's Eve, Italians wear red underclothes for good luck.

Last night in Palermo, July 12th, Saturday, at Kris's flat. Give her the last jar of marmalade but it's not enough. More than anyone, she is responsible for launching me here. The Feast of Santa Rosalia which goes on for 5 days is underway.

'The fireworks are to-morrow night, maybe the day after, so you will miss them,' she says. 'But Sicily has been very kind to you. Nothing has harmed you. Even the medusas in the sea at Selinunte did not touch you. Every door has been open. Even the Palazzo Gangi, which is closed up, opens for you.'

'It was full of canaries in cages.'

'Whose?'

'I asked Mr Cucchiara that and he said in a low tone "the Principessa's".'

A dusty yellow ballroom in the heart of the old town, with stupendous chandeliers, was empty but echoed faintly in the mind's ear. Likewise a saloon with large ottomans and divans and a pierced 2-tier ceiling lit from above. Old court robes were propped in a glass case and photographs of Victor Emmanuel II, George V and Queen Mary stood on the grand piano. The rarest smell of antiquated and forlorn grandeur, of abandonment at its most sumptuously frayed and calm, goes deeper than nostalgia, suggesting a remote and forgotten ideal of perfection. Now the palace's perfection lies in its emptiness, the alluring void of infinite time and space at the centre of a whirling universe.

We are eating on Kris's balcony and can see prisoners in the lit-up windows of the prison. Palermo, town of the 3 'F's: farina, feste, forca. Are Palermitans happier than Londoners or Parisians or New Yorkers? Or less happy? Palermo the Incurable has cured something in me. And another thing – I haven't stood on my head once in Sicily. Usually I stand on it half-a-dozen or more times a week. But in Sicily I forgot. It never entered my head to stand on it. At this point in my rumination the fireworks go up on the Marina.

'OK, OK,' laughs Kris through her rings of smoke, 'they send up the fireworks a day early – just for you!'

Morning of departure. Natale helps with the bags which include a giant pot wedding present for my brother who's about to take the plunge. The temptation to model an ending, to fill it with symbols and theories, to wrench conclusions, I've resisted. Natale, Kris, perhaps others here – they will stay in my life. I do not want 'an end'. My thoughts are haphazard, in free association, contradictory. Conflict is the refusal of a being to accept its contradictions and I do not want that. Sicily's paradoxes challenge. The Sicilians are so cynical and at the same time so innocent. The culture is so insistent and yet so reticent. The clash of beauty and ugliness is painful – but terribly absorbing. There can be no resolution. And in the end one has to release the conclusions and let them fly up like birds into the indeterminate sky. The car is covered with birdshit but unbroken on the dockside.

The sense of life's terribilità is very strong here. Sicily's readiness to express its contradictions gives intense visibility to problems we all share. And it occurs to me that everything I have said about the Sicilians applies to us all in varying degrees, so that perhaps the secret of this island's spell is the way it reveals the universal processes of human nature in an especially vivid and moving form. That is, in a form you do not 'understand' and are therefore unable to dismiss. Sicily's revelations are dynamic, untrappable. There is an astonishing beauty in this, a beauty that is not always tolerable. Do I love this place? Love changes you. If it doesn't, then it's sex. Sex is OK. With sex you can keep your distance. Home is love. But everyone must leave home to find love. Yes, somehow I do feel changed. As the Greeks tell us, Love is the child of Chaos.

Sitting up on deck. Woman opposite is squeezing blackheads from her husband's back.

The boat pushes off. The body slackens as the tension of land-fight leaves it and you feel a softness enter. Natale waves from the dockside. In a plane you are wrapped in metal and lift off quickly. In a car you battle through traffic to get out. In both cases it is only in retrospect that you appreciate you've left. But on a ship there is the smooth, slow, subdued, tearing sensation, a massive and ineluctable event beneath your feet and in your emotion: the long smooth tear of departure through your softness.

And as the ship moves out on a sea of bubbles in the midday midsummer heat, pushing north again, you feel that brilliant odd feathers have sprouted from your heart and wag there mockingly, giving you pain and pleasure, giving you character, so that you are both humiliated and strengthened, made less mysterious and more wonderful. . . . . Oh yes, let the end disintegrate. We do not peter out, we move away . . . A small figure waving . . . Moist eyes . . . Pieces of Palermo fade into the heat. . . . .

Index